Learning the Yahoo! User Interface Library

Get started and get to grips with the YUI JavaScript development library!

Dan Wellman

BIRMINGHAM - MUMBAI

Learning the Yahoo! User Interface Library

First published: March 2008

Production Reference: 1120308

Published by Packt Publishing Ltd.
32 Lincoln Road
Olton
Birmingham, B27 6PA, UK.

ISBN 978-1-847192-32-5

www.packtpub.com

Cover Image by Vinayak Chittar (vinayak.chittar@gmail.com)

Credits

Author
Dan Wellman

Reviewer
Jon Trelfa

Senior Acquisition Editor
Douglas Paterson

Development Editor
Nikhil Bangera

Technical Editor
Bhupali Khule

Editorial Team Leader
Mithil Kulkarni

Project Manager
Abhijeet Deobhakta

Project Coordinator
Snehal Raut

Indexer
Hemangini Bari

Proofreaders
Martin Brook
Angie Butcher

Production Coordinator
Shantanu Zagade

Cover Work
Shantanu Zagade

About the Author

Dan Wellman lives with his wife and three children in his home town of Southampton on the south coast of England. By day his mild-mannered alter-ego works for a small yet accomplished e-commerce agency. By night he battles the forces of darkness and fights for truth, justice, and less intrusive JavaScript.

Dan has been writing web-design tutorials and articles for around five years and is rarely very far from a keyboard of some description. This is his first book.

I'd like to say a special thank you to James Zabiela for the use of his Mac, and Eamon O'Donoghue for the exceptional art work that features in some of the examples; the book would simply not be the same without your help guys. A nod of respect is also directed at Steve Bishop for his invaluable advice.

This book is dedicated to my wife Tammy and
my children Bethany, Matthew and James.

Table of Contents

Preface

Learning the Yahoo! User Interface Library was written to help people with a basic knowledge of JavaScript and web design principles to quickly get up to speed with the UI library developed by Yahoo. The book covers a selection of some of the most established utilities and controls found in the library, but it does not go into detail on any of the beta or experimental components.

Each chapter of the book focuses on one, or a maximum of two, individual utilities or controls, and is broken down into theory and practice sections. The theory sections of each chapter discuss the benefits of the component being looked at, the situations it would be most useful in and looks at the classes from which it is constructed. The code sections walk you through implementing and configuring the component in step by step detail.

No previous experience of the YUI library is required, although an understanding of JavaScript, HTML, and CSS is assumed. Other technologies such as PHP and mySQL are used in places throughout the book, although these are not explained in great detail as they fall outside of the book's scope.

By the time you finish this book you'll be well on your way to mastering the library and will have increased the number of web design tools and techniques at your disposal exponentially.

What This Book Covers

In *Chapter 1* we look at the library as a whole covering subjects such as how it can be obtained, how it can be used, the structure and composition of it, and the license it has been released under. We also look at a coding example featuring the Calendar control.

Chapter 2 covers the extensive CSS tools that come with the library, specifically the Reset and Base tools, the Fonts tool, and the extremely capable Grids tool. Examples on the use of each tool are covered.

In *Chapter 3* we look at the all important DOM and Event utilities. These two comprehensive utilities can often form the backbone of any modern web application and are described in detail. We look at the differences between traditional and YUI methods of DOM manipulation, and how the Event utility unites the conflicting Event models of different browsers. Examples in this chapter include how the basic functions of the DOM utility are used, and how custom events can be defined and subscribed to.

AJAX is the subject of *Chapter 4*, where we look in detail at how the Connection Manager handles all of our XHR requirements. Examples include obtaining remote data from external domains and the sending and recieving of data asynchronously to our own servers.

Chapter 5 looks first at how the Animation utility can be used to add professional effects to your web pages. It then moves on to cover how the Browser History Manager re-enables the back and forward buttons and bookmarking functionality of the browser when used with dynamic web applications.

The Button family of controls and the TreeView control are the focus of *Chapter 6*. We first cover each of the different buttons and look at examples of their use. We then implement a TreeView control and investigate the methods and properties made available by its classes.

In *Chapter 7* we look at one of the most common parts of any web site—the navigation structure. The example looks at the ease at which the Menu control can be implemented. We also look at the AutoComplete control and create both array and XHR-based versions of this component.

Chapter 8 looks at the container family of controls as well as the tabView control. Each member of the container family is investigated and implemented in the coding examples. The visually engaging and highly interactive TabView control is also looked at and implemented.

Drag-and-Drop, one of DHTML's crowning acheivements is wrapped up in an easy to use utility, forms the first part of *Chapter 9*. In the second part of this chapter we look at the related Slider control and how this basic but useful control can be added to pages with ease.

In *Chapter 10* we cover the Logger control in detail and work through several examples that include how the Logger is used to view the event execution of other controls and how it can be used to debug existing controls and custom classes.

What You Need for This Book

This book expects and requires you to have a prior knowledge and understanding of at least JavaScript, HTML, and CSS. While the use of the utilities, controls, and CSS tools will be explained in detail throughout the book, any HTML, CSS, or PHP code that is featured in any of the examples may not be explained in detail. Other skills, such as the ability to install and configure a web server, are required. A PC or Mac, a browser, text editor, the YUI, and a web server are also required.

Who is This Book for

This book is for web developers comfortable with JavaScript and CSS, who want to use the YUI library to easily put together rich, responsive web interfaces. No knowledge of the YUI library is presumed.

Conventions

In this book, you will find a number of styles of text that distinguish between different kinds of information. Here are some examples of these styles, and an explanation of their meaning.

There are three styles for code. Code words in text are shown as follows: "we can also add the `lang` attribute to the opening `<html>` tag..."

A block of code will be set as follows:

```
//get the date components
Var dates = args[0];
Var date = dates[0];
Var theYear = date[0];
Var theMonth = date[1];
Var theDay = date[2];
```

When we wish to draw your attention to a particular part of a code block, the relevant lines or items will be made bold:

```
<body>
    <div id="doc3">
      <div id="hd">This is your Header</div>
      <div id="bd">This is the body
   <div class="yui-b">This is the secondary block</div>
   <div class="yui-main">
    <div class="yui-b">This is the main block</div>
```

```
        </div>
      </div>
      <div id="ft">This is your footer</div>
    </div>
  </body>
```

New terms and **important words** are introduced in a bold-type font. Words that you see on the screen, in menus or dialog boxes for example, appear in our text like this: " the default category of message is **INFO**".

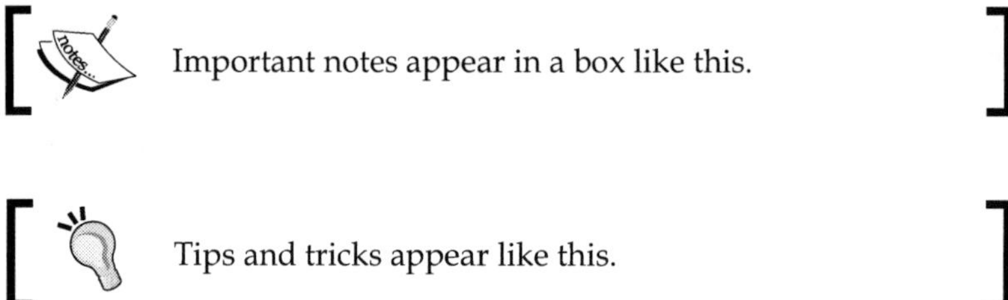

Important notes appear in a box like this.

Tips and tricks appear like this.

Reader Feedback

Feedback from our readers is always welcome. Let us know what you think about this book, what you liked or may have disliked. Reader feedback is important for us to develop titles that you really get the most out of.

To send us general feedback, simply drop an email to `feedback@packtpub.com`, making sure to mention the book title in the subject of your message.

If there is a book that you need and would like to see us publish, please send us a note in the **SUGGEST A TITLE** form on `www.packtpub.com` or email `suggest@packtpub.com`.

If there is a topic that you have expertise in and you are interested in either writing or contributing to a book, see our author guide on `www.packtpub.com/authors`.

Customer Support

Now that you are the proud owner of a Packt book, we have a number of things to help you to get the most from your purchase.

Downloading the Example Code for the Book

Visit http://www.packtpub.com/files/code/2325_Code.zip, to directly downlad the example code.

The downloadable files contain instructions on how to use them.

Errata

Although we have taken every care to ensure the accuracy of our contents, mistakes do happen. If you find a mistake in one of our books—maybe a mistake in text or code—we would be grateful if you would report this to us. By doing this you can save other readers from frustration, and help to improve subsequent versions of this book. If you find any errata, report them by visiting http://www.packtpub.com/support, selecting your book, clicking on the **Submit Errata** link, and entering the details of your errata. Once your errata are verified, your submission will be accepted and the errata added to the list of existing errata. The existing errata can be viewed by selecting your title from http://www.packtpub.com/support.

Questions

You can contact us at questions@packtpub.com if you are having a problem with some aspect of the book, and we will do our best to address it.

1
Introducing the YUI

Welcome to the first chapter of "Web Development with the Yahoo! User Interface Library". Throughout this book, we'll be exploring what makes up the library and what it can do for you. By implementing a selection of the available utilities and controls, we can see exactly how each one works and what functionality and tools it leaves at your disposal.

During this chapter we're going to introduce ourselves to the library by taking an overall view of it. The topics that we are going to cover include:

- How to get the library, where to get it from, how to install it, and how to work with it in your own web pages.
- Where it came from, what inspired its creation, who made it, and the core ideas behind it.
- Exploring the library and investigating what components form its constituent parts.
- Where we can find important information and news about the library and places where we can go to for help if we need it.
- The gallery, where you can see who else is using it and what they've been able to achieve.
- The licensing issues that surround its legal use.
- Who would make the most of it.

We'll also go over a brief coding example where you will get down to some proper scripting and find out for yourself just how easy it is to get up and running with the components themselves. This is where you will see the power provided by the library at first-hand.

What is the YUI?

The Yahoo! User Interface (YUI) Library is a free collection of utilities and controls, written primarily in JavaScript, that has been produced by the expert developers at Yahoo! to make your life easier as a web developer or front-end user interface designer.

It consists of a series of JavaScript and CSS components that can be used to quickly and easily build the rich and highly interactive applications that today's web consumer expects and demands.

The premise of the library is simple; often when writing JavaScript, you'll come up with a function that works perfectly in one browser, yet badly (or worse, not at all) in alternative browsers. This means that you'll often need a set of different functions to do exactly the same thing in different browsers.

This can be done for some of the major browsers without too much difficulty using standard object detection methods within `if` statements. However, this can lead to massively increased script files and unwieldy code that takes longer to debug and troubleshoot, and longer to write in the first place.

The YUI wraps both sets of code up into one object that can be used programmatically with one constructor, so instead of dealing with different sets of code for different browsers, you deal with the library and it makes the different calls depending on the browser in use.

Another important aspect of the library that I should mention at this point is its respect for the Global Namespace. All objects created by the library and its entire code run within, and can only be accessed through, the `YAHOO` Global Namespace object. This means that the entire library, including every utility and every control, and its numerous classes, create just one namespace object within the Global Namespace.

The Global Namespace is the global collection of JavaScript object names, and it is very easy to litter it with potentially conflicting objects, which can become a problem when code is shared between applications. Yahoo minimises its impact on the Global Namespace and so shall we; all of the code that we'll write throughout the course of this book will reside within its own namespace object.

Essentially, the YUI is a toolkit packed full of powerful objects that enables rapid front-end GUI design for richly interactive web-based applications. The utilities provide an advanced layer of functionality and logic to your applications, while the controls are attractive pre-packed objects that we can drop onto a page and begin using with little customization.

Who Is It for and Who Will It Benefit the Most?

The YUI is aimed at and can be used by just about anyone and everyone, from single-site hobbyists to creators of the biggest and best web applications around. Developers of any calibre can use as much or as little of it as they like to improve their site and to help with debugging.

It's simple enough to use for those of you that have just a rudimentary working knowledge of JavaScript and the associated web design technologies, but powerful and robust enough to satisfy the needs of the most aspiring and demanding developers amongst you.

The library will be of interest primarily to front-end developers, as the main aim of the YUI is to provide a framework within which robust and attractive interfaces can be quickly and easily designed and built. It can help you to side-step what can otherwise be insurmountable compatibility issues.

There is no set standard that says you must know this much or that much before you can begin to use the YUI. However, the more you know and understand about JavaScript itself, the more the library will make sense to you and the more that you will be able to gain from using it.

Trying to learn how to make use of the YUI without first knowing about the JavaScript language itself, at least to a basic working standard, is an endeavour likely to end in frustration and disappointment. It would be a great shame if a lack of understanding prevented you from enjoying the benefits that using the library can bring to both your creativity and creations.

So to get the most out of the YUI, you do need to have at least a basic understanding of JavaScript and the principles of object oriented programming. However, a basic working understanding is all that is required and those developers that have less knowledge of scripting will undoubtedly find that they come out of the experience of developing with the YUI knowing a whole lot more than they did to begin with.

The YUI can teach you advanced JavaScript scripting methods, coding and security best practices, and more efficient ways of doing what you want to do. It will even help more advanced programmers streamline their code and dramatically reduce their development time, so everyone can get something from it.

For some, the YUI is also a challenge; it's an excellent opportunity for developers to get involved in a growing community that is creating something inspiring. The Firefox browser is a great example of an open-source, community-driven, collaborative effort of separate but like-minded individuals. Some people may not want to develop web pages or web applications using the library: they may just want to be involved in evolving it to an even greater accomplishment.

I should also point out at this stage that like the library itself, this book expects you to have a prior knowledge and understanding of JavaScript, HTML, and CSS. While the use of the utilities, controls, and CSS tools will be explained in detail throughout the book, any HTML, CSS, or PHP code that is featured in any of the examples may not be explained in detail. Other skills, such as the ability to install and configure a web server, are also required.

Why the Yahoo! User Interface Library?

Using any JavaScript library can save you great amounts of time and frustration when coding by hand, and can allow you to implement features that you may not have the knowledge or skill to make use of. But why should you use the YUI rather than the many other libraries available?

To start with, as I'm sure you already know, Yahoo! is extremely well established, and at the forefront of cutting edge web technology and front-end design principles. The utilities and controls provided by the library have already been tried and tested in their world-class service provision environment. Hence you know that the components are going to work, and work in the way that you expect them to work and that Yahoo! says that they will.

The YUI library is not the only developer-centric offering to come from these world-class leaders and go on to achieve high levels of accomplishment and a following amongst developers; other very successful projects include the extensive Design Pattern library, Yahoo! Widgets, and the Yahoo! Music Engine. They also have a wide range of APIs for you to experiment and work with, so they have already shown a commitment of providing open-source tools designed to succeed.

Additionally, the library has already been publicly available for over a year and in this time has undergone rapid and extensive improvement in the form of bug fixes and additional functionality. Overall, it is not still in beta stage, and has been proven to be an effective addition to your development toolset. Like the Mozilla and Firefox browsers, it has a huge, world-wide following of developers, all seeking to further enhance and improve it.

There are some libraries out there that have been developed which seek to alter the JavaScript language itself, building capabilities into the language that the developers felt should already have been present and extending the language in new and interesting ways.

While these libraries can provide additional functionality at a deeper and more integrated level, their use can often be hampered by technical implementation difficulties that will be too difficult to overcome for all but the most advanced and seasoned developers.

The YUI is not like this; it is extremely well documented, stuffed full of examples, and is extremely easy to use. It doesn't get bogged down in trying to alter the JavaScript language at a fundamental level, and instead sits on top of it as a complimentary extension.

There's also no reason why you can't use the YUI library in conjunction with other JavaScript libraries if a particular feature, such as the rounding of box corners as provided by MochiKit for example, is required in your application but not provided by the YUI.

Graded Browser Support

Whichever browser you prefer, there's one thing that I think we can all agree on; all browsers are not created equal. Differing support and a lack of common standards implementation are things that have confounded web developers for as long as there have been web developers.

Although the situation is improving with agreed standards from the W3C, and better and more consistent support for these standards, we are far from being in a position where we can write a bit of code and know that it is going to function on any of the many browsers in use.

There may never come a time when this can be said by developers, but with the YUI, you can already count on the fact that the most popular browsers in use, on all manner of operating systems, are going to be able to take full advantage of the features and functionality you wish to implement.

It doesn't, and can't be expected to support every single web browser that exists, but it does group together common browsers with common capabilities into a graded support framework that provides as much as it can to visitors whichever browser they happen to be using.

Every single browser in existence falls into one of the defined grades; the most common class of browser are the A-grade variety of browsers, which are the browsers that the creators of the library actively support. These are modern, generally standards compliant, and capable of rendering in full the enhanced visual fidelity and advanced interface functionality provided by the library as well as the inner core of content.

X-grade browsers are generally unknown and untested, and account for a wide range of less common, often highly specific browsers that are simply assumed to be able to access the full, enhanced experience. Any browser that has not been extensively tested by the YUI development team is automatically an X-grade browser regardless of its capabilities; IE7 on Vista was classed as X-grade for some time after its release simply because it had not been fully tested by the Yahoo! team.

C-grade browsers are able to access the base or core content and functionality of the library components, but cannot handle the enhanced content. These are browsers that are simply not supported by the library.

Currently, the complete spectrum of A-grade browsers supported by the library includes the following browser and platform configurations:

- IE7 on Windows XP and Vista
- IE6 on Windows 98, 2000, Server 2003 and XP
- Firefox 2.x on Windows 98, 2000, XP and Vista, and Mac OS 10.3 and 10.4
- Firefox 1.5 on Windows 98, 2000 and XP, and Mac OS 10.3 and 10.4
- Opera 9 on Windows 98, 2000 and XP, and Mac OS 10.3 and 10.4
- Safari 2 on Mac OS 10.4
- Safari 3 on Mac OS 10.4 and 10.5, Windows XP and Vista

These 27 common configurations are able to make use of not just the core content of any applications we create with the YUI, but also all of the enhanced functionality brought on by the library. Any browser not on this list will still receive either an A or C-grade experience, but may be classed as an X-grade browser if it has not been extensively tested.

The graded browser support strategy is based on the notion of progressive enhancement as opposed to graceful degradation. "Graceful degradation" is a term that I'm sure you've heard at some point and involves designing content so that, when it breaks in older browsers, it retains some semblance of order.

This method involves designing a page with presentation in your supported browsers as your main priority while still allowing unsupported browsers to view at least some kind of representation of your content.

Progressive enhancement approaches the problem of supporting browsers with different capabilities from the other way by providing a core of accessible content and then building successive layers of presentation and enhanced functionality on top of this inner core of generalized support.

This screenshot shows how the Rich Text Editor control appears in a C-grade browser. Older readers may recognize the browser used in this experiment as Netscape Navigator version 4, a popular browser approximately a decade ago.

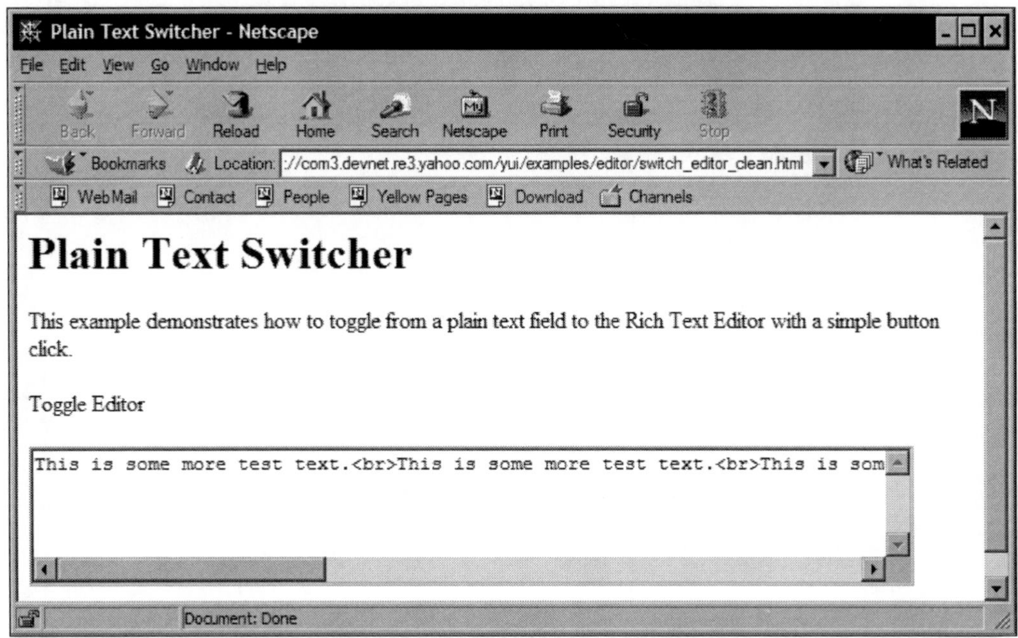

As you can see from this example, the inner core of the page content is a standard HTML `<textarea>` element, which is displayed completely normally. The page doesn't break, but the high fidelity content is not displayed. Using graceful degradation techniques, the browser would probably attempt to display the Editor, but it would probably look very poor and would certainly not function.

The following screenshot shows how the editor appears in an A-grade browser:

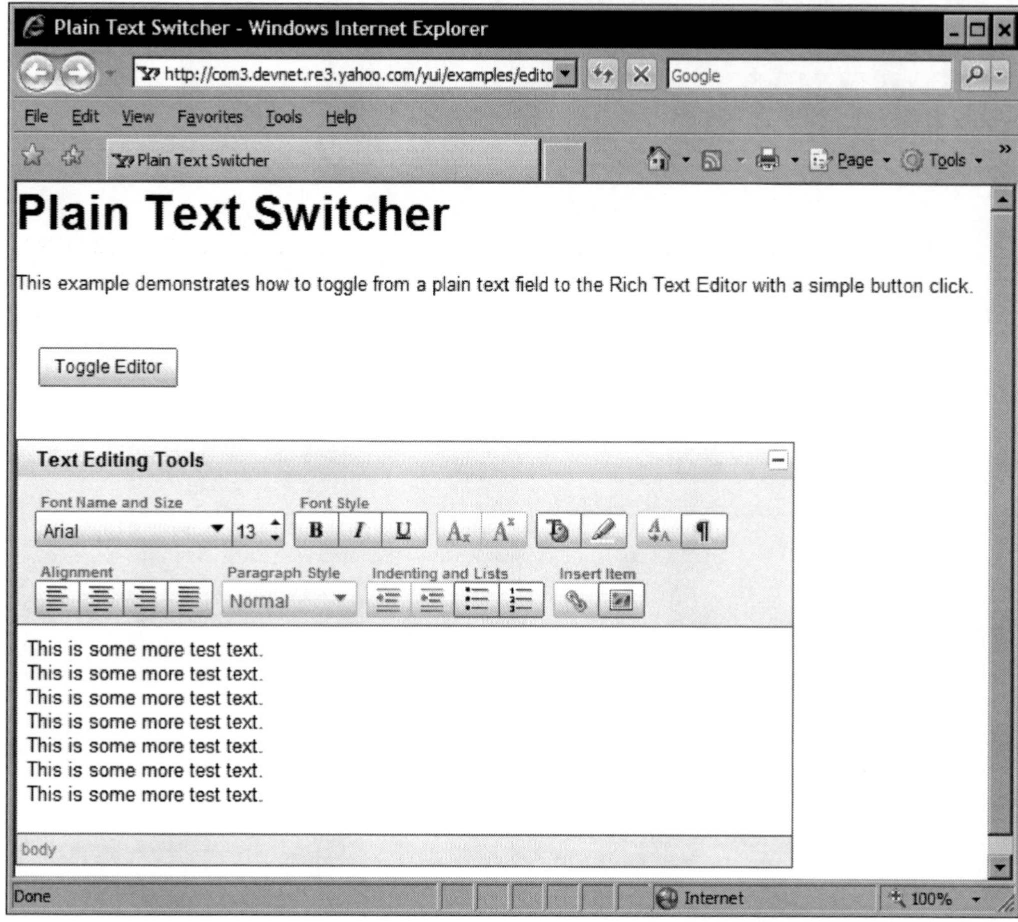

In a capable, supported browser the library can transform the `<textarea>` element into the full Rich Text Editor control. Now, the following screenshot shows exactly the same page in exactly the same browser but with JavaScript switched off:

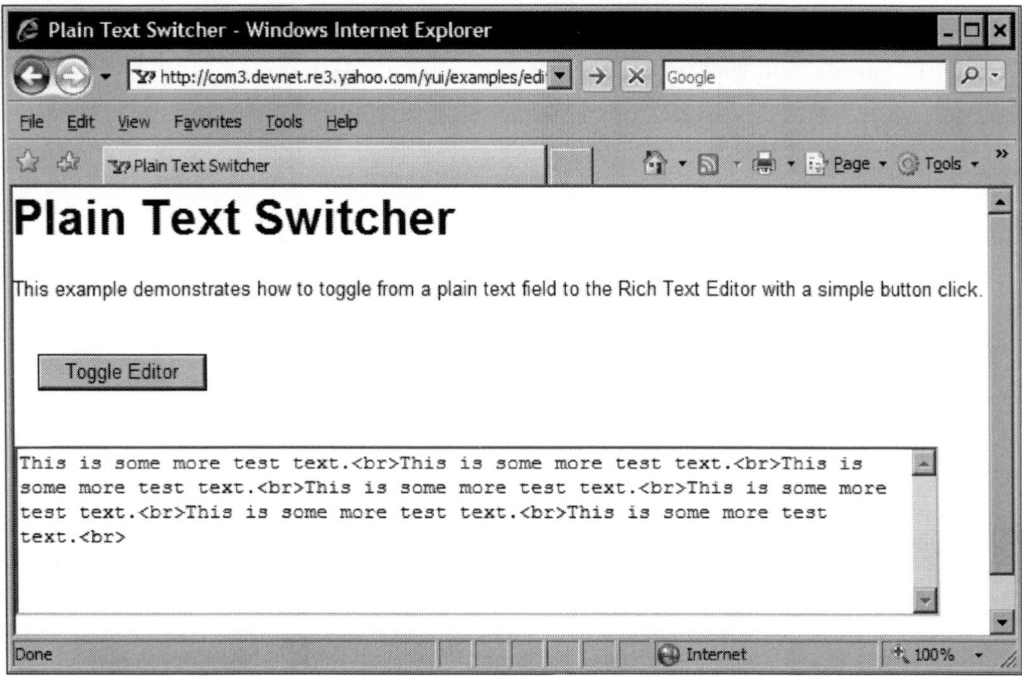

Notice the similarity between a C-grade browser and an A-grade browser with JavaScript switched off.

The knowledge that has enabled Yahoo! to use the concept of graded browser support has been gained from wide variety of user-agents that hit their site every single day. They've been accessed by over 10,000 different software and platform configurations since they began focusing on who and how their portal is accessed.

Approximately 96% of this total have received an A-grade experience when using the Yahoo! site, leaving just three percent that are classed as C-grade, and a minimal one percent classed as X-grade.

What Comes with the YUI?

Some JavaScript libraries are condensed into a single script file such as the jQuery library. While this can make linking to them easier, it can be inefficient depending on how much of the library you actually use.

The YUI Library is split into its constituent components, making it easy to pick and mix which utilities and controls are used, and making it much more efficient to implement. In addition to the large collection of JavaScript files the library provides a great deal more.

The Library Topography

The library is currently divided into four distinct sections; the library core files, a series of utilities, a set of controls, and some excellent CSS tools. There are a total of 33 different components, at the time of writing, and the library is continually growing and being refined.

There are also three versions of most of the library's utilities and controls, including a full version of the underlying JavaScript file that powers each component, complete with white space and comments for better readability and understanding, which can help your learning and development.

As well as the full versions, there are also `-min.js` and `-debug.js` versions of all the utilities and controls; the **min** (for minified) files have had all white space and comments removed, and variable names have been shortened where possible to cut down drastically on file size.

The min versions of each component are the ones served by Yahoo! and are perfect for production-release applications. These are the ones that you should be using most of the time in your own implementations, and the ones that we will be using throughout for most of the coding examples included in this book.

The debug version of each component is designed to be used in conjunction with the Logger Control rather than presented to your visitors. Along with white space and comments, these files also contain additional code which logs messages to the Logger console during key interactions within the components.

The differences between the full and min versions of each file can be quite large, with the min versions often being less than half the size of the full version. The only comment in each of the min files is the copyright notice, which has to stay intact in every file. Other than that, these files are pretty much solid chunks of hard code and readability is therefore very poor.

There are also three different file designations that each component can be classed as; fully released components are termed GA (for General Availability). GA components are typically the oldest, have been tested extensively, and had most of the bugs weeded out. They are reliable and have been considerably refined.

Beta designated utilities and controls are still in the process of being ironed out, but they have been released to the development community for wider testing, bug highlighting, and feature suggestion.

Any component termed experimental is still in the conceptual phase of its design and may or may not be promoted to Beta or GA status.

The Core Files

The core of the library consists of the following three files:

- YAHOO Global Object
- DOM Collection
- Event Utility

The Global Object sets up the Global YUI namespace and provides other core services to the rest of the utilities and controls. It's the foundational base of the library and is a dependant of all other library components (except for the CSS tools). A useful browser detection method is also available via this utility.

The DOM Collection provides a series of convenience methods that make working with the Document Object Model much easier and quicker. It adds useful selection tools, such as those for obtaining elements based on their class instead of an id, and smoothes out the inconsistencies between different browsers to make interacting with the DOM programmatically a much more agreeable experience.

The Event utility provides a unified event model that co-exists peacefully with all of the A-grade browsers in use today and offers a consistent method of accessing the event object. Most of the other utilities and controls also rely heavily upon the Event utility to function correctly.

Since the core files are required in most YUI implementations, they have been aggregated into a single file: `yahoo-dom-event.js`. Using this one file instead of three individual files helps to minimise the number of HTTP requests that are made by your application.

The Utilities

The utilities provide you with different sets of user-interface functionality that you can implement within your web pages. They provide programming logic and deal specifically with the behaviour and interactions between your visitors and the different objects and elements on your pages.

They are more of a concept that you begin with and then build upon, and they provide the foundation from which you create your vision. They provide unseen behaviour; for example, the Animation utility isn't something your visitors will see directly, but its effects on the element being animated will of course be visible.

Like the core files of the library, the utilities have all been rolled up into one easy to link to master file: `utilities.js`. Again, this can be used to make your application run more efficiently when using all of the utilities together.

The set of utilities included in the current release of the library (which is constantly changing and growing) are as follows:

- Animation Utility
- Browser History Manager
- Connection Manager
- Cookie Utility [beta]
- DataSource Utility [beta]
- Drag and Drop Utility
- Element Utility [beta]
- Get Utility
- ImageLoader Utility
- JSON Utility
- Resize Utility [beta]
- Selector Utility [beta]
- YUILoader Utility

The Controls

The controls on the other hand are a collection of pre-packaged objects that can be placed directly on the page as they are, with very little customization. Your visitors can then interact with them.

These are objects on the page that have properties that you can adjust and control, and are the cornerstone of any web-based user interface.

These controls will be highly recognisable to most visitors to your site and will require little or no learning in order to use. The complete suite of controls currently included with the library is:

- AutoComplete Control
- Button Control
- Calendar Control
- Charts Control [experimental]
- Color Picker Control
- Container
- DataTable Control [beta]
- ImageCropper [beta]
- Layout Manager [beta]
- Menu Control
- RichTextEditor Control [beta]
- Slider Control
- TabView Control
- TreeView Control
- Uploader [experimental]

The CSS Tools

The CSS Tools form the smallest, but by no means the least useful, component of the library. The utilities and controls are designed to be used almost independently (although some of the files do depend on other files in the library to function properly), but the CSS tools are designed to be used together (although they can also be used separately if desired) and provide a framework for standardising the visual representation of elements on the page.

The following four tools make up the current CSS section of the library:

- Reset CSS
- Fonts CSS
- Grids CSS
- Base CSS

The CSS tools have just two versions of each CSS file instead of three: a full version and a minimum version; there are no debug versions in this section of the library. Like with the `yahoo-dom-event` utility, some of the CSS files have also been combined into one file for your convenience. You can use `reset-fonts-grids.css` or `reset-fonts.css` depending on your requirements.

The Library's Structure

Once the library has been unpacked, you'll see that there are a series of folders within it; the **build** folder contains production-ready code that you can use immediately on your web site. This is where the code that makes each component work, and all of its associated resources, such as images and style-sheets can be found.

The **docs** directory contains the complete API documentation for every library component. This is where you can find the classes that make up each component, look at the underlying code, and review the properties and methods available to you.

The **examples** folder contains a series of demonstrative web pages that highlight the key functionality or behaviour of each library component and mirrors the example space found online.

The **tests** folder contains a series of pages which use the Logger Control to check that each component is functioning correctly for the platform on which it is being run. Each method for the component being tested is called, and the results are logged for you to examine.

Another set of folders that you'll need frequently when using the library controls are the **assets** folders. Each of the controls has its own **assets** folder which contains things like supporting images and style-sheets, as well as the **sam** skin files (if applicable) for display purposes.

There are some other files and folders within the library, such as an index for the library so that you can easily look for documentation or examples and release notes. The screenshot on the next page shows the folder structure of the library.

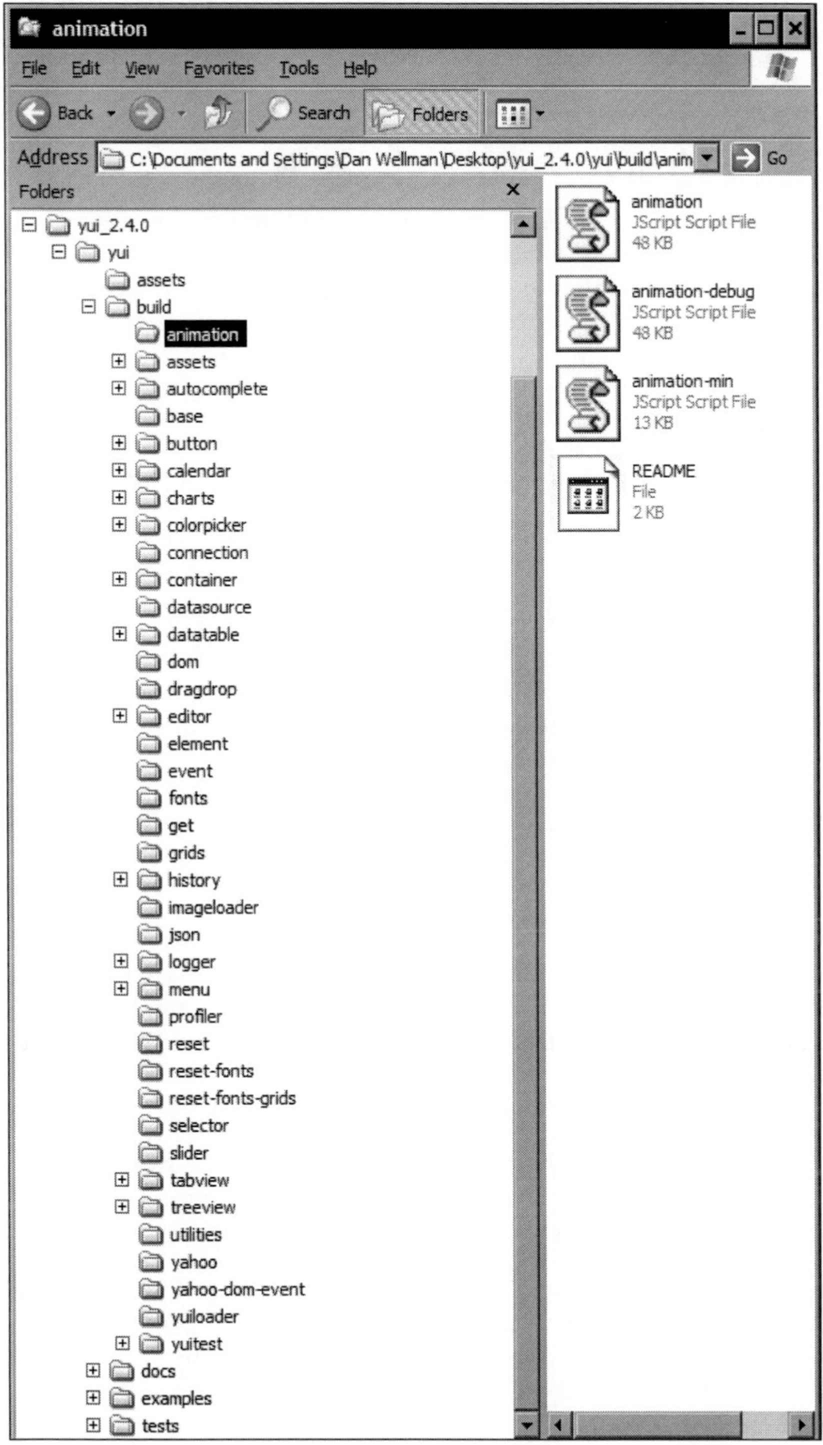
animation
File Edit View Favorites Tools Help
Back
Search
Folders
Address C:\Documents and Settings\Dan Wellman\Desktop\yui_2.4.0\yui\build\anim
Go
Folders
yui_2.4.0
yui
assets
build
animation
assets
autocomplete
base
button
calendar
charts
colorpicker
connection
container
datasource
datatable
dom
dragdrop
editor
element
event
fonts
get
grids
history
imageloader
json
logger
menu
profiler
reset
reset-fonts
reset-fonts-grids
selector
slider
tabview
treeview
utilities
yahoo
yahoo-dom-event
yuiloader
yuitest
docs
examples
tests
animation
JScript Script File
48 KB
animation-debug
JScript Script File
48 KB
animation-min
JScript Script File
13 KB
README
File
2 KB

Due to the changing nature of the beta, and the experimental utilities and controls, we will not be looking at them in any great detail in this book. For information regarding any of these components, see the YUI site and API guides.

What Else Does Yahoo! Provide?

There are some additional resources that are available courtesy of Yahoo! to help you use the library to its maximum potential. There are a series of very helpful "Cheat Sheets" that you can view online from any of the individual component's information pages, and which have also been bundled up into a zip file for you to download for offline viewing.

These resources provide a useful and centralised reference manual which lists the key methods, properties, and syntax patterns of each of the fully released components and gives some basic examples of their implementation.

Some of the beta and experimental components do not have their own cheat sheets as these are still subject to change. The cheat sheets for the rest of the components however, are extremely useful and act as an invaluable reference whilst working with the library.

There is a discussion forum which developers can use to discuss their projects and get help from experts. It's not a proper forum as such; it's actually a Yahoo! Group, which is kind of like a cross between a forum and a mailing list.

Nevertheless, if you've got a problem with getting a utility or control to do what you want it to, you can search the list of messages in the group to see what you're doing wrong, or submit a question if there is no information listed.

If you're a member of any other Yahoo! Groups already, you just need to join the `ydn-javascript` group. If not, you'll need to sign up for a free Yahoo! account and then join the group. There are tens of thousands of registered members and the number is growing on a daily basis, so if you do have any problems and find that you need to ask a question, there's a very good chance that someone, including the library's creators, will be willing and able to help.

The forum is home to a growing community of developers that have been brought together by the YUI; community involvement is an excellent way to connect with developers and can take a project in new and impressive directions.

To keep up-to-date on developments in the YUI and read associated news statements and technical articles about the library and the Yahoo! Developer Network in general, or to watch screen casts from the development team and other experts, you can visit the YUI blog at `http://yuiblog.com`.

This is a companion blog not just for the YUI library but also for the Yahoo! Design Pattern Library. This is separate from the YUI and is not something that we'll be looking at in this book, but it is worth mentioning because the two libraries can be used together in many situations.

The entire selection of different video screencasts and podcasts are brought together in one place for easy searching in the YUI theatre. Both the blog and the theatre are subscribable via RSS, so that you can have up-to-date news and announcements surrounding the library.

There is also a section of the YUI site where you can look at the implementations of the library by other people and on other web sites. There are only a few showcase examples listed on this page, and some of the examples link to other parts of the Yahoo! network rather than to external sites, but there are a couple of high profile sites using YUI and this page can be a great place to find inspiration.

This page is also where you can find links to the online component examples. These are detailed examples that demonstrate the default, core abilities of each module in an uncluttered environment and have been provided by the actual developers of the utilities and controls.

Finally, there are a few interesting articles about different aspects of the library that can be found on the YUI developer site. The first article is an FAQ that provides some standard answers to some standard questions.

Other articles discuss topics such as Yahoo's approach to graded browser support, the benefits of serving library files from Yahoo! servers, and current best practice with regard to security measures.

For those of you that want to join the YUI development community and give something back to the Yahoo! Developers that have bestowed this awesome tool upon us, there is also the facility to submit bug reports or feature requests.

This is an excellent channel of feedback and as the YUI team point out, many useful features have been added to the library following a feature request. It also allows the team to remove errors and refine the features of existing components.

Are There Any Licensing Restrictions?

All of the utilities, controls, and CSS resources that make up the YUI have been publicly released, completely for free, under the open-source BSD license. This is a very unrestrictive license in general and is popular amongst the open-source community.

For those of you who don't know anything about what the license stands for and what it allows you to do, I'll give you quick overview now so that you need not worry about it again. Consider these next few paragraphs your education in open-source software licensing!

BSD stands for Berkeley Software Distribution and was originally designed and used by a team of developers who created an open-source operating system of the same name that was similar in many ways to the UNIX platform (and even shared part of its code-base with it). Many of today's most popular operating systems, including Windows and OSX are derived from or contain code from the original BSD operating system.

The current BSD version, sometimes known as the New BSD license, differs from the original in that it has had the restrictive UC Berkeley advertising clause removed, making it almost equivalent to the MIT license but with the addition of a brief final clause prohibiting the use of the copyright owners name for endorsement without obtaining prior consent.

This means that you can pretty much do whatever you want to do with the library source code; you can use it as it is, you can modify it as you wish, add to it, or even remove bits. You can use the files in the format in which they are provided, or you can use the code within them in the distribution of a compiled, closed-source application.

You can use it in your own personal projects, as part of a commercial venture or even within an educational framework. You can do all of this provided that you retain the copyright notice in your source code, or the copyright notice present on each of the library files remains intact.

If you're using the library files as the original JavaScript files as they come in the library, all you need to do is make sure that the existing copyright notice is left at the top of every file that you use. In a compiled application, it should be clearly visible in the help section or user manual.

Installing the YUI

The YUI is not an application in its own right, and it doesn't need to be installed as such. Getting started with the YUI is extremely simple; you first choose whether to download all of the source files from Yahoo and use them locally as part of your web sites' hierarchy, or whether to use the URLs provided on the YUI developer pages to reference the library files stored on Yahoo's web server.

These are the exact same files that are used in many different interface implementations across the Yahoo! network and as such can be depended on for being almost continuously available, and even if Yahoo! does decide to take these files down at some point in the future, I'm sure that this will be announced in a timely manner.

Another benefit of using Yahoo's network bandwidth to provide the functionality behind your application is that their network is global in nature, with servers running in many geographically distinct parts of the world.

Being able to serve library files from a location closer to your visitors' location results in a better response from your application; this is good news for your visitors and therefore good news for your business.

Additionally, as I mentioned earlier, there are different versions of each of the working files in the library including a 'minified' file that has been stripped of whitespace and comment blocks. The Yahoo servers provide these minified versions of the files, but in addition, they also serve the files in a GZIP format, making the files up to 90% smaller and therefore, much more efficient for transportation across the Internet. Finally, Yahoo! also helps the cache hit rates by issuing `expires` headers with expiration dates set far in the future. But best of all, these benefits are all provided for free.

If you've decided that you want to download the YUI in its entirety, you'll find a link on the YUI home page at `http://developer.yahoo.com/yui` which will lead you to the library's project site at SourceForge.net.

SourceForge is renowned as the world's largest open-source software development site and currently host over 100,000 different projects. All you really need from there is the library itself as virtually all of the documentation and useful information resides on the YUI site on the Yahoo! portal.

So as far as installing the library goes, the most that you'll need to do is to download the library to your computer and unpack it to a local directory where you can easily find the files, assets, and resources that you require for your current project, and if you choose to let Yahoo! host the files for you, you won't even need to do that.

Creating an Offline Library Repository

In order to follow the examples in this book, you will need to download a copy of the library and ensure that it is accessible to the pages that we are going to make. So you will need to create a new folder on your hard drive called `yuisite`. This folder is where all of our examples will reside.

Inside this folder, create another new folder called **yui**. When you unpack the library, you will see a folder called **build** inside it (as in the previous screenshot). You will need to copy and paste the entire **build** directory into the **yui** folder that you have just created. You won't need to add any files to the build directory, all of the files that we create will sit in the **yuisite** folder.

It is important that this structure is correct; otherwise none of the examples that we create as we progress through this book will work. A common indicator that library files are not accessible is a JavaScript error stating that YAHOO is undefined.

Using the Library Files in Your Own Web Pages

One thing that you need to check when using different controls and utilities from the library is which, if any, of the other utilities will be needed by the component that you wish to use; fortunately the online documentation and cheat sheets will list out any dependencies of any component that you choose, so finding out isn't hard.

There is only one file that must be used in every implementation of any of the various components: the YAHOO Global Object. This utility creates the namespaces within which all of the YUI library code resides, and contains some additional methods that are used by other files throughout the library.

It must appear before any of the other library files because if references to other component files appear before the Global Object, none of the namespaces used will be recognised by your script. This will cause a JavaScript error stating that YAHOO is undefined.

The CSS files should be linked to in the `<head>` section of your page, as any other CSS file would be. For SEO purposes, and to support the notions of progressive enhancement, the JavaScript that invokes and customises the library components should be as close to the bottom of the page as possible. Also, you can easily separate your JavaScript from your HTML altogether and keep your scripts in separate files.

To use the animation utility from the Yahoo! servers for example, the following script tag would be required:

```
<script type="text/javascript" src="http://yui.yahooapis.com/
          current_version/build/animation/animation-min.js">
</script>
```

As the animation utility also depends on the YAHOO Global Object, and the Event and DOM utilities, the `yahoo-dom-event` utility should also be used (but don't forget that the YAHOO Global Object must appear first), so the script tag shown below would actually have to appear before the above one:

```
<script src="http://yui.yahooapis.com/current_version/build/
                        yahoo-dom-event/yahoo-dom-event.js">
</script>
```

Once these script tags have been added to your page, the code required to animate your object or element would go into its own script tag in the `<body>` section of the page.

Now, we'll take our first look at one of the library components in detail: the Calendar control. We can take a quick look at its supporting classes to see what methods and properties are available to us, and can then move on to implement the control in the first of our coding examples.

Code Placement

Good coding practice should always be adhered to, whether designing with the YUI or not. Keeping your JavaScript and CSS code in separate files helps to minimise the amount of code that a search engine spider has to index, which could help contribute to a better results page listing. But it does have its downsides too; every file that your page links to adds another HTTP request to the interaction between your visitor and your server, which can result in slower performance.

In real-world implementations, we would always keep as much of our JavaScript and CSS in separate files as possible, keeping a clear distinction between content, behaviour, and presentation layers. For the purpose of this book however, we will be keeping the HTML and JavaScript code in one file. I stress that this is not the correct way to do things and is done purely so that the examples do not become bloated with numerous files.

Perfect Date Selection with the Calendar Control

For our first coding example, we'll take a quick look at the Calendar Control. The YUI Calendar allows you to easily create a variety of attractive and highly functional calendar interfaces which can allow your visitors to quickly and easily select single dates, or range of dates.

It's an easy component to master, making it ideal for our very first coding example. Not much coding is required for a basic calendar implementation, and the control can easily be customized using the Calendar classes' extensive range of properties, or by over-riding the default styling.

There is also a range of different formats of Calendar that we can create; there's the basic, single-select, one-page calendar control which displays one month at a time, or there's a larger, multi-page calendar which allows multiple months to be displayed at once. Multi-select calendars can come in either single or multiple month display formats.

The rendered calendar is instinctively intuitive to use and is presented in a very attractive manner. Almost anyone being presented with it will instantly know how to use it. By default, it features a clear and sensible interface for selecting a date, arranging the dates of the current or starting month in a grid headed by the day of the week.

It also features automatic rollovers for valid or selectable dates, automatic current date selection, and an infinite date range both forwards and backwards in time that the visitor can move through to select the date of their choice. When navigating between months, the individual days automatically reorder themselves so that the correct date appears in the correct day of the week.

Several supporting classes make up the Calendar control; two separate classes represent the two different types of calendar that can be rendered and another class contains math utilities which allow you to add, subtract, or compare different dates. We will take a look at the classes that make up this control to see what is available and exactly how it works before we begin coding.

The Basic Calendar Class

The most basic type of calendar is the single-panel Calendar which is created with the `YAHOO.widget.Calendar` class. To display a calendar, an HTML element is required to act as a container for the calendar. The screenshot shows a basic Calendar control:

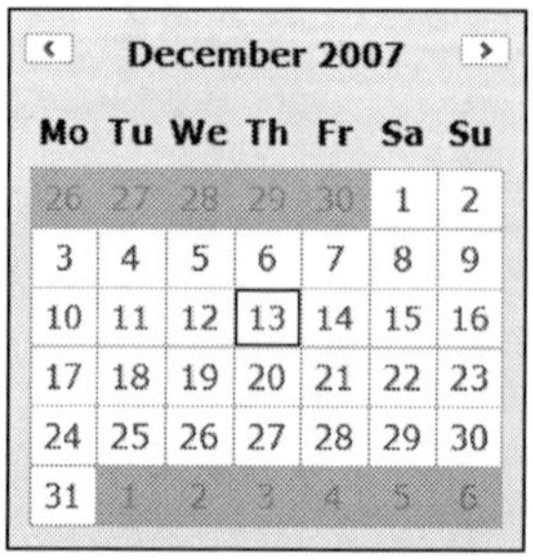

The constructor can then be called specifying, at the very least the `id` of the container element as an argument. You can also specify the `id` of the Calendar object as an argument, as well as an optional third argument that can accept a literal object containing various configuration properties.

The configuration object is defined within curly braces within the class constructor. It contains a range of configuration properties and keys that can be used to control different Calendar attributes such as its title, a comma-delimited range of pre-selected dates, or a close button shown on the calendar.

There are a large number of methods defined in the basic Calendar class; some of these are private methods that are used internally by the Calendar object to do certain things and which you normally wouldn't need to use yourself. Some of the more useful public methods include:

- Initialisation methods including `init`, `initEvents`, and `initStyles` which initialise either the calendar itself or the built-in custom events and style constants of the calendar.
- A method for determining whether a date is outside of the current month: `isDateOOM`.
- Navigation methods such as `nextMonth`, `nextYear`, `previousMonth`, and `previousYear` that can be used to programmatically change the month or year displayed in the current panel.
- Operational methods such as `addMonths`, `addYears`, `subtractMonths`, and `subtractYears` which are used to change the month and year shown in the current panel by the specified number of months or years.
- The `render` method is used to draw the calendar on the page and is called in for every implementation of a calendar, after it has been configured. Without this method, no Calendar appears on the page.
- Two reset methods: `reset` which resets the Calendar to the month and year originally selected, and `resetRenderers` which resets the render stack of the calendar.
- Selection methods that select or deselect dates such as `deselect`, `deselectAll`, `desellectCell`, `select`, and `selectCell`.

As you can see, there are many methods that you can call to take advantage of the advanced features of the calendar control.

The CalendarGroup Class

In addition to the basic calendar, you can also create a grouped calendar that displays two or more month panels at once using the `YAHOO.widget.CalendarGroup` class. The control automatically adjusts the Calendar's UI so that the navigation arrows are only displayed on the first and last calendar panels, and so that each panel has its own heading indicating which month it refers to.

The `CalendarGroup` class contains additional built-in functionality for updating the calendar panels on display, automatically. If you have a two-panel calendar displaying, for example, January and February, clicking the right navigation arrow will move February to the left of the panel so that March will display as the right-hand panel. All of this is automatic and nothing needs to be configured by you.

There are fewer methods in this class; some of those found in the basic `Calendar` class can also be found here, such as the navigation methods, selection methods, and some of the render methods. Native methods found only in the `CalendarGroup` class include:

- The subscribing methods `sub` and `unsub`, which subscribe or unsubscribe to custom events of each child calendar.
- Child functions such as the `callChildFunction` and `setChildFunction` methods which set and call functions within all child calendars in the calendar group.

Implementing a Calendar

To complete this example, the only tool other than the YUI that you'll need is a basic text editor. Native support for the YUI is provided by some web authoring software packages, most notably Aptana, an open-source application that has been dubbed 'Dreamweaver Killer'. However, I always find that writing code manually while learning something is much more beneficial.

It is very quick and easy to add the calender, as the basic default implementations require very little configuration. It can be especially useful in forms where the visitor must enter a date. Checking that a date has been entered correctly and in the correct format takes valuable processing time, but using the YUI calendar means that dates are always exactly as you expect them to be.

So far we've spent most of this chapter looking at a lot of the theoretical issues surrounding the library; I don't know about you, but I think it's definitely time to get on with some actual coding!

The Initial HTML Page

Our first example page contains a simple text field and an image which once clicked will display the Calendar control on the page, thereby allowing for a date to be selected and added to the input. Begin with the following basic HTML page:

```
<!DOCTYPE HTML PUBLIC "-//W3C//DTD HTML 4.01//EN"
                       "http://www.w3.org/TR/html4/strict.dtd">
<html lang="en">
  <head>
    <meta http-equiv="content-type" content="text/html;
                                         charset=utf-8">
    <title>YUI Calendar Control Example</title>
    <link rel="stylesheet"
          type="text/css"
          href="yui/build/calendar/assets/skins/sam/calendar.css">
    <script type="text/javascript"
            src="yui/build/yahoo-dom-event/
                                      yahoo-dom-event.js"></script>
    <script type="text/javascript"
            src="yui/build/calendar/calendar-min.js"></script>
    <style type="text/css">
      input {
               margin:0px 10px 0px 10px;
            }
    </style>
  </head>
  <body class="yui-skin-sam">
    <div>
      <label>Please enter your date of birth:</label>
      <input type="text" name="dobfield" id="dobfield">
      <img id="calico" src="icons/cal.png"
           alt="Open the Calendar control">
    </div>
    <div id="mycal"></div>
  </body>
</html>
```

We begin with a valid `DOCTYPE` declaration, a must in any web page. For validity, we can also add the `lang` attribute to the opening `<html>` tag and for good measure, enforce the `utf-8` character set. Nothing so far is YUI-specific, but coding in this way every time is a good habit.

We link to the stylesheet used to control the appearance of the calendar control, which is handled in this example by the `sam` skin within the `<link>` tag. Accordingly, we also need to add the appropriate class name to the `<body>` tag.

Following this, we link to the required library files with `<script>` tags; the calendar control is relatively simple and requires just the YAHOO, DOM, and Event components (using the aggregated `yahoo-dom-event.js` file for efficiency), as well as the underlying source file `calendar-min.js`.

A brief `<style>` tag finishes the `<head>` section of the page with some CSS relevant to this particular example, and the `<body>` of the page at this stage contains just two `<div>` elements: the first holds a `<label>`, text field, and a calendar icon (which can be used to launch the control), while the second holds the calendar control. When viewed in a browser, the page at this point should appear like this:

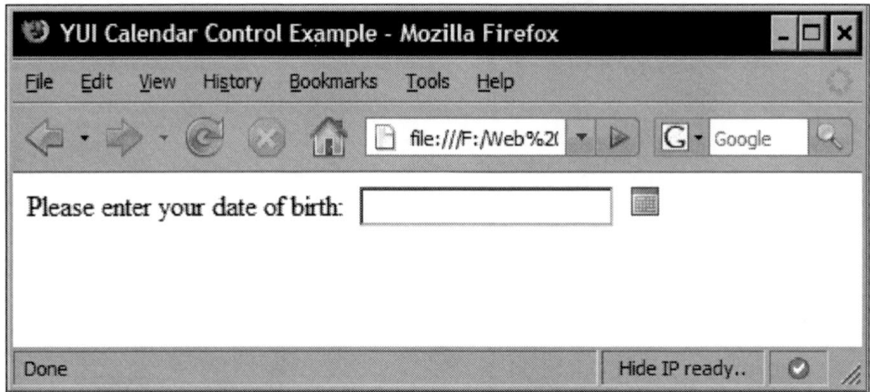

The calendar icon used in this example was taken, with gratitude from Mark Carson at `http://markcarson.com`.

Beginning the Scripting

We want the calendar to appear when the icon next to the text field is clicked, rather than it being displayed on the page-load, so the first thing we need to do is to set a listener for the click event on the image.

Directly before closing `</body>` tag, add the following code:

```
<script type="text/javascript">
  //create the namespace object for this example
  YAHOO.namespace("yuibook.calendar");
```

```
    //define the lauchCal function which creates the calendar
    YAHOO.yuibook.calendar.launchCal = function() {

    }

    //create calendar on page load
    YAHOO.util.Event.onDOMReady(YAHOO.yuibook.calendar.launchCal);
  </script>
```

Let's look at each line of the above code. We first use the `.namespace()` method of the YAHOO utility to set up the namespace object used for this example. Next we define the anonymous `launchCal` function, which will hold all of the code that generates the calendar control.

Then we use the `.onDOMReady()` method of the Event utility to execute the `launchCal` function when the DOM is in an usable state. We'll be looking at the DOM utility in much greater detail later in the book.

Now we can add the extremely brief code that's required to actually produce the Calendar. Within the braces of our anonymous function, add the following code:

```
//create the calendar object, specifying the container
Var myCal = new YAHOO.widget.Calendar("mycal");

//draw the calendar on screen
myCal.render();

//hide it again straight away
myCal.hide();
```

This is all that we need to create the Calendar; we simply define `myCal` as a new `Calendar` object, specifying the underlying container HTML element as an argument of the constructor.

Once we have a `Calendar` object, we can call the `.render()` method on it to create the calendar and display it on the page. No arguments are required for this method. Since we want the calendar to be displayed when its icon is clicked, we hide the calendar from view straight away.

To display the calendar when the icon for it is clicked, we'll need one more anonymous function. Add the following code beneath the `.hide()` method:

```
//define the showCal function which shows the calendar
Var showCal = function() {

  //show the calendar
  myCal.show();
}
```

Now we can attach a listener which detects the click event on the calendar icon:

```
//attach listener for click event on calendar icon
YAHOO.util.Event.addListener("calico", "click", showCal);
```

Save the file that we've just created as `calendar.html` or similar in your `yuisite` directory. If you view it in your browser now and click the Calendar icon, you should see this:

The calendar is automatically configured to display the current date, although this is something that can be changed using the configuration object mentioned earlier.

If you use a DOM explorer to view the current DOM of a page with an open calendar on it, you'll see that a basic Calendar control is rendered as a table with eight rows and seven columns.

The first row contains the images used to navigate between previous or forthcoming months and the title of the current month and year. The next row holds the two-letter representations of each of the different days of the week, and the rest of the rows hold the squares representing the individual days of the current month. The screenshot on the next page show some of the DOM representation of the Calendar control used in our example page:

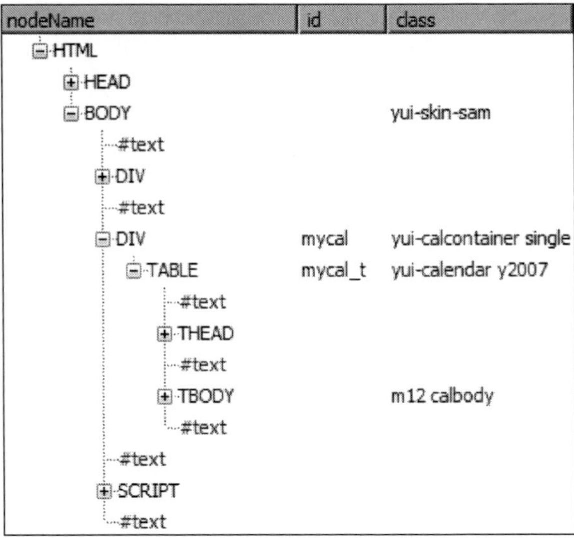

Now that we can call up the Calendar control by clicking on our Calendar icon, we need to customize it slightly. Unless the person completing the form is very young, they will need to navigate through a large number of calendar pages in order to find their date of birth. This is where the Calendar Navigator interface comes into play.

We can easily enable this feature using a configuration object passed into the `Calendar` constructor. Alter your code so that it appears as follows:

```
//create the calendar object, using container & config object
myCal = new YAHOO.widget.Calendar("mycal", {navigator:true});
```

Clicking on the **Month** or **Year** label will now open an interface which allows your visitors to navigate directly to any given month and year:

The configuration object can be used to set a range of calendar configuration properties including the original month and year displayed by the Calendar, the minimum and maximum dates available to the calendar, a title for the calendar, a close button, and various other properties.

Let's update our `Calendar` instance so that it features a title and a close button. Add the following properties to the literal object in our constructor:

```
//create the calendar object, specifying the container and a literal
//configuration object
myCal = new YAHOO.widget.Calendar("mycal",
     {navigator:true, title:"Choose your Date Of Birth", close:true});
```

This is what our Calendar should now look like:

Configuration properties like those we have just set, can also be set outside of the constructor using the `.queueProperty()` and `.fireQueue()` methods, or by using the `.setProperty()` method. Let's use these to alter our Calendar so that the first column header is set to Monday instead of Sunday. Add the following code directly before the call to the `.render()` method:

```
//configure the calendar to begin on Monday
myCal.cfg.setProperty("start_weekday", "1");
```

When the calendar is displayed now, Monday will be the first day instead of Sunday:

Finally, we need to add some additional code that will allow the date that is selected to be inserted into the text field. We can do this using some of the custom events defined by the calendar classes.

Highly Eventful

Both the `Calendar` and `CalendarGroup` classes have a series of custom events defined for them which allow for easily listening and reacting to interesting moments during any calendar or calendar group interaction.

The two classes both have the same set of events defined for them, including:

- `beforeDeselectEvent`: Fired before a cell is deselected, allowing you to abort the operation if needed
- `beforeHideEvent`: Fired just before the calendar is hidden
- `beforeHideNavEvent`: Fired just before the calendar navigator is hidden
- `beforeRenderEvent`: Fired before the calendar is drawn on screen
- `beforeSelectEvent`: Fired before a cell is selected
- `beforeShowEvent`: Fired just before the calendar is shown
- `beforeShowNavEvent`: Fired just before the calendar navigator is shown
- `changePageEvent`: Fired once the current calendar page has been changed
- `clearEvent`: Fired once the calendar has been cleared
- `deselectEvent`: Fired once the cell has been deselected

- `hideEvent`: Fired once the calendar has been hidden
- `hideNavEvent`: Fired once the calendar navigator has been hidden
- `renderEvent`: Fired once the calendar has been drawn on screen
- `resetEvent`: Fired once the calendar has been reset
- `selectEvent`: Fired once a cell, or range of cells, has been selected
- `showEvent`: Fired once the calendar has been shown
- `showNavEvent`: Fired once the calendar navigator has been shown

This rich event system allows you to easily watch for cells being selected or deselected, month panel changes, render events, or even the reset method being called, and add code to deal with these key moments effectively. As you can see, most of the events form pairs of before and after events, which allows you to easily cancel or abort an operation before it has any visual impact.

Let's now take a look at how these custom Calendar events can be used. First define the function that will handle the `select` event; add the following code directly after the `showCall()` function:

```
//attach listener for click event on calendar icon
YAHOO.util.Event.addListener("calico", "click", showCal);
//define the ripDate function which gets the selected date
var ripDate = function(type, args) {
}
//subscribe to the select event on Calendar cells
myCal.selectEvent.subscribe(ripDate);
```

Every time the `select` event is detected, our `ripDate` function will be executed. The `type` and `args` objects are automatically created by the control; the `args` object is what we are interested in here, because it gives us easy access to an array of information about our Calendar.

Now, within the curly braces of the `ripDate()` function set the following variables:

```
//get the date components
Var dates = args[0];
Var date = dates[0];
Var theYear = date[0];
Var theMonth = date[1];
Var theDay = date[2];
```

The first item in the `args` array is an array of selected dates, so we first save this to the variable `dates`. As this is a single-select calendar, only the first item of the `dates` array will contain data, so this is also saved to a variable: the `date` variable.

Each date is itself an array, with the first item corresponding to the year, the second item equaling the month, and the third item mapped to the individual date. All of these values are saved into variables.

```
Var theDate = theMonth + "/" + theDay + "/" + theYear;
```

This part of the function uses standard concatenation techniques to build a string containing the individual date components in the format in which we want to present them (so that, for example, it would be extremely easy to express dates in UK format, where the date appears before the month):

```
//get a reference to the text field
Var field = YAHOO.util.Dom.get("dobfield");

//insert the formatted date into the text field
field.value = theDate;

//hide the calendar once more
myCal.hide();
```

Finally, we use the very handy DOM utility's `.get()` method to grab a reference to the text field, set the value of the text field to our date string, and then hide the calendar once more.

Save the file once more and view it again in your browser of choice. After clicking the Calendar icon and choosing a date, it should be displayed in the text field:

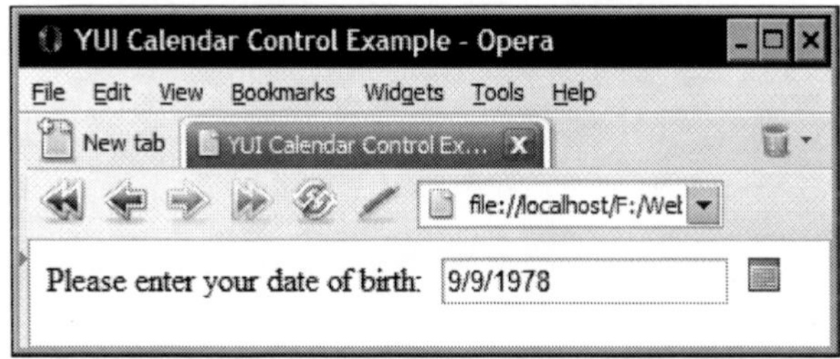

At this point, we can take a brief look at how we can override the default styling of the calendar. I think we should change the calendar's close button and make it look a little more like a traditional close button. This can be done with the following simple CSS rule, which should be inserted into the `<style>` tag in the `<head>` of our document:

```
.yui-skin-sam .yui-calcontainer .calclose {
  background:url("icons/myclose.gif") no-repeat;
}
```

Because we're using the default `sam` skin, we should begin the selector with this class name and then target the name of the container and close elements. Other elements of the calendar, such as the navigation arrows, can easily be styled in this way. Using a DOM explorer to expose the names of other parts of the calendar is also an easy way to change other elements of the calendar. Our Close button should now appear like this:

The DateMath Class

In addition to the two classes catering for two different types of calendar, a class, `YAHOO.widget.DateMath`, defines a series of utilities for performing simple mathematical calculations or comparisons on dates. It has only a small number of static properties and a small set of methods. There are no events defined in this class and no configuration attributes.

All of its methods return either a boolean value indicating whether the comparison was true or false, or a modified date object. Some of them will be used very frequently, while others will be used only rarely (but are still very useful).

Our date of birth calendar isn't really appropriate for seeing how the `DateMath` calls can be used. In order to examine some of the available methods, we should create a new calendar. In a blank page of your text editor, begin with the following HTML:

```
<!DOCTYPE HTML PUBLIC "-//W3C//DTD HTML 4.01//EN"
                       "http://www.w3.org/TR/html4/strict.dtd">
<html lang="en">
  <head>
```

```
      <meta http-equiv="content-type" content="text/html;
                                       charset=utf-8">
      <title>YUI MathDate Class Example</title>
      <link rel="stylesheet"
            type="text/css"
            href="yui/build/calendar/assets/skins/sam/calendar.css">
      <script type="text/javascript"
              src="yui/build/yahoo-dom-event/yahoo-dom-event.js">
      </script>
      <script type="text/javascript"
              src="yui/build/calendar/calendar-min.js"></script>
    </head>
    <body class="yui-skin-sam">
      <div id="mycal"></div>
      <div id="results"></div>
    </body>
  </html>
```

This very simple page will form the basis of our example. Next, add the following `<script>` tag to the `<body>` tag of the page, directly below the results `<div>` tag:

```
<script type="text/javascript">
  //create the namespace object for this example
  YAHOO.namespace("yuibook.calendar");

  //define the initCal function which creates the calendar
  YAHOO.yuibook.calendar.initCal = function() {

  }
  //create calendar on page load
  YAHOO.util.Event.onDOMReady(YAHOO.yuibook.calendar.initCal);
</script>
```

We create the same namespace object for this page and initially generate the calendar using the `.onDOMReady()` method and an anonymous function in exactly the same way as we did before. Next, add the following code to the `YAHOO.yuibook.calendar.initCal()` function:

```
//create the calendar object, specifying the container
var myCal = new YAHOO.widget.Calendar("mycal");

//draw the calendar on screen
myCal.render();
```

We create the calendar in the same way as in the previous example and render it on the page. This time, we don't need to worry about hiding it again as it will be a permanent fixture of the page.

Before we start looking at the `DateMath` methods, let's get a reference to the current date. Add the following code directly below the `.render()` method call:

```
//get and display today's date
var dayNum = myCal.today.getDay();
var dayString = myCal.Locale.WEEKDAYS_LONG[dayNum];
var date = myCal.today.getDate();
var monthNum = myCal.today.getMonth();
var monthString = myCal.Locale.MONTHS_LONG[monthNum];
var year = myCal.today.getFullYear();
var results1 = document.createElement("div");
results1.innerHTML = "Today is " + dayString + ", " + date + "
                                        " + monthString + " " + year;

YAHOO.util.Dom.get("results").appendChild(results1);
```

It is easy to obtain today's date in UTC format using the `today` property of the `Calendar` class. Once we have this, we can get references to the date and month numerical representations and from these we can get the full day name and month name using `Locale.WEEKDAYS_LONG[dayNum]` and `Locale.MONTHS_LONG[monthNum]`.

The `Locale` object is automatically created by the control and contains localised day and month names. It is primarily used to add new locales and specify alternative day and month names, but because it defaults to English, we can simply read the properties and pull out what we want.

Once we have the information we need, it is simple enough to create a new `<div>` element, populate it with our formatted date string and then attach it to our results `<div>` element. Your page should look similar to the following screenshot:

Now we can have some fun with a few of the `DateMath` methods. First, add the following directly beneath our last block of code:

```
//work out date in 10 days time
var futureDate = YAHOO.widget.DateMath.add(myCal.today,
                                    YAHOO.widget.DateMath.DAY, 10);

var results2 = document.createElement("div");
results2.innerHTML = "In ten days time it will be " + futureDate;

YAHOO.util.Dom.get("results").appendChild(results2);
```

We can use the `.add()` method of the `YAHOO.widget.DateMath` class to add a specified amount of time to a date object. In this example, the date object is obtained using the `myCal.today` property once more (as we can't use the `date` variable that already exists as this is a number not a full date object), but any date object could be used.

The `.add()` method takes three arguments. The first is the date object on which the addition should be carried out, the second is one of the built-in field constants representing the unit to be added (which could be days, weeks, months, years), and the final argument is the actual amount to be added.

For the purposes of this example, I have left the `futureDate` field in full UTC format, but we could easily extract just the parts of the date that we want, just as we did to get the today date.

Let's now look at the almost identical `.subtract()` method. Add the following code:

```
//work out date two months ago
var pastDate = YAHOO.widget.DateMath.subtract(myCal.today,
                                YAHOO.widget.DateMath.MONTH, 2);
var results3 = document.createElement("div");
results3.innerHTML = "Two months ago the date was " + pastDate;
YAHOO.util.Dom.get("results").appendChild(results3);
```

You can see how easy the `DateMath` class makes addition and subtraction of date objects. The class has other useful methods such as the `.getDayOffset()` and `.getWeekNumber()` methods. We can expose the functionality of these two methods with the following code:

```
//work out day and week numbers of current date
var numberOfDays = YAHOO.widget.DateMath.getDayOffset(myCal.today,
                                                          year);

var weekNumber = YAHOO.widget.DateMath.getWeekNumber(myCal.today,
                                                          year);
```

```
results4 = document.createElement("div");
results4.innerHTML = numberOfDays + " days have elapsed so far this
                                                              year";

results5 = document.createElement("div");
results5.innerHTML = "We are in week number " + weekNumber;
YAHOO.util.Dom.get("results").appendChild(results4);
YAHOO.util.Dom.get("results").appendChild(results5);
```

Save the file as `datemath.html` and view it in your browser of choice:

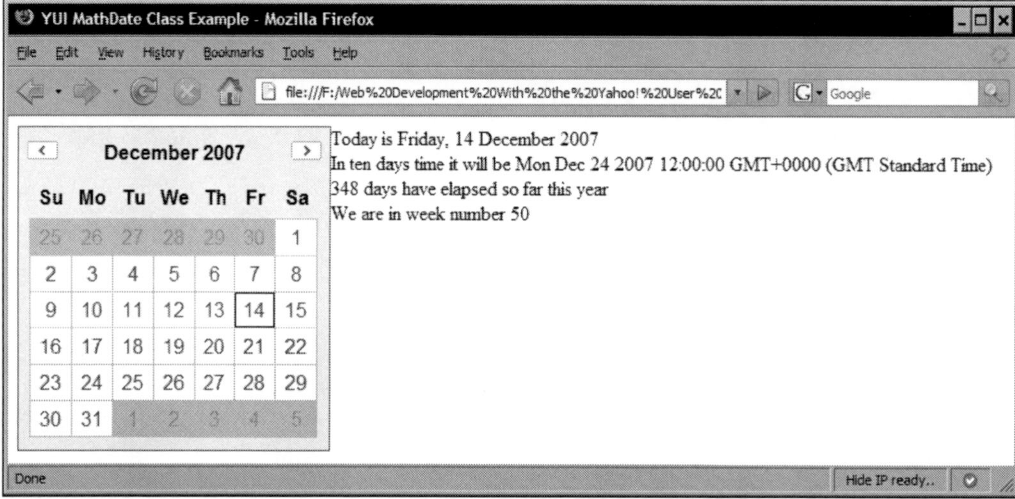

Summary

During the course of this chapter we have taken an in-depth view into what the YUI is, where it came from, and the things that spurred it into existence. We have seen everything that the license gives us permission to do and investigated the different ways of serving the files that power it. We've also looked at who can make the most of the library, how to install it, and how to use it in your own web pages.

Lastly, we finished off all the theory with a practical example that had you creating and customising your first user interface control: a calendar, and working with one of its supporting classes: the `DateMath` class. I hope that this first example has made you eager to experiment with the library further and has shown you how easy it is to implement YUI components.

2

Creating Consistency With The CSS Tools

Not only does the library provide you with a rich selection of easily implemented utilities and UI controls that save you time and effort when developing and debugging, it is also a gift that keeps on giving with a selection of CSS tools that every developer should have to hand.

The CSS tools that form the fourth and final section of the library are separate from the CSS files required by some of the controls in order to be displayed correctly; some of the controls contain a folder within their unpacked directories called 'assets', and in this folder there may be images, a stylesheet, or sometimes both depending on the control.

But the CSS files discussed in this chapter do not reside within the assets folders, tucked away deep within the library's hierarchy. The CSS tools each have folders of their own within the library's directory structure, and are on a level with both the utilities and controls.

In this chapter we're going to examine these tools in detail and learn exactly what they can do for your web pages and applications, whether used in conjunction with other components of the library, or completely on their own.

We will look at the following:

- What each of the four tools do
- Rules contained within each CSS file
- Why and how you should use the tools
- How and why elements are normalised
- Solid foundation provided by the base tool
- How fonts are styled with the fonts tool
- Some of the different templates found within the grids CSS tool

Tools of the Trade

There are some similarities between the CSS tools and the other components of the library and there are of course some differences. Like each of the other components, there is also a full version of each file with comments and whitespace preserved for readability, and a minified production version.

If you wish, you can also have Yahoo! serve the CSS files used by the tools to you across the internet by linking to the files held on their servers, just like you can with the other library components.

Several different configurations of the CSS tools have also been put together, which combine some of the different tools into single files, making them easier and more efficient to use together. `resets.css` and `fonts.css` have been amalgamated into one file for your convenience, which is probably because the YUI team recommend the use of these two tools in all YUI implementations. A `reset-fonts-grids.css` file has also been created due to the high likelihood that the huge range of page templates available in `grids.css` will also be used very frequently.

There is also a cheat sheet that combines information on all four of the CSS Tools, which makes more sense than supplying one sheet per tool. There wouldn't be much point providing a whole sheet for each of the tools anyway, as on the whole the CSS tools will do their job provided you use the correct class names and nesting structures in your mark up.

The one sheet provided does give you enough basic information about each of the tools for you to get started, and lists information such as how you should structure your basic pages for best effect with grid layouts, or the percentages you should specify to make use of different font sizes, and some of the different template class names, so it can still be an invaluable reference when working with these tools.

Element Normalisation with reset.css

Often, one of the most painful exercises in web development is simply getting everything to look consistent across the major browser platforms. Developers will often design and test an implementation in one particular browser, and then when everything is working and rendering correctly in their browser of choice, they will then refine it and tweak it until it works and renders similarly in all of the other major browsers.

Due to the differences between the default stylesheet in use in the various browsers, getting pages to render in the same way can be a challenge. Something that lines up perfectly in IE will undoubtedly be misaligned in other browsers, and of course when you correct the difference so that it renders in the way that you want it to in Safari, for example, you go back to IE and it's out of alignment there once again.

For a quick example of CSS inconsistencies at work, take a look at screenshot below; there are two `<div>` elements on the page, one nested within the other. Both of the `<div>` elements have specified `width` and `padding` values. The outer `<div>` is absolutely positioned while the inner `<div>` is fixed. In IE6 on Windows, you can see that the two `<div>` elements nest as intended. In Firefox however, the nesting is broken:

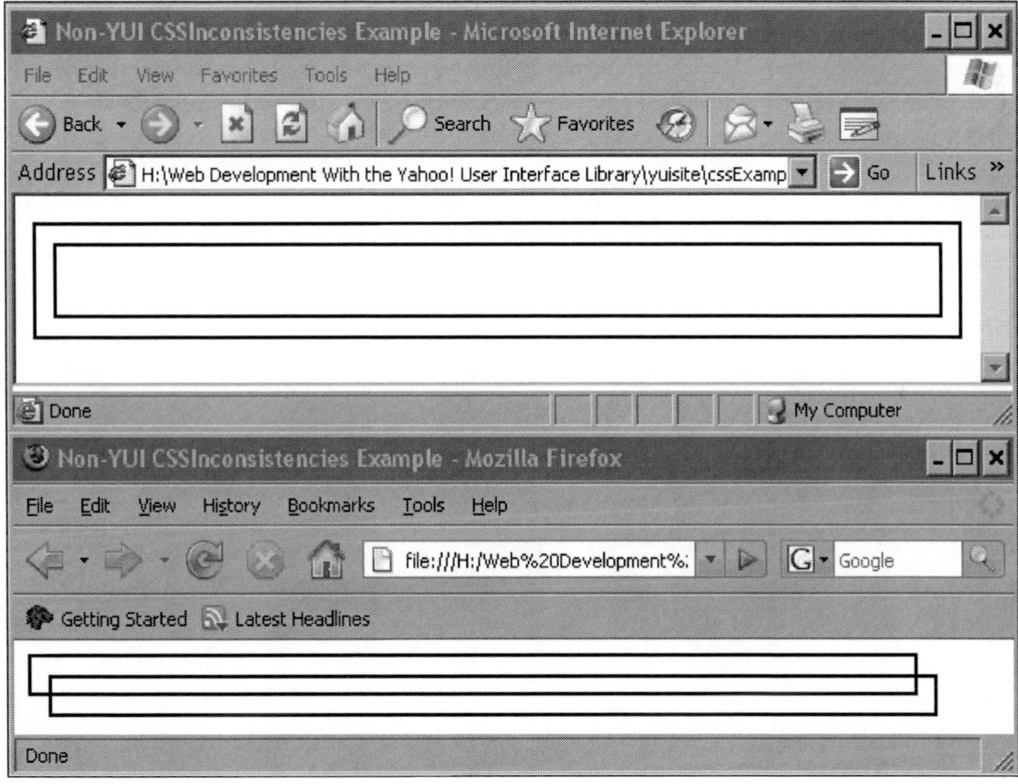

Until now, the quickest way around these issues has been to use a compliant browser to design in and resort to hacks or filters so as to make the various versions of IE play along, or to use the IE-specific conditional-comments method of supplying a different stylesheet for different versions of IE.

While both of these methods can make designing a site easier in the short-term, there is no guarantee that future browsers will not choke on any hacks or filters that you may be using in your stylesheet, so it is best to try avoid them whenever it is possible for you to do so.

Using a range of different stylesheets for different browsers and browser versions can also be problematic in terms of maintenance, as you will find that, when you want to make a change to the way in which your site is displayed, there are many more files that need to be updated.

The CSS tools can provide a firmer guarantee that future browsers will still display everything correctly and can cut down on the number of files that you need to actively maintain (as Yahoo will kindly maintain these for you).

The `resets.css` file provided by the YUI library avoids the need to use most hacks or workarounds by standardizing the default rendering of all of the most common HTML elements across the different browsers, saving you the tricky troubleshooting that sometimes needs to be done to get everything lined up and looking right in all browsers.

Margins and some of the other preset styles of various elements have been removed or set to zero in the resets stylesheet, so you can worry about presenting your content, without trying to remember whether additional padding in a particular browser is going to put everything out of place.

Element Rules

`reset.css` consists mostly of element selectors that match nearly all content containing HTML elements and resets them to a non-styled state. This enables the designer to apply consistent styling that works across all browsers.

The following common and frequently used elements each have their `margin` and `padding` values normalised to zero:

- The document body
- `div` and `p` elements
- All of the list elements: `dl`, `dt`, `dd`, `ul`, ol, `li`
- All of the heading elements: `h1`, `h2`, `h3`, `h4`, `h5`, `h6`
- `pre` and `blockquote` elements
- Some of the form elements: `form`, `fieldset`, `input`, `textarea`
- The table elements `th` and `td`

The next element to be standardized is the `table` element, which has its borders automatically collapsed and set to zero. Following on from this, `fieldset` elements and images both have their borders set to zero as well, as do any `abbr` and `acronym` elements that you use.

To prevent certain types of font-specific elements from rendering in either italic or bold typefaces in some of the more common browsers, the following list of elements all have their `font-style` and `font-weight` properties set to `normal`:

- `address`
- `caption`
- `cite`
- `code`
- `dfn`
- `em`
- `strong`
- `th`
- `var`

The next rule targets the standard ordered and unordered HTML list elements and sets their `list-style` property to `none` thereby removing the standard list item marker from the text that makes up each list item, easily allowing you to explicitly define your own if necessary. Following on from this, both `caption` and `th` elements are aligned strictly to the left with no indentation.

All heading elements (`h1` through `h6`) are standardised to a `font-size` of `100%` and a `font-weight` of `normal`, effectively setting all heading types to the same size and weight as standard text. The size that the text actually ends up is of course wholly dependent on the visitor's browser settings.

The final style rules supplied by the `reset.css` stylesheet are the two `:before` and `:after` pseudo-elements which act upon any `q` (a single-line or short quotation) elements used in the document. The rule specifies that no content should be placed directly before or after this element using the `content:'';` rule.

As an example of what `reset.css` does to elements, the screenshot below shows a collection of all of the elements targeted by this CSS tool, before `resets.css` has been applied. Most of the elements have visible styling applied to them by the browser, and this varies slightly between different browsers.

I've chosen Firefox on Windows to highlight this example because the `<fieldset>` element is one of the few examples of this browser styling an element badly. Note that, no `<br>` elements or positional CSS has been used in this example at all; all of the styling has been applied automatically by the browser.

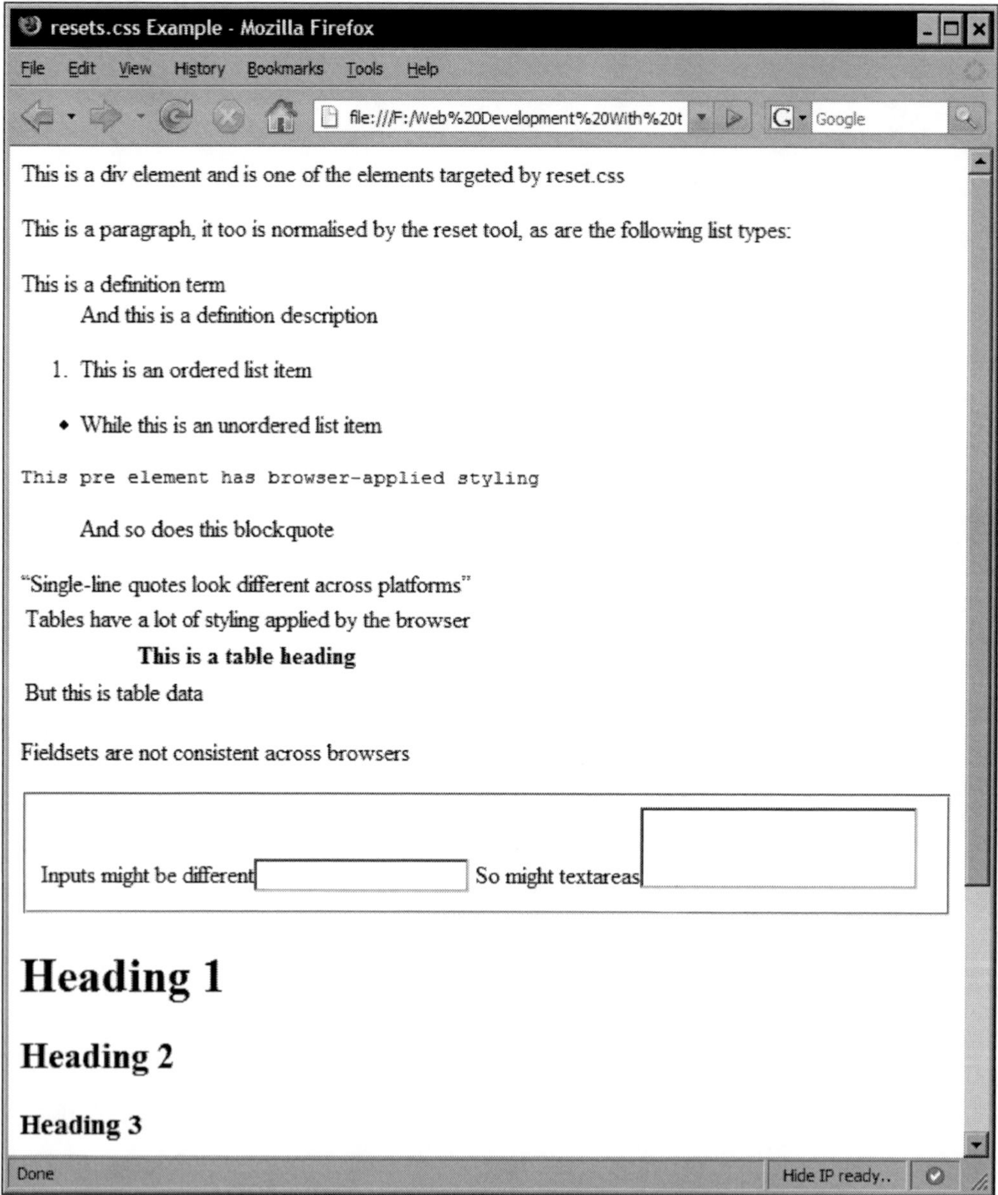

Next, we can see what a difference `reset.css` makes to this page by including a reference to the file in the `<head>` of the page. With `reset.css` linked, all elements are reset.

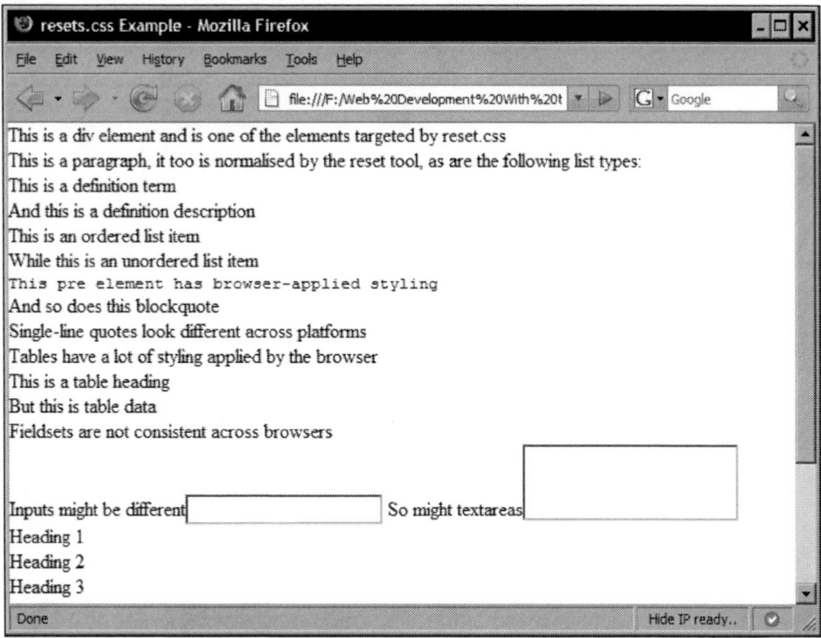

Hence, the resets CSS tool can be an invaluable asset when either used as part of a YUI implementation, or completely isolated from the rest of the library, and linked to by pages entirely of your own design. This tool is completely compatible across the A-grade browser spectrum. (Refer to Chapter 1 for details).

It's also very easy to change the default rendering provided by this file. You may wish to have certain images that do have a border, so all you need to do is add your own class attribute to the `<image>` and define a new CSS class in a separate CSS file of your own making.

If you only ever use one file from the library, this one alone could provide the most benefit in the long-term (but of course you won't want to exclude the rest of the fantastic functionality provided by the YUI!).

First Base

Where the `resets.css` tool breaks down the default stylesheets of the different browsers, the `base.css` tool then builds upon this level foundation to provide basic styling across a range of commonly used elements.

There are certain elements on your page that just should be styled differently from other elements. Heading text for example, simply should stand out from body text; aside from any SEO benefits, that's the whole point of heading text in the first place.

So the base tool reintroduces some of the presentational styles of the common elements that the resets tool neutralizes, but it does so in a way that is consistent across browsers. Let's look at the basic stylesheet provided by the `base.css` tool.

Headings

The first three levels of heading elements are scaled up to sizes more appropriate for headings (so that they are bigger than standard body text). The new sizes are specified in percentages as follows:,

- `<h1>` elements are set to `138.5%` which corresponds to a `px` size of `18`
- `<h2>` elements are set to `123.1%` which corresponds to a `px` size of `16`
- `<h3>` elements are set to `108%` which corresponds to a `px` size of `14`

Additionally, the above three heading levels are also given a top and bottom margin equal to the height of one line, and left and right margins of zero. All of the heading elements (`<h1>` through `<h6>`) are also given back their bold `font-weight` properties.

Lists

Ordered, unordered, and definition lists are given a left margin to indent them by two lines. Ordered lists are given a decimal marker positioned outside, while unordered lists are given a disc marker, also placed on the outside of the list item's box.

The `<li>` elements of definition lists are given a `left-margin` setting of `1em` to indent the text within the list item slightly. These lists are not given an item marker like the other two list types.

Tables

Both table header and table data cells are given a solid, black, 1 pixel border and an overall padding of half an `em`. This helps to space things out and make tables a little more readable. `<th>` elements are also given a `bold` style to set them out from `<td>` elements.

Like the `<th>` cells in a table, the caption element is also given the same overall margin of `0.5em` and a centred appearance, and the entire table is given a `bottom-margin` of one line height as well.

Miscellaneous Rules

The base tool provides a couple of other rules as well; `<abbr>` and `<acronym>` elements are both given a dotted bottom and a help icon so that visitors can easily find extra information by hovering the mouse, and `<em>` elements are given an `italic` style.

Block quote elements, like the list family, are given an overall margin of `1em` to help them stand out from standard body text, as are `<p>` and `<fieldset>` elements.

If we include a reference to the `base.css` stylesheet in our test page, some of the elements that were normalised by the reset tool will have styling applied, as demonstrated by the following screenshot:

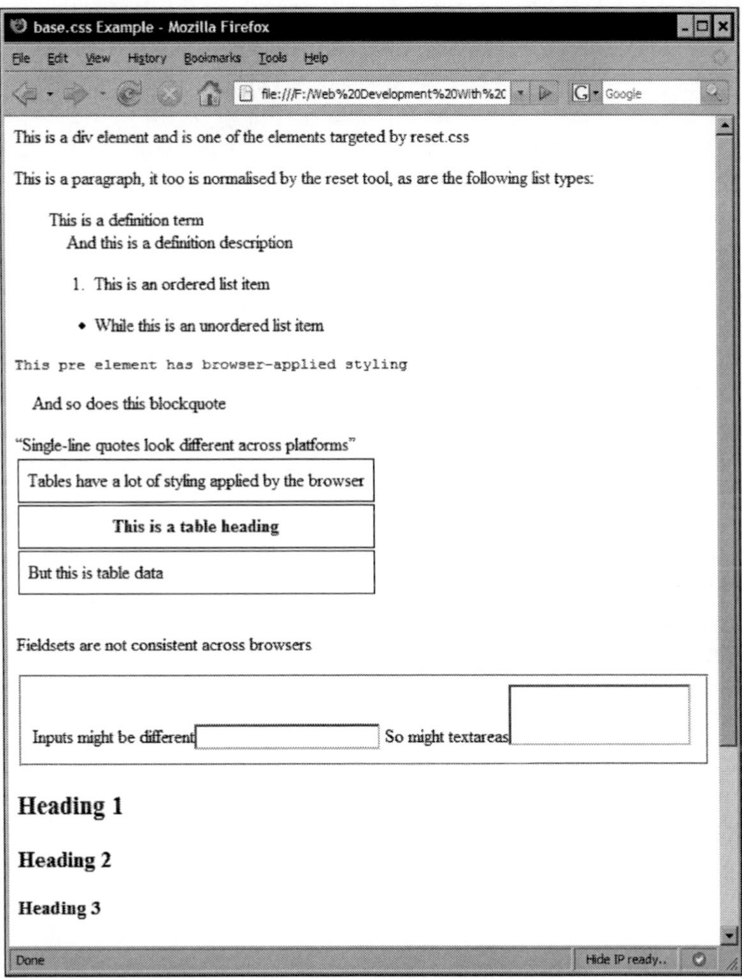

Tidying up Text with fonts.css

The next CSS tool, `fonts.css`, is provided so that you can easily standardize all of your text to a single font-face, font-size, and line-height. It standardises all rendered text on the page to the `Arial` font, except for text within `<pre>` and `<code>` tags, which instead use the `monospace` typeface.

In terms of the amount of actual code, this file is tiny, much smaller in fact than the reset tool we looked at earlier, providing just five rules in total, and unlike the other tools provided in the library, the fonts tool does need to resort to a few filters to bring older versions of IE back into line.

The Body

The first rule targets the `<body>` tag and sets the `font` property to `13px`, `arial`, `Helvetica`, `clean`, or `sans-serif`. This provides a clear font degradation path; if browsers or operating systems don't have Arial installed or for some reason can't display it, the platform tries Helvetica next, and so on, right down to sans-serif if necessary (although it's unlikely that the browser would need to travel all the way down to the end of the degradation path).

This is also important for Unicode support; if the font in use cannot map a Unicode character to a font-glyph in the current font set, it can use the font degradation path to map a Unicode character from another defined font set.

This helps to avoid those unsightly little squares that sometimes appear in emails or on web pages when the authors decide to use unusual or foreign font families (I use the word "foreign" hesitantly, because clearly this is relative to the visitors nationality and location.).

The final two rules in the `<body>` selector, `*font-size:small` and `*font:x-small`, are used to set the `font-size` in IE (which makes better use of the CSS keywords for `font-size` than it does of percentages) and addresses text-rendering peculiarities in older versions of IE, which can incorrectly interpret the `font-size` keywords specified by the CSS1 standard thus making all of your fonts appear bigger than they should.

Tables

Rule number two targets `<table>` elements and forces them to inherit the `font-styles` that are specified by their parent elements. This is especially important to overcome inheritance problems when browsers are running in quirks mode. It also sets all table text to the standardized size of `100%`.

> Quirks mode describes a mode of operation for browsers whereby they render pages according to the support of older, non-standards compliant versions of their browsers instead of according to W3C standards. If you don't include a complete DOCTYPE in the head of your page, it will trigger quirks mode in any browsers that view it.

The final rule targets elements containing content that may be used to display some kind of programming code. The following elements receive the monospace font family:

- `pre`
- `code`
- `kbd`
- `samp`
- `tt`

An IE hack can also be found in this rule to correct a misinterpretation in this browser of the font-size calculated on these elements; as IE renders them slightly too small, the font-size is bumped up to `108%`. In other browsers, it is set to 100% instead.

Like the resets CSS Tool, `fonts.css` is extremely easy to use and requires no further participation from you once you have linked to the stylesheet. You don't need to use any particular class names or give elements specific `id` attributes in order to make use of the normalization services provided by these two tools, and the fonts CSS tool is compatible with all A-grade browsers.

Remember from Chapter 1 that A-grade browsers are browsers that have been tested extensively by the YUI developers and confirmed to support the highest level of visual presentation and interactivity that the library can provide.

As before, we can see the effect that `fonts.css` has on our dummy page in the screenshot below. This is exactly the same page as shown before except that it links to `fonts.css` instead of reset or base.

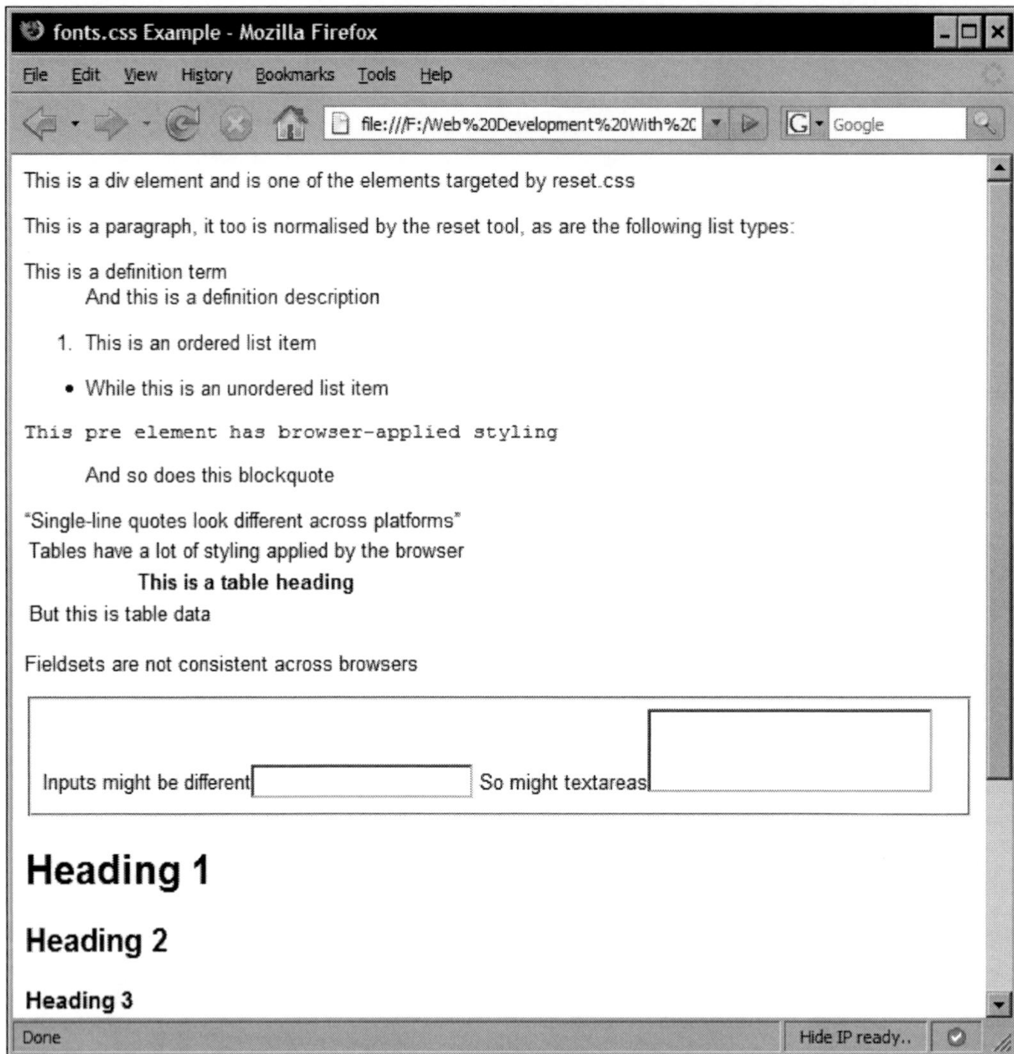

So far we've looked at how these files act upon elements when used individually, so for completeness, let's have a look at all three in action at once on our test page:

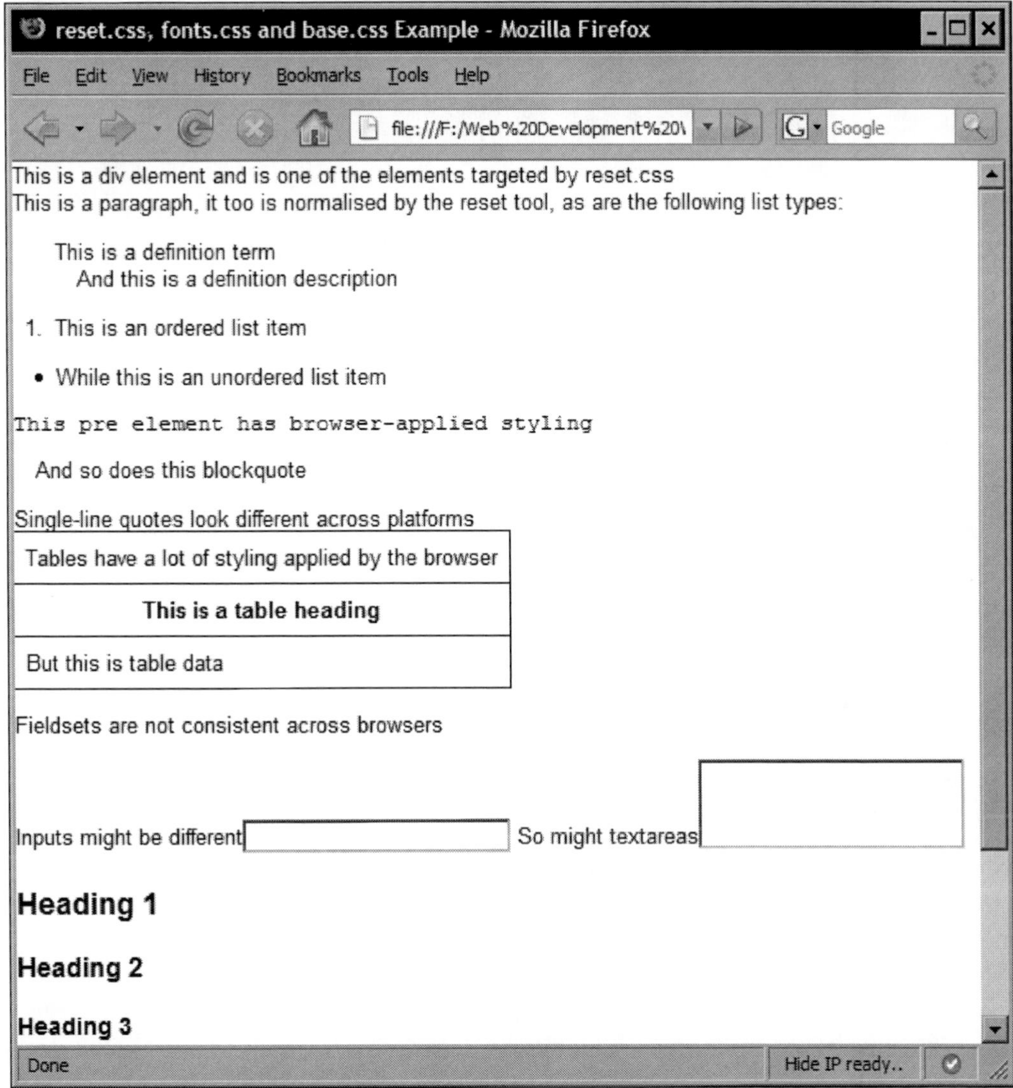

Firefox has been used in all of the screenshots so far so that you can see the differences that each file makes relative to a single browser. For brevity, let's look at the page in Safari on OS-X:

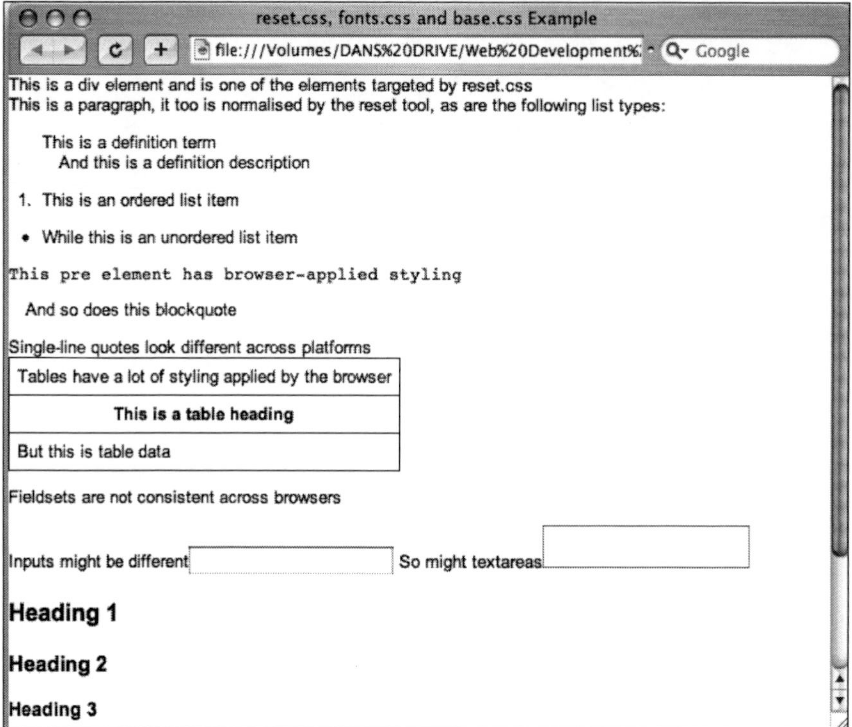

Layout Pages with Ease Using grids.css

In comparison to the other three CSS tools, the `grids.css` file is a lot bigger, containing a much wider range of selectors and rules. This tool is used in a different way than the other two; instead of just linking to the file and forgetting about it, you will need to make use of specific class names, give elements-specific ids, and use the correct nesting structures in order to have your pages laid out in the format that you want.

One of the features of the grids tool is that it automatically centres your content in the viewport, which is achieved with the first very simple rule. Another of its features is the fact that the footer, if you wish to use it, is self-clearing and stays at the bottom of the page, whichever layout template you're using.

Setting up Your Page Structure

Yahoo! recommend a particular basic structure to use when building web pages; your document should be broken up into three different content sections: a header <div>, a body <div>, and a footer <div>. All three of these different sections should also be wrapped in an outer containing <div>. The following code shows how pages should initially be structured:

```
<!DOCTYPE HTML PUBLIC "-//W3C//DTD HTML 4.01//EN"
                                "http://www.w3.org/TR/html4/strict.dtd">
<html lang="en">
  <head>
    <meta http-equiv="content-type" content="text/html;
          charset=utf-8">
    <title>Mark-up Example</title>
      <link rel="stylesheet" type="text/css"
            href="reset-fonts-grids.css">
  </head>
  <body>
    <div>
      <div id="hd">This is your Header</div>
      <div id="bd">This is the body</div>
      <div id="ft">This is your footer</div>
    </div>
  </body>
</html>
```

You can use one of the four preset page widths when constructing pages linked to the grids tool by giving the outer containing <div> element one of the following values for its `ids` attribute:

- `doc` for a 750 pixel wide page geared towards resolutions of 800x600
- `doc2` for a 950 pixel wide page that is aimed at 1024x768 resolutions
- `doc3` for a full 100% fluid page width suitable for all monitor resolutions
- `doc4` for a 974 pixel page width, an increasingly popular and robust width

These widths are controlled by three fairly straightforward selectors and rules defined near the top of the `grids.css` file.

The following screenshot shows how the four different page templates appear. To make the example clearer and to enable you to see the different page widths easily, I've added style rules that set the borders and heights of the different `<div>` elements making up the page:

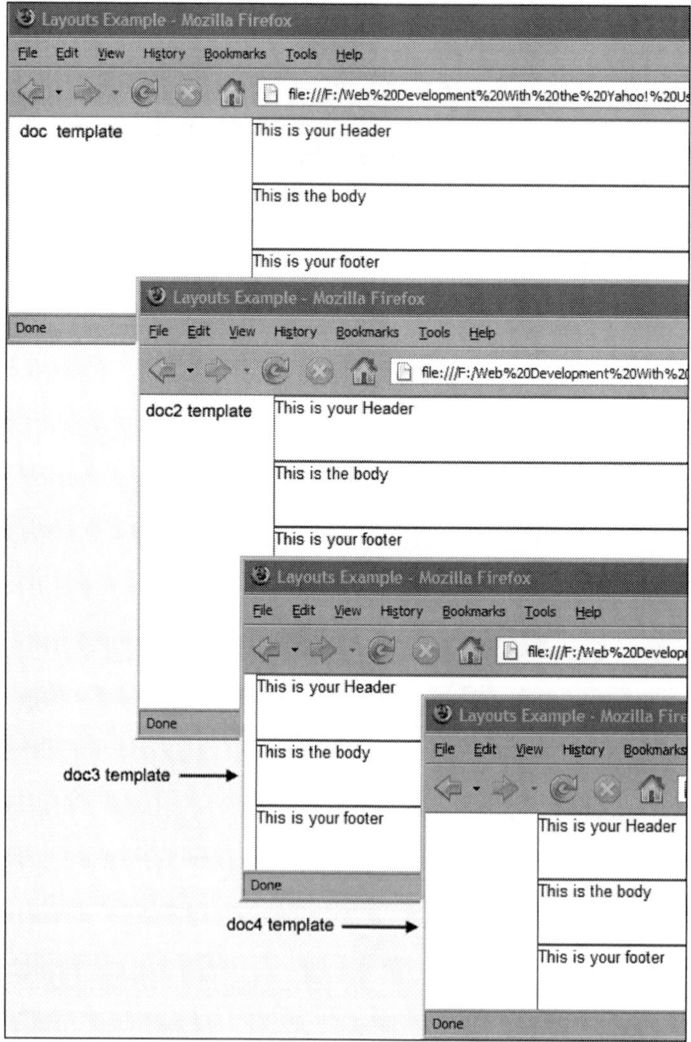

All four of these page width specifications, as well as the six different templates (`yui-t1` to `yui-t6`) have auto margins and have their content aligned to the left. The width is specified in `em` units, as these units of measurement scale better across platforms during text-size changes driven by the visitor. Using a combination of templates and different class attributes in your mark up you can specify a wide range of different page layouts.

The `*width` property is a filter used to specify the width specifically for IE versions six or under, which calculates `ems` slightly too large so that it needs to specify less of them. The third layout, for `100%` page widths, includes a `10 pixel margin` on both sides of the page so as just to prevent any bleed between the page contents and the browser's user interface chrome.

The Basic Building Blocks of Your Pages

Going back to the recommended layouts of pages, the developers at Yahoo! recognise that the main content, the body `<div>`, of your page will probably be split into different blocks itself, featuring perhaps a navigation menu on one side of the page as well as a main block of content.

These blocks of content can be represented in your HTML code by `<div>` elements with a class attribute of `yui-b` to denote a basic block. The main block should then be wrapped in a container `<div>` with a class attribute of `yui-main`. The main block is where your primary page content should reside. Although the basic `yui-b` block that is not nested within a `yui-main` block is known as the secondary block, it can still appear before the main block in your code and can appear either on the left or right-hand side of the page:

```
<!DOCTYPE HTML PUBLIC "-//W3C//DTD HTML 4.01//EN"
                                    "http://www.w3.org/TR/html4/strict.dtd">
<html lang="en">
  <head>
    <meta http-equiv="content-type" content="text/html;
                                       charset=utf-8">
    <title>YUI Grids Page</title>
      <link rel="stylesheet" type="text/css"
            href="reset-fonts-grids.css">
  </head>
  <body>
    <div id="doc3">
      <div id="hd">This is your Header</div>
      <div id="bd">This is the body
        <div class="yui-b">This is the secondary block</div>
        <div class="yui-main">
          <div class="yui-b">This is the main block</div>
        </div>
      </div>
      <div id="ft">This is your footer</div>
    </div>
  </body>
</html>
```

This is great from an SEO perspective as it allows you to define your navigation model (probably based on a simple list of links in your mark up, which search engine crawlers and spiders love) before the code making up the main content block. As any budding SEO enthusiast knows, content near the beginning of a page can be treated by search engines as more important and is more likely to be indexed.

In order to use these content-organizing blocks, you'll also need to specify one of six preset templates. These block templates specify the width of the two blocks in much the same way as the three page templates specify page width. The following block templates are available:

- `.yui-t1` for a 160 pixel secondary block on the left
- `.yui-t2` for a 180 pixel secondary block on the left
- `.yui-t3` for a 300 pixel secondary block on the left
- `.yui-t4` for a 160 pixel secondary block on the right
- `.yui-t5` for a 180 pixel secondary block on the right
- `.yui-t6` for a 300 pixel secondary block on the right

In all of these templates, the main content block will take up the remaining space on the page (which is dependent on the page template in use). To use these templates, you just need to add one of them as a class attribute of the outer containing `<div>`, element, whichever template you wish to use.

```
<!DOCTYPE HTML PUBLIC "-//W3C//DTD HTML 4.01//EN"
                            "http://www.w3.org/TR/html4/strict.dtd">
<html lang="en">
  <head>
    <meta http-equiv="content-type" content="text/html;
                                   charset=utf-8">
    <title>YUI Grids Page</title>
      <link rel="stylesheet" type="text/css"
           href="reset-fonts-grids.css">
  </head>
  <body>
    <div id="doc3" class="yui-t1">
      <div id="hd">This is your Header</div>
      <div id="bd">
        <div class="yui-b">This is a block</div>
        <div class="yui-main">
          <div class="yui-b">This is the main block</div>
        </div>
      </div>
      <div id="ft">This is your footer</div>
    </div>
  </body>
</html>
```

The addition of the blocks and additional template will produce a page with a layout as shown in screenshot below. Again styling has been used for clarity:

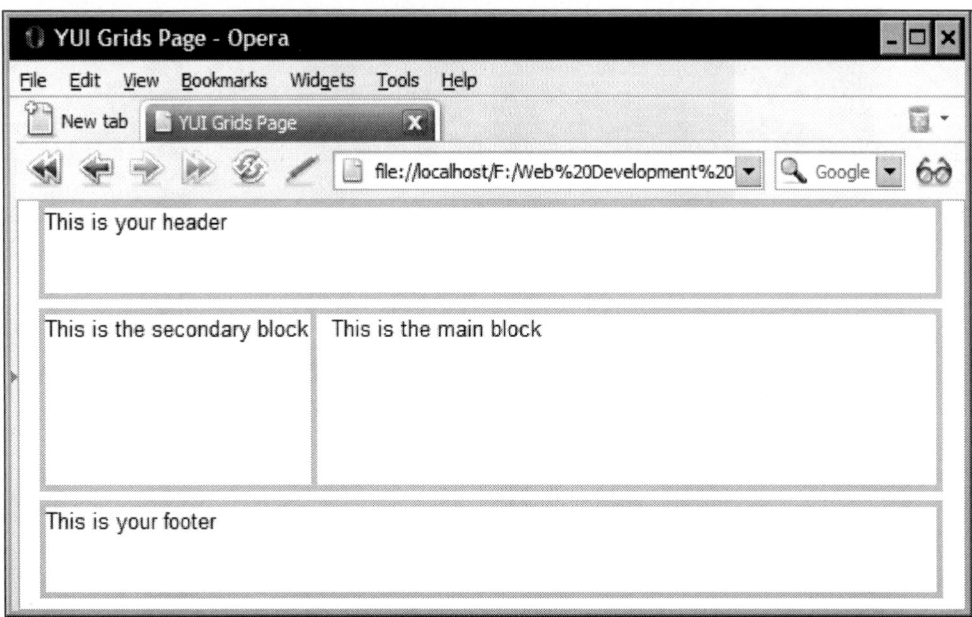

These templates, combined with the three different document widths and the two types of class attributes, added to the different block configurations give you a total of up to 42 different visual presentation models. But that's not all; your main content block can be further subdivided with grids and units.

Grid Nesting

If you would like to split your main block of content into two or more different columns, you can nest some more `<div>` elements within your main block. You need to add a container `<div>` to the main block. This is known as a grid. The two new columns that are formed in the grid are known as units and are made up of two nested `<div>` elements within the grid `<div>`.

To make a grid, the container `<div>` within the main block `<div>` should be given a class attribute of `yui-g` and each unit `<div>` should have a class attribute of either `yui-u first` for the first unit or `yui-u` for the second unit, as illustrated by the following code sample:

```
<!DOCTYPE HTML PUBLIC "-//W3C//DTD HTML 4.01//EN"
                                  "http://www.w3.org/TR/html4/strict.dtd">
<html lang="en">
  <head>
```

```
      <meta http-equiv="content-type" content="text/html;
                                      charset=utf-8">
      <title>YUI Grids Page</title>
        <link rel="stylesheet" type="text/css"
              href="reset-fonts-grids.css">
    </head>
    <body>
      <div id="doc" class="yui-t1">
        <div id="hd">This is your header</div>
        <div id="bd">
         <div class="yui-b">This is the secondary block</div>
         <div id="yui-main">
           <div class="yui-b">This is the main block
             <div class="yui-g">
               <div class="yui-u first">This is a unit</div>
               <div class="yui-u">This is another unit</div>
             </div>
           </div>
         </div>
        </div>
        <div id="ft">This is your footer</div>
      </div>
    </body>
  </html>
```

This screenshot shows how the grid units will appear on the page:

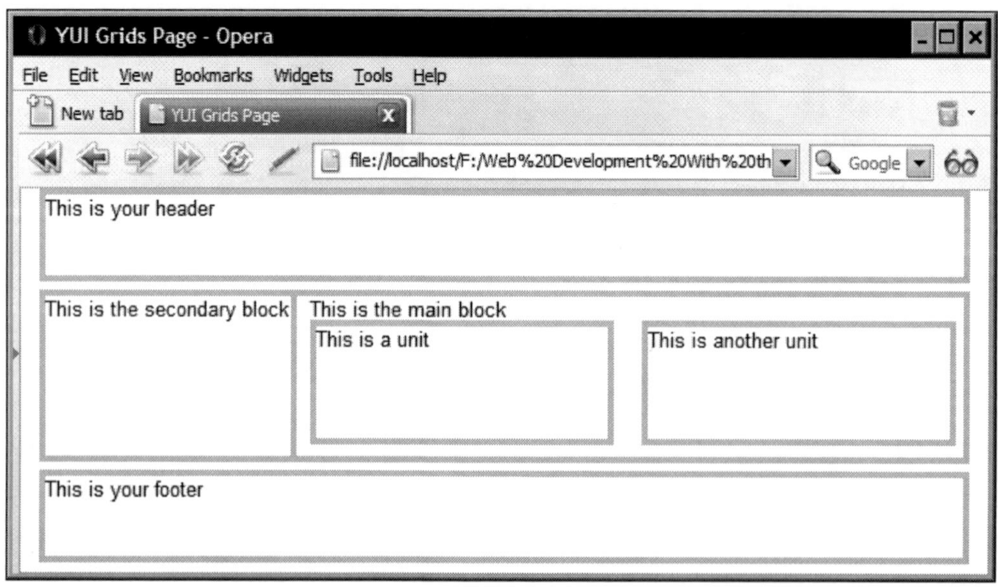

This is necessary due to the lack of support of the `:first-child` pseudo-selector in some A-grade browsers. When nesting grids within grids (to make four columns within the main content block for example), the first grid should have a `class` attribute of `yui-g first`.

By default, the two unit columns that make up a grid are of equal width, but you can easily deviate from this by using one of five 'special grids' which specify more than two columns or a range of different column proportions. The five special grids have class selectors of:

- `.yui-gb` for three columns of equal width
- `.yui-gc` for two columns where the first has double the width of the second
- `.yui-gd` for two columns where the second has double the width of the first
- `.yui-ge` for two columns where the first has three times the width of the second
- `.yui-gf` for two columns where the second has three times the width of the first

We can see one of these special grids in action by simply changing the class name of our grid in the previous example:

```
<!DOCTYPE HTML PUBLIC "-//W3C//DTD HTML 4.01//EN"
                              "http://www.w3.org/TR/html4/strict.dtd">
<html lang="en">
  <head>
    <meta http-equiv="content-type" content="text/html;
                                    charset=utf-8">
    <title>YUI Grids Page</title>
      <link rel="stylesheet" type="text/css"
            href="reset-fonts-grids.css">
  </head>
  <body>
    <div id="doc" class="yui-t1">
      <div id="hd">This is your header</div>
      <div id="bd">
        <div class="yui-b">This is the secondary block</div>
        <div id="yui-main">
          <div class="yui-b">This is the main block
           <div class="yui-gb">
             <div class="yui-u first">This is a unit</div>
             <div class="yui-u">This is another unit</div>
             A third unit created with the yui-gb special grid
           </div>
          </div>
      </div>
    </div>
```

```
        <div id="ft">This is your footer</div>
      </div>
    </body>
  </html>
```

This change in class name will result in our grid appearing as in the screenshot below:

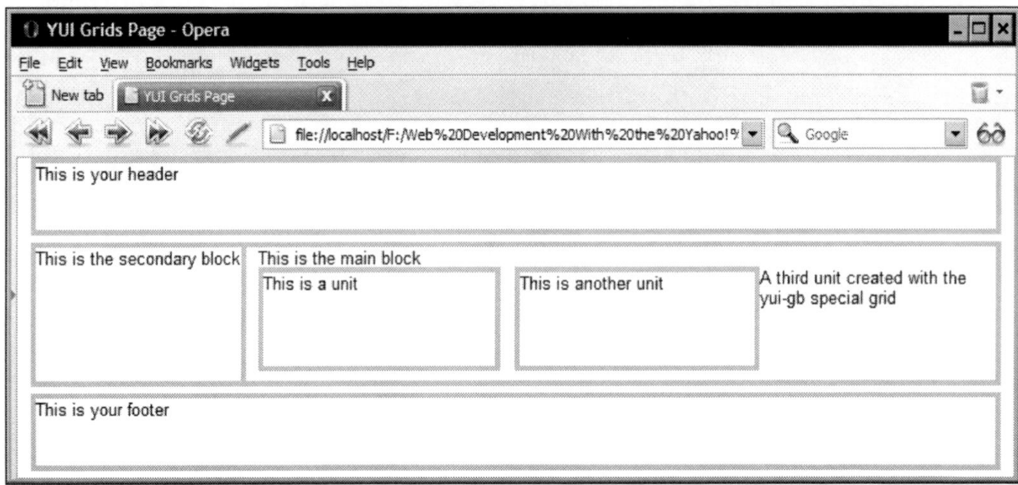

There is a large number of different variations of page layouts that the grids tool allows you to implement. All you need to do is define your pages in the correct structure, and give the right elements the right `class` attributes and ids. It may seem a little daunting at first, trying to remember all those different class names and nesting rules, but with a little bit of practice, it all becomes second nature.

In addition to the online documentation and cheat sheets, the CSS Grids page on the YUI developer site also contains a very nifty little tool that allows you to generate page templates for use with the `grids.css` tool. Simply choose your desired layout, add in any header or footer text and the tool will then generate the basic template code for you to copy and paste into your own files:

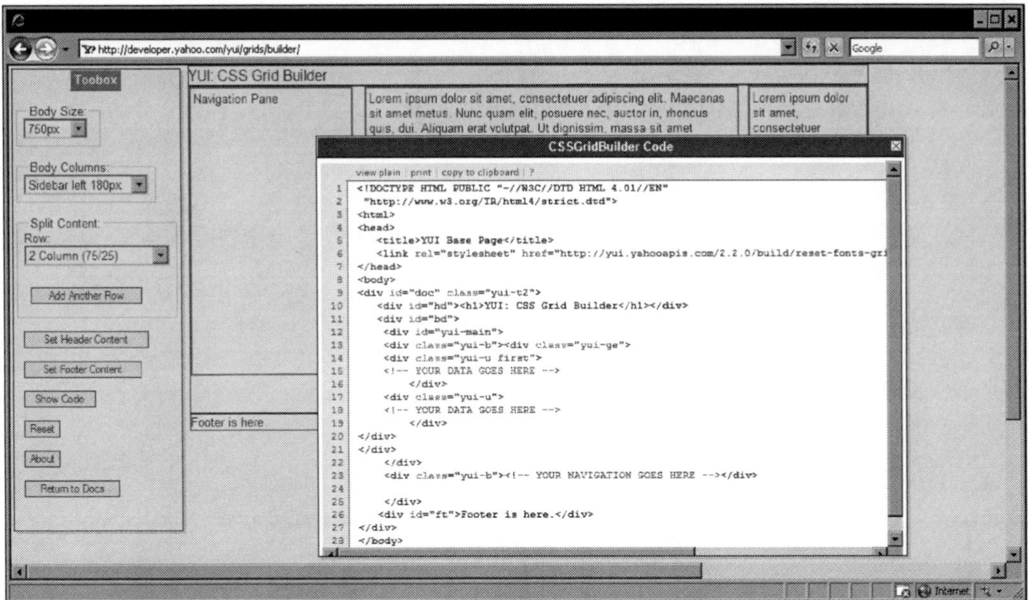

A Word on Sam

Completely separate from the CSS tools, but still composed entirely of CSS, the Sam skin provides a default theme for each of the library's controls. Each control contains a skin CSS file in its assets folder and should be linked to using the standard `<link>` tag in the `<head>` of any pages on which the controls are displayed.

In order to use the skin files, as well as linking to the stylesheet used by the skin, you will also need to give the containing element (whether that is the `<body>` or a `<div>`) a special class name:

```
<body class="yui-skin-sam">
```

Or:

```
<div class="yui-skin-sam">
  <div id="someControl"></div>
</div>
```

This makes using the skin extremely easy. The Sam skin takes its name from its creator Sam Lind. New skins will be provided by the YUI developers in future releases of the library and there's nothing stopping you from creating your own.

Summary

The CSS tools are the smallest and without doubt the easiest component of the library to use, but their contribution in the form of time-saving and functionality provided is no less than that of the utilities and controls.

First the reset tool provides normalization services to the most common HTML elements so that borders, margins, and padding, among other things, are set to zero across all of the most common browsers.

The base tool then builds upon the level foundation provided by resets to give certain elements back some of the styling that marks them out from other elements. This tool is the only one that isn't part of the minified aggregated `resets-fonts-grids.css` file.

Next, all of your page text is standardized to the Arial font and is given a fixed line height. Sizes are also fixed to a consistent size across the document with the fonts tool.

Finally, the precise layout of your page can be declared through the use of a range of CSS classes, ids, and templates defined for you in the grids tool.

3
DOM Manipulation and Event Handling

Every time you view a web page in your browser a tree-like structure representing the page and all of its elements is created. This is the Document Object Model (DOM), and it provides an API which you can use to obtain, add, modify, or remove almost any part of the web page, and without which modern web design as we know it would not exist. The YUI makes accessing and working with the DOM much easier, and allows you to perform a variety of common DOM scripting tasks with ease.

An integral part of any web application is the ability to react to different events that occur upon the different elements found on your pages. Browsers have had their own event models for some time now, allowing you to easily add code that handles something being clicked on for example, or something being hovered over. The YUI takes this one step further, replacing the existing browser event model with its own, which is more powerful, yet easier to use.

In this chapter, we're going to look at some of the issues surrounding the use of the DOM and the event model and how the YUI overcomes common obstacles that surround their use. We're also going to get stuck into some more coding examples where you'll get to work with these two fundamentally useful library components directly.

Working with the DOM

You may have worked with the DOM and not even realized it; if you've ever used `getElementById` or `getElementsByTagName` for example (two common methods), then you have worked with the DOM.

The first of the above two methods returns the element that has a matching `id` attribute from the document. The second method returns either an element with the matching tag name, a `<table>` element for example, or it returns an array of matching elements.

In a nutshell, the DOM gives you access to the structure and content of a web page (or XML document), and allows you to make modifications to either using almost any common scripting or web programming language around.

Most of you, I'm sure, would have at least come across these two basic DOM methods and understood the concepts behind their use. I would be surprised if a high percentage of you have not used them frequently.

DOM Concepts

Each of the DOM level recommendations defined by the W3C have been designed to promote interoperability between different platforms and to be language independent, so the DOM can be accessed and manipulated not just by JavaScript, but by other popular programming languages such as Java or Python.

The different levels are also designed to be backwards compatible and to function on any browser which implements them. However since Level 2, the DOM has not been one single specification but a range of specifications where each supply one or more interfaces that tackle a particular aspect of DOM manipulation.

The methods and properties that you make use of in order to work with the DOM are exposed through these interfaces, but except for each level's Core Specification, the specifications do not have to be implemented in full.

So different browsers, after implementing the Core Specification may pick and choose which, if any, of the other specifications, they wish to implement.

This often leads to inconsistencies between browsers, and when working with the DOM you'll often find that certain features you wish to make use of are not universally implemented.

The `setAttribute` method for example, often fails to have the desired effect in IE depending on the attribute that you wish to set. Using it to set an element's class attribute will not work in IE, although Firefox is happy enough to let you use it.

Firefox has pretty much always had a built-in DOM viewer (and one can easily be installed for IE on Windows, or Web Inspector can be used for Safari on Mac), and this can be an invaluable tool when putting pages together.

Using any of these tools, you can easily see how the DOM breaks documents down into a series of nodes in a tree-like structure. The screenshot on the next page shows the top-level DOM representation of the Google homepage in the Firefox DOM inspector:

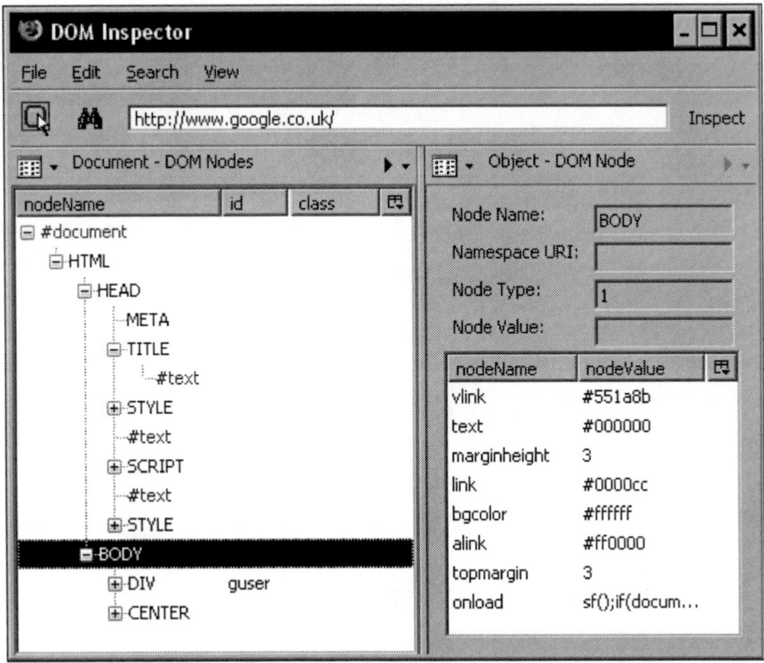

As you can see, the left-hand pane shows a logical tree representation of the page's structure and makes it easy for you to see which elements are parents, which are siblings, and which are child elements. The right-hand pane gives information about a selected node and its attributes and properties. This can be a very useful tool for checking that any DOM scripting (such as adding or removing elements) is going according to plan.

Common DOM Scripting Techniques

The DOM is best known among web developers for its ability to dynamically alter the structure and content of web pages using easily implemented scripting techniques. JavaScript contains a useful (although somewhat restricted) set of built-in methods for accessing, manipulating, and even replacing DOM nodes.

Nodes are a fundamental part of the DOM; each object represented in the DOM is represented as a node. Each node may be a branch node, which has child nodes and possibly parent nodes and sibling nodes, or it may be a leaf node which may have siblings and parents but not children of its own.

In the above screenshot, you can clearly see that the page is made up of a series of objects, where each individual object is a node. The nodes shown in that example are a branch nodes because each one has at least one child. The **HTML** node, for example, has **HEAD** and **BODY** child nodes, and both of these have their own child nodes.

Every single element that makes up a page is represented as either a branch or leaf node (if this isn't making much sense now, it should become a lot clearer when we move on to the TreeView example in Chapter 5).

A special node is the document node, commonly referred to as the document object. When you call a method such as `document.getElementById(someid)` you are calling it on the document object. It has a special set of methods which can only be called on the document node, such as `document.implementation.hasFeature(somefeature, someversion)`. Other methods may be called on any type of node.

Common DOM Methods

We've already seen the two main ways of obtaining elements from the DOM— `.getElementById()` and `.getElementsByTagName()`. Once an element has been obtained, it's very easy to navigate your way through the tree using properties such as: `firstChild`, `parentNode`, or `previousSibling` for example.

So you can grab an element from the page and then move up, down, or sideways across the tree, navigating parents, siblings, or child elements alike. Each branch node also has an accessible `childNodes[]` collection which exposes information about each of the child nodes.

The DOM gives you methods which allow you to create different objects such as `.createElement()` or `.createTextNode()`. Both of these methods are only available under the document node.

Once you've created your new element or text node, you can insert it into the DOM (and therefore the document) using `.appendChild()`, `.insertBefore()`, `.replaceChild()`, or `.innerHTML()`. You can also copy nodes using `.cloneNode()`, or remove elements using the `.removeChild()` method.

Each node in the document has a series of properties which allow you to determine various bits of information about it, such as the `data` it holds, its `id`, its `nodeName`, `nodeType`, `tagName`, or even its `title`. You can also use the `.hasChildNodes()` method to determine whether the node is a branch node or a leaf node.

Any attributes of each node are available to you under the `attributes` collection. The methods `.getAttribute()`, `.setAttribute()`, and `.removeAttribute()` are also available for use by the discerning web programmer to make working with element attributes easier, although this is one area in which browser support can vary wildly between platforms.

Further Reading

The DOM, together with events (see the second half of this chapter) are the cornerstones of modern web development and web application design, and some fascinating documentation exists to further your understanding of these two important concepts. The W3C site for example, provides detailed descriptions of all of the standardized DOM levels.

DOM—the Old Way

To better understand the benefits that using the YUI DOM utility introduces, it may be useful to see a brief example of how the DOM can be used with just plain old JavaScript. We can then recreate the same example but this time using the YUI so that you can instantly see the difference in the two approaches.

Those of you who are familiar with the workings of the traditional DOM (by this I mean non-YUI techniques) can safely skip this section, but any of you that have not had much exposure to it may find this example beneficial.

We'll create a very simple `form` with just a single text `input` field on it and a `submit button`. If the `submit button` is clicked while the text `input` field is empty, we'll then use the DOM to add a simple warning message to the `form`. In your text editor add the following html:

```
<!DOCTYPE HTML PUBLIC "-//W3C//DTD HTML 4.01//EN"
                              "http://www.w3.org/TR/html4/strict.dtd">
<html lang="en">
  <head>
    <meta http-equiv="content-type" content="text/html;
                                    charset=utf-8">
    <title>Traditional DOM Example</title>
  </head>
  <body>
    <form id="form" action="">
```

```
        <div id="container">
          <label for="input1">Enter some text</label>
          <input type="text" id="input1">
          <button id="submit" type="submit">Submit</button>
        </div>
      </form>
    </body>
  </html>
```

This all we need for the HTML code; we won't worry about any presentational or positional CSS. Now for some JavaScript, all we have to really concern ourselves with is getting the contents of the text field and checking that it is not empty. If it is empty, we can then create the error message and add it to the page.

We'll also need a way of calling the function into action once the submit button is clicked. We can do all of this using the following set of functions which can be added to the `<head>` section of the HTML code in a single `<script>` block:

```
<script type="text/javascript">
  //define the checkInput function
  function checkInput() {
    //get the value of the input
    var input = document.getElementById("input1").value;
    //if the value is an empty string...
    if (input == "") {
      //create a new element and a new text node
      var newspan = document.createElement("span");
      var newtext = document.createTextNode("You didn't enter
                                                       anything!");
      //get the container element
      var newparent = document.getElementById("container");
      //add the new text node to the new element
      newspan.appendChild(newtext);
      //add the new element to the container
      newparent.appendChild(newspan);
      return false;
    }
  }
  //the init function adds a listener for the submit event
  function init() {
    document.getElementById("form").attachEvent("onsubmit",
                                                       checkInput);
  }
  //execute the init function when the window loads
  window.onload = init;
</script>
```

I would like to point out that the above example is absolutely how things should *not* be done. This is very common, but very bad coding practice, and is something that we can thankfully leave behind when working with the YUI.

Save the file and view it in IE; if you click the button without entering anything into the text field, our message is added to the page.

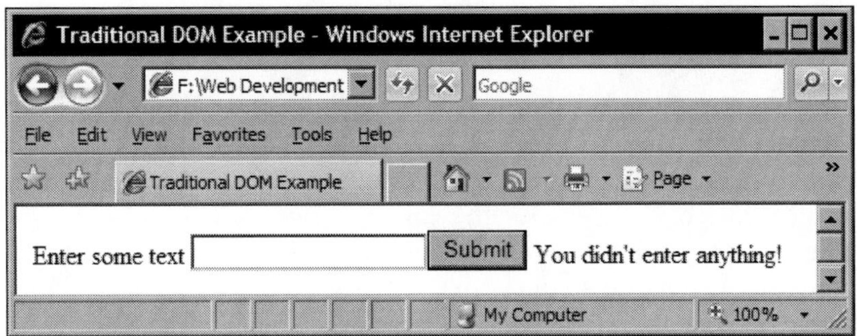

The way it works is very simple. We've used a mixed bag of DOM methods to achieve this basic functionality, such as getting the value of the data entered into the text field and obtaining the `container` element using `.document.getElementBy()`, and creating our new content with the `.createElement()` and `.createTextNode()` methods.

We've also made use of the `.appendChild()` method to first add the new `textNode` to the new `<span>` element, then to add the `<span>` element to the container element. The final DOM maneuver involves using the `.attachEvent()` method to attach the `onsubmit` listener to the form and calls the `.checkInput()` function when the event occurs.

You'll notice that the form does not work when viewed in Firefox, which highlights a classic problem of working with the DOM. The `.attachEvent()` method is a Microsoft only event and so is not understood by Firefox. To get this example to work in Firefox, we must detect which browser is in use and provide the `.addEventListener()` method to Firefox instead:

```
function init() {
  if (document.addEventListener) {
    document.getElementById("form").addEventListener
                                ("submit",checkInput, false);
  } else {
    document.getElementById("form").attachEvent
                                ("onsubmit",checkInput);
  }
}
```

Additional code routines like this are commonplace when using the traditional DOM methods because of the inconsistencies between different browsers. There are other ways of avoiding the above problem, for example, we could use the following statement in the `init()` function instead:

```
document.getElementById("form").onsubmit = checkInput;
```

But I thought it would be more interesting to show one of the common pitfalls of traditional DOM manipulation.

While not important in this example, Search Engine Optimization (SEO) and download times are an important consideration when developing for real world implementations. Thus, allowing your event handlers to reside in the JavaScript code instead of as attributes of the elements they are attached to help to reduce the file size of the page when a separate script file is used. It also cuts down on the amount of code that any search engine spiders have to wade through in order to get at your optimized content.

DOM—the YUI Way

Now let's change our basic `form` from the previous example so that it makes use of the YUI DOM utility instead of relying on standard JavaScript methods. The HTML markup can stay the same, but remove the entire `<script>` block from the `<head>` of the page.

You'll need to link to the DOM utility; with this file saved in your `yuisite` folder, the `build` directory will be accessible. Link to the DOM utility using the following `<script>` block:

```
<script type="text/javascript" src="yui/build/yahoo-dom-event/
                                    yahoo-dom-event.js"></script>
```

We're linking to the `yahoo-dom-event.js` file because the YAHOO object is required, and we can make good use of some the Event utility's methods (we'll be looking at the Event utility in detail later in this chapter).

In the `<body>` of the page, just after the closing `</form>` tag, add the following code:

```
<script type="text/javascript">
  //set up the namespace object for this example
  YAHOO.namespace("yuibook.yuiform");
  //define the checkInput function
  YAHOO.yuibook.yuiform.checkInput = function() {
    //work out whether the input field is empty
    if (YAHOO.util.Dom.get("input1").value == "") {
```

```
        //create a new element and a new text node
        var newspan = document.createElement("span");
        var newtext = document.createTextNode("You didn't enter
                                                      anything!");
        //add the textnode to the element
        newspan.appendChild(newtext);
        //insert the new element after the submit button
        YAHOO.util.Dom.insertAfter(newspan, "submit");
        return false;
      }
    }
```

This is our main function, used to check the input and add the message when appropriate. Next we need to add a `listener` for the `submit` event:

```
    //initForm adds a listener for the submit event
    YAHOO.yuibook.yuiform.initForm = function() {
      YAHOO.util.Event.addListener("form", "submit",
                                   YAHOO.yuibook.yuiform.checkInput);
    }
```

This time we don't need to worry about catering for different browsers, the YUI will do that for us. Our final task is to execute the `.initForm()` function so that the event listener is added as soon as the page has loaded:

```
    //when the DOM is ready execute the initForm function
    YAHOO.util.Event.onDOMReady(YAHOO.yuibook.yuiform.initForm);
  </script>
```

Run this code in any browser. It will look exactly the same as the page in the previous screenshot, but under the hood, things are working much better. We use less code this way and although there's only one input field to validate (and only very basic validation at that), imagine the benefits of using the YUI for form validation on an entire form with many input elements.

DOM Manipulation in YUI

The YUI DOM utility enhances your DOM toolkit in several important ways, giving you more power and more control. First of all, it adds a whole range of new methods for obtaining DOM nodes such as:

- `getAncestorByTagName`
- `getAnscestorByClassName`
- `getChildren`
- `getElementsByClassName`.

These give you much more flexibility than the standard DOM node retrieval methods built into JavaScript. As if these additions weren't enough in themselves, the YUI DOM utility also gives you a range of methods for defining your own parameters with which to obtain elements. These include:

- `getAncestorBy`
- `getChildrenBy`
- `getElementsBy`
- `getFirstChildBy`
- `getLastChildBy`
- `getNextSiblingBy`
- `getPreviousSiblingBy`

The utility also adds a series of convenience methods that makes it easier to traverse the DOM including `.getFirstChild()`, `.getLastChild()`, `.getNextSibling()`, and `.getPreviousSibling()`, so you can navigate your way through the tree with ease.

It also introduces methods for obtaining positional properties of nodes like `.getRegion()`, `.getX()`, and `.getY()`. You can also change these positional properties as well using `.setX()`, `.setY()`, and `.setXY()`.

Another important point is that you don't need to worry about whether these methods should be called on the special document node or on standard nodes. All of the methods defined by the classes making up the DOM utility are used in conjunction with the library namespace `YAHOO.util.DOM` prefixed to the method name.

If you look through the W3C Level 1 Core Specification, which defines most of the basic DOM manipulation and traversal methods, you'll notice that an `insertAfter` method does not exist. The YUI DOM utility kindly adds this method to our toolset, giving you more flexibility when adding new content to your pages, as we saw in our first YUI DOM example.

Although a specification exists for working with stylesheets using the traditional DOM, support for class names is limited and is sometimes not implemented by browsers. The YUI rectifies this lack of support by providing several methods that allow you to work closely with class names such as:

- `addClass`
- `hasClass`
- `removeClass`
- `replaceClass`

Many DOMs Make Light Work

Traditionally, the DOM is sometimes regarded as a bit of a pain to work with, but all of that ends when using the DOM Collection utility. A lot of the other utilities and controls make use of the functionality that it provides, so it is usually part of any library implementation you create.

The DOM utility has just two classes (with one subclass) and is relatively small compared to some of the other utility files. It provides browser normalization functions that help to iron out the differences between DOM implementations among some of the more common browsers, and is made up mostly of convenience methods. Let's look at these two classes in more detail.

The DOM Class

The first class is `YAHOO.util.DOM`. All of its members are methods, there are no properties at all. The methods available deal mainly with element positioning, setting CSS classes and styles, and getting elements by a range of different means, although there are also a couple of useful methods used to obtain the viewport height, and other information like that.

In order to provide the different browser normalizations, the `YAHOO.util.DOM` class also contains an automatic browser detection method that is used in various places throughout the utility.

The DOM utility allows you to use the shorthand `.get()` method to get an element using a reference to it, such as its `id`, but you can also get elements based on class name, or by using the `.getElementsBy()` method to create a custom test, such as by attribute.

This method takes three arguments: the first is a reference to a function that checks objects based on a particular test, the second is optional and is used to specify the tag name of the elements you require, and the third (also optional) is the root tag.

If you're ever using a utility which assigns default `id`s to elements dynamically, and you wonder where these `id`s come from, the answer is the `.generateId()` method found here in the DOM class. It generates either a single `id` or array of `id`s for either an element or array of elements passed into it as an argument. It can also generate a prefix for the `id` if this is passed as a second, optional parameter.

Using the DOM Class

Let's put some of the available methods from the DOM class to work in a basic page. In your text editor, begin with the following HTML page:

```
<!DOCTYPE HTML PUBLIC "-//W3C//DTD HTML 4.01//EN"
                          "http://www.w3.org/TR/html4/strict.dtd">
<html lang="en">
  <head>
    <meta http-equiv="content-type" content="text/html;
                                        charset=utf-8">
    <title>YUI Dom Utility Example 1</title>
    <script type="text/javascript"
            src="yui/build/yahoo-dom-event/yahoo-dom-event.js">
    </script>
    <style type="text/css">
      #info {
        width:300px;
        border:2px solid black;
        padding:5px;
      }
    </style>
  </head>
  <body>
    <div id="info">
      <h2 class="header">Information</h2>
      <p><span id="portWidth">The current viewport width in pixels
                              is: </span></p>
      <p><span id="portHeight">The current viewport height in pixels
                               is: </span></p>
      <p><span id="childClass">The first child of this div has a
                               class of: </span></p>
      <p><span>This div has: </span>
         <span id="children"> child elements</span></p>
    </div>
  </body>
</html>
```

You can see from the `<span>` elements the kind of information we are going to obtain in this example. Using the DOM utility we can easily obtain information regarding the `viewport` dimensions, as well as details of class names and child elements.

All of this information can be extracted from the page using the following, relatively simple `<script>` tag, which should be added to the document directly after the final `</div>` closing tag:

```
<script type="text/javascript">
  //create the namespace object for this example
  YAHOO.namespace("yuibook.domExamples");
  //define the getPageInfo function
  YAHOO.yuibook.domExamples.getPageInfo = function() {
    //get viewport size
    var portWidth = YAHOO.util.Dom.getViewportWidth();
    var portHeight = YAHOO.util.Dom.getViewportHeight();
    //get first child of the info div
    var child1 = YAHOO.util.Dom.getFirstChild("info").className;
    //get number of children
    var childs = YAHOO.util.Dom.getChildren("info").length;
```

The first part of our script is where all of the required data is obtained. The DOM methods we are using are wrapped in the `getPageInfo()` function.

First, the veiwport width and height properties are obtained using the `.getViewportWidth()` and `.getViewportHeight()` methods, and this information is stored in a couple of variables for later use.

Next, the `.getFirstChild()` method returns the HTML element that appears as the first child of the `<div>` element. This is an object which has many attributes of the element mapped to its properties. The first child of our `<div>` is a `<h2>` element. It only has one attribute which is the class name, so this information can be obtained from the `className` property.

Finally, we can get the number of children found in our `<div>` element using the `length` property of the array returned by the `.getChildren()` method. Now that we have a series of variables holding the information we wanted to get, we need to do something with them.

As I mentioned before, the DOM utility is not meant to replace existing JavaScript DOM methods, but to enhance them. As there are already `.createElement()` and `.appendChild()` methods built into JavaScript, these are not provided by the library.

This means that we need to fall back on these traditional DOM methods in order to create new `<span>` elements and populate them with new `textNodes` so that they hold the information obtained with the first part of our script.

We can make use of the DOM utility's `.addClass()` method however, to easily give our new `<span>` elements class names.

```
        //create new span elements to hold viewport info
        var newspan = document.createElement("span");
        var width = document.createTextNode(portWidth);
        newspan.appendChild(width);
        YAHOO.util.Dom.addClass(newspan, "infoText");
        var newspan2 = document.createElement("span");
        var height = document.createTextNode(portHeight);
        newspan2.appendChild(height);
        YAHOO.util.Dom.addClass(newspan2, "infoText");
        var newspan3 = document.createElement("span");
        var className = document.createTextNode(child1);
        newspan3.appendChild(className);
        YAHOO.util.Dom.addClass(newspan3, "infoText");
        var newspan4 = document.createElement("span");
        var children = document.createTextNode(childs);
        newspan4.appendChild(children);
        YAHOO.util.Dom.addClass(newspan4, "infoText");
```

We will also need to add some styling for the new class, the following selector and rule can be added to the existing `<style>` tag in the `<head>` of the document:

```
    .infoText {
      color:red;
    }
```

Once we have created the new `<span>` elements and each one has had its `textNode` appended and an appropriate `class` set, we can insert them into the page. This example uses both the YUI `.insertAfter()` and the standard JavaScript `.insertBefore()` methods to put the new elements in their correct locations on the page:

```
        //insert the new elements in the page
        YAHOO.util.Dom.insertAfter(newspan, "portWidth");
        YAHOO.util.Dom.insertAfter(newspan2, "portHeight");
        YAHOO.util.Dom.insertAfter(newspan3, "childClass");
        YAHOO.util.Dom.insertBefore(newspan4, "children");
      }
```

This is everything that our `getPageInfo` function needs to do, so we can safely close it off. We can then use the Event utility to execute the function when the `<div>` with an `id` of `info` is available in the DOM:

```
      //get info when the info div is available
      YAHOO.util.Event.onAvailable("info",
                                   YAHOO.yuibook.domExamples.getPageInfo);
    </script>
```

Make sure the page is saved in your `yuisite` folder and view it in a browser; you should find that you end up with a page looking like the one displayed below:

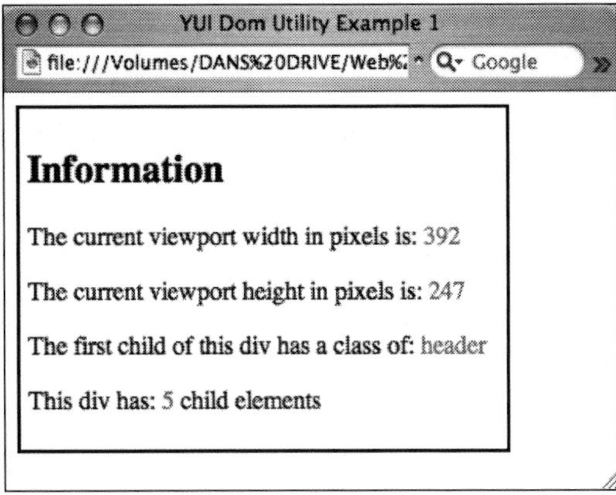

Additional Useful DOM Methods

Another useful set of methods found in the DOM class are the get and set methods which are used to determine an element's current location on the page using X and Y page coordinates. As well as getting the location, there are also methods provided to set an element's location.

There are also some useful tools for working with CSS. Methods are provided to add a class, remove a class, and replace a class or even to determine whether an element has a particular class in the first place.

Different browsers often have different means of setting styles to newly created elements, particularly IE. So these tools provide a useful layer that smoothes out these differences and allows you to use the same methods to consistently work with styles across browser platforms.

We can put the X and Y methods to good use in another brief example. Begin with the following basic page:

```
<!DOCTYPE HTML PUBLIC "-//W3C//DTD HTML 4.01//EN"
                          "http://www.w3.org/TR/html4/strict.dtd">
<html lang="en">
  <head>
    <meta http-equiv="content-type" content="text/html;
                                    charset=utf-8">
    <title>YUI Dom Utility Example 2</title>
    <script type="text/javascript" src="yui/build/
```

```
                    yahoo-dom-event/yahoo-dom-event.js"></script>
    <style type="text/css">
      #positions {
        width:250px;
        border:2px solid black;
        padding:5px;
      }
    </style>
  </head>
  <body>
    <div id="positions">
      <h2 class="header">Positional Methods</h2>
      <p><span id="elemX">The X position of this div
                                                    is: </span></p>
      <p><span id="elemY">The Y position of this div
                                                    is: </span></p>
      <button id="move" type="button">Move this div!</button>
    </div>
  </body>
</html>
```

Now let's move on to the script. This time we'll have two functions; the first will get the current X and Y positions of the `<div>` element, the second function will deal with moving the `<div>` to a new location on the page. Add the code for the first function directly above the closing `</body>` tag:

```
<script type="text/javascript">
  //create the namespace object for this example
  YAHOO.namespace("yuibook.domExamples");
  //define getPositions function
  YAHOO.yuibook.domExamples.getPositions = function() {
    //get positions x and y coordinates
    var x = YAHOO.util.Dom.getX("positions");
    var y = YAHOO.util.Dom.getY("positions");
    var newspan = document.createElement("span");
    var posx = document.createTextNode(x);
    newspan.appendChild(posx);
    YAHOO.util.Dom.addClass(newspan, "infoText");
    var newspan2 = document.createElement("span");
    var posy = document.createTextNode(y);
    newspan2.appendChild(posy);
    YAHOO.util.Dom.addClass(newspan2, "infoText");
    //insert the new elements in the page
    YAHOO.util.Dom.insertAfter(newspan, "elemX");
```

```
        YAHOO.util.Dom.insertAfter(newspan2, "elemY");
      }
      //execute getPositions when positions div available
      YAHOO.util.Event.onAvailable("positions",
                                   YAHOO.yuibook.domExamples.getPositions);
```

The current X and Y positions of the <div> are obtained using the `.getX()` and `.getY()` methods from the library. These positions are then added to the <div> in exactly the same way as in the previous example.

Now let's add a second function:

```
      //define move function
      YAHOO.yuibook.domExamples.move = function() {
        //get input values
        var xmove = YAHOO.util.Dom.get("moveX").value;
        var ymove = YAHOO.util.Dom.get("moveY").value;
        //remove input values
        YAHOO.util.Dom.get("moveX").value = "";
        YAHOO.util.Dom.get("moveY").value = "";
        //set new position
        YAHOO.util.Dom.setX("positions", xmove);
        YAHOO.util.Dom.setY("positions", ymove);
        //remove existing position information
        var info = YAHOO.util.Dom.getElementsByClassName("infoText")
        for (x = 0; x < info.length; x++) {
          info[x].parentNode.removeChild(info[x]);
        }
        //call getPositions to get new position info
        YAHOO.yuibook.domExamples.getPositions();
      }
      //execute move function when button is clicked
      YAHOO.util.Event.addListener("moveElem", "click",
                                   YAHOO.yuibook.domExamples.move);
    </script>
```

First we get the values entered into the two text inputs and store these values in a couple of variables. To keep things tidy, we can also remove the values entered into the text fields once we have gotten their value.

Next we use the `.setX()` and `.setY()` methods to physically move the <div> element, passing in its `id`, and the values obtained from the text inputs, as arguments. Following this we use the `.getElementsByClassName()` method to select all of the elements that have a `className` of `infoText`.

The resulting object will be an array, so we can easily loop through each item in the array, move up to the element's parent, then call the standard JavaScript `removeChild()` method to get rid of any pre-existing info text. Once this has been done we can call the `getPositions()` function again to get and display the new position.

Once the element has moved, we call the `getPositions()` function again so that the new location details can be added to the page. This is all the `move()` function needs to do, and all that remains for us to do is to add the listener for the `moveElem` button's click event.

If you save the file and view it in your browser, then enter some values into each field and hit the button, you should end up with a page similar to that shown below:

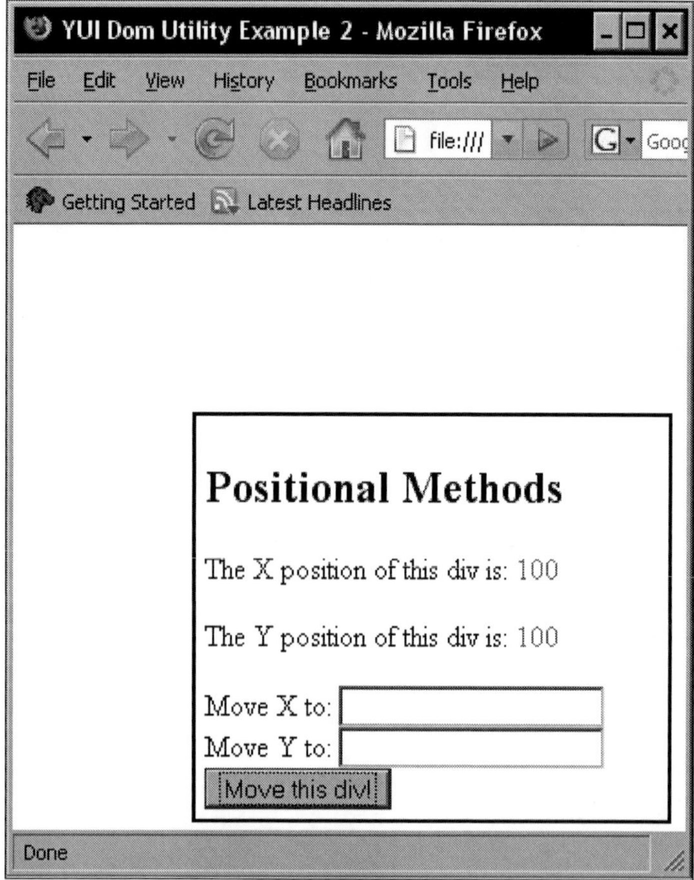

The Region Class

The other class is `YAHOO.util.Region`, which in turn has the subclass `YAHOO.util.Point`. A region defines a rectangular or square area of an imaginary grid covering the page, although as Yahoo! points out, you could extend the class to allow other shapes. The constructor `YAHOO.util.Region` takes four arguments and each argument is a reference to each sides furthest extent (top, right, bottom, and left naturally).

There are six properties defined in this class, one for each of the rectangular regions sides and two indices, 0 and 1, which correspond to the left and top extents of the region for symmetry with the `.getXY()` and `.setXY()` methods.

There are just six methods in this class also, and these deal with testing whether a region contains another region, getting the area of the region, getting the region itself, getting any overlap between regions (the region of the overlap is returned), obtaining the properties of the region as a string, or getting the union region, which represents the smallest region that can contain two other regions.

For a brief example of the region class at work, we can continue with the information box theme and create a simple `<div>` element to get some of its region properties. Begin with the following basic HTML page:

```
<!DOCTYPE HTML PUBLIC "-//W3C//DTD HTML 4.01//EN"
                            "http://www.w3.org/TR/html4/strict.dtd">
<html lang="en">
  <head>
    <meta http-equiv="content-type" content="text/html;
                                      charset=utf-8">
    <title>YUI Dom Utility Example 3</title>
    <script type="text/javascript"
            src="yui/build/yahoo-dom-event/yahoo-dom-event.js">
    </script>
    <style type="text/css">
      #region {
        width:280px;
        border:2px solid black;
        padding:5px;
      }
      .infoText {
        color:red;
      }
    </style>
  </head>
  <body>
    <div id="region">
```

```
        <h2 class="header">Region Information</h2>
        <p><span id="divRegion">The region of this div
                                              is: </span></p>
        <p><span id="topSideLength">The length of the top edge in
                                         pixels is: </span></p>
        <p><span id="area">Its total area in pixels
                                              is: </span></p>
      </div>
    </body>
  </html>
```

The script required for this example is minimal, but should highlight the basic functionality of the region class. Add the following `<script>` block after the final closing `</div>` tag:

```
<script type="text/javascript">
  //define the namespace object
  YAHOO.namespace("yuibook.domExamples");
  //define the getElemRegion function
  YAHOO.yuibook.domExamples.getElemRegion = function() {
    //get the region of the region element
    var elemRegion = YAHOO.util.Dom.getRegion("region");
    //work out length of top side
    var rightSide = elemRegion.right;
    var leftSide = elemRegion.left;
    var length = rightSide - leftSide;
    //work out area of div
    var bottomEdge = elemRegion.bottom;
    var topEdge = elemRegion.top;
    var height = bottomEdge - topEdge;
    var area = length * height;
    //create new span elements to hold region info
    var newspan = document.createElement("span");
    var region = document.createTextNode("Top: " + elemRegion.top +
      ", right: " + elemRegion.right + ", bottom: " +
      elemRegion.bottom + ", left: " + elemRegion.left);
    newspan.appendChild(region);
    YAHOO.util.Dom.addClass(newspan, "infoText");
    var newspan2 = document.createElement("span");
    var lengthText = document.createTextNode(length);
    newspan2.appendChild(lengthText);
    YAHOO.util.Dom.addClass(newspan2, "infoText");
    var newspan3 = document.createElement("span");
    var areaText = document.createTextNode(area);
```

```
        newspan3.appendChild(areaText);
        YAHOO.util.Dom.addClass(newspan3, "infoText");
        YAHOO.util.Dom.insertAfter(newspan, "divRegion");
        YAHOO.util.Dom.insertAfter(newspan2, "topSideLength");
        YAHOO.util.Dom.insertAfter(newspan3, "area");
    }
  YAHOO.util.Event.onAvailable("region", YAHOO.yuibook.domExamples.
  getElemRegion)
  </script>
```

We start off by using the `.getRegion()` method; this returns a literal object in the following format: `Region {top: 17, right: 306, bottom: 171, left: 12}`

Once we have the region of the `<div>` element. We can easily work out the length of one or more edges by subtracting one value from the other. We can also work out the area by working out the length of two perpendicular sides and then multiplying them.

We can access each extent of the region object returned by `.getRegion()` using the `.left`, `.right`, `.top`, and `.bottom` properties, and then construct a formatted string for display on the page. The screenshot below shows how the resulting page should look:

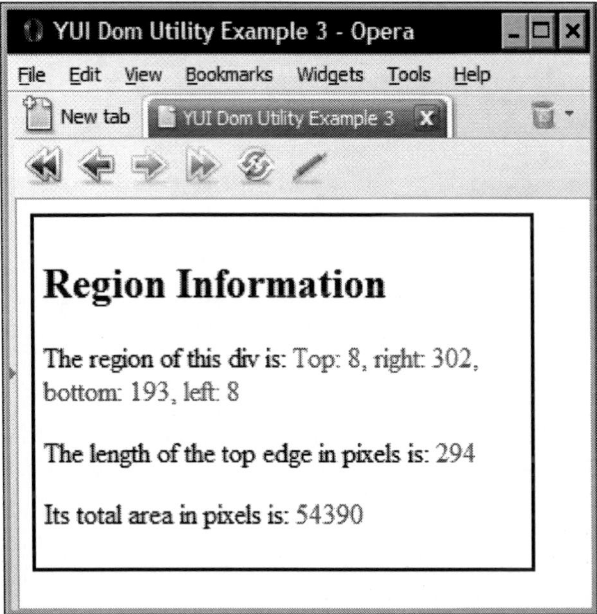

I See Your Point

The `YAHOO.util.Point` class extends the region class and is used to define a special region which represents a single point on a grid. It inherits all of the properties of the region class, and all of the methods except `.getRegion()`. It has no methods of its own and only two properties, `x` and `y`, which shouldn't really need explaining! Its constructor `YAHOO.util.Point` takes just two arguments, the X and Y positions of the point.

Listening for Events the Easy (YUI) Way

The event utility makes listening for any event extremely easy. The events you may wish to listen for could be traditional events that are available under the browser's own event model, such as the `click` event, or they may be custom events that you define yourself. This is where the real power of this utility resides. You should avoid working with events in the traditional way and give in completely to the ways of the Event Utility.

The Event Utility provides a framework that makes it easier to create event-driven applications, where interesting moments defined by the utilities, as well as in your own application, can be listened for and reacted to accordingly. It has many features to help you create rich and interactive internet applications including:

- Automatic handler deferral—If the HTML element to which the event listener is attached is not found by the script immediately, it is deferred for up to 15 seconds after the page has loaded to give the element time to appear. This only works when using the elements `id` directly in the listener function, not when using a variable representing the element.
- Automatic scope correction—The event utility automatically adjusts the scope of your event handler so that the `this` variable always refers to the DOM object that the event is attached to, rather than the window object. This frequently happens in IE or other non-standards based browsers when handling events.
- Automatic browser abstraction—Obtaining properties of the event object is another area of current web design where huge incompatibilities between IE and other browsers exist. The event utility doesn't care which browser is in use, it overcomes the differences by always passing the actual event object to the callback function as a parameter. A series of utility methods exist that allow you to easily access the properties of this event object, which we'll look at in just a minute.

- Easy event handler attachment—Any event handler for any DOM events or any custom events can be attached to any DOM element or series of elements using either a string variable (which could also be an array) representing the DOM element(s) or a literal reference to the DOM element itself.
- Automatic listener cleanup—when the `onUnload` event is detected, the event utility will automatically try to remove listeners it has registered. It does this using the `_simpleRemove()` and `_unload()` methods which are private members of the `YAHOO.util.Event` class. You can also remove listeners manually when they are no longer required using the `.removeListener()` or `.purgeElement()` methods.

Event Models

Browser event support started way back in second generation browsers when the individual browsers of the time began exposing certain events to JavaScript through their respective object models.

This was the real turning point for the interactive web and laid the foundations for the event-driven web applications that proliferate on the Internet and the language of JavaScript as it stands at the present time. As I mentioned earlier in the chapter, the event model is very closely related to the Document Object Model and events are made possible by the DOM.

Event History

Early events such as `onclick`, `onmouseover`, and `onmouseout` allowed developers to add event-handling code that reacted to user-initiated changes, and `onload` and `onunload` events allowed scripts to react to browser initiated events like page loads.

Each browser implemented its own object model in the early days, and therefore its own event model. The prevailing browsers at the time were Internet Explorer and Netscape Navigator, a distant predecessor of Firefox, and the event models used by each were largely incompatible.

The mighty W3C came to the rescue with a standardized event model, based loosely on the original Netscape model. The W3C DOM Events specification became a full recommendation on 13 November 2000, bringing consistency and coherence between the Netscape and Explorer models.

Today there are two main event models; the IE event model and the W3C event model. IE supports much of the W3C standard but also, unsurprisingly, adds support for a lot of non-standard events too. It is best to avoid using these, as browsers that are not IE will not work with them.

W3C Events

The latest event specification from the W3C is the DOM Level 3 Events specification, which although still at working draft status, promises enhancements to the existing W3C Event model, and adds support for keyboard events, as well as range of new methods.

Although some aspects of DOM Level 3 are full recommendations, and have been since 2004, DOM Level 3 events are not, but the working draft was last updated in 2006 and development is moving forward.

The Event Object

As well as different event models, different browsers deal with the `event` object in different ways. The event object contains information about the most recent event that has occurred, so if a visitor clicks on a link for example, the event object's type property will be set to `click`, and other information will also be made available, such as the `EventTarget` property, which indicates the target element that the event was originally dispatched to.

One of the main differences in how the event object is used in different browsers centers on how the object is accessed. In IE the event object is accessed through the `window` object, whereas in Firefox, the event object is automatically passed to your event handler as an argument.

YUI Event Capturing

The YUI provides a unified event model that works across all A-grade browsers. It also introduces an interface that allows you to create your own custom events. These are important enhancements in several ways.

Firstly, you can save yourself a lot of code as the event handlers can be attached to almost any element without the worry that the events will fail to successfully fire in different browsers. Handlers can even be attached to multiple elements with ease or multiple handlers can be attached to a single element.

The event object and how it is accessed has also been refined so that it can be obtained in the same way regardless of the browser to a certain extent. You don't need to add separate code routines that look for the object under `window.event` as well as an argument of your handler because the YUI always passes the event object to your event handler, making it available whenever you need to access it.

Evolving Event Handlers

In the early event models event handlers were attached directly to their HTML elements as attributes. For example, a click handler would go into the HTML for the link as an `onclick` attribute:

```
<a href="someurl" onclick="someFunction(); return false">
```

Once the W3C provided the standardized event model, handlers could be implemented directly in the accompanying script without cluttering the HTML mark up that defined the page:

```
document.getElementById('someElement').onclick = someFunction;
```

The YUI Event utility takes the direct implementation method one step further, giving you a standard method of attaching certain listeners to selected elements:

```
YAHOO.util.Event.addListener(someElement, "someEvent",
                             someHandler);
```

The Event utility provides an extensive range of methods, all of them equally as useful in their own way as the `addListener()` method and all designed to make coding an event-driven application quicker and easier.

Reacting When Appropriate

Traditionally, the easiest way to execute some code without any event being initiated by the visitor to the page was to use the `window` object's `onload` event. We even made use of this when we looked at the traditional DOM example earlier in this chapter.

This method can cause unpredictable behavior in some browsers if the code that is executed by the `onload` event targets elements of the page that do not yet exist and therefore should not be used.

The Event utility brings with it several methods that help to avoid this problem including: `.onDOMReady()`, `.onAvailable()`, and `.onContentReady()`. They are all similar, but have their subtle differences.

The `.onDOMReady()` method allows you to execute arbitrary code as soon as the DOM is structurally complete. It is a much more effective method than reacting to the old school `onLoad` event of the `window` object. The event fires as soon as the DOM is complete.

You can also target specific elements with ease using either `.onAvailable()` or `.onContentReady()`. These two methods allow you to execute some code as soon as an element is detected in the DOM. The syntax and use of these two methods are very similar, except that `.onContentReady()` does not fire until the target element, as well as its next sibling are detected in the DOM.

Let's put something basic together that illustrates the above methods. As this is just a minor example, the page will again be very basic and will simply serve to exhibit the methods described above. The page will need to be saved into your `yuisite` directory.

Create the following basic web page:

```
<!DOCTYPE HTML PUBLIC "-//W3C//DTD HTML 4.01//EN"
                              "http://www.w3.org/TR/html4/strict.dtd">
<html lang="en">
  <head>
    <meta http-equiv="content-type" content="text/html;
                                    charset=utf-8">
    <title>Content Loading Examples</title>
    <script type="text/javascript"
            src="yui/build/yahoo/yahoo-min.js"></script>
    <script type="text/javascript"
            src="yui/build/event/event-min.js"></script>
  </head>
  <body>
    <div id="div1">I am div number 1</div>
  </body>
</html>
```

This is all we'll need on the HTML front. Save the file as `contentLoadingExample.html`. Next, before the closing `</body>` tag of the document, add the following code:

```
    function onAvailableHandler() {
      alert("Div number 1 has loaded!");
    }
    YAHOO.util.Event.onAvailable("div1", onAvailableHandler);
  </script>
```

In this very basic example we send an alert when the target element has been detected in the DOM.

As `.onContentReady()` is syntactically identical to `.onAvailable()`, you can simply substitute `.onAvailable()` in the above code for `.onContentReady()` and the outcome, in this very limited example, will be exactly the same.

Using this example, we can also look at the difference in Event order between IE and Firefox. Add the following function to the main script block:

```
function onLoadHandler() {
  alert("window.onload fired!");
}
window.onload = onLoadHandler;
```

When you open the new page in IE, the `load` event fires first, then the `onAvailable` event, however in Firefox, the `onAvailable` event correctly fires first, followed by the window's load event. This is the case for both `onAvailable` and `onContentReady`, and is why traditional and YUI events should not be mixed.

A Look at the Event Class

There are five classes defined within the Event Utility. The first, `YAHOO.util.Event` provides the mechanism for defining the event handling callback functions and for adding the listeners to the elements.

Other classes include the `YAHOO.util.CustomEvent` class which deals with non-standard events you define yourself, `YAHOO.util.EventProvider`, which provides a wrapper for firing and subscribing to events by name and is used by some of the other utilities to extend event functionality (such as the Element utility). `YAHOO.util.KeyListener` is a special class that deals solely with listening for keyboard events, and finally, the `YAHOO.util.Subscriber` class is another specialized class used to store subscriber information that is used when events fire.

Listeners

The `.addListener` (alias `.on`) method is the event method you'll use most often as this is the method that adds the listener which executes the callback function whenever the event in question occurs. It takes up to five arguments: the first is the HTML element to bind the event to,the second argument is the type of event to listen for, and the third is a reference to the callback function to execute on detection of the event. The fourth optional argument is an arbitrary object to pass to the callback and the fifth, also an optional argument is a boolean that specifies the execution scope.

If this last argument is true, the object passed in the preceding argument becomes the execution scope instead of the element that the event occurred on. These arguments are known as the event signature.

Removing listeners is just as easy as adding them. The `.removeListener()` method unbinds bound events and takes three arguments, the element the listener is defined for, the type of event, and optionally, a third argument specifying the callback function originally used to register the event. The `.purgeElement()` method may also be used to remove any listeners defined on an element for any event registered with the `.addListener()` method.

The `.stopEvent()` method combines the functionality of the `.stopPropagation()` and `.preventDefault()` methods for your convenience so you can achieve the effect of two useful methods with minimal code. So `.stopPropagation()` stops the event from bubbling up to the document level, while `.preventDefault()` prevents the default action of the event from being carried out by the browser automatically.

Custom Events

Most of each of the different utilities and controls featured in the library make use of custom events defined by the library's authors. This has been done because the W3C event model doesn't define a lot of the actions that the library allows your visitors to take.

The extra functionality provided by the library brings with it a whole host of fresh events that allow you to intercept interactions made between your visitors and the components of the library.

Not all of the components bring new custom events with them, but most of them do, and don't forget that if a utility or control lacks an event that you wish to capture, you can always define it yourself using the custom event interface.

The Animation utility features three custom events which define important moments during an animation such as when the animation begins (`onStart`), when it ends (`onComplete`), and during every frame of the animation (`onTween`).

The DataSource utility provides a series of both interaction and execution events that mark the occurrence of things like a request being made of the live data source, or a response being returned from the data source.

Some of the components of the library simply define too many events to list. The DataTable control for example defines 59 different things that may occur while the control is onscreen, allowing you to handle everything from a header cell being clicked to a row being double-clicked, as well as a series of events linked to records including the `keyUpdateEvent` and `resetEvent`.

The Custom Event Class

The IE and W3C/Netscape event models have a wide range of events that you can detect and react to via listeners and callback functions, but there are going to be occurrences during the use of your applications where you would like to listen for an event that simply doesn't exist by default. The `CustomEvent` object allows you to define and listen for non-default events. These events could be something like `onTabChange` for when a visitor changes tabs in a module on the page, for example, or anything else you deem important.

To define a custom event, the `YAHOO.util.CustomEvent` constructor is used, it takes up to four parameters. The first is the name of the custom event that will be listened for, the second is optional and sets the object scope the event will fire from, the optional third argument is a boolean that either allows or prevents the event from writing to the debug system (the default is false if this is left out). Finally, the fourth argument is an integer that represents the event signature that the custom event listener will use.

A simple case use would involve just specifying the first argument and none of the optional ones, so don't get too bogged down in the technical details at this stage. The `.fire()` method is provided to allow you to create the mechanism by which your custom event notifies a callback function that it has occurred. The fire method supplies the data that the callback function will make use of. This data is provided as an object literal which contains a series of name:value pairs.

The custom event class also provides a `.subscribe()` method so that you can add handlers for your custom events. It takes three arguments: the first is the function to execute when the custom event occurs, the second is an optional object to be passed to the function, and the third is an optional override which can be either a boolean or an object.

If true is supplied, the object passed in becomes the execution scope, if false the object which contains the event becomes the scope. Once the previous three steps have been completed, you can create the handlers that are invoked by the fire method and react to the event accordingly.

Creating a Custom Event

We've seen the event class and its properties and methods in detail, let's now take things one step further and define our own custom event. This is probably going to be the best way to learn how to use the custom event interface to a basic degree.

We'll be making use of different methods provided by the event utility throughout the rest of the coding examples so a full-blown coding example focused on the Event utility itself will probably be less beneficial than an example of a custom event in action.

What we'll do is create a basic `display` event which will fire whenever a hidden `<div>` element is displayed on screen. It'll be a very short example, but should help you to understand the use of custom events. Let's start with the following basic HTML page:

```
<!DOCTYPE HTML PUBLIC "-//W3C//DTD HTML 4.01//EN"
                          "http://www.w3.org/TR/html4/strict.dtd">
<html lang="en">
  <head>
    <meta http-equiv="content-type" content="text/html;
                                      charset=utf-8">
    <title>YUI Custom Event Example</title>
    <script type="text/javascript" src="yui/build/
            yahoo-dom-event/yahoo-dom-event.js"></script>
    <style type="text/css">
      .hidden {
        display:none;
        border:2px solid black;
        width:200px;
        padding:10px;
        margin-top:10px;
      }
    </style>
  </head>
  <body>
    <div>
      <a id="link" href="#">Click to open the hidden div</a>
      <div id="hiddendiv" class="hidden">I am the hidden div!</div>
    </div>
  </body>
</html>
```

We have a basic page featuring an anchor element and a `<div>` element. We want the `<div>` hidden initially, and we can also add some borders and padding to make it stand out a little more. You can add the following CSS `<style>` tag to the `<head>` of the document to achieve this:

```
<style type="text/css">
  .hidden {
    display:none;
    border:2px solid black;
    width:200px;
    padding:10px;
    margin-top:10px;
  }
</style>
```

Next, we can add the script in which our custom event will be defined. This should be added after the final closing </div> tag:

```
<script type="text/javascript">
  //create the namespace object for this example
  YAHOO.namespace("yuibook.customEvent");

  //define our custom event
  YAHOO.yuibook.customEvent.onDisplay = new
                              YAHOO.util.CustomEvent("onDisplay");
  //the displayDiv function is executed on a click of the link
  YAHOO.yuibook.customEvent.displayDiv = function() {
    //show the hidden div
    YAHOO.util.Dom.setStyle("hiddendiv", "display", "block");
    //fire our custom event
    YAHOO.yuibook.customEvent.onDisplay.fire();
  }
```

First we set a new variable that holds an instance of our custom event object. The object is generated using the `YAHOO.util.CustomEvent` constructor, specifying the event as an argument.

One of our objectives is to display the hidden <div>, so we set a function called `displayDiv()` which uses the `setStyle()` convenience method to set the hidden <div> element's `display` property to `block`. We then fire our custom event, using the `.fire()` method, because the display action has occurred.

```
  //execute code when the custom event fires
  YAHOO.yuibook.customEvent.displayEvent = function() {
    alert("The Display event fired!");
  }
```

Next we add the `displayEvent()` callback function to execute when our custom event fires. In this example it's just an (ugly) alert which notifies us that our event has occurred.

```
  //subscribe to our custom event
YAHOO.yuibook.customEvent.onDisplay.subscribe
                        (YAHOO.yuibook.customEvent.displayEvent);
  //add a listener for the click event on the link
  YAHOO.util.Event.addListener("link", "click",
                              YAHOO.yuibook.customEvent.displayDiv);
</script>
```

The `.subscribe()` method allows us to listen for the custom event and then execute the callback function when the event fires. To initiate the displaying of the hidden `<div>` we can use the Event utility to attach a listener to the anchor element, which in turn calls the `displayDiv()` function.

Save the file and run it in your browser. When you click the link the hidden `<div>` is displayed and the custom event is fired, causing the alert to display. This is just a very basic example of the power of the custom event.

All we do in this example is display a simple alert when our custom event fires, but we could add any arbitrary code in order to react in any way to events that may occur in an application. Traditionally, we would have had to have added any code we wanted to execute in a callback function for the click event, so rather than reacting to unique interactions we would always be reacting to the click event.

To prove that this is the case, add in another alert call directly after the `displayDiv()` function declaration:

```
alert("The Click event fired");
```

Run the file in your browser again; the first alert fires as soon as the link is clicked because it is part of the callback function that the click listener invokes.

Once the hidden `<div>` is displayed, the second alert is produced by the subscriber to the custom event. If this were still part of the click event, both alerts would be displayed before the hidden `<div>` was displayed.

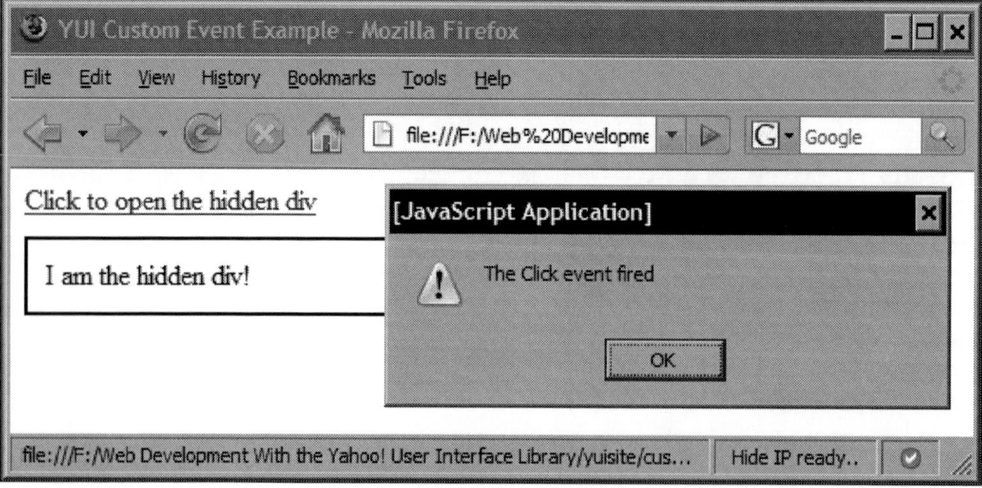

Summary

The YUI DOM utility isn't meant to replace the DOM specifications from the W3C. It uses them as a foundation to develop the tools available to you when working with the DOM. It enhances the existing DOM specifications, giving you more power in the fight for cleaner code.

It may seem a little complicated at first, but the DOM utility is actually one of the easiest utilities to use. You don't need to create any objects using constructors or factory methods, you just include the utility reference in your code and make use of the methods you need. If you've already got some experience in manipulating the DOM using traditional methods, picking up the new methods defined by the YUI DOM utility won't take long at all.

The DOM and events go hand-in-hand and the latter would certainly not exist as we know them without the former. Like manipulating the DOM, intercepting and reacting to common events that are initiated as a result of user interaction forms the basis of modern web design. Any web solution is going to rely on events to a certain degree and they are something that you should already be very familiar with.

The YUI harmonizes the different event models at work in different browsers allowing you to do the same things but with less code and less browser detection. It also extends the capabilities of each browser's event model, adding new event tools to the already well defined set and even introduces new tools that allow you to define and react to your own custom events.

4
AJAX and Connection Manager

As far as web interface design techniques are concerned, AJAX is definitely the way to go. So what JavaScript library worth its salt these days wouldn't want to include a component dedicated to this extremely useful and versatile method of client/server communication?

The term AJAX has been part of the mainstream development community's vocabulary since early 2005 (with the advent of Google Mail). Although some of the key components that AJAX consists of, such as the XMLHttp object, have been around for much longer (almost a decade in fact). The goal of asynchronously loading additional data after a web page has rendered is also not a new concept or requirement.

Yet AJAX reinvented existing technologies as something new and exciting, and paved the way to a better, more attractive, and interactive web (sometimes referred to loosely as web 2.0) where web applications feel much more like desktop applications.

AJAX can also perhaps be viewed as the godfather of many modern JavaScript libraries. Maybe it wasn't the sole motivating factor behind the growing plethora of available libraries, but it was certainly highly influential and orchestral in their creation and was at least partly responsible for the first wave of modern, class-based JavaScript libraries.

Like many other cornerstone web techniques developed over the years, AJAX was (and still is) implemented in entirely different ways by different browsers. I don't know if developers just finally had enough of dealing with these issues.

The very first JavaScript libraries sprang into existence as a means of abstracting away the differences in AJAX implementation between platforms, thereby allowing developers to focus on the important things in web design instead of worrying about compatibility issues.

The result in many cases is a quick and easy way for developers to cut down on the amount of code they are required to produce, and a better more interactive experience for end users and website visitors.

The Connection Manager—A Special Introduction

The Connection Manager utility is by no means the smallest, most light-weight component included with the YUI, but it's certainly not the largest either, yet it packs so much functionality into just 12Kb (for the `-min` version).

Connection Manager provides a fast and reliable means of accessing server-side resources, such as PHP or ASP scripts and handling the response. A series of supporting objects manage the different stages of any asynchronous transactions, whilst providing additional functionality where necessary.

Connection is one of just a few of the utilities that are supported by a single class; this makes looking up its methods nice and straight-forward. It also doesn't have any properties at all (although the objects that it creates all have their own members which hold various pieces of information), which makes using it even easier!

This utility is what is known as a singleton utility, which means that there can only be one live instance of the utility at any one time, differing from many of the other components of the library. Don't worry though, this doesn't restrict you to only making one request; Connection will manage as many separate requests as you need.

Because this utility is a singleton, there are important considerations that advanced coders may want to take note of. Unlike some of the other library components, Connection cannot be subclassed—all of its class's members are static, meaning that they won't be picked up when using the YAHOO global `.extend()` method.

It wraps up the cross-browser creation of the `XMLHttpRequest` (XHR) object, as well as a simple to use object-based method of accessing the server response and any associated data, into a simple package which handles the request from start to finish. This requires minimal input from you, the developer, saving time as well as effort.

Another object created by Connection is the response object, which is created once the transaction has completed. The response object gives you access via its members to a rich set of data including the `id` of the transaction, the HTTP status code and status message, and either the `responseText` and `responseXML` members depending on the format of the data returned.

Like most of the other library components, Connection Manager provides a series of global custom events that can be used to hook into key moments during any transaction. We'll look at these events in more detail later on in the chapter but rest assured, there are events marking the start and completion of transactions, as well as success, failure, and abort events.

The Connection utility has been a part of the YUI since its second public release (the 0.9.0 release) and has seen considerable bug fixing and refinement since this time. This makes it one of the more reliable and better documented utilities available.

Connection is such a useful utility that it's used by several other library components in order to obtain data from remote sources. Other components that make use of Connection Manager include the AutoComplete control, DataTable, DataSource, and Tabview.

It is one of the only library components not dependant on the DOM utility. All it requires are the YAHOO global utility and the Event utility. That doesn't mean that you can't include a reference to the DOM utility, however, to make use of its excellent DOM manipulation convenience methods.

The XMLHttpRequest Object Interface

When working with the Connection utility you'll never be required to manually create or access an XHR object directly. Instead, you talk to the utility and this works with the object for you using whichever code is appropriate for the browser in use. This means that you don't need separate methods of creating an XHR object in order to keep each browser happy.

A transaction describes the complete process of making a request to the server and receiving and processing the response. Connection Manager handles transactions from beginning to end, providing different services at different points during a request.

Transactions are initiated using the `.asyncRequest()` method which acts as a constructor for the connection object. The method takes several arguments: the first specifies the HTTP method that the transaction should use, the second specifies the URL of your server-side script while the third allows you to add a reference to a callback object.

A fourth, optional, argument can also be used to specify a `POST` message if the HTTP method is set to use `POST` giving you an easy means of sending data to the server as well as retrieving it. This is rarely required however, even when using the `POST` method, as we shall see later in the chapter.

It's also very easy to build in query string parameters if these are required to obtain the data that you are making the request for. It can be hard coded into a variable and then passed in as the second argument of the Connection constructor instead of setting the second argument manually within the constructor.

Connection Manager takes these arguments and uses them to set up the XHR object that will be used for the transaction on your behalf. Once this has been done, and Connection has made the request, you then need to define a new object yourself that will allow you to react to a range of responses from the server.

A Closer Look at the Response Object

I briefly mentioned the response object that is created by the utility automatically once a transaction has completed, let's now take a slightly more in-depth view at this object. It will be created after any transaction, whether or not it was considered a success.

The callback functions you define to handle successful or failed transactions (which we'll examine in more detail very shortly) are automatically passed to the response object as an argument. Accessing it is extremely easy and requires no additional intervention from yourself.

If the transaction fails, this object gives you access to the HTTP failure code and HTTP status message which are received from the server. Examining these two members of the response object can highlight what happened to make the request fail, making it integral to any Connection implementation.

If the transaction was a success, these two members will still be populated but with a success code and status message, and additional members such as `responseText` or `responseXML` will also contain data for you to manipulate.

If you need to obtain the HTTP response headers sent by the server as part of the response, these can be obtained using either the `getResponseHeader` collection, or the `getAllResponseHeaders` member.

In the case of file uploads, some of these members will not be available via the response object. File uploads are the one type of transaction that do not make use of the XHR object at all, so the HTTP code and status message members cannot be used. Similarly, there will not be either a textual or XML-based response when uploading files.

Managing the Response with a Callback Object

In order to successfully negotiate the response from the server, a literal callback object should be defined which allows you to deal quickly and easily with the information returned whether it is a success, failure, or another category of response.

Each member of this object invokes a callback function or performs some other action relevant to your implementation. These members can be one of several types including another object, a function call or even a string or integer depending on the requirements of your application.

The most common members you would use in your callback object would usually be based upon `success` and `failure` function calls to handle these basic response types, with each member calling its associated function when a particular HTTP response code is received by the response object.

It's also very easy to add an additional member to this object which allows you to include data which may be useful when processing the response form the server. In this situation, the `argument` object member can be used and can take a string, a number, an object, or an array.

Other optional members include a `customevents` handler to deal with custom, per-transaction events as opposed to the global events that are available to any and all transactions, a `scope` object used to set the scope of your handler functions, and a timeout count used to set the wait time before Connection aborts the transaction and assumes failure.

The remaining member of the callback object is the `upload` handler which is of course a special handler to deal specifically with file uploads. As I already mentioned, the response object will be missing success of failure details when dealing with file uploads, however, you can still define a callback function to be executed once the upload transaction has completed.

Working with responseXML

In this example we're going to look at a common response type you may want to use—`responseXML`. We can build a simple news reader that reads headlines from a remote XML file and displays them on the page.

We'll also need an intermediary PHP file that will actually retrieve the XML file from the remote server and pass it back to the Connection Manager. Because of the security restrictions placed upon all browsers we can't use the XHR object to obtain the XML file directly because it resides on another domain.

This is not a problem for us however, because we can use the intermediary PHP file that we're going to have to create anyway as a proxy. We'll make requests from the browser to the proxy thereby sidestepping any security issues, and the proxy will then make requests to the external domain's server. The proxy used here in this example is a cut down version of that created by Jason Levitt that I modified specifically for this example.

In order to complete this example you'll need to use a full web server setup, with PHP installed and configured. Our proxy PHP file will also make use of the cURL library, so this will also need to be installed on your server.

The installation of cURL varies depending on the platform in use, so full instructions for installing it is beyond the scope of this book, but don't worry because there are some excellent guides available online that explain this quick and simple procedure.

Even though Connection Manager only requires the YAHOO and Event utilities to function correctly, we can make use of some of the convenient functionality provided by the DOM utility, so we will use the aggregated `yahoo-dom-event.js` instead of the individual YAHOO and Event files. We'll also need `connection-min.js` and `fonts.css` so make sure these are all present in your `yui` folder and begin with the following HTML:

```
<!DOCTYPE HTML PUBLIC "-//W3C//DTD HTML 4.01//EN"
                              "http://www.w3.org/TR/html4/strict.dtd">
<html lang="en">
  <head>
    <meta http-equiv="content-type" content="text/html;
                                     charset=utf-8">
    <title>Yui Connection Manager Example</title>
    <script type="text/javascript"
            src="yui/yahoo-dom-event.js"></script>
    <script type="text/javascript"
            src="yui/connection-min.js"></script>
    <link rel="stylesheet" type="text/css"
          href="yui/assets/fonts-min.css">
    <link rel="stylesheet" type="text/css" href="responseXML.css">
  </head>
  <body>
    <div id="newsreader">
      <div class="header">Recent News</div>
```

```
        <div id="newsitems"></div>
        <div id="footer"><a class="link"
                            href="http://news.bbc.co.uk/1/hi/
                                  help/rss/4498287.stm">
                                  Copyright: &copy; British
                                  Broadcasting Corporation</a></div>
      <div>
    </body>
  </html>
```

We'll start off with this very simple page which at this stage contains just the markup for the newsreader and the references to the required library files. There's also a `<link>` to a custom stylesheet which we'll create in a little while.

Adding the JavaScript

Directly after the final closing `</div>` tag, add the following `<script>`:

```
<script type="text/javascript">
  //create namespace object for this example
  YAHOO.namespace("yuibook.newsreader");

  //define the initConnection function
  YAHOO.yuibook.newsreader.initConnection = function() {

    //define the AJAX success handler
    var successHandler = function(o) {

      //define the arrays
      var titles = new Array();
      var descs = new Array();
      var links = new Array();

      //get a reference to the newsitems container
      var newsitems = document.getElementById("newsitems");

      //get the root of the XML doc
      var root = o.responseXML.documentElement;

      //get the elements from the doc we want
      var doctitles = root.getElementsByTagName("title");
      var docdescs = root.getElementsByTagName("description");
      var doclinks = root.getElementsByTagName("link");

      //map the collections into the arrays
      for (x = 0; x < doctitles.length; x++){
        titles[x] = doctitles[x];
        descs[x] = docdescs[x];
```

```
    links[x] = doclinks[x];
  }

  //removed the unwanted items from the arrays
  titles.reverse();
  titles.pop();
  titles.pop();
  titles.reverse();
  descs.reverse();
  descs.pop();
  descs.reverse();
  links.reverse();
  links.pop();
  links.pop();
  links.reverse();

  //present the data from the arrays
  for (x = 0; x < 5; x++) {

    //create new elements
    var div = document.createElement("div");
    var p1 = document.createElement("p");
    var p2 = document.createElement("p");
    var a = document.createElement("a");

    //give classes to new elements for styling
    YAHOO.util.Dom.addClass(p1, "title");
    YAHOO.util.Dom.addClass(p2, "desc");
    YAHOO.util.Dom.addClass(a, "newslink");

    //create new text nodes and the link
    var title =
         document.createTextNode(titles[x].firstChild.nodeValue);
    var desc =
         document.createTextNode(descs[x].firstChild.nodeValue);
    var link = links[x].firstChild.nodeValue;
    a.setAttribute("href", link);

    //add the new elements to the page
    a.appendChild(desc);
    p1.appendChild(title);
    p2.appendChild(a);
    div.appendChild(p1)
    div.appendChild(p2)
    newsitems.appendChild(div);
  }
```

```
        }

        //define the AJAX failure handler
        var failureHandler = function(o) {

          //alert the status code and error text
          alert(o.status + " : " + o.statusText);
        }

        //define the callback object
        var callback = {
          success:successHandler,
          failure:failureHandler
        };

        //initiate the transaction
        var transaction = YAHOO.util.Connect.asyncRequest("GET",
                                          "myproxy.php", callback, null);
      }

      //execute initConnection when DOM is ready
      YAHOO.util.Event.onDOMReady( YAHOO.yuibook.newsreader.
    initConnection);
    </script>
```

Once again, we can make use of the `.onDOMReady()` method to specify a callback function that is to be executed when the YUI detects that the DOM is ready, which is usually as soon as the page has finished loading.

The code within our master initialization function is split into distinct sections. We have our `success` and `failure` callback functions, as well as a callback object which will call either the success or failure function depending on the HTTP status code received following the request.

The failure handler code is very short; we can simply alert the HTTP status code and status message to the visitor. The callback object, held in the variable `callback`, is equally as simple, just containing references to the success and failure functions as values.

The pseudo-constructor which sets up the actual request using the `.asyncRequest()` method is just a single line of code, It's arguments specify the response method (`GET`), the name of the PHP file that will process our request (`myproxy.php`), the name of our callback object (`callback`), and a null reference.

Connection Manager is able to accept URL query string parameters that are passed to the server-side script. Any parameters are passed using the fourth argument of the `.asyncRequest()` method and as we don't need this feature in this implementation, we can simply pass in `null` instead.

Most of our program logic resides in the `successHandler()` function. The response object (`o`) is automatically passed to our callback handlers (both success and failure) and can be received simply by including it between brackets in the function declaration. Let's break down what each part of our `successHandler()` function does.

We first define three arrays; they need to be proper arrays so that some useful array methods can be called on the items we extract from the remote XML file. It does make the code bigger, but means that we can get exactly the data we need, in the format that we want. We also grab the `newsitems` container from the DOM.

The `root` variable that we declare next allows us easy access to the root of the XML document, which for reference is a news feed from the BBC presented in RSS 2.0 format. The three variables following `root` allow us to strip out all of the elements we are interested in.

These three variables will end up as collections of elements, which are similar to arrays in almost every way except that array methods, such as the ones we need to use, cannot be called on them, which is why we need the arrays. To populate the arrays with the data from our collections, we can use the `for` loop that follows the declaration of these three variables.

Because of the structure of the RSS in the remote XML file, some of the `title`, `description`, and `link` elements are irrelevant to the news items and instead refer to the RSS file itself and the service provided by the BBC. These are the first few examples of each of the elements in the file.

So how can we get rid of the first few items in each array? The standard JavaScript `.pop()` method allows us to discard the last item from the array, so if we reverse the arrays, the items we want to get rid of will be at the end of each array.

Calling reverse a second time once we've popped the items we no longer need puts the array back into the correct order. The number of items popped is specific to this implementation, other RSS files may differ in their structural presentation and therefore their `.pop()` requirements.

Now that we have the correct information in our arrays, we're ready to add some of the news items to our reader. The RSS file will contain approximately 20 to 30 different news items depending on the day, which is obviously far too many to display all at once in our reader.

There are several different things we could do in this situation. The first and arguably the most technical method would be to include all of the news items and then make our reader scroll through them. Doing this however would complicate the example and take the focus off of the Connection utility. What we'll do instead is simply discard all but the five newest news items. The `for` loop that follows the `.reverse()` and `.pop()` methods will do this.

The loop will run five times and on each pass it will first create a series of new `<p>`, `<div>`, and `<a>` elements using standard JavaScript techniques. These will be used to hold the data from the arrays, and to ultimately display the news items.

We can then use the DOM utility's highly useful `.addClass()` method (which IE doesn't ignore, unlike `setAttribute("class")`) to give class names to our newly created elements. This will allow us to target them with some CSS styles.

Then we obtain the `nodeValue` of each item in each of our arrays and add these to our new elements. Once this is done we can add the new elements and their `textNodes` to the `newsitems` container on the page. Save the file as `responseXML.html`.

Styling the Newsreader

To make everything look right in this example and to target our newly defined classes, we can add a few simple CSS rules. In a fresh page in your text editor, add the following selectors and rules:

```
#newsreader {
  width:240px;
  border:2px solid #980000;
  background-color:#cccccc;
}
.header {
  font-weight:bold;
  font-size:123.1%;
  background-color:#980000;
  color:#ffffff;
  width:96%;
  padding:10px 0px 10px 10px;
}
.title {
  font-weight:bold;
  margin-left:10px;
  margin-right:10px;
}
```

```
.desc {
  margin-top:-14px;
  *margin-top:-20px;
  margin-left:10px;
  margin-right:10px;
  font-size:85%;
}
.newslink {
  text-decoration:none;
  color:#000000;
}
.link {
  text-decoration:none;
  color:#ffffff;
}
#footer {
  background-color:#980000;
  color:#ffffff;
  font-size:77%;
  padding:10px 0px 10px 10px;
}
```

Save this file as `responseXML.css`. All of the files used in this example, including the YUI files, will need to be added to the content-serving directory of your web server in order to function correctly.

Finally, in order to actually get the XML file in the first place, we'll need a little PHP. As I mentioned before, this will act as a proxy to which our application makes its request. In a blank page in your text editor, add the following PHP code:

```
<?php

  define ('HOSTNAME', 'http://newsrss.bbc.co.uk/rss/
                       newsonline_uk_edition/world/rss.xml');
  $session = curl_init();
  curl_setopt($session, CURLOPT_URL, HOSTNAME);
  curl_setopt($session, CURLOPT_RETURNTRANSFER, true);
  $xml = curl_exec($session);
  curl_close($session);

  if (empty($xml))
  {
    print "Error extracting RSS file!";
  }
  else
  {
```

```
        header("Content-Type: text/xml");
        echo $xml;
    }

?>
```

Save this as myproxy.php. The newsreader we've created takes just the first (latest) five news items and displays them in our reader. This is all we need to do to expose the usefulness of the Connection utility, but the example could easily be extended so scroll using the Animation and DragDrop utilities.

Everything is now in place, if you run the HTML file in your browser (not by double-clicking it, but by actually requesting it properly from the web server) you should see the newsreader as in the following screenshot:

Useful Connection Methods

As you saw in the last example, the Connection Manager interface provides some useful methods for working with the data returned by an AJAX request. Let's take a moment to review some of the other methods provided by the class that are available to us.

The `.abort()` method can be used to cancel a transaction that is in progress and must be used prior to the `readyState` property (a standard AJAX property as opposed to YUI-flavoured) being set to `4` (complete).

The `.asyncRequest()` method is a key link in Connection's chain and acts like a kind of pseudo-constructor used to initiate requests. We already looked at this method in detail so I'll leave it there as far as this method is concerned.

A public method used to determine whether the transaction has finished being processed is the `.isCallInProgress()` method. It simply returns a boolean indicating whether it is true or not and takes just a reference to the connection object.

Finally `.setForm()` provides a convenient means of obtaining all of the data entered into a form and submitting it to the server via a `GET` or a `POST` request. The first argument is required and is a reference to the form itself, the remaining two arguments are both optional and are used when uploading files. They are both boolean: the first is set to `true` to enable file upload, while the third is set to `true` to allow SSL uploads in IE.

A Login System Fronted by YUI

In our first Connection example we looked at a simple `GET` request to obtain a remote XML file provided by the BBC. In this example, let's look at the sending, or Posting of data as well.

We can easily create a simple registration/login system interface powered by the Connection utility. While the creation of session tokens or a state-carrying system is beyond the scope of this example, we can see how easy it is to pass data to the server as well as get data back from it.

Again, we'll need to use a full web server set up, and this time we can also include a mySQL database as the end target for the data posted to the server. You'll probably want to create a new table in the database for this example.

In order to focus just on the functionality provided by the YUI, our form will have no security checks in place and data entered into the form will go directly into the database. Please do not do this in real life!

Security in a live implementation should be your primary concern and any data that goes anywhere near your databases should be validated, double-checked, and then validated again if possible, and some form of encryption is an absolute must. The MD5 hashing functions of PHP are both easy to use and highly robust.

Create a new table in your database using the mySQL Command Line Interface and call it **users** or similar. Set it up so that a `describe` request of the table looks like that shown in the screenshot overleaf:

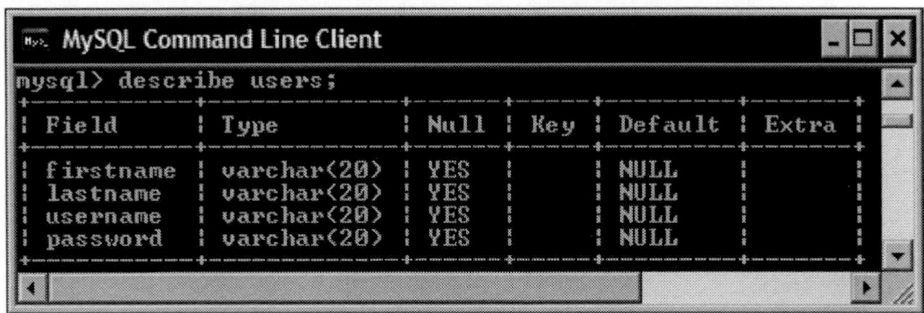

For the example, we'll need at least some data in the table as well, so add in some fake data that can be entered into the login form once we've finished coding it. A couple of records like that shown in the figure below should suffice.

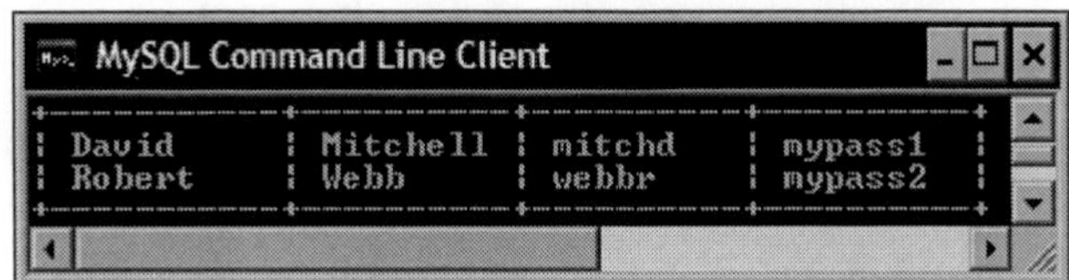

Start off with the following basic web page:

```
<!DOCTYPE HTML PUBLIC "-//W3C//DTD HTML 4.01//EN"
                              "http://www.w3.org/TR/html4/strict.dtd">
<html lang="en">
  <head>
    <meta http-equiv="content-type" content="text/html;
                                    charset=utf-8">
    <title>Yui Connection Manager Example 2</title>
    <script type="text/javascript"
            src="yui/yahoo-dom-event.js"></script>
    <script type="text/javascript"
            src="yui/connection-min.js"></script>
</head>
  <body>
    <form id="signin" method="get" action="#">
```

```
        <fieldset>
          <legend>Please sign in!</legend>
          <label>Username</label><input type="text" id="uname"
                                        name="uname">
          <label>Password</label><input type="password" id="pword"
                                        name="pword">
          <button type="button" id="login">Go!</button>
          <button type="reset">Clear</button>
        </fieldset>
      </form>
      <form id="register" method="post" action="#">
        <fieldset>
          <legend>Please sign up!</legend>
          <label>First name:</label><input type="text" name="fname">
          <label>Last name:</label><input type="text" name="lname">
          <label>Username:</label><input type="text" name="uname">
          <label>Password:</label><input type="password" name="pword">
          <button type="button" id="join">Join!</button>
          <button type="reset">Clear</button>
        </fieldset>
      </form>
    </body>
  </html>
```

The `<head>` section of the page starts off almost exactly the same as in the previous example, and the body of the page just contains two basic forms. I won't go into specific details here. The mark up used here should be more than familiar to most of you. Save the file as `login.html`.

We can also add some basic styling to the form to ensure that everything is laid out correctly. We don't need to worry about any fancy, purely aesthetic stuff at this point, we'll just focus on getting the layout correct and ensuring that the second form is initially hidden.

In a new page in your text editor, add the following `css`:

```
fieldset {
    width:250px;
    padding:10px;
    border:2px solid lightblue;
  }
  label {
    margin-top:3px;
    width:100px;
    float:left;
```

```
    }
    input {
      margin-top:2px;
      *margin-top:0px;
    }
    button {
      float:right;
      margin:5px 3px 5px 0px;
      width:50px;
    }
  #register {
    display:none;
  }
```

Save the file as `login.css` and view it in your browser. The code we have so far should set the stage for the rest of the example and appear as shown in the figure below:

Now let's move on to the real nuts and bolts of this example—the JavaScript that will work with the Connection Manager utility to produce the desired results. Directly before the closing `</body>` tag, add the following `<script>`:

```
<script type="text/javascript">
  //create namespace object
  YAHOO.namespace("yuibook.login");

  //define the submitForm function
  YAHOO.yuibook.login.submitForm = function() {

    //have both fields been completed?
    if (document.forms[0].uname.value == "" ||
                                  document.forms[0].pword.value == "") {
      alert("Please enter your username AND password to login");
      return false;
```

```
      } else {

        //define success handler
        var successHandler = function(o) {
          alert(o.responseText);

          //if user not found show register form
          if (o.responseText == "Username not found") {
            YAHOO.util.Dom.setStyle("register", "display", "block");
            document.forms[0].uname.value = "";
            document.forms[0].pword.value = "";
          }
        }

        //define failure handler
        var failureHandler = function(o) {
          alert("Error " + o.status + " : " + o.statusText);
        }

        //define callback object
        var callback = {
          success:successHandler,
          failure:failureHandler
        }

        //harvest form data ready to send to the server
        var form = document.getElementById("signin");
        YAHOO.util.Connect.setForm(form);

        //define a transaction for a GET request
        var transaction = YAHOO.util.Connect.asyncRequest("GET",
                                                   "login.php", callback);
      }
    }

    //execute submitForm when login button clicked
    YAHOO.util.Event.addListener("login", "click", YAHOO.yuibook.login.
  submitForm);
  </script>
```

We use the Event utility to add a listener for the `click` event on the login button. When this is detected the `submitform()` function is executed. First of all we should check that data has been entered into the login form. As our form is extremely small, we can get away with looking at each field individually to check the data has been entered into it.

Don't forget that in a real-world implementation, you'd probably want to filter the data entered into each field with a regular expression to check that the data entered is in the expected format, (alphabetical characters for the first and last names, alphanumerical characters for the username, and password fields).

Provided both fields have been completed, we then set the success and failure handlers, the callback object and the Connection Manager invocation. The failure handler acts in exactly the same way as it did in the previous example; the status code and any error text is alerted. In this example, the success handler also sends out an alert, this time making use of the `o.responseText` member of the response object as opposed to `responseXML` like in the previous example.

If the function detects that the response from the server indicates that the specified username was not found in the database, we can easily show the registration form and reset the form fields.

Next, we define our callback object which invokes either the `success` or `failure` handler depending on the server response. What we have so far is pretty standard and will be necessary parts of almost any implementation involving Connection.

Following this we can make use of the so far unseen `.setForm()` method. This is called on a reference to the first form. This will extract all of the data entered into the form and create an object containing `name:value` pairs composed of the form field's names and the data entered into them. Please note that your form fields must have `name` attributes in addition to `id` attributes for this method to work.

Once this has been done, we can initiate the Connection Manager in the same way as before. Save the HTML page as `login.html` or similar, ensuring it is placed into a content-serving directory accessible to your web server.

As you can see the `.setForm()` method is compatible with `GET` requests. We are using the `GET` method here because at this stage all we are doing is querying the database rather than making physical, lasting changes to it. We'll be moving on to look at `POST` requests very shortly.

Now we can look briefly at the PHP file that can be used to process the login request. In a blank page in your text editor, add the following code:

```
<?php
  $host = "localhost";
  $user = "root";
  $password = "mypassword";
  $database = "mydata";
  $uname = $_GET["uname"];
  $pword = $_GET["pword"];
  $server = mysql_connect($host, $user, $password);
```

```
    $connection = mysql_select_db($database, $server);
    $query = mysql_query("SELECT * FROM users WHERE username LIKE
                        '$uname%'");
    $rows = mysql_num_rows($query);
    if ($rows != 0)
    {
      $row = mysql_fetch_array($query);
      $pass = $row['password'];
      if ($pass != $pword)
        echo "Password incorrect";
      else
       echo "Hello ".$row['firstname'].", thanks for signing in";
    }
    else
    {
      echo "Username not found";
    }
    mysql_close($server);
  ?>
```

Here we set up the variables required to query our database and then extract any records where the username entered into our form matches the username associated with a user. There should only be one matching record, so we can then compare the stored password with that entered into our form.

All we're doing here is passing back an appropriate message to be displayed by our `successHandler` function back in the HTML page. Normally, after entering the correct credentials, the visitor would be redirected to their account page or some kind of personal home page, but a simple alert gives us everything we need for this example. Save the above file as `login.php` in the same directory as the web page and everything should be good to go.

Try it out and reflect upon the ease with which our task has been completed. Upon entering the username and password of one of our registered users, you should see something similar to the figure below:

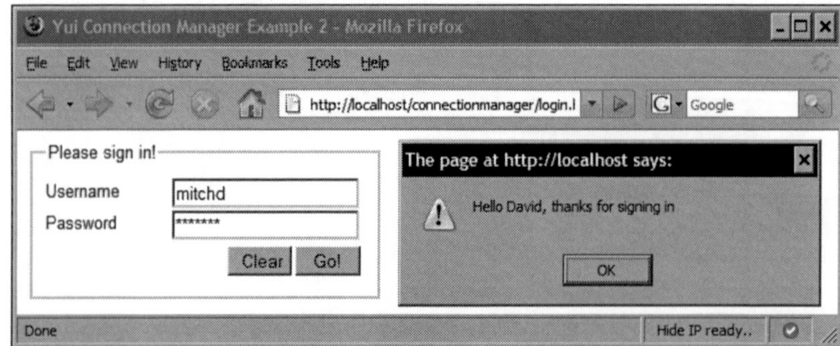

So that covers GET requests, but what about POST requests? As I mentioned before, the .setForm() method can be put to equally good use with POST requests as well. To illustrate this, we can add some additional code which will let unregistered visitors sign up.

Add the following function directly before the closing </script> tag:

```
//define registerForm function
  YAHOO.yuibook.login.registerForm = function() {
    //have all fields been completed?
    var formComp = 0;
    for (x = 1; x < document.forms[1].length; x++) {
      if (document.forms[1].elements[x].value == "") {
        alert("All fields must be completed");
        formComp = 0;
        return false;
      } else {
        formComp = 1;
      }
    }
    if (formComp != 0) {
      //define success handler
      var successHandler = function(o) {
        //show succes message
        alert(o.responseText);
      }
      //define failure handler
      var failureHandler = function(o) {
        alert("Error " + o.status + " : " + o.statusText);
      }
      //define callback object
      var callback = {
        success:successHandler,
        failure:failureHandler
      }
      //harvest form data ready to send to the server
      var form = document.getElementById("register");
      YAHOO.util.Connect.setForm(form);
      //define transaction to send stuff to server
      var transaction = YAHOO.util.Connect.asyncRequest(
                      "POST", "register.php", callback);
    }
  }
  //execute registerForm when join button clicked
  YAHOO.util.Event.addListener("join", "click",
            YAHOO.yuibook.login.registerForm);
```

In the same way that we added a listener to watch for clicks on the `login` button, we can do the same to look for clicks on the `join` button. Again we should check that data has been entered into each field before even involving the Connection Manager utility. As there are more fields to check this time, it wouldn't be efficient to manually look at each one individually.

We use a for loop and a control variable this time to cycle through each form field; if any field is left blank the `formComp` control variable will be set to `0` and the loop will exit. We can then check the state of `formComp` and provided it is not set to `0`, we know that each field has been filled in.

The success and failure handlers are again based on simple alerts for the purpose of this example. We again use the `.setForm()` method to process the form prior to sending the data. We can then proceed to initiate the Connection Manager, this time supplying POST as the HTTP method and a different PHP file in the second argument of the `.asyncRequest()` method.

All we need now is another PHP file to process the registration request. Something like the following should suffice for this example:

```
<?php
  $host = "localhost";
  $user = "root";
  $password = "mypassword";
  $database = "mydata";
  $fname = $_POST["fname"];
  $lname = $_POST["lname"];
  $uname = $_POST["uname"];
  $pword = $_POST["pword"];
  $server = mysql_connect($host, $user, $password);
  $connection = mysql_select_db($database, $server);
  $query = mysql_query("INSERT INTO users VALUES ('$fname', '$lname',
                                                  '$uname',
                                                  '$pword')");
  echo "Thanks for joining us ".$fname;
  mysql_close($server);
?>
```

As we're using `POST` this time, we can use the `$_POST` superglobal to pull our values out, and can then run a simple `INSERT` query to add them to the database. Upon entering an unrecognized name into the first form, the registration form should then be displayed, as in the following screenshot:

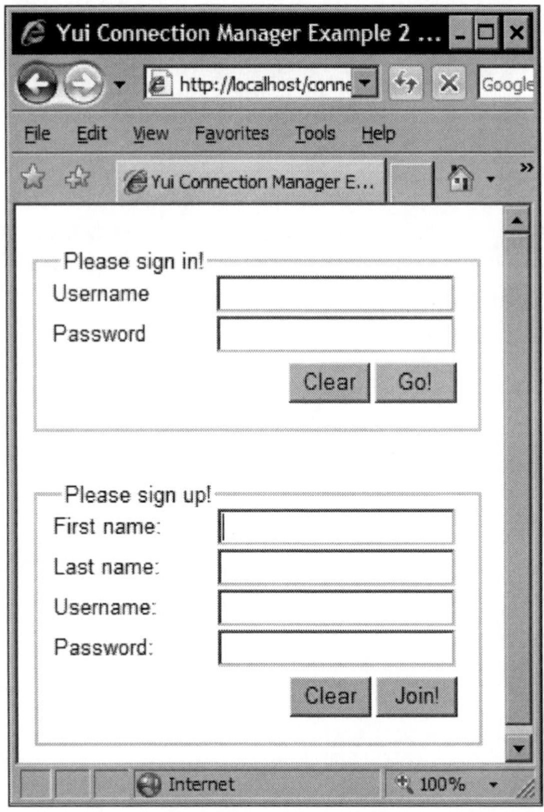

If you register a new user now and then take a look at your database with the mySQL Command Line Client, you should see the new data appear in your database:

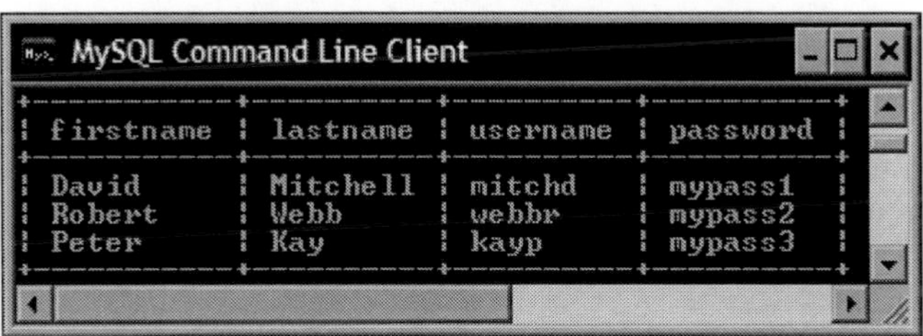

firstname	lastname	username	password
David	Mitchell	mitchd	mypass1
Robert	Webb	webbr	mypass2
Peter	Kay	kayp	mypass3

Summary

The YUI Connection Manager utility provides an almost unequalled interface to AJAX scripting methods used today among the many JavaScript libraries available. It handles the creation of a cross-platform XHR object and provides an easy mechanism for reacting to success and failure responses among others.

It handles common HTTP methods such as `GET` and `POST` with equal ease and can be put to good use in connection (no pun intended) with a PHP (or other form of) proxy for negotiating cross-domain requests.

5

Animation and the Browser History Manager

The Animation utility is used to add a variety of effects to your pages that can really bring your web application to life. It's a very easy component of the library to use, but delivers a powerful and robust mechanism by which elements can be made to grow, move, and even change color.

When using web-based applications that are based on DOM-scripted or AJAX-driven dynamic page changes, it is usually impossible to return to a previous page state using the back button of the browser. The Browser History Manager (BHM) utility provided in the YUI is the first step towards a web of online applications where the functionality of the back and forward browser buttons has been restored.

In this chapter we will look at:

- Enhancing our pages with attractive animations
- Why the BHM is needed and how it can be implemented
- The different components of the BHM
- Recording state changes
- Retrieving bookmarked state

Introducing the Animation Utility

The Animation utility provides a quick and easy solution to adding a variety of animations to elements on your pages. You can specify that elements should grow, shrink, or even scroll across the page, and you have complete control over how and when these animations should occur. Almost any property of an element with a numerical value, such as `width` or `height` for example, can be animated.

The Class Structure of the Animation Utility

`YAHOO.util.Anim` is the base class that provides most of the basic properties and methods that are used to create animations. It features a constructor which is used to create an instance of the animation object, a series of methods which allow you to control the animation, and a set of custom events which are fired at different moments during the animation.

The Animation Constructor

Animating an object is as simple as creating a new instance of an Animation object and applying it to an element on your page. The constructor used to create this object takes four arguments. The first is a string that represents the element to animate, the second is an object which can have one of four properties and defines how the element should be animated. Only the first of these arguments is actually mandatory, but no animation will take place if the second is not supplied.

The third argument, which is optional, is a number representing the approximate duration of the animation. If this is not specified the animation will default to 1 second. The fourth also an optional argument is a reference to one of the members of the `easing` class. If this argument is not supplied `YAHOO.util.Easing.easeNone` is used.

Easing, a feature we will be looking at in just a little while, allows the beginning or end of your animation speed up, slow down, change direction, or any combination of these behaviours briefly before continuing as normal, This is an easy way to add interest to a basic animation.

Animation's Properties

One of the most important properties provided by the `Anim` class is the attributes object. It is this object which allows you to specify exactly which property of the specified element is animated, and exactly how it is animated. The structure of this object is a little misleading at first glance, but is actually very simple.

An attributes object may be created in one of two ways. It can be defined as a separate object and then passed into the `Anim` constructor, or it can be defined inline entirely within the constructor. An attributes object defined outside of the constructor would look something like that shown below:

```
Var attsObj = {
  height:{by:100},
  width:{by:100}
};
```

The attributes object above has two members. Each member is a `name:value` pair where the `name` specifies the element property that we want to animate. The `value` of each member is also an object which also consists of a `name:value` pair.

This second object uses one of four attributes as the `name` and an integer for the `value`. In this example, the element to which the animation was applied would have its `height` and `width` properties increased by 100 pixels. The four attributes are as follows:

- `by` – the element should change by a specified amount from the current
- `to` – the element should go to the specified value from the current value
- `from` – the element should begin from the specified value instead of the current value
- `unit` – this specifies the units, such as pixels or em's, that the other properties should be measured in

The value of the second object varies depending on which of the attributes is specified. When the `YAHOO.util.Motion` constructor is used, for example, the value of the second object will be an array consisting of the X and Y coordinates required for the animation.

It is important that these attributes are used in the correct way. The `from` and `to` attributes are often used together, and the `unit` can be used with any other property. The `by` property however, should never be used with the `to` property as they are inherently contradictory in nature.

You can't move an element by 50 pixels while at the same time moving it to 300 pixels from the top of the page (unless it happens to be exactly 250 pixels from the edge of the screen, in which case either property would suffice anyway). If both attributes are supplied, the `to` attribute will override the `by` attribute, and become the attribute that is used.

You can specify any number of different element properties and values that you want to animate within this object, which allows you to create complex and visually appealing animations with very little effort and in very little time at all.

Custom Animation Events

The custom events defined in the base animation class are:

- `onStart`
- `onTween`
- `onComplete`

It should be plainly obvious to all when each of them fire, but for the record `onStart` is fired when the animation begins, `onTween` occurs during every frame of the animation and `onComplete` is fired when the animation ends.

The `onTween` event has the potential to bring your application down if it is not used in the correct way. Since this event fires on every single frame of the animation, the code that it executes needs to be highly efficient, otherwise the animation, and potentially your entire application, will grind to a halt. Generally, you won't need to use this event for this exact reason and it will only become useful in highly specific situations. If using it can be avoided, it should be.

The Subclasses

The animation class has three subclasses: `YAHOO.util.ColorAnim`, `YAHOO.util.Motion`, and `YAHOO.util.Scroll`. Each of these provides an additional constructor with which to create a different type of animation. None of them have their own properties, and only the `ColorAnim` class has its own method, but all three of them inherit the methods and properties they need from the base class.

`YAHOO.util.ColorAnim` extends the base animation class by allowing you to animate the color of an element. Unlike the base class, the `ColorAnim` class does allow you to work with element properties that are specified using HEX or RGB rather than just numerical values.

The attributes object used by `colorAnim` is extremely flexible and can accept any style property that has a numerical value as its first member. To change the color of text within an element to white for example, you could use the following object:

```
var attsObj {
  color: {to: #ffffff}
};
```

The `YAHOO.util.Motion` subclass allows you to specify a path of points which an object can follow across the page to reflect movement. The path is specified using the `points` attribute where the second member of the `value` object is an array with `X` and `Y` coordinates. Note that the use of the motion class results in paths that follow straight lines.

The `points` attribute is used in the same way as the four attributes looked at earlier on. To move an element 100 pixels along both the `X` and `Y` axis, for example, you could use the following attributes object:

```
var attsObj {
  points: { to: [100, 100] }
};
```

`YAHOO.util.Scroll` extends the base animation class by allowing you to scroll overflowing elements. The amount of scroll is specified using the `scroll` attribute in the attributes object, where once again the second member of the value object is an array containing the number of units to scroll the element across or down the page.

The following object could be used to `scroll` the hidden contents of an element into view vertically:

```
Var attsObj {
  Scroll: { by: [0, 200] }
};
```

To `scroll` an element horizontally you simply specify a positive value for the first array item.

Additional Classes

As well as the above subclasses two other classes are also defined within the Animation utility; the `YAHOO.util.Bezier` class and the Animation Manager `YAHOO.util.AnimMgr`. The `Bezier` class is used in conjunction with the `motion` class and allows for motion that follows a curved path.

To use this class a second member, the `control` member, should be defined within the attributes object supplied to the `motion` constructor. We will look at implementing motion later on in the chapter but an example of an attributes object making use of the `Bezier` class is as follows:

```
var attsObj {
  points: { to: [100, 100],
  control: [[40, 120], [-40, 240]]
}
```

The final class defines the Animation Manager. It's unlikely that you'll need to use this class directly, but it is present in any animation implementation and controls the animation queue. Animations are executed one at a time and when several animations are registered it is the Animation Manager that organizes them into a controlled queue.

Members of the Easing Class

The members of the `easing` class provide a series of animation enhancements used to add visual interest and appeal to your animations. They are based on easing equations created by Robert Penner in 2001. The members of the easing class are as follows:

- `backIn` - animation backtracks slightly at the beginning before proceeding as normal
- `backOut` - animation begins as normal, but overshoots the end slightly, then returns to the correct end-point
- `backBoth` - animation backtracks slightly, proceeds as normal, then overshoots the end before returning to the correct end-point
- `bounceIn` - animation bounces at the start-point then proceeds as normal
- `bounceOut` - animation begins as normal but bounces at the end-point
- `bounceBoth` - animation bounces both at the start and end-points of the animation
- `easeIn` - animation begins slowly before building up to normal speed
- `easeInStrong` - same as above but to a higher degree
- `easeNone` - No easing (the default if no easing method is specified in the animation constructor)
- `easeOut` - animation begins at normal speed and slows down towards the end
- `easeOutStrong` - same as above but to a higher degree
- `easeBoth` - animation begins slowly, builds up to normal speed, then slows down again towards the end of the animation
- `easeBothStrong` - same as above but to a higher degree
- `elasticIn` - animation bounces exaggeratedly at the beginning before proceeding as normal to the end
- `elasticOut` - animation begins normally but bounces at the end in an exaggerated way
- `elasticBoth` - animation bounces exaggeratedly at both the beginning and end-points of the animation but proceeds normally during the middle

Using Animation to Create an Accordion Widget

We can put the Animation utility to good use to create a simple, yet visually appealing, accordion-style content area. Begin with the following web page:

```
<!DOCTYPE HTML PUBLIC "-//W3C//DTD HTML 4.01//EN"
                          "http://www.w3.org/TR/html4/strict.dtd">
<html lang="en">
  <head>
    <meta http-equiv="content-type" content="text/html;
                                     charset=utf-8">
    <title>YUI Animation Example</title>
    <script type="text/javascript" src="yui/build/yahoo-dom-event/
                                        yahoo-dom-event.js"></script>
    <script type="text/javascript"
            src="yui/build/animation/animation-min.js"></script>
    <link rel="stylesheet" type="text/css" href="animation.css">
  </head>
  <body>
  </body>
</html>
```

This is the basic shell of the page. As you can see, only the `yahoo-dom-event.js` and the animation source file `animation-min.js` are required. We've also linked to a custom stylesheet which we'll create in just a moment. Now add the following content to the `<body>` of the page:

```
<div id="accordion">
  <div id="section1Head">Section 1</div>
  <div id="section1">
    <p>Lorem ipsum etc...</p>
  </div>
  <div id="section2Head">Section 2</div>
  <div id="section2">
    <p>Lorem ipsum etc...</p>
  </div>
  <div id="section3Head">Section 3</div>
  <div id="section3">
    <p>Lorem ipsum etc...</p>
  </div>
</div>
```

Save the page as `animation.html` in your `yuisite` folder. We'll also need some CSS for this example, in a fresh page in your text editor add the following selectors and rules:

```
#section1Head, #section1 {
  background-color:#99ccff;
  color:white;
  border:1px solid #000000;
  cursor:pointer;
  width:400px;
  text-align:center;
}
#section1 {
  height:140px;
  text-align:left;
  cursor:default;
  overflow:hidden;
}
#section2Head, #section2 {
  background-color:#ffcccc;
  color:white;
  border:1px solid #000000;
  cursor:pointer;
  width:400px;
  text-align:center;
}
#section2 {
  height:0px;
  text-align:left;
  cursor:default;
  overflow:hidden;
}
#section3Head, #section3 {
  background-color:#ffcc99;
  color:white;
  border:1px solid #000000;
  cursor:pointer;
  width:400px;
  text-align:center;
}
#section3 {
  height:0px;
  text-align:left;
  cursor:default;
```

```
    overflow:hidden;
  }
  p {
    margin-top:0px;
  }
```

Save this as `animation.css`, also in your `yuisite` folder. At this point, you should have a page that appears like the following screenshot:

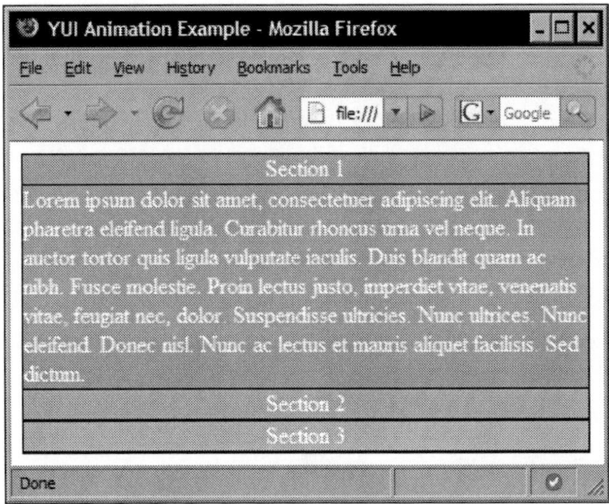

A Basic Animation Script

Now let's look at the JavaScript need to turn this collection of `<div>` elements into an accordion-style widget. Directly before the closing `</body>` tag, add the following `<script>` tag:

```
<script type="text/javascript">
  //create the namespace object used in this example
  YAHOO.namespace("yuibook.accordion");

  //define the initAccordian function
  YAHOO.yuibook.accordion.initAccordion = function() {
    //define the attributes objects
    var openObj = {
      height: {to: 140}
    };
    var closeObj = {
      height: {to: 0}
    };
    //define fnClick function
```

```
        var fnClick = function() {

          //get the element to open/close
          var section = YAHOO.util.Dom.getNextSibling(this);
          var height = YAHOO.util.Dom.getStyle(section, "height");

          //call the doAnim function
          doAnim(section, height);
        }

        //execute fnClick when a sectionHead is clicked
        YAHOO.util.Event.addListener("section1Head", "click", fnClick);
        YAHOO.util.Event.addListener("section2Head", "click", fnClick);
        YAHOO.util.Event.addListener("section3Head", "click", fnClick);

        function doAnim (section, height) {

          //is the element open or closed?
          if (height > "0px") {

            //define and run the animation
            var anim = new YAHOO.util.Anim(section, closeObj, 0.5);
            anim.animate();
          } else if (height == "0px") {

            //define and run the animation
            var anim = new YAHOO.util.Anim(section, openObj, 0.5);
            anim.animate();
          }
        }
      }

      //execute initAccordion when DOM is ready
      YAHOO.util.Event.onDOMReady( YAHOO.yuibook.accordion.initAccordion);
    </script>
```

The first thing we do after namespacing our code is set up the main initialization function, `initAccordian`, which will execute all subsequent code. The DOM utility's `.onDOMReady()` method is used to call our function when the DOM is structurally complete.

Next, we define our attributes objects; these are used for expanding for collapsing or different accordion sections. We use these objects to either set the height to `140px` or `0px` to simulate the opening and closing of the different content sections on the accordion element.

We want the different content sections to open or close when the corresponding header element is clicked, so next we define a callback function, `fnClick`. We can then add listeners for click events on the header elements, and execute the callback function when they occur. Each listener subscribes to the same function for efficiency.

The callback function's scope will automatically be set to the element that was clicked on. We can safely use the `this` keyword in conjunction with the `.getNextSibling()` method to obtain the content section that follows the header element that was clicked.

We also get the current height of the relevant content section so that we know whether to expand or collapse the content section. The last thing our callback function does is call the `doAnim` function, passing along the element object and height property to the next function as arguments.

The `doAnim` function is relatively straightforward and simply checks whether or not the relevant section is currently open or closed, then defines an animation that does the opposite. The constructor uses the element passed into the function as its first argument, whichever attributes object is required as the second argument, and a duration of half a second for the third argument.

Now when the page is run the different accordion sections can be opened or closed with a simple click and the Animation utility kindly provides the smooth opening and closing effects:

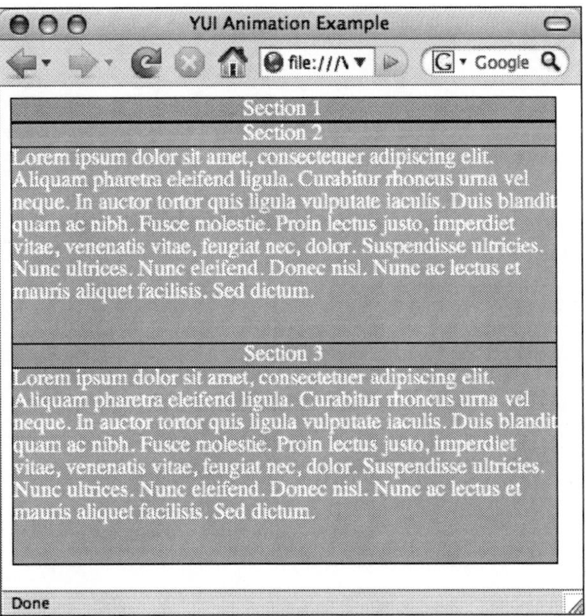

Dealing With Motion

Each of the other Animation constructors are as easy to use as the basic `Anim` constructor that we just looked at. Another example that does warrant further attention however is the Motion constructor due to its complexity. Let's implement basic motion along a curve so that we can explore the functionality exposed by the `Motion` and `Bezier` classes.

In this example, we'll animate a simple `<div>` element so that it travels across its parent page. Begin with the following HTML:

```
<!DOCTYPE HTML PUBLIC "-//W3C//DTD HTML 4.01//EN"
                         "http://www.w3.org/TR/html4/strict.dtd">
<html lang="en">
  <head>
    <meta http-equiv="content-type" content="text/html;
                                    charset=utf-8">
    <title>YUI Motion Example</title>
    <script type="text/javascript" src="yui/build/yahoo-dom-event/
                                       yahoo-dom-event.js"></script>
    <script type="text/javascript"
            src="yui/build/animation/animation-min.js"></script>
    <link rel="stylesheet" type="text/css" href="motion.css">
  </head>
  <body>
    <div id="box"></div>
  </body>
</html>
```

Save this in your `yuisite` folder as `motion.html`. We'll also need a little CSS, in a fresh page in your text editor add the following brief selector and rule set:

```
#box {
  width:100px;
  height:100px;
  background-color:#e3a8f2;
  border:1px solid gray;
}
```

This can be saved as `motion.css`. This should give you a page that looks like the following screenshot:

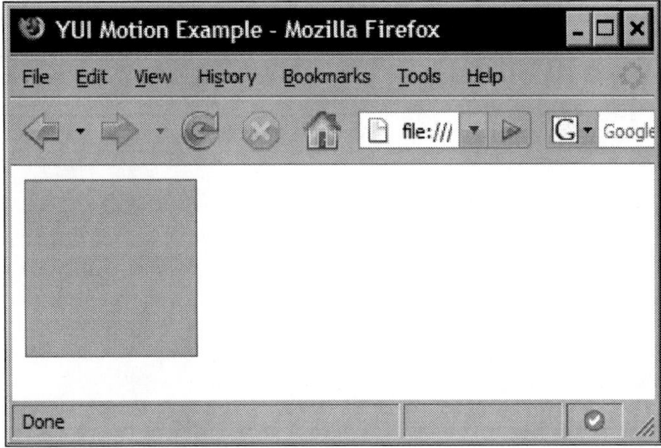

We'll look at standard, linear motion along a fixed axis first. Add the following `<script>` block directly after the box `<div>`:

```
script type="text/javascript">
  //create the namespace object used in this example
  YAHOO.namespace("yuibook.motion");

  //define the initMotion function
  YAHOO.yuibook.motion.initMotion = function() {

    //define the points object
    var moveObj = {
      points: {by: [300, 300]}
    };

    //define fnClick function
    var fnClick = function() {

      //define and run the animation
      var anim = new YAHOO.util.Motion(this, moveObj);
      anim.animate();

    }

    //execute fnClick when the box is clicked
    YAHOO.util.Event.addListener("box", "click", fnClick);

  }

  //execute initMotion when DOM is ready
  YAHOO.util.Event.onDOMReady( YAHOO.yuibook.motion.initMotion);
</script>
```

This script is even simpler than that in the previous example. Within our master initialization function we first define the attributes object which furnishes the Animation utility with the necessary information that defines the animation.

The `moveObj` object contains a `points` object, which in turn contains another object specifying the `by` attribute and an array of `X` and `Y` coordinates. We have specified `300` as the `X` item and `300` as the `Y` item so the box will move by `300` pixels across the page and `300` pixels down the page diagonally.

The call to the `YAHOO.util.Motion()` constructor is wrapped within a callback function which is triggered when the box `<div>` is clicked on. If you run the page now and click the purple box, the animation should proceed as expected and end with the square `300` pixels away from its original starting point:

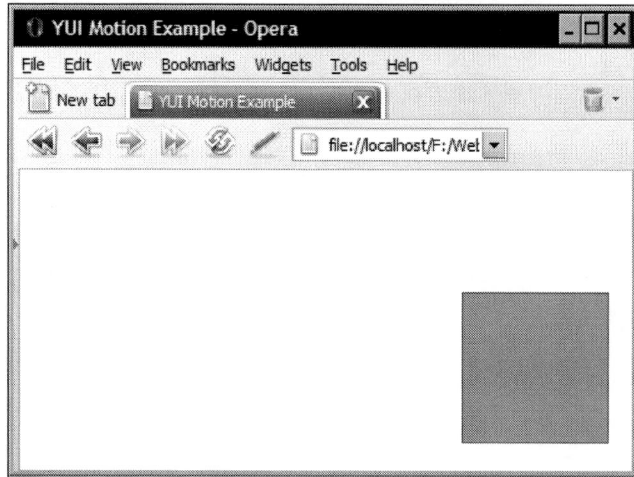

Curvature

We can easily make our little purple `<div>` travel along a curved path instead of the straight path that we have so far achieved. All we need to do is define another object within our existing `points` object. Change the `<script>` so that it appears as follows (new code is shown in bold):

```
<script type="text/javascript">
      //create the namespace object used in this example
      YAHOO.namespace("yuibook.motion");

      //define the initAccordian function
      YAHOO.yuibook.motion.initMotion = function() {

        //define the points object
        var moveObj = {
          points: {
```

```
            by: [300, 300],
            control:[600, 150]
          }
        };
        //define fnClick function
        var fnClick = function() {
          //define and run the animation
          var anim = new YAHOO.util.Motion(this, moveObj);
          anim.animate();
        }
        //execute fnClick when the box is clicked
        YAHOO.util.Event.addListener("box", "click", fnClick);
      }
      //execute initMotion when DOM is ready
      YAHOO.util.Event.onDOMReady(YAHOO.yuibook.motion.initMotion);
    </script>
```

To invoke a curved path of travel all we need to do is specify a `control` object after the `by` object within our `points` object. We have specified values of `600` for the `X` axis and `150` for the Y axis so the curve will be more pronounced along the `X` axis. To invert the curve, all we need do is reverse the values supplied for `X` and `Y`. The following screenshot shows the box occupying a region of the page that without the `control` object it would not otherwise cross:

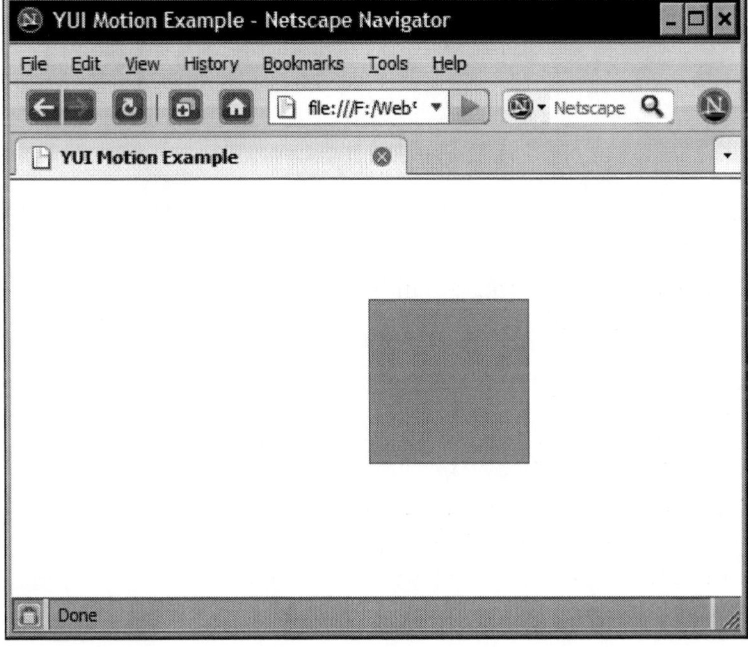

Restoring the Browser's Expected Functionality

The BHM utility allows you to register different steps in the interactions that mark changes in your application's state. Viewing different months of the Calendar control, for example, marks a change in state, and you may have noticed when we looked at this control earlier in the book that the back button of the browser remained grayed out and unavailable to us no matter how many different months were viewed.

Once a step has occurred that is defined within the BHM as a change in state, the back button of the browser becomes available and when clicked, takes the application back one of these steps. The expected functionality of the browser's interface is restored.

As well as defining different changes in state that may occur within your application, the BHM utility also tackles the problem of web application bookmarking. A simple method can be called that retrieves the initial state of the application according to the state that it was bookmarked in.

The BHM Class

The BHM is supported entirely by just one class, the `YAHOO.util.History` class. The members of this class number surprisingly few and consist of eight methods and a single custom event. The methods available include:

- `.getBookmarkedState()` – used to get the state of the application as stored in the bookmark URL fragment identifier
- `.getCurrentState()` – gets the current state of your application
- `.getQueryStringParameter()` – returns the specified parameter from the query string
- `.initialize()` – initializes the BHM
- `.navigate()` – used to store application states
- `.onReady()` – the preferred method of detecting when the BHM is ready to be used
- `.register()` – registers an application with the BHM

The custom event defined by the `History` class is the `onLoadEvent` which fires when the BHM has finished loading, however you must subscribe to this event before calling the `.initialize()` method so Yahoo! recommends that the `.onReady()` method be used instead.

Using BHM

Let's build a page that makes use of the BHM utility to record state information about one of the Controls that we looked at earlier in the book—the Calendar control. The BHM works asynchronously, and as such it must be run from a content-serving directory accessible to a web server. It is also important to note that the Opera browser is not currently supported by the BHM.

Begin with the following initial HTML:

```
<!DOCTYPE HTML PUBLIC "-//W3C//DTD HTML 4.01 Transitional//EN"
                              "http://www.w3.org/TR/html4/loose.dtd">
<html lang="en">
  <head>
    <meta http-equiv="content-type" content="text/html;
                                         charset=utf-8">
    <title>YUI Browser History Manager Utility Example</title>
    <script type="text/javascript"
            src="http://yui.yahooapis.com/2.4.1/build/
                 yahoo-dom-event/yahoo-dom-event.js"></script>
    <script type="text/javascript"
            src="http://yui.yahooapis.com/2.4.1/build/
                 calendar/calendar-min.js"></script>
    <script type="text/javascript"
            src="http://yui.yahooapis.com/2.4.1/build/
                 history/history-min.js"></script>
    <link rel="stylesheet" type="text/css"
          href="yui/build/calendar/assets/skins/sam/calendar.css">
    <link rel="stylesheet" type="text/css" href="bhmCalendar.css">
  </head>
  <body class="yui-skin-sam">
    <iframe id="yui-history-iframe" src="yahoo.gif"></iframe>
    <input id="yui-history-field" type="hidden">
    <div id="mycal"></div>
  </body>
</html>
```

Save this file as `bhmCalendar.html` in the appropriate folder. There are several important changes to this code compared with the original Calendar example. We link to the `yahoo-dom-event.js` and `calendar-min.js` files as we did before and of course need the BHM source file `history-min.js`. The Calendar container element is still the `<div>` element with an `id` of `mycall`.

This time you'll notice however that we're linking to the YUI files hosted on the Yahoo! servers. The reason for this is because, due to an inherent peculiarity, the Calendar will not work from a local library source (even the basic Calendar from Chapter 1 is the same).

You can also see that we're using the HTML 4.01 Transitional DTD in this example also. This is because the page will not validate against the strict DTD with the `<iframe>` element included.

The other major change is the addition of an `<iframe>` and a hidden `<input>` field. The `<iframe>` is required for the sole purpose of making the BHM compatible with Internet Explorer. The hidden `<input>` element is used to record the initial state of the Calendar, as well as the current state. The `<iframe>` must be linked to a pre-existing file on your web server—an empty HTML file will do, or an image, as in this example, that is already being used in your site.

We don't have the text `<input>` or the calendar icon to worry about this time, but we still need to make sure the `<iframe>` doesn't interfere with the rest of the page content. In a fresh page in your text editor add the following CSS:

```
#yui-history-iframe {
  position:absolute;
  top:0;
  left:0;
  width:1px;
  height:1px;
  visibility:hidden;
}
```

Save this file as `bhmCalendar.css` in the same folder as the accompanying HTML file.

The BHM Script

We can now move on to add the initial JavaScript for this example. Directly after the Calendar container in the HTML file add the following `<script>` block:

```
<script type="text/javascript">
  //create the namespace object for this example
  YAHOO.namespace("yuibook.bhm");

  //define the initBHM function
  YAHOO.yuibook.bhm.initBHM = function() {

    //get present date and define initial state for calendar
    var today = new Date();
```

```
var defaultState = (today.getMonth() + 1) + "/" + today.
                                              getFullYear();
var myCal;

//define the stateChanger callback
var stateChange = function(state) {

  //set calendar page and render calendar
  myCal.cfg.setProperty("pagedate", state);
  myCal.render();
};

//register the calendar with BHM
YAHOO.util.History.register("myCal", defaultState, stateChange);

//define the beforeRender function
var beforeRender = function() {

  //get the current calendar date
  var calDate = myCal.cfg.getProperty("pageDate");
  var newState = (calDate.getMonth() + 1) + "/" +
                 calDate.getFullYear();

  //get the current state according to BHM
  var currentState = YAHOO.util.History.getCurrentState("myCal");

  //is calendar date different from BHM date?
  if (newState != currentState) {

    //add a new state to BHM
    YAHOO.util.History.navigate("myCal", newState);
  }
};

//define the lauchCal function which creates the calendar
var launchCal = function(startDate) {

  //create the calendar object
  myCal = new YAHOO.widget.Calendar("myCal", "mycal", startDate);

  //configure the calendar to begin on Monday
  myCal.cfg.setProperty("start_weekday", "1");

  //subscribe to the beforeRenderEvent
  myCal.beforeRenderEvent.subscribe(beforeRender, myCal, true);
  myCal.render();
}

//create calendar when BHM is ready
YAHOO.util.History.onReady(function () {
  launchCal({ pagedate: defaultState });
```

```
      });

      //initialise BHM
      YAHOO.util.History.initialize("yui-history-field",
                                    "yui-history-iframe");

    };

    //initialise components on page load
    YAHOO.util.Event.onDOMReady(YAHOO.yuibook.bhm.initBHM);
  </script>
```

As before, the code is wrapped up in a namespace object to preserve the global namespace. Like our other examples, the rest of the code is held within a master initialization function (the `initBHM()` function) that is executed using the Event utility's `.onDOMReady()` method.

The first thing our master function does is retrieve the current date and process it so that it appears in the format `MM/YYYY`. This is then stored in the `defaultState` variable and is used, as I'm sure you can guess, as the default state of the Calendar control. The Calendar object variable is also declared here so that it can be passed between functions (although the Calendar control is not actually initialized at this stage).

Next we define the `stateChange` callback function, which is called every time the BHM detects that our Calendar has changed state. This may happen when we interact with the Calendar by navigating through month panels, or it may occur when the back or forward button of the browser is used. Programmatically, there is no difference between the two.

As we are responsible for updating the Calendar following a change in state, the `stateChange()` function sets the page date according to the new state that it receives as an argument and re-renders the Calendar. We register our Calendar with the BHM using the `.register()` method; this involves supplying the `id` of the object we wish to register as the first argument, the default state of the Calendar as the second argument, and lastly the `stateChange` callback function as the third argument. The default state is one of the items stored in the hidden `<input>` field.

Next we define the `beforeRender()` function. This function is executed prior to every render of the Calendar, which occurs on the initial page load, as well as every time our `stateChange` function is evoked. First the `beforeRender()` function gets the current date from the calendar and processes it so that it appears in the `MM/YYYY` format. The result is then saved in the `newState` variable.

The current state according to the BHM is then obtained using the `.getCurrentState()` method and stored in the `currentState` variable. The `newState` and `currentState` variables are then compared. If they are found to be different, the BHM knows that the state of the Calendar has changed and can add the `newState` variable as the next step in the BHM using the `.navigate()` method.

If the `.navigate()` method is called, the `stateChange()` function will be executed once more, which will in turn trigger the `beforeRender()` function again. The `if` statement here is really important as it prevents this perpetual loop of our functions.

Our next function is the `launchCal()` function, which deals with the creation of the Calendar control. The `startDate` variable is used to display the present date, and the `beforeRenderMethod` is subscribed to.

Our final function makes use of the BHM's `.onReady()` method to call the `launchCal()` function, which enables us to ensure that the Calendar is not created before the BHM is ready to work. The BHM runs asynchronously and needs a little time to start up before we start calling its methods.

The final step is to initialize the BHM. This is done using the `.initialize()` method, which takes references to the hidden `<input>` and the hidden `<iframe>` elements as its two arguments.

If you now run the application and navigate to a new month on the Calendar, you should see that the back button of the browser becomes available, and that a fragment identifier is appended to the URL in the browser's address bar. This is the mechanism by which the BHM is able to recall the history of the various states the Calendar has passed through. The screenshot below illustrates both the enabled back button and the URL fragment identifier:

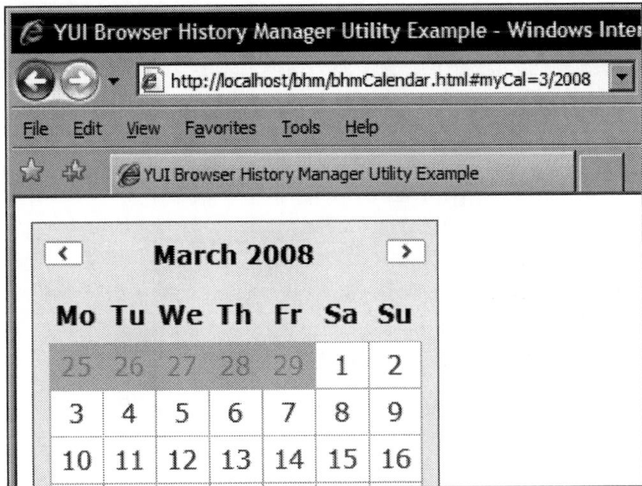

The BHM can also be used to return an application to the state it was in when it was bookmarked by a visitor. Little additional coding is required and we can easily modify the previous example so that bookmarking is taken into consideration. Here's the new version of our script, with the changes and new additions to the code highlighted:

```
<script type="text/javascript">
  //create the namespace object for this example
  YAHOO.namespace("yuibook.bhm");

  //define the initBHM function
  YAHOO.yuibook.bhm.initBHM = function() {

    //get present date and define initial state for calendar
    var today = new Date();
    var defaultState = (today.getMonth() + 1) + "/" + today.
                                                   getFullYear();
    var bookmarkState =
                      YAHOO.util.History.getBookmarkedState("myCal");
    var initialState = bookmarkState || defaultState;
    var myCal;

        //define the stateChanger callback
        var stateChange = function(state) {

          //set calendar page and render calendar
          myCal.cfg.setProperty("pagedate", state);
          myCal.render();
        };

        //register the calendar with BHM
        YAHOO.util.History.register("myCal", initialState,
                                      stateChange);

        //define the beforeRender function
        var beforeRender = function() {

          //get the current calendar date
          var calDate = myCal.cfg.getProperty("pageDate");
          var newState = (calDate.getMonth() + 1) + "/" +
                          calDate.getFullYear();

          //get the current state according to BHM
          var currentState =
                        YAHOO.util.History.getCurrentState("myCal");

          //is calendar date different from BHM date?
          if (newState != currentState) {

            //add a new state to BHM
```

```
            YAHOO.util.History.navigate("myCal", newState);
          }
        };

        //define the lauchCal function which creates the calendar
        var launchCal = function(startDate) {

          //create the calendar object
          myCal = new YAHOO.widget.Calendar("myCal", "mycal",
                                            startDate);

          //configure the calendar to begin on Monday
          myCal.cfg.setProperty("start_weekday", "1");

          //subscribe to the beforeRenderEvent
          myCal.beforeRenderEvent.subscribe(beforeRender, myCal,
                                            true);

          myCal.render();
        }

        //create calendar when BHM is ready
        YAHOO.util.History.onReady(function () {
          launchCal({ pagedate: initialState });
        });

        //initialise BHM
        YAHOO.util.History.initialize("yui-history-field",
                                      "yui-history-iframe");

      };

      //initialize components on page load
      YAHOO.util.Event.onDOMReady(YAHOO.yuibook.bhm.initBHM);
    </script>
```

As you can see, the additional bookmarking facility can be initiated using very few changes; we need just two additional variables at the start of the script. The first of these, `bookmarkState`, holds a reference to the bookmarked state according to the BHM, which will either be `null` if no bookmarked state is found, or it will contain a string representing the actual state.

The `initialState` variable will contain either the contents of the `bookmarkState` variable, or if this variable is null it will contain the contents of the `defaultState` variable instead. After these two new variables have been declared, it is simply a case of substituting any references to `defaultState` to `initialState`.

If the page containing the BHM utility and Calendar is accessed using a bookmark or favorite, the initial requesting URL will already contain the URL fragment identifier, which will be stored in the bookmarked state property of the BHM. If the `.getBookmarkedState()` method returns null, we know that a bookmark has not been used to access the page and can continue the same as before.

Summary

The Animation utility makes it easy to add a variety of animations covering movement, changes in size and even changes in color. It's a very easy utility to use and is limited only by your imagination.

The BHM utility is extremely powerful, despite its relatively small supporting class. It gives you the power to define discrete steps or changes in the state of your applications in which the back and forward button functionality is restored. It also allows your visitors to bookmark your application in a particular state and when they return to your application, the state is set so that it resembled their last visit.

6
Buttons and Trees

In this chapter we are going to look at two very useful controls provided by the library: the Button and TreeView controls. Both provide the rich and engaging functionality expected of web-based interface controls, and both are highly configurable and customizable.

The standard buttons used in practically every web form ever created are an intrinsic part of HTML. These buttons are so ingrained in the average surfer's psyche that they are used without a moments thought. But don't you ever want to do more than just push them? No? Well the good people at Yahoo! think that you should, and so they've created a new breed of button—the YUI Button control.

The TreeView control allows us to easily create a variety of hierarchical tree structures in almost no time at all. These are traditionally something that you would expect to find in a desktop application (like Windows Explorer) rather than a web application, but with the distinction between the desktop and the web becoming more blurred by the day, this control is only ever going to get more useful.

In this chapter we will cover the following topics:

- Why we should use YUI's Button control
- The different button objects that can be implemented and how they can be added to our pages
- The classes behind the buttons
- How TreeView is implemented
- The properties and methods that make up the TreeView classes
- How Trees can be styled
- Dynamic Trees
- Loading remote node data

Why Use the YUI Button Family?

Standard web buttons are one element whose default appearance can vary wildly between browsers and platforms, and they are also very difficult to style consistently across browsers. Styled buttons also look far less 'buttony' to the average web user than unstyled buttons, and they can often just feel not very much like buttons. Styled buttons also often lack the inverted bevel effect that makes them look like they are being depressed when they are clicked.

The YUI button family overcomes these difficulties with ease, providing rich and attractive buttons, whose styling is consistent across A-grade browsers and whose functionality far exceeds that of traditional buttons. Another important factor of the Button control as opposed to standard HTML buttons is that the Button control can have a label that is entirely different from its value.

Meet the Button Control

The Button control gives you the ability to easily create a range of innovative different button types that extend standard HTML form buttons and allow for much more advanced behavior than just submitting or resetting a form.

The Button family consists of eight individual Button types, each with their own advanced behavior:

- A basic push button which acts like a normal web button but looks much better
- A link button which navigates visitors to a specified URL when clicked
- A submit button which automatically submits the data entered into its parent form
- A reset button which automatically clears any input entered into its parent form
- Checkbox buttons which are a group of controls that look like normal buttons but act like standard checkboxes
- Radio buttons which are a group of controls that look like push buttons but behave like traditional radio controls
- A menu button that can be expanded to show a series of options when clicked
- A split button with two clickable regions. The first region initiates some kind of action as any standard button would do, but the second region shows a menu when clicked which allows action of the first region to be changed

Button controls can be created in one of three ways: from standard HTML form elements like `<input>` or `<select>` elements, entirely through JavaScript, or by using a special kind of mark up called Button Control HTML. This is where the `<button>` element is wrapped in two container `<span>` elements and then fed to the relevant constructor.

Two classes are defined by the Button control: `YAHOO.widget.Button` and `YAHOO.widget.ButtonGroup`. Both classes are subclasses of the Element utility and inherit properties and methods from it.

The Button class takes care of all of the different types of button except the radio style button, which is handled exclusively by the `ButtonGroup` class. Let's take a look into each of the classes and see the properties and methods available for us to use.

YAHOO.widget.Button

The `Button` class is huge, as it needs to be in order to cover all those different types of button. Many of the properties and methods defined within it are private or protected and wouldn't normally need to be used by you, the programmer, during a normal implementation of any of the types of button control.

The `YAHOO.widget.Button` constructor takes just two arguments, but because there are three different ways to create a button, the first argument can take one of three different forms. It can be a string specifying the `id` of the element used to create the button, an element reference, or an object containing configuration properties used to initialise the button. If a string or element reference is supplied, the configuration object can still be specified as the second argument.

There are a huge range of methods available to you through the `Button` class. Although many of them are protected or private and therefore used internally by the control itself, there are still some that you may want to make use of, including:

- `.addHiddenFieldsToForm()` – to ensure that values selected with Radio, Checkbox, MenuButton, and SplitButton controls are submitted with the form, this method adds the value of each control to a hidden text field
- `.blur()` —causes the Button to lose focus and the blur event to fire
- `.destroy()` —removes the Button control and any associated event handlers
- `.focus()` —causes the Button to gain focus and the focus event to fire
- `.getForm()` —gets a reference to the parent form
- `.getHiddenField()` —gets the `<input>` used when the form is submitted
- `.getMenu()` —obtains the Button's menu control

- `.hasFocus()`—returns true if the Button has focus
- `.isActive()`—returns true if Button is active
- `.onFormKeyDown()`—a handler for keydown events of the Buttons parent form
- `submitForm`—submits the form that the Button is a child of
- `toString`—returns a string representing the Button instance

Like some of the other controls provided by the library, the Button control also makes use of a literal configuration object. This allows you to define attributes as its members in a `key:value` format in order to configure different aspects of the Button instance.

Configuration attributes include, but are not limited to:

- `checked`—indicates whether Radio or Checkbox Buttons are checked by default. The default is false
- `disabled`—indicates whether the Button should be disabled but does not apply to link buttons. The default is false again
- `href`—if the Button is a link it needs this to define its `href` attribute
- `label`—the text label or `innerHTML` of the Button
- `menu`—if the Button is a Menu Button this property allows you to specify the Menu to use. It can take the form of an object specifying a Menu instance, a string or object specifying the `id` of the element used to create the Menu, or finally, an array of object literals. Each specifies a set of `MenuItem` configuration attributes or strings representing the `MenuItem` labels
- `name`—the name of the Button
- `tabIndex`—a number representing the tab index of the Button
- `target`—if the Button is a link Button, this specifies the target of the link
- `title`—the title of the Button
- `type`—this is used to specify the different types of Button
- `value`—the value of the Button

YAHOO.widget.ButtonGroup

As I mentioned before, the `ButtonGroup` class is used solely to define Buttons with the behavior of radio `<input>` elements. To clarify this behavior; out of any number of buttons in a ButtonGroup, only one can be selected at any given time.

The `YAHOO.widget.ButtonGroup()` constructor accepts exactly the same arguments as that for the Button. Methods you may wish to make use of include:

- Methods for adding Buttons to the group like `.addButton()` or `.addButtons()`
- `.check()` — checks the Button at the specified index
- `.destroy()` — removes the whole group and handlers (if any have been registered)
- Methods for getting Button instances like `.getButton()` and `.getButtons()`
- `.getCount()` — gets the number of Buttons in the group
- `.removeButton()` — removes a single Button from the group

Like the `Button` class, the `ButtonGroup` class defines a series of configuration attributes for use in an object literal passed into the constructor allowing you to set attributes such as:

- `checkedButton` — allows you to specify which Button of the group is checked by default
- `container` — allows you to specify the `id` of the element that the `ButtonGroup` should be rendered into
- `disabled` — allows you to specify whether the group should be disabled
- `name` — the name for the `ButtonGroup`
- `value` — an object that specifies the value for the group

Using the Button Control

Let's play with some of the available Button controls. During this example, we'll create the page displayed in the figure below:

In a blank page of your text editor, begin with the following HTML:

```
<!DOCTYPE HTML PUBLIC "-//W3C//DTD HTML 4.01//EN"
                              "http://www.w3.org/TR/html4/strict.dtd">
<html lang="en">
  <head>
    <meta http-equiv="content-type" content="text/html;
                                    charset=utf-8">
    <title>YUI Buttons Example</title>
    <script type="text/javascript" src="yui/build/yahoo-dom-event/
                                        yahoo-dom-event.js"></script>
    <script type="text/javascript"
            src="yui/build/element/element-beta-min.js"></script>
    <script type="text/javascript"
            src="yui/build/button/button-min.js"></script>
    <link rel="stylesheet" type="text/css"
          href="yui/build/assets/skins/sam/button.css">
  </head>
  <body class="yui-skin-sam">
    <div>
      <h1>Please complete this form</h1>
      <form method="post" action="processForm.php">
        <div class="formdiv"><label>Please enter your first
           name: </label><input class="field" type="text"
           name="fname"></div>
        <div class="formdiv"><label>Please enter your last
           name: </label><input class="field" type="text"
           name="lname"></div>
        <div class="formdiv"><label>Please enter your
           email: </label><input class="field" type="text"
           name="email"></div>
        <div id="buttons"><button type="reset" id="myReset"
             name="myReset">Reset</button> <button type="submit"
             id="mySubmit" name="mySubmit">Submit</button></div>
      </form>
    </div>
  </body>
</html>
```

The required library files are referenced in the `<head>` of the document and the `<body>` is given the required skin `class` attribute so that the `sam` skin can style our YUI Button objects.

Following this we have a very basic `<form>` element with some `<label>` elements, some `<input>` fields and a couple of standard HTML `<button>` elements. This will form the basis of our example. Save the file as `buttons.html` in your **yuisite** folder.

We also reference a non-library stylesheet in the <head> of this page. This is so we can style our form with some basic CSS so that everything lines up for this example. In a blank page in your text editor, add the following selectors and rules:

```
.formdiv {
  position:relative;
  width:400px;
  margin-bottom:10px;
}
.field {
  position:absolute;
  right:0px;
  margin-right:4px;
  width:183px;
}
#buttons {
  width:400px;
  margin-top:20px;
  padding-top:10px;
  border-top:2px solid black;
}
```

Save this file as `buttons.css` also in the `yuisite` folder. We've already linked to this file in the <head> of `buttons.html`. Our page should at this stage look the same as figure below:

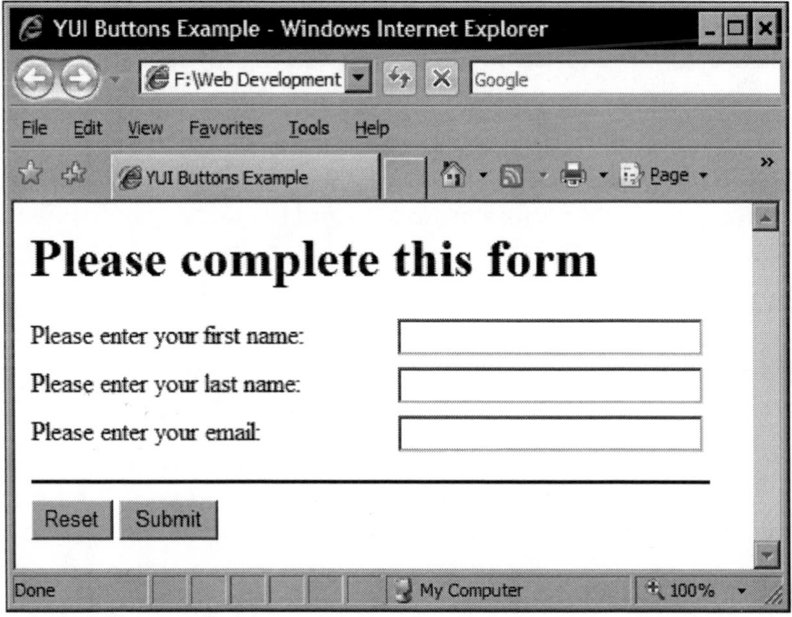

Creating the YUI Button Objects

We can now construct our shiny new Button objects to replace the existing, boring, standard `<button>` elements. Add the following `<script>` block to `buttons.html`, directly before the closing `</body>` tag:

```
<script type="text/javascript">
  //set up the namespace object for this example
  YAHOO.namespace("yuibook.buttons");

  //define the initButtons function
  YAHOO.yuibook.buttons.initButtons = function() {

    //define a reset Button object
    var yuiReset = new YAHOO.widget.Button("myReset");

  }

  //execute initButtons when the underlying button is available
  YAHOO.util.Event.onContentReady("myReset", YAHOO.yuibook.buttons.
                                  initButtons);
</script>
```

This very simple script uses the `YAHOO.widet.Button()` constructor, with the name of the standard `<button>` element that we want to transform into a Button control passed in as an argument. The constructor is wrapped in a function, which is called using the `.onContentReady()` method of the Event utility.

Instead of waiting for the entire DOM to be complete before our Button control is created, it will be done as soon as the underlying `<button>` element is detected in the DOM.

This is extremely useful because it helps to minimize the content flicker that can sometimes occur if a page is a little slow to load and the underlying element is initially visible for a few seconds before the script kicks in.

This is also a great example of **Progressive Enhancement**. If the visitor has JavaScript switched off, or if their browser cannot handle the script, the original HTML buttons will still be available for use. Supported browsers, on the other hand, will see our rich `Button` objects as we intend.

There are two `<button>` elements on the page that we want to transform. We could add another `onContentReady` handler for the second `<button>` element and use a second initialization function to create the second `Button` object.

This would be inefficient however, so instead we can use the `.onContentReady()` method in conjunction with the `<button>` elements container, which is a simple `<div>` element with an `id` of `buttons`.

Change the script so that it appears as follows:

```
//set up the namespace object for this example
YAHOO.namespace("yuibook.buttons");

//define the initButtons function
YAHOO.yuibook.buttons.initButtons = function() {

  //define a reset Button object
  var yuiReset = new YAHOO.widget.Button("myReset");

  //define a submit Button object
  var yuiSubmit = new YAHOO.widget.Button("mySubmit");
}

//execute initButtons when the button container is available
YAHOO.util.Event.onContentReady("buttons",
                              YAHOO.yuibook.buttons.initButtons);
```

The figure below shows how our page should look at this stage. As you can see, the YUI Button controls are a big improvement on their original counterparts:

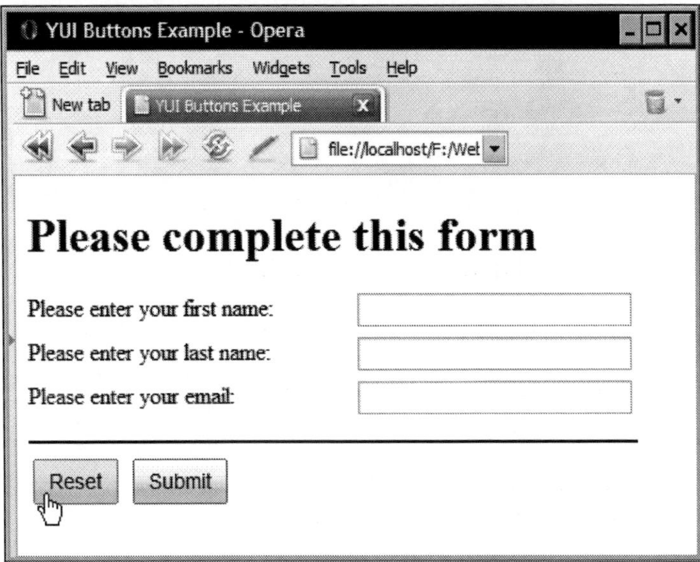

Now that we have our `Button` objects, we can begin to add some functionality to them. We'll start off by disabling both of the Buttons, which can be done using a configuration object within each Button's constructor. Change the `<script>` so that it appears as follows:

```
//set up the namespace object for this example
YAHOO.namespace("yuibook.buttons");

//define the initButtons function
YAHOO.yuibook.buttons.initButtons = function() {

  //define a reset Button object
  var yuiReset = new YAHOO.widget.Button("myReset",
                                        {disabled:true});

  //define a submit Button object
  var yuiSubmit = new YAHOO.widget.Button("mySubmit",
                                         {disabled:true});
}

//execute initButtons when the button container is available
YAHOO.util.Event.onContentReady("buttons",
                                YAHOO.yuibook.buttons.initButtons);
```

The configuration object is added as the second argument of each constructor and allows us to specify a series of `key:value` pairs. In this example, we use the `disabled` key and a value of `true` to disable each button. When the page initially loads, both Button objects will be grayed out and will not respond in any way:

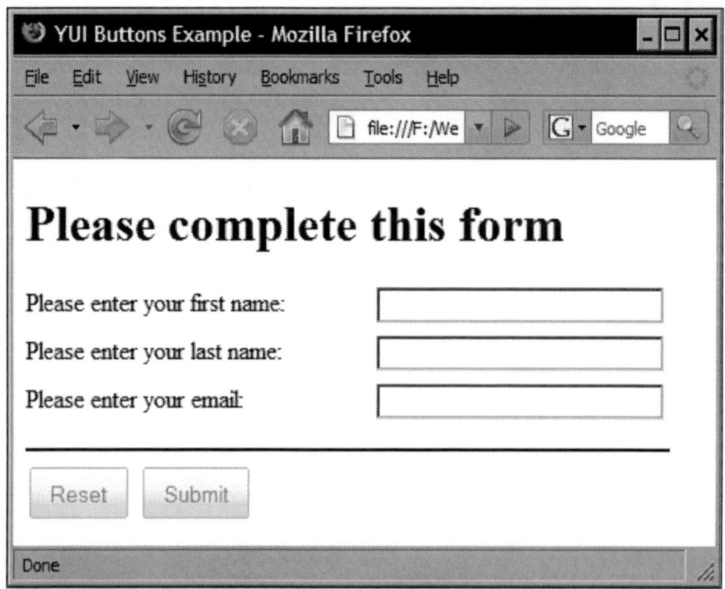

Configuration attributes that are set in the constructor can be easily accessed and changed if necessary using the `.get()` or `.set()` methods. Let's set a function so that as soon as one of the text fields is typed into, the `Reset` button becomes available for use. Change the script so that it appears as follows:

```
//set up the namespace object for this example
YAHOO.namespace("yuibook.buttons");

//define the initButtons function
YAHOO.yuibook.buttons.initButtons = function() {

  //define a reset Button object
  var yuiReset = new YAHOO.widget.Button("myReset",
                                          {disabled:true});

  //define a submit Button object
  var yuiSubmit = new YAHOO.widget.Button("mySubmit",
                                           {disabled:true});

  //define the unDisableReset function
  var unDisableReset = function() {

    //set disabled state to false
    yuiReset.set("disabled", false);
  }

  //execute unDisableReset when change event detected
  var fields = YAHOO.util.Dom.getElementsByClassName("field");
  YAHOO.util.Event.addListener(fields, "keypress", unDisableReset);
}

//execute initButtons when the button container is available
YAHOO.util.Event.onContentReady("buttons",
                                 YAHOO.yuibook.buttons.initButtons);
```

The `unDisableReset()` function calls the `.set()` method on the reset Button; the property and the value to set the property to are specified as arguments. We then simply add a listener for the `keypress` event on the collection of `<input>` elements obtained using the `YAHOO.util.Dom.getElementsByClassName()` convenience method. As soon as any of the text fields are typed in, the `Reset` button becomes available and its rollover states begin working again:

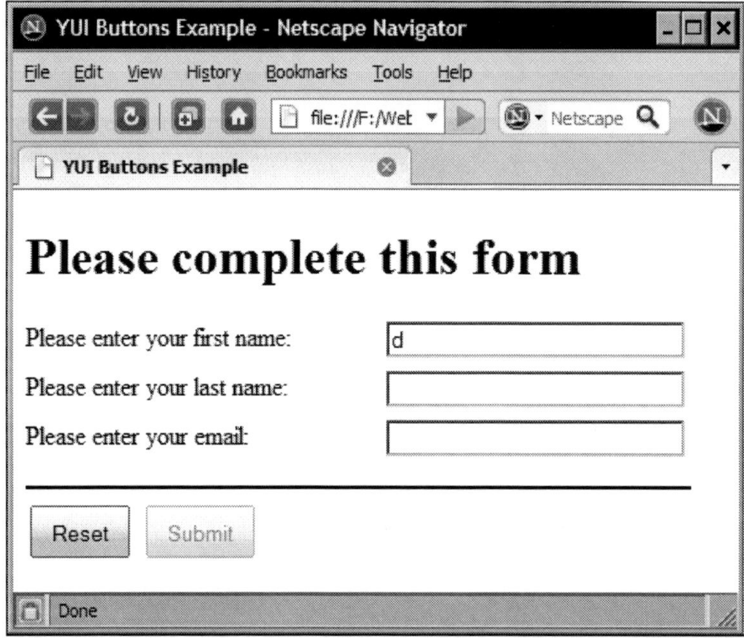

We can add a similar function that will allow us to enable the `Submit` button once all of the fields have been completed. Alter the script so that it appears as follows:

```
//set up the namespace object for this example
YAHOO.namespace("yuibook.buttons");

//define the initButtons function
YAHOO.yuibook.buttons.initButtons = function() {

  //define a reset Button object
  var yuiReset = new YAHOO.widget.Button("myReset",
                                        {disabled:true});

  //define a submit Button object
  var yuiSubmit = new YAHOO.widget.Button("mySubmit",
                                         {disabled:true});
```

```
    //define the unDisableReset function
    var unDisableReset = function() {

      //set disabled state to false
      yuiReset.set("disabled", false);
    }

    //execute unDisableReset when keypress event detected
    var fields = YAHOO.util.Dom.getElementsByClassName("field");
    YAHOO.util.Event.addListener(fields, "keypress", unDisableReset);

    //define the unDisableSubmit function
    var unDisableSubmit = function() {

      var count = 0;

      //check each field completed
      for (x = 0; x < fields.length; x++) {
        if (fields[x].value != "") {
          count++;
          if (count == fields.length) {
            //if each field completed set disabled state to false
            yuiSubmit.set("disabled", false);
          }
        }
      }
    }

    //execute unDisableSubmit when keypress event detected
    YAHOO.util.Event.addListener(fields, "keypress", unDisableSubmit);

  }

  //execute initButtons when the button container is available
  YAHOO.util.Event.onContentReady("buttons",
                                  YAHOO.yuibook.buttons.initButtons);
```

We first define the `unDisableSubmit()` function. This relies on a simple `count` variable which is initially set to zero each time the function is executed. A `for` loop then cycles through each `<input>` element and checks to see whether it contains any text, if it does, the variable is incremented by one.

The variable is then checked again and if it is found to equal the number of `<input>` elements the script knows that each field has been typed into and the `Submit` button can be enabled.

After the `unDisableSubmit()` function we add a listener for the `keypress` event to each item in the `fields` array. Every time a key is pressed while one of the `<input>` fields has focus, the function will be executed.

Now when each field has been completed, both buttons become available, as shown in the figure below:

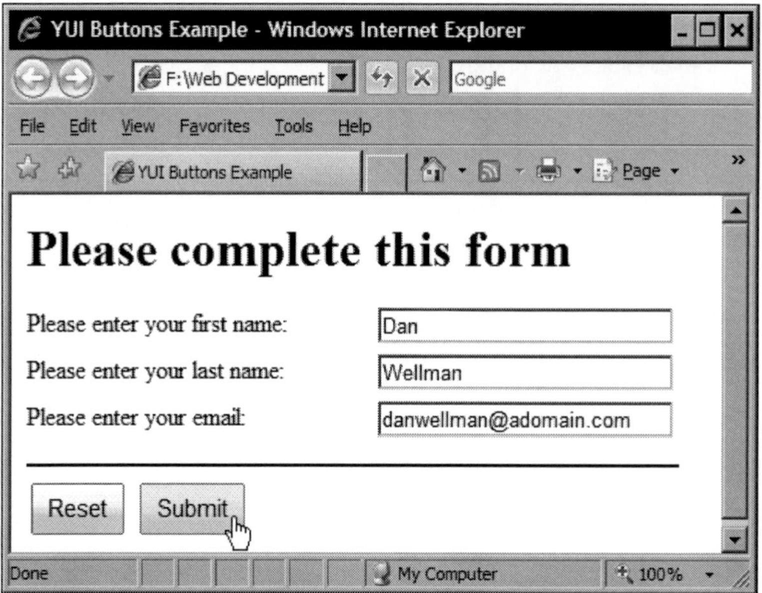

Additional Button Types

Let's now look at some of the other Button types available to us. We can easily add a Link Button and a couple of Radio Button objects to our page. This time we can use Yahoo's Button Control HTML as the underlying mark up for some of our new buttons. Change the `<body>` of the page so that it appears as below:

```
<body class="yui-skin-sam">
  <h1>Please complete this form</h1>
  <form method="post" action="#" id="testform" name="testform">
    <div class="formdiv"><label>Please enter your first
      name: </label><input class="field" type="text"
                                name="fname"></div>
    <div class="formdiv"><label>Please enter your last
```

```
      name: </label><input class="field" type="text"
                                 name="lname"></div>
    <div class="formdiv"><label>Please enter your
      email: </label><input class="field" type="text"
                                 name="email"></div>
    <div class="formdiv"><button id="tacs" name="tacs"
      type="button">Please Read our T&Cs</button></label>
      <div id="buttonGroup1" class="yui-buttongroup">
        <span id="radio1"
              class="yui-button yui-radio-button yui-button-checked">
          <span class="first-child">
            <button type="button" name="termsRadio"
                    value="disagree">I Do Not Agree</button>
          </span>
        </span>
        <span id="radio2" class="yui-button yui-radio-button">
          <span class="first-child">
            <button type="button" name="termsRadio" value="agree">
              I Agree</button>
          </span>
        </span>
      </div>
    </div>
    <div id="buttons"><button id="myReset" name="myReset"
         type="reset">Reset</button> <button id="mySubmit"
         name="mySubmit" type="submit">Submit</button></div>
  </form>
  <script type="text/javascript">
    //our script here...
  </script>
</body>
```

Our first new Button, which is given an `id` and a `name` of `tacs` is a standard `<button>` element, will become our Link Button. Next we define two Radio Buttons using Yahoo's Button Control Format. This consists of a standard `<button>` element wrapped in two `<span>` elements that represent one Button object. As these two buttons will become our Radio Buttons, they are wrapped in a container `<div>` which is given an `id` of `buttonGroup1` and a `class` of `yui-buttongroup`.

Each of the top-level `<span>` elements in our ButtonGroup has a class of `yui-button yui-radio-button`, which enables appropriate styling by the `sam` skin. The first top-level `<span>` also has the additional `yui-button-checked` identifier. This is the Radio Button that will be selected by default.

Now let's look at the additional JavaScript required to create the new Button Controls. Change your `<script>` block so that it appears as follows:

```
<script type="text/javascript">
  //set up the namespace object for this example
  YAHOO.namespace("yuibook.buttons");

  //define the initButtons function
  YAHOO.yuibook.buttons.initButtons = function() {

    //define a reset Button object
    var yuiReset = new YAHOO.widget.Button("myReset",
                                            {disabled:true});

    //define a submit Button object
      var yuiSubmit = new YAHOO.widget.Button("mySubmit",
                                            {disabled:true});

    //define a link button
    var tacs = new YAHOO.widget.Button("tacs", {
      type:"link",
      href:"tacs.html",
      target:"_blank",
    });

    //define a radio buttongroup
    var buttonGroup1 = new YAHOO.widget.ButtonGroup("buttonGroup1",
                                                  {disabled:true});

    //define the unDisableReset function
    var unDisableReset = function() {

      //set disabled state to false
      yuiReset.set("disabled", false);
    }

    //execute unDisableReset when keypress event detected
    var fields = YAHOO.util.Dom.getElementsByClassName("field");
    YAHOO.util.Event.addListener(fields, "keypress", unDisableReset);

    //define the unDisableSubmit function
    var unDisableSubmit = function() {

      var count = 0;

      //check each field completed
      for (x = 0; x < fields.length; x++) {
        if (fields[x].value != "") {
          count++;
          if (count == 3) {
            //if each field completed set disabled state to false
            yuiSubmit.set("disabled", false);
```

```
                }
            }
        }
    }
    //execute unDisableSubmit when keypress event detected
    YAHOO.util.Event.addListener(fields, "keypress",
                                  unDisableSubmit);
  }
  //execute initButtons when the button container is available
  YAHOO.util.Event.onContentReady("buttons",
                                  YAHOO.yuibook.buttons.initButtons);
</script>
```

The first of the new additions to our code creates a new `Button` object in the same way as before, but because the Button is a Link Button, the `type`, `href`, and `link` configuration attributes must also be set.

Our Radio Button objects use the `YAHOO.widget.ButtonGroup()` constructor which accepts the `id` of the container `<div>` as the first argument. The second argument is a literal object. We've set the `disabled` attribute to `true`, so all Button objects within the ButtonGroup will be disabled.

When the page loads now, it should appear as in the figure below:

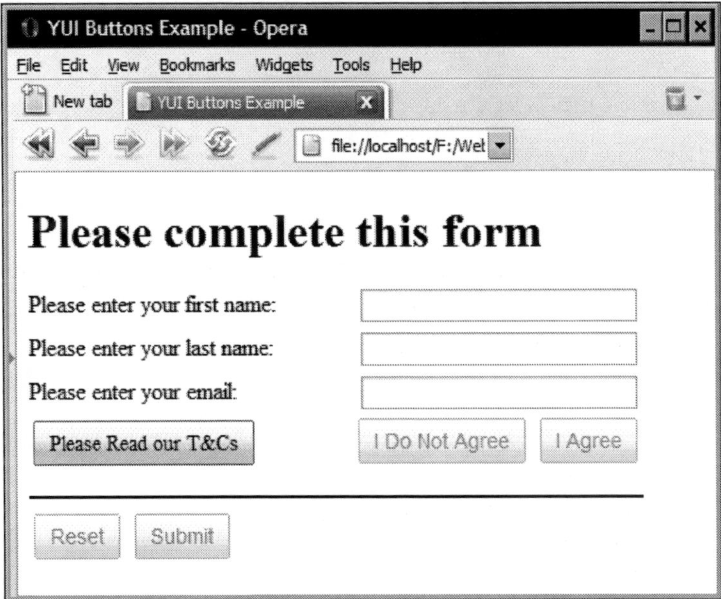

In order to make the `Link` Button work completely, the page it links to must exist. Create a basic web page with some text on it and save it as `tacs.html` in the `yuisite` folder. Now when you click the Link Button, the new page should open in its own window, just like in the figure below:

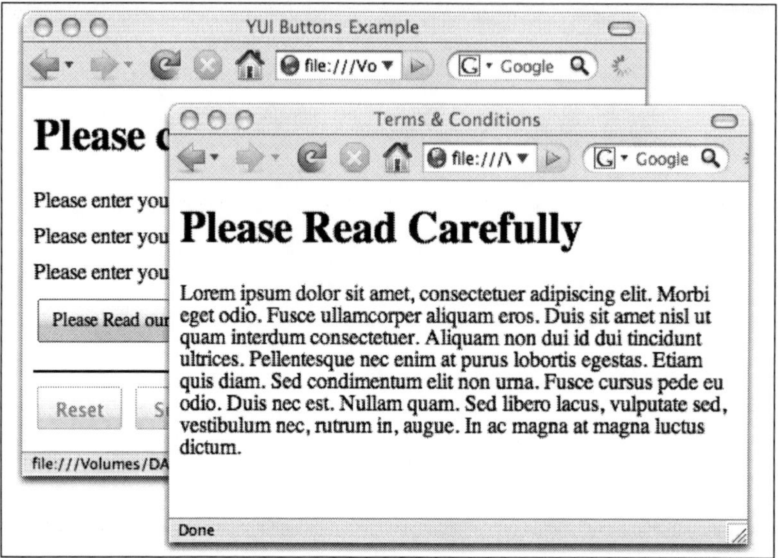

At this stage our Radio ButtonGroup is disabled. Why don't we add some code that enables the ButtonGroup once the `tacs.html` page has been opened? You'll need to create a new callback function and add a new configuration attribute to the Link Button:

```
//define the unDisableButtonGroup function
var unDisableButtonGroup = function() {

  //set disabled state to false
  buttonGroup1.set("disabled", false);
}

//define a link button
var tacs = new YAHOO.widget.Button("tacs", {
  type:"link",
  href:"tacs.html",
  target:"_blank",
  onclick:{
    fn:unDisableButtonGroup
  }
});
```

We can set the `disabled` state of the `ButtonGroup` to `false`, just like we did with the Reset and Submit Buttons, but instead of attaching a listener for the `click` event on the Link Button using the Event utility, we can use the `onclick` configuration attribute to specify a function to execute when the Button is clicked.

Our `Submit` Button currently becomes available when all of the fields on the form have been completed (or aren't empty at least). We can easily make use of one of the `ButtonGroup` control's custom events in order to change this so that the Submit Button becomes available when the `I Agree` Radio Button is selected, as well as all of the fields having been completed.

Directly after the `YAHOO.widget.ButtonGroup()` constructor add the following code:

```
//define radioChange function
var radioChange = function() {
  unDisableSubmit();
}

//add a listener for the checkedButtonChange event
buttonGroup1.addListener("checkedButtonChange", radioChange);
```

We can call the `.addListener()` method directly on the `buttonGroup1` object, specifying `checkedButtonChange` as the event to listen for and our newly created `radioChange()` callback as the function to execute. All our `radioChange()` function does is call the `unDisableSubmit()` function.

We need to make a minor change to our `unDisableSubmit()` function as well. Update it so that it appears as below:

```
//define the unDisableSubmit function
var unDisableSubmit = function() {

  var count = 0;

  //check each field completed and Agree button selected
  for (x = 0; x < fields.length; x++) {
    if (fields[x].value != "") {
      count++;
      if ((count == 3) && (buttonGroup1.get("checkedButton") ==
                                        "Button radio2")) {

      //if each field completed set disabled state to false
        yuiSubmit.set("disabled", false);
      }
    }
  }
}
```

The `.get()` method of the `Button` object allows us to check the current value of any Button object's configuration attributes. As long as all of the fields have been completed, and the `checkedButton` attribute is equal to the `id` of the Agree Button, the Submit Button will become available. At this point, you should now have a page that looks like the figure from the start of this example.

Using the Split Button Type

Using most of the different Button controls is similar to what we did in `buttons.html`, each Button can be initially configured via a series of attributes, and those attributes can be easily set or obtained at any point in the script. As we saw in the previous example, using the custom Events defined by each class is equally as simple.

Two Button types that we didn't cover in the last example were the Menu Button and Split Button types, both of which are highly specialized controls not available natively under HTML.

The Menu Button displays a Menu when it is clicked, allowing you to bundle up a series of related actions into a single `Button` object. The Split Button is similar but its face is split into two sections—the Button itself and a drop-down which allows the Menu to be opened.

In this example, we'll look at the Split Button, which is similar in many ways to the Menu Button. By the end of the example, we'll have a page the same as in the figure below:

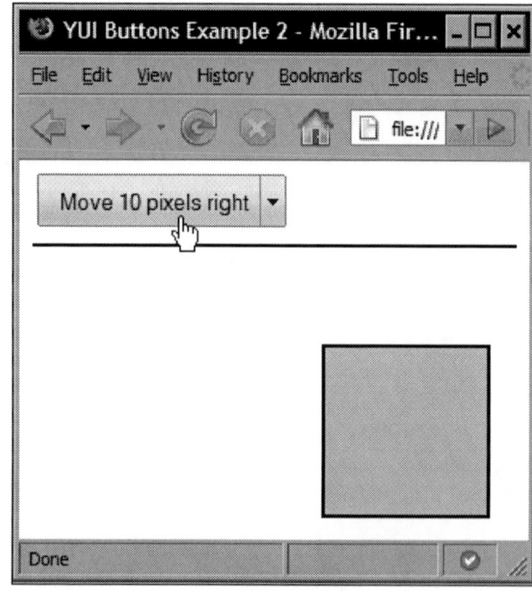

Getting Started

Our page will require the following markup:

```
<!DOCTYPE HTML PUBLIC "-//W3C//DTD HTML 4.01//EN"
                              "http://www.w3.org/TR/html4/strict.dtd">
<html lang="en">
  <head>
    <meta http-equiv="content-type" content="text/html;
                                     charset=utf-8">
    <title>YUI Buttons Example 2</title>
    <script type="text/javascript" src="yui/build/yahoo-dom-event/
                                          yahoo-dom-event.js"></script>
    <script type="text/javascript"
            src="yui/build/element/element-beta-min.js"></script>
    <script type="text/javascript"
            src="yui/build/container/container_core-min.js"></script>
    <script type="text/javascript"
            src="yui/build/menu/menu-min.js"></script>
    <script type="text/javascript"
            src="yui/build/button/button-min.js"></script>
    <link rel="stylesheet" type="text/css"
          href="yui/build/button/assets/skins/sam/button.css">
    <link rel="stylesheet" type="text/css"
          href="yui/build/menu/assets/skins/sam/menu.css">
    <link rel="stylesheet" type="text/css" href="splitButton.css">
  </head>
  <body class="yui-skin-sam">
    <div id="splitContainer"></div>
    <div id="parent">
      <div id="square"></div>
    </div>
  </body>
</html>
```

As well as the same library files required by the Button, the Split (and Menu) Button type is also dependant on the `container_core-min.js`, the `menu-min.js` and the `menu.css` files. The only elements in the <body> of our page is an element for the Split Button control to be rendered into and an empty `<div>` element. Save this page as `splitButton.html` in the `yuisite` folder.

Next we'll need a little CSS to layout the elements on the example page correctly. In a new file in your text editor, add the following code:

```
#parent {
  position:relative;
  padding-top:10px;
  margin-top:10px;
  border-top:2px solid black;
```

```
}
#square {
  position:absolute;
  width:100px;
  height:100px;
  background-color:lightblue;
  border:2px solid darkblue;
  left:100px;
  top:100px;
}
```

Save this as `splitButton.css`, also in the `yuisite` folder.

Scripting the Split Button

Everything is in place, we can now move on to adding the JavaScript that will bring our Split Button control to life. Re-open `splitButton.html` in your text editor and directly above the closing `</body>` tag, add the following `<script>` block:

```
<script type="text/javascript">
  //set up namespace object
  YAHOO.namespace("yuibook.buttons");

  //define the initSplitButton function
  YAHOO.yuibook.buttons.initSplitButton = function() {

    //define an array of menuitem objects
    var splitMenu = [
      {text: "Move 10 pixels up", value:"up",
             onclick:{fn:menuSelect}},
      {text: "Move 10 pixels right", value:"right",
             onclick:{fn:menuSelect}},
      {text: "Move 10 pixels down", value:"down",
             onclick:{fn:menuSelect}},
      {text: "Move 10 pixels left", value:"left",
             onclick:{fn:menuSelect}}
    ];

    //generate a splitButton
    var splitButton1 = new YAHOO.widget.Button({ type: "split",
      label: "Choose a Direction", name: "splitbutton1", menu:
      splitMenu, container: "splitContainer" });

  }

  //execute initSplitButton when DOM is ready
  YAHOO.util.Event.onDOMReady( YAHOO.yuibook.buttons.initSplitButton);
</script>
```

The `initSplitButtons()` function wraps up the Menu items array definition and the constructor used to create our Button object. The function is evoked with the `.onDOMReady()` method.

The options to be displayed on the Split Button's Menu are defined using a simple array of objects. Each object has a `text` property which reflects the text displayed on the Menu. It also has `value` and `onclick` properties.

The `onclick` property of each MenuItem is also an object. The only member of the object we've used in this example is the `fn` property, which defines a callback function to execute when the Menu item is clicked on. The Menu used in this example is illustrated in the figure below:

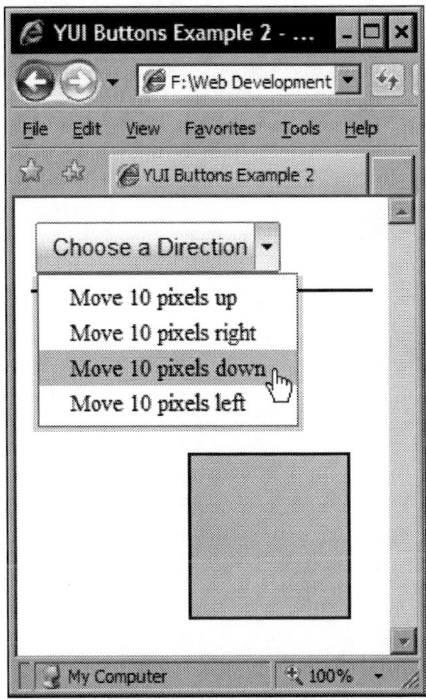

The Split Button uses exactly the same constructor as the other Button types, but additional arguments, such as `menu`, which uses our `splitMenu` array, should also be used in the configuration object.

We haven't based this button on any underlying HTML, this time it is created entirely from script. We simply specify the container (the empty `<div id="splitContainer">` element) on the page which the Button control should be rendered into. If you use a DOM explorer to look at the page, you'll see that the control created by the library follows the standard Button Definition mark up pattern.

Each MenuItem specifies the `menuSelect` callback function which is executed when it is clicked. Let's add this function now. Here is how the existing code should look with the addition of the `menuSelect()` function, new code is shown in bold:

```
<script type="text/javascript">
  //set up namespace object
  YAHOO.namespace("yuibook.buttons");

  //define the initSplitButton function
  YAHOO.yuibook.buttons.initSplitButton = function() {

    var direction;

    //define the menuSelect function
    var menuSelect = function(type, args, item) {

      //set the button label to the selected menuitem text
      splitButton1.set("label", this.cfg.getProperty("text"));
      direction = item.value;
    }

    //define an array of menuitem objects
    var splitMenu = [
      {text: "Move 10 pixels up", value:"up",
             onclick:{fn:menuSelect}},
      {text: "Move 10 pixels right", value:"right",
             onclick:{fn:menuSelect}},
      {text: "Move 10 pixels down", value:"down",
             onclick:{fn:menuSelect}},
      {text: "Move 10 pixels left", value:"left",
             onclick:{fn:menuSelect}}
    ];

    //generate a splitButton
    var splitButton1 = new YAHOO.widget.Button({ type: "split",
      label: "Choose a Direction", name: "splitbutton1", menu:
      splitMenu, container: "splitContainer" });
  }

  //execute initSplitButton when DOM is ready
  YAHOO.util.Event.onDOMReady(YAHOO.yuibook.buttons.initSplitButton);
</script>
```

We first define the `direction` variable, which will be populated by the `menuSelect()` function, and then used later on in the script. The `menuSelect()` function accepts three objects, these are passed into the function automatically by each MenuItem. We don't need to use the first two in this example, but we need to define them so that the third argument is the correct object.

The `type` object for example will tell us the type of event that called the function, in this example it would contain the string `click` to represent the click event. The `args` object is an array. It contains the URL that the Menu item links to, which is not needed in this example.

The `item` object contains further information about the MenuItem that the click event occurred on, such as the `value` property, which we use to fill the `direction` variable with the required information.

We use the `.set()` method to set the Button's `label` to the text from the MenuItem, which is obtained using the `this.cfg.getProperty()` method to obtain the `text` property of whichever MenuItem was clicked. We use `this` because the object representing the MenuItem is the current execution context. Once an item from the Menu has been selected, the Button will display it's text, as shown in the figure below:

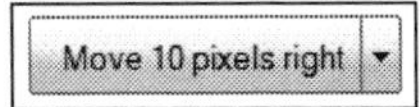

We need just one more function now; the function that actually moves the square once the direction has been selected and the Button is clicked. Change your script so that the new function is included, new code is again shown in bold:

```
<script>
  //set up namespace object
  YAHOO.namespace("yuibook.buttons");

  //define the initSplitButton function
  YAHOO.yuibook.buttons.initSplitButton = function() {

    var direction;

    //define the menuSelect function
    var menuSelect = function(type, args, item) {

      //set the button label to the selected menuitem text
      splitButton1.set("label", this.cfg.getProperty("text"));
      direction = item.value;
    }
```

```
//define an array of menuitem objects
var splitMenu = [
  {text: "Move 10 pixels up", value:"up",
          onclick:{fn:menuSelect}},
  {text: "Move 10 pixels right", value:"right",
          onclick:{fn:menuSelect}},
  {text: "Move 10 pixels down", value:"down",
          onclick:{fn:menuSelect}},
  {text: "Move 10 pixels left", value:"left",
          onclick:{fn:menuSelect}}
];

//generate a splitButton
var splitButton1 = new YAHOO.widget.Button({ type: "split",
  label: "Choose a Direction", name: "splitbutton1", menu:
  splitMenu, container: "splitContainer" });

//define the moveSquare function
var moveSquare = function() {

  //check direction has been selected
  if (splitButton1.get("label") == "Choose a Direction") {
    alert("Please choose a direction");
  } else {

    //get the square div and its existing coordinates
    var square = YAHOO.util.Dom.get("square");
    var x = YAHOO.util.Dom.getX(square);
    var y = YAHOO.util.Dom.getY(square);

    //move the square
    if (direction == "up") {
      var newy = y - 10;
      YAHOO.util.Dom.setY(square, newy);
    } else if (direction == "right") {
      var newx = x + 10;
      YAHOO.util.Dom.setX(square, newx);
    } else if (direction == "down") {
      var newy = y + 10;
      YAHOO.util.Dom.setY(square, newy);
    } else if (direction == "left") {
      newx = x - 10;
      YAHOO.util.Dom.setX(square, newx);
```

```
            }
         }
      }

      //execute moveSquare when button is clicked
      splitButton1.addListener("click", moveSquare);
   }

   //execute initSplitButton when DOM is ready
   YAHOO.util.Event.onDOMReady(YAHOO.yuibook.buttons.initSplitButton);
</script>
```

The `moveSquare()` function is really very simple. We first check that a direction has actually been selected by checking the `label` property of the Button. If it's still the same as when the page loaded we know a direction has not been selected and emit an appropriate alert.

Once it has been established that a direction has been selected we then get a reference to the element that has an `id` of `square`. We also obtain the current X and Y page coordinates of the square using the DOM utility's `.getX()` and `.getY()` methods.

It is then just a matter of determining which direction has been selected and manipulating the X and Y properties using `.setX()` and `.setY()`, which results in the `<div>` being moved. The `moveSquare()` function is executed when the `click` event is detected on the Button. You should now have a page exactly like that shown in the figure at the start of this section.

Tree-like Structures with the TreeView Control

Back in Chapter 3 when we looked at the DOM utility, we looked at the DOM Inspector provided by Firefox (under the heading DOM Concepts). DOM viewers are an excellent example of a useful tree-like representation of a series of objects (in that example the objects making up a web page), and the TreeView control can be used to create tree-like structures that are just as useful. File system explorers, such as Windows Explorer or the Finder application on the Mac, are also common examples of tree-structures at work.

This component is extremely versatile and provides essential methods for adding and removing nodes programmatically, as well as loading node data dynamically. It also has a set of default behaviours that can be manipulated to give you the effects you want.

It even allows you to override the default behavior of allowing several parent nodes to be expanded at once in order to use the tree control as a navigation menu, and has the capability to be combined with the Animation utility to provide transition effects when opening and closing nodes.

The TreeView control is created mostly from script rather than any underlying HTML, although an empty container, such as a `<div>` element, for the TreeView object to be rendered into should be provided.

Class of Nine

We'll be learning about the TreeView control very soon but, before we do, let's have a look at its capabilities by diving head first into its classes—all nine of them, to make sure that the most useful aspects of this control are highlighted.

YAHOO.widget.TreeView

The `TreeView` class is used to manage the state data of the TreeView control and contains the root node of the tree. The constructor found within this class is the main constructor used when generating an instance of a basic TreeView control. There aren't many properties useful to you as an implementer as many of them are private and are used internally by the control.

There are however, a wide range of useful methods that are defined by this class, which mostly allow you to control the appearance and object model of a TreeView control instance. These include, but are certainly not limited to, the following:

- `.collapseAll()`—used to collapse all expanded nodes in the current tree instance
- `.collapseComplete()`—automatically called when a collapse animation completes
- `.draw()`—renders the tree on the page
- `.expandAll()`—expands all collapsed child nodes unless the `multiExpand` property is set to `false` (that is, `MenuNode` in use), in which case only the last child node with children will be expanded
- `.expandComplete()`—automatically called when an expand animation completes
- `.getNodeByProperty()`—gets a node with the property and value specified as arguments
- `.getNodesByProperty()`—gets a collection of nodes with the property and value specified by arguments

- `.getRoot()` — gets the root node of the current tree
- `.popNode()` — removes the specified node but doesn't delete it entirely thereby making it easy to insert the node somewhere else in the current, or another tree instance
- `.removeChildren()` — deletes the child nodes of the specified node, collapses the node and resets the dynamic load flag, allowing the node to fetch its data dynamically again
- `.removeNode()` — removes the specified node and all of it child nodes
- `.setCollapseAnim()` and `.setExpandAnim()` — specifies the of animation for expanding and/or collapsing nodes
- `.setDynamicload()` — configures the tree to load its node data dynamically. Can only be called once before the node needs to be reset using the `.removeChildren()` method above
- `.setUpLabel()` — sets up the node label

As you'd expect, the class also defines a series of custom events that let you detect things like an animation starting or completing, a collapse or expand event beginning and ending or a label being clicked.

YAHOO.widget.Node

Next up is the `YAHOO.widget.Node` class, which acts as the base class for all of the different types of node available. It does have its own constructor method so generic or non-specific nodes can be created, but you'd probably invoke one of its subclass's constructors instead. I won't go into too much detail about it.

A huge range of properties are defined by this class and then inherited when required by the various node subclasses. Some of the properties you have available for to use include:

- `children` — the collection of the current child nodes
- `data` — an object literal holding node-specific information like `label` or `href`
- `depth` — an integer representing the depth of the node, beginning at -1 for the root node
- `dynamicLoadComplete` — set to `true` once dynamic data has been loaded once
- `expanded` — a boolean indicating the state of the node
- `hasIcon` — a boolean used to show or hide the toggle icon

- `href` — the `href` attribute of the node's label. If not specified, the label toggles the node between collapsed and expanded states. It is set to `null` by default
- `iconMode` — overrides the default of using a toggle icon on a dynamic child with no children
- `index` — the index of the current node
- `isLoading` — a boolean that is set to `true` while the loading of dynamic node data occurs
- `multiExpand` — a boolean indicating whether more than one node can be expanded at once. False when using `MenuNode`
- `nextSibling` and `previousSibling` — the next and previous siblings respectively
- `nowrap` — a boolean indicating whether the content of the node should wrap. False is the default
- `parent` — the nodes parent
- `target` — the target window of the label's `href` attribute. Default is `_self`
- `tree` — the tree instance the node belongs to

There are quite a few of them, but you have to remember that they are shared out between all three of the subclasses. You also have a number of methods at your disposal including:

- `.appendChild()` — takes one argument, the child node to append
- `.appendTo()` — appends the current node to the specified node
- `.collapseAll()` — collapses all of the current nodes child nodes
- `.expandAll()` — expands all of the current node's child nodes
- `.getAncestor()` — returns the node at the specified depth
- `.getSiblings()` — returns the siblings of the current node in an array
- `.insertAfter()` and `.insertBefore()` — inserts the current node after or before the specified node
- `.isDynamic()` — returns a boolean indicating whether the child nodes are loaded dynamically
- `.isRoot()` — returns a boolean indicating whether the current node is the root node
- `.refresh()` — a useful way of showing new child nodes that have been added to an expanded node
- `.toggle()` — expands or collapses a node depending on its current state

A custom event, `parentChange`, is also defined by the `Node` class, which fires when a parent node is applied to the current node. This can be useful when moving a node from one tree to another. Next let's take a look at the subclasses of this class.

YAHOO.widget.TextNode

The TextNode is the basic, default type of TreeView node. Its constructor takes three arguments. The first can be either a string which is used as the label of the TextNode, or an object containing arbitrary data, including a `label` property. The second argument is the parent that the new TextNode will belong to, and the third argument is an optional boolean that indicates whether the node should be expanded by default.

Most of its properties and methods, as well as its only event are inherited, but native properties include the `label` property. This is the text to use as the node's label, and `labelStyle` which can be used to change from the default CSS class of `ygtvlabel` to a custom class of your own.

YAHOO.widget.HTMLNode

The `HTMLNode` class allows you to generate nodes that use customized HTML for their labels. It's a very compact class, defining just a few of its own native members. The constructor though is slightly more complex (but really only slightly) than that of other node types, taking four arguments. The first argument is again either a string or an object that holds information used to create the node. The second argument specifies the parent, the third specifies whether the node is expanded by default, and the fourth and final argument is another boolean that specifies whether the node has an icon or not.

The configuration object optionally specified as the second argument in the constructor should have a property defined within it called `content` which refers to the HTML content of the node. Other properties defined by the class include the `contentStyle` and `contentElId` properties.

YAHOO.widget.RootNode

This class is ultra-specific and extremely compact. Its only native member is its very simple constructor, which takes just one argument—the TreeView instance that the root node belongs to. All of its other members are inherited.

The root node is a container, which holds all of the nodes and child nodes of the tree and is created automatically by the control. You probably won't need to call this directly in a standard implementation, but it is something that is created by the control once for every TreeView that gets instantiated.

YAHOO.widget.MenuNode

The MenuNode is a subclass of the TextNode, and is another very minimal class that just defines its constructor natively. Everything else including properties, methods, and events, are inherited from other classes. The multiExpand property, which this class inherits from the Node class, is set to false by default. Its constructor is identical to the TextNode constructor.

The Animation Classes

The TreeView control provides a built-in mechanism for displaying fade-in and fade-out animations which occur when a node is expanded or collapsed. Three classes are defined to facilitate these animations: YAHOO.widget.TVAnim, YAHOO.widget.TVFadeIn, and YAHOO.widget.TVFadeOut.

The first class defines two constant properties which you use to specify the different animations when calling the setCollapseAnim or setExpandAnim methods. It also contains a couple of methods which can be used to obtain an animation instance or query it for validity.

The other two classes each contain a constructor which you can use to invoke callback functions once animation has been completed. In a basic implementation, where all you want to do is create the default animations and not react to them in anyway, you won't need to use the properties or methods of either of these two classes.

I should point out now that the TreeView control still relies on the Animation utility to actually perform the animation, so you'll still need to include a reference to the animation-min.js file. The dom-min.js file is likewise required.

Implementing a Tree

In this example we'll build a basic Tree object that could be put to good use as a file explorer in an online content management system. Start off with the following basic HTML page:

```
<!DOCTYPE HTML PUBLIC "-//W3C//DTD HTML 4.01//EN"
                              "http://www.w3.org/TR/html4/strict.dtd">
<html lang="en">
  <head>
    <meta http-equiv="content-type" content="text/html;
                                    charset=utf-8">
    <title>YUI Tree Control Example</title>
    <script type="text/javascript" src="yui/build/yahoo-dom-event/
                                       yahoo-dom-event.js"></script>
    <script type="text/javascript"
```

```
            src="yui/build/treeview/treeview-min.js"></script>
    <link rel="stylesheet" type="text/css"
          href="yui/build/treeview/assets/skins/sam/treeview.css">
    <link rel="stylesheet" type="text/css" href="treecontrol.css">
  </head>
  <body class="yui-skin-sam">
    <div id="treeDiv"></div>
  </body>
</html>
```

In the `<head>` of the document we link to the library files required for the Tree Control to function, as well as the `sam` skin file and a custom stylesheet that we'll create shortly. The `<body>` of our page contains a simple `<div>` element, which will be used as the container for our TreeView object. Save this as `treecontrol.html` in your `yuisite` folder.

Begin the Scripting

Next we need to add the code that will create and render our TreeView object on the page. Directly after the `<div>` tag on the page we've just created, add the following `<script>` block:

```
<script type="text/javascript">
  //create the namespae object
  YAHOO.namespace("yuibook.tree");

  //define the initTree function
  YAHOO.yuibook.tree.initTree = function() {

    //create a TreeView object
    var tree = new YAHOO.widget.TreeView("treeDiv");

    //define the root of the tree
    var root = tree.getRoot()

    //add the tree nodes
    var usr = new YAHOO.widget.TextNode("usr", root, true);
    var mail = new YAHOO.widget.TextNode("mail", usr);
    var ftp = new YAHOO.widget.TextNode("ftp", usr);
    var www = new YAHOO.widget.TextNode("www", usr);

    //generate the tree
    tree.draw()
  }

  //execute initTree when DOM is ready
  YAHOO.util.Event.onDOMReady( YAHOO.yuibook.tree.initTree);
</script>
```

Our first task (after creating the namespace object used in this example, and setting up the initialization function) is to create the TreeView object using the `YAHOO.widget.TreeView` constructor. It accepts the `id` of the underlying HTML container for the control as an argument.

Once this has been done we need to use the `.getRoot()` method to get a reference to the root of the tree. The root is the fundamental building block of the tree and is what the first node that we create is appended to.

Creating the Tree Nodes

The `.TextNode()` methods in the above code creates each node that appears on the tree and takes three parameters to do so. The first parameter is the text to be used as the label of the node, the second parameter is the parent that the node should be attached to.

The third argument is an optional Boolean flag that tells the script whether the node should be expanded by default when the control is initially loaded by the script. It has been omitted from the three child nodes as they cannot be expanded at this stage due to not having child nodes of their own.

Drawing the Tree On-Screen

The `.draw()` method renders the tree control on the screen. It automatically uses the object variables created using the `.TextNode()` constructors and inserts the control into the `<div>` container. If you view the page in a browser at this stage, it should appear as in the figure shown here:

The library has automatically created several different things for us. It has added the images used to expand or collapse parent nodes, the logical lines linking the nodes, and it has created the rollover effects. By default, parent nodes can be opened and closed by clicking either the icon at the node's left, or its text label.

Using Custom Icons

In a new file in your text editor, add the additional selectors and rules required to add custom icons to our tree:

```
icon-drive {
  padding-left:20px;
  background:url(icons/drive.png) no-repeat;
}
icon-folder {
  padding-left:20px;
  background:url(icons/folder.png) no-repeat;
}
```

We define a set of class selectors that will target each of the different types of TextNode that we have created, which we'll be applying to the nodes in just a moment. The rules for the selector specify an area directly to the left of the text label twenty pixels wide.

We then specify a URL pointing to the image file we wish to use as the icon for the node being targeted by the class. Save this file as `treecontrol.css` in the same folder as its accompanying HTML file.

Applying the Icon Styles

Next we need to apply these styles to the relevant nodes in the tree. Alter the <script> tag so that it appears as follows:

```
<script type="text/javascript">
  //create the namespae object
  YAHOO.namespace("yuibook.tree");

  //define the initTree function
  YAHOO.yuibook.tree.initTree = function() {

    //create a TreeView object
    var tree = new YAHOO.widget.TreeView("treeDiv");

    //define the root of the tree
    var root = tree.getRoot()
```

```
        //add the tree nodes
        var usr = new YAHOO.widget.TextNode("usr", root, true);
        var mail = new YAHOO.widget.TextNode("mail", usr);
        var ftp = new YAHOO.widget.TextNode("ftp", usr);
        var www = new YAHOO.widget.TextNode("www", usr);

        //customize the node icons
        usr.labelStyle = "icon-drive";
        mail.labelStyle = "icon-folder";
        ftp.labelStyle = "icon-folder";
        www.labelStyle = "icon-folder";

        //generate the tree
        tree.draw()
      }

      //execute initTree when DOM is ready
      YAHOO.util.Event.onDOMReady(YAHOO.yuibook.tree.initTree);
    </script>
```

These property changes can be added after the `.TextNode()` constructors that create our text nodes, but they should appear before the call to draw the tree or they will not be applied. The icons should appear as shown in the figure below:

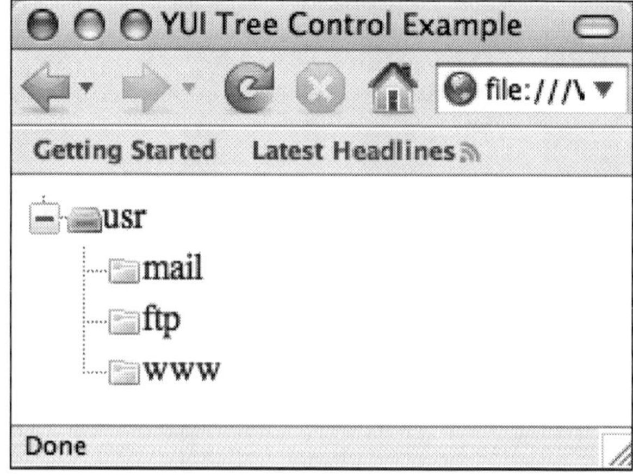

The icon images I used in the example were taken, with gratitude, from the Silk Icons package available at `www.famfamfam.com`, produced by Mark James.

Dynamic Nodes—Making the Library Work Harder

One way to make the tree more efficient is to only load the tree data that is required when the tree is initially drawn, and then dynamically load the children of parent nodes only when their parent is expanded.

The TreeView component provides built-in methods that handle this for you and tapping into them is really easy. To illustrate the point, we can add some child nodes to the `www` directory and then adjust the script so that the child nodes are not loaded until the parent node is actually expanded.

Instead of just hard-coding the new child nodes into the Tree object however, we can make use of the Connection Manager and a little PHP to actually get the contents of a `www` folder. You'll need to create this folder and make sure there are a few folders and files within it. This example, like others involving the Connection utility, will need to be run from a content-serving directory of a web server.

Let's look at the new script and then break down each new part so that we can see exactly what it does. The script will now need to appear as follows (with new code shown in bold):

```
<script type="text/javascript">
  //create the namespae object
  YAHOO.namespace("yuibook.tree");

  //define the initTree function
  YAHOO.yuibook.tree.initTree = function() {

    //create a TreeView object
    var tree = new YAHOO.widget.TreeView("treeDiv");

    //define the root of the tree
    var root = tree.getRoot()

    //add the tree nodes
    var usr = new YAHOO.widget.TextNode("usr", root, true);
    var mail = new YAHOO.widget.TextNode("mail", usr);
    var ftp = new YAHOO.widget.TextNode("ftp", usr);

    //create a node objext
    var nodeObj = {
      label:"www",
      id:"www"
```

```
};

var www = new YAHOO.widget.TextNode(nodeObj, usr, false);
www.setDynamicLoad(loadData);

//customize the node icons
usr.labelStyle = "icon-drive";
mail.labelStyle = "icon-folder";
ftp.labelStyle = "icon-folder";
www.labelStyle = "icon-folder";

//define the loadData function
function loadData(node, onCompleteCallback) {

  //define the success handler
  var handleSuccess = function(o) {

    //get individual filenames into an array
    var contents = o.responseText.split("\n");

    //remove the last array item
    contents.pop();

    //define an array for our new TextNodes
    var newNode = {};

    //check each item in contents array
    for (x = 0; x < contents.length; x++) {

      //if it doesn't have a . in it its a folder
      if (contents[x].indexOf(".") == -1) {

        //create a new Node and set its icon style
        newNode[x] = new YAHOO.widget.TextNode(contents[x], www);
        newNode[x].labelStyle = "icon-folder";

      } else {  //else its a file

        //create an array to hold the filename and extension
        var file = contents[x].split(".");
```

```
            //create a new Node and set its icon style
            newNode[x] = new YAHOO.widget.TextNode(contents[x], www);
            var iconStyle = "icon-" + file[1];
            newNode[x].labelStyle = iconStyle;
          }
        }

        //notify Tree that loadData function has ended
        onCompleteCallback();
      }

      //define failure handler
      var handleFailure = function(o) {
        alert("Error " + o.status + " : " + o.statusText);
      }

      //define the callback object
      var callback = {
        success:handleSuccess,
        failure:handleFailure
      };

      //request directory list from getdir.php
      var transaction = YAHOO.util.Connect.asyncRequest("POST",
        "getdir.php", callback, "dir=" + node.data.id);
    }

    //generate the tree
    tree.draw()

  }

  //execute initTree when DOM is ready
  YAHOO.util.Event.onDOMReady( YAHOO.yuibook.tree.initTree);
</script>
```

We first specify that the contents of the `www` folder should be retrieved dynamically using the `.setDynamicLoad()` method, which takes the name of the function to execute when the node is expanded as an argument.

The `loadData()` function receives two parameters: the object representing the node that is being expanded, and a callback function that is executed once the dynamic nodes have been created.

As we are using Connection Manager to obtain a list of the contents of the `www` directory we then define our `handleSuccess` and `handleFailure` callback functions, as well as the `callback` object. It executes either of the handlers depending on whether the transaction was successful or not.

The failure handler simply sends an appropriate alert; most of our logic is in the success handler. First we define the `contents` variable, which is populated by the data held in `o.responseText`. We can break this data apart using the new-line character `\n`, so each item within `contents` will relate to one file or folder name.

As the very last item in `contents` will be empty (a result of the last `\n` character in the file) we can use the standard JavaScript `.pop()` method to lose this empty item. Following this, we then define the `node` array, which we can populate with the new nodes for a tree next.

To populate the `nodes` array we use a `for` loop to cycle through each item in the `contents` collection one item at a time. The purpose of the `if` conditional branch statement within the loop is to determine whether the current item that is being looked at is a file or folder.

We can use the standard JavaScript `.indexOf()` method to see if the current item has a period character in it. If it doesn't then it's definitely a folder. We can then create a new `TextNode` in the same way as before and set its `iconStyle` property to our existing `icon-style` class to give it the correct icon.

If the current `contents` item does have a period in it, we know that it is a file. First we create the `file` variable, which is populated with the text before and the text after the period as separate items. We then create a new `TextNode` in the normal way, and use the second item in `file` to set an appropriate `icon-style`.

Once the for loop has finished executing, we call the method that was passed into the `loadData()` function as the second argument to notify the Tree that the dynamic node has loaded. This removes the loading icon and replaces it with the standard expand or collapse icon used for parent nodes.

The AJAX transaction is initiated using the `.asyncRequest()` method of the Connect utility. This method is used with four arguments. The first is the HTTP method, the second is the name of the PHP resource, the third links to our `callback` object, and the final one sets the query string which tells the PHP file the name of the folder to search.

The new part of our script sets a series of new icon styles to reflect the different files that are found in our www directory. We'll also need to define these new styles in the stylesheet associated with this page. In `treecontrol.css` add the following new selectors and rules:

```
icon-html {
  padding-left:20px;
  background:url(icons/html.png) no-repeat;
  text-decoration:none;
}
icon-css {
  padding-left:20px;
  background:url(icons/css.png) no-repeat;
  text-decoration:none;
}
icon-js {
  padding-left:20px;
  background:url(icons/script.png) no-repeat;
  text-decoration:none;
}
icon-txt {
  padding-left:20px;
  background:url(icons/text.png) no-repeat;
  text-decoration:none;
}
icon-php {
  padding-left:20px;
  background:url(icons/php.png) no-repeat;
  text-decoration:none;
}
```

We also need an accompanying PHP file that gets the request via Connection to search the www directory and passes back the resulting list of files and folders. The following file can easily accomplish this:

```
<?php

  $dir = $_POST['dir'];
  $dirHandle = opendir($dir);

  while(($item = readdir($dirHandle)) !== false) {
    $dirArray[] = $item;
  }

  closedir($action);
```

```
    sort($dirArray);
    $total = count($dirArray);

    for($x = 0; $x < $total; $x++) {
      if (substr("$dirArray[$x]", 0, 1) != ".") {
        echo "$dirArray[$x]" . "\n";
      }
    }

  ?>
```

Save the file again and view it in your browser. When the www node is expanded, the loading icon should appear briefly while the Connection Manager requests and processes the directory list, and then the new nodes should be added to the Tree. Because we're running the example on a localhost setup, the delay should be minimal and the loading icon will only be shown for a second or two. Our Tree should now appear as in the figure below:

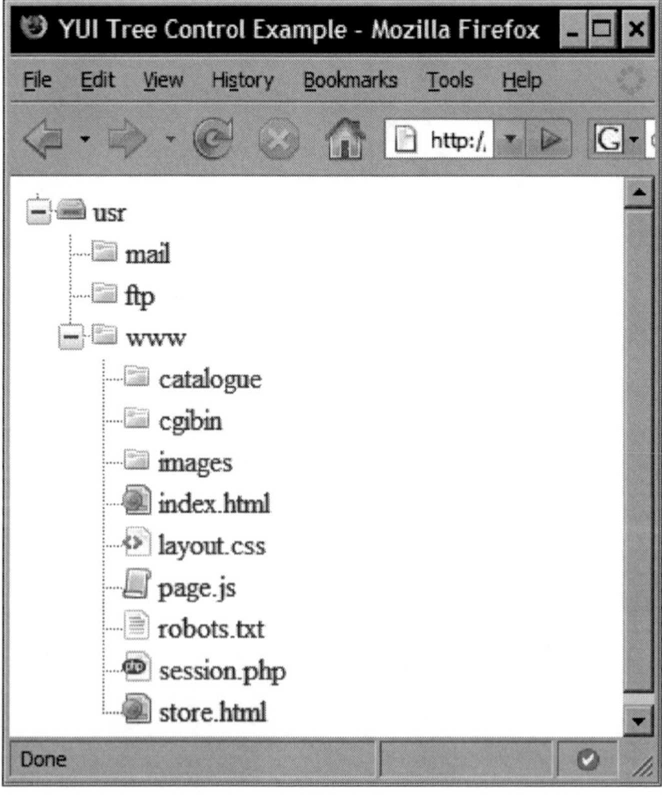

The loadData() function will only be executed once—the first time the www node is expanded. In order to make subsequent expand events work dynamically we have to remove the child nodes of the www node each time the node is collapsed. This is very easy to achieve and can be done be subscribing to the Tree's collapse event. Add the following new code directly after the call to draw the tree:

```
    //generate the tree
    tree.draw()

    //subscribe to the trees collapse event
    tree.subscribe("collapse", function(node) {

        //was the www node collapsed?
        if (node.data.id == "www") {

        //remove www child nodes
        tree.removeChildren(www);
      }
    });

}
```

Because the collapse event is a Tree event rather than a Node event, we have to determine whether or not it was the www node that was collapsed. This is achieved using the if conditional branch and the id member of the node's data object.

It is then just a case of calling the .removeChildren() method and specifying the node to remove the children from. Now the Tree will retrieve the directory contents afresh every time the www node is expanded.

Summary

The Button family of controls is a versatile replacement to the dusty old native HTML button element, providing enhanced features and functionality, wrapped up in an attractive and aesthetically appealing package.

The TreeView control is an important component of the library that creates an object with no analogous native counterpart. It creates a tree-like control which enables you to show the relationship between different objects in an intuitive and easy to use interface.

Both controls are backed up by rich and feature-packed classes which add the functionality and behavior that you'd expect from web design aids of the caliber found in the YUI.

7
Navigation and AutoComplete

In this chapter, we're going to look at two more very common web page elements: navigation menus and auto-complete text fields. Both of these widgets provide timesaving and code-efficient solutions to common website application requirements.

The skills that you will take away from this chapter include:

- How to implement a basic navigation menu
- How to override the default `sam` skin
- How to create an application style menu bar
- How to use the `ContextMenu` type
- How to implement an auto-complete text field linked to a live data source
- When the different types of data source should be used

Common Navigation Structures

All but the most limited of websites must have a mechanism by which visitors can navigate around the pages of the site from the home page. In order to meet accessibility guidelines, several methods of navigation will usually be available, including at least a navigation menu and a site map.

There have been many different implementation styles that have been popular over the years. Before anyone really worried about accessibility or standards compliance, a common way of designing a navigation menu was to use a series of images that linked to other pages of the site, and there was also the popular frame-based navigation structure. While these methods saved the designer a lot of time, effort, and any real skill, it led to hugely increased page load times and a legacy of bad coding practice.

Thankfully, these days have long since passed, and with the continued development of CSS, it's now possible to design an effective navigation structure based on semantic HTML and styled with CSS.

Designing a navigation menu that is effective, robust, and presented effectively can still pose a challenge however, and troubleshooting the compatibility of a menu between different browsers can be a very time-consuming process. This is where the YUI steps in.

Instant Menus—Just Add Water (or a Menu Control)

The Menu control is used to add one of several different menus to your web site, saving you the chore of adding this almost essential feature yourself. It's another control that takes a complex, difficult, or time consuming task, and one which is an almost inherent requirement of any website, and packages it up into a convenient and easy to use module. The three different types of menu you can create are:

- A standard navigation menu
- An application style menu bar
- A right-click contextmenu

The navigation menu can be implemented as either a vertical or horizontal menu and generates a clean and attractive interface which your visitors can use to navigate to different areas of your site. The navigation model of any site is key to whether using the site is easy and enjoyable; nothing turns off visitors more than a poorly designed or inconsistent navigation structure.

Another type of menu that the Menu control is able to create is an application style menu bar, which stretches across the screen horizontally, building on the current trend in the online world to blur the distinction between the browser and the desktop.

As well as taking care of navigation for you, it can also be used to add right-click context menus to any part of your web application, which again can give a web application a definite desktop feel to it.

The Menu control is very flexible and can be built from either underlying HTML using a clean and logical list structure, or it can be generated entirely through JavaScript and built at runtime. Each of the different menu types are also given a default appearance with the `sam` skin so there is very little that is required to generate the attractive and highly functional menus.

We'll be looking at implementing each of the different types of menu ourselves in just a moment. Before we do this, let's take a quick look at the classes that go together to make the Menu control.

The Menu Classes

This control, much like the button that we looked at earlier, is made up of a small family of different types of menu. There are a range of different classes that work together to bring the functionality of the different types of menu to you.

The three main classes behind the menu family are:

- `YAHOO.widget.Menu`
- `YAHOO.widget.ContextMenu`
- `YAHOO.widget.Menubar`

These classes are all subclasses of the Overlay class (the Overlay is a member of the Container family which we'll be looking at soon). Other classes that make up the Menu control and which are subclasses (by this I mean that they inherit properties and methods of the above classes) of the three classes above include:

- `YAHOO.widget.MenuItem`
- `YAHOO.widget.ContextMenuItem`
- `YAHOO.widget.MenuBarItem`
- `YAHOO.widget.MenuManager`

Many of the methods defined by the Menu class are private as well so we won't worry about them, and a large number of those that aren't private are event handlers. Useful methods that don't fit into either of the above categories include:

- `addItem`—appends a new, dynamically generated `MenuItem` to the existing menu
- `addItems`—adds an array of dynamically generated `MenuItems` to the existing menu
- `getItem`—returns the `MenuItem` at the specified index
- `getItemGroups`—returns a multidimensional array representing the `MenuItems` as they appear in the menu
- `getItems`—returns an array of all `MenuItems`
- `getRoot`—finds the root element of the menu

- `insertItem`—inserts a new `MenuItem` at the specified index
- `removeItem`—removes the specified `MenuItem`

Most of the components of the library are able to accept a literal object as an argument of their constructor. The parts of the API that will be used most frequently when implementing the Menu control will probably be the configuration attributes defined as members of this object. Attributes we can make use of include:

- `clicktohide`—a boolean indicating whether the menu will be hidden if the visitor clicks outside of it. Default is true
- `constrainviewport`—a boolean indicating whether the menu will try to remain inside the viewable area of the screen. Default is true
- `hidedelay`—the number of milliseconds that the menu should remain open after the user has moused out of it. Default is zero
- `maxheight`—maximum height of the menu before the contents are scrolled.
- `position`—indicates whether the menu should be static or dynamic (the two possible values). A static menu is visible by default and resides in the normal flow of the document. Dynamic menus are hidden by default and are outside the flow of the document, overlaying other elements if need be. Navigation menus are usually static, while context menus are dynamic
- `showdelay`—number of milliseconds the menu should wait before displaying when it is moused-over. Default is 250
- `submenuhidedelay`—same as `hidedelay` but for submenus. Default is 250
- `visible`—a boolean indicating whether the menu is visible

Menu Subclasses

The ContextMenu is a specialized version of the control that provides a menu hidden from view until the element that it is associated with, the trigger element, is clicked with the right mouse button (except in Opera on Windows and OS-X which requires the left-click + Ctrl key combination). The trigger element is defined using the `trigger` configuration attribute; this is the only configuration attribute natively defined by the `ContextMenu` class, all others are inherited.

The MenuBar is similar to the standard Menu, but is horizontal instead of vertical. It can behave like an application style menu bar, where the top-level menu items must be clicked in order for them to expand, or it can behave more like a web menu where the menu items expand on a simple mouse-over and have submenu indicators. This is controlled with the `autosubmenudisplay` boolean configuration attribute.

The MenuItem Class

Each menu type has a subclass representing the individual menu items that form choices within the menu. Individual menu items can be generated entirely through HTML and are created using the base mark up `<li>` or `<option>` elements when the Menu is instantiated.

This is fine for most basic implementations in most situations, but there may come a time when you need or want to create new menu items programmatically. The `MenuItem` class defines its own constructor specifically for this purpose.

The `YAHOO.widget.MenuItem` constructor is almost identical to that of the standard Menu but the first argument can take a couple of different types depending on your requirements; the first argument can be either a string representing the text of the MenuItem or it can be an object specifying the `<li>`, `<optgroup>`, or `<option>` element of the MenuItem. I shouldn't need to tell you that the second argument is the optional configuration object literal used to specify particular configuration attributes.

This class does not inherit any of its members so there are quite a few that are defined natively. Some of the properties defined by the `MenuItem` class which you will probably find most useful include:

- `browser` — the browser in use
- `element` — an object reference to the `MenuItems` `<li>` element
- `id` — the `id` attribute of the `MenuItems` root `<li>` element
- `srcElement` — the element the `MenuItem` has been created from
- `value` — an object reference to the value of the `MenuItem`

MenuItem Subclasses

The two subclasses `YAHOO.widget.ContextMenuItem` and `YAHOO.widget.MenuBarItem` both extend the `MenuItem` class, providing a constructor and some basic properties and methods for programmatically working with individual ContextMenu or MenuBar menu items.

Most of the members of these two classes are inherited, and very few members are defined natively. There are only one or two native properties and methods in each subclass. Neither class defines their own configuration attributes.

Creating a Basic Navigation Menu

Let's now put together a basic navigation menu and use some of those methods and properties that we looked at in the classes. Our menu will be built from underlying HTML rather than from script.

Since the `grids.css` tool that we looked at earlier in the book allows us to easily define a region of the page to be used to hold a navigation structure, we can make use of the tool in this example. The Yahoo! team also recommends using `font.css` with the Menu control, so we may as well use `reset-fonts-grids.css`.

For the purpose of this example, let's pretend that we're setting up a portfolio site for a freelance graphic designer. We don't need to do anything intricate, just a few pages will illustrate the power of the menu control. The additional pages we need to create can be simple pages with little or no content themselves.

Once complete, our navigation menu should appear like this:

The Initial HTML Page

Begin by adding the following basic HTML to a blank page in your text editor:

```
<!DOCTYPE HTML PUBLIC "-//W3C//DTD HTML 4.01//EN"
                             "http://www.w3.org/TR/html4/strict.dtd">
<html lang="en">
  <head>
    <meta http-equiv="content-type" content="text/html;
                                   charset=utf-8">
    <title>YUI Vertical Navigation Menu Example</title>
    <script type="text/javascript"
            src="yui/build/yahoo-dom-event/yahoo-dom-event.js">
    </script>
```

```
        <script type="text/javascript"
                src="yui/build/container/container_core-min.js"></script>
        <script type="text/javascript"
                src="yui/build/menu/menu-min.js"></script>
        <link rel="stylesheet" type="text/css"
              href="yui/build/assets/skins/sam/menu.css">
        <link rel="stylesheet" type="text/css"
              href="yui/build/reset-fonts-grids/reset-fonts-grids.css">
      </head>
      <body class="yui-skin-sam">
        <div id="doc" class="yui-t1">
          <div id="hd">
            <h1>DigitalDesigns</h1>
          </div>
          <div id="bd">
            <div class="yui-b">
            </div>
            <div id="yui-main">
              <div class="yui-b">
                <p class="content-head">Welcome to DigitalDesigns!
                                                          </p><br>
                <p>Lorum ipsum etc...</p><br>
                  <p>Lorum ipsum etc...</p>
              </div>
            </div>
          </div>
          <div id="ft">
            <p class="ftext">Copyright&copy; Mr Freelance 2007</p>
          </div>
        </div>
      </body>
    </html>
```

Our page <head> links to the required files; yahoo-dom-event.js is a must for this control, as is the source file menu-min.js. As the menu is a subclass of the Overlay, it is also dependant on the container_core-min.js file.

The appearance of the menu is controlled by the sam skin, so the skin file for the menu, menu.css, should also be included, and the <body> tag given the appropriate class attribute of yui-skin-sam.

Some of our page elements have class names, this is for presentational purposes later in the example. The remainder of the code above is the page layout and <div> nesting structure required for the CSS grid we are using for this example.

The Underlying Menu Mark Up

As I mentioned before, a Menu object can be created using pure JavaScript or HTML combined with JavaScript. There are different reasons for using each, but the main reason for relying on underlying mark up is for the SEO benefit.

We know that search engine spiders love links, and giving them a whole list of links in the first few lines of your code is guaranteed to please them! In the first yui-b <div>, add the following <div> and <ul> elements:

```
<div id="navmenu" class="yuimenu">
  <div class="bd">
    <ul class="first-of-type">
      <li class="yuimenuitem"><a class="yuimenuitemlabel"
          href="aboutme.html">About Me</a></li>
      <li class="yuimenuitem"><a class="yuimenuitemlabel"
          href="images.html">My Images</a></li>
      <li class="yuimenuitem"><a class="yuimenuitemlabel"
          href="blog.html">My Blog</a></li>
      <li class="yuimenuitem"><a class="yuimenuitemlabel"
          href="contact.html">Contact Me</a></li>
      <li class="yuimenuitem"><a class="yuimenuitemlabel"
          href="imagelinks.html">Image Resources</a></li>
    </ul>
  </div>
</div>
```

Our menu wouldn't be a proper navigation menu if there weren't, at least, a couple of submenus, it would just be a list of links. Let's add a couple of submenus now:

```
<div id="navmenu" class="yuimenu">
  <div class="bd">
    <ul class="first-of-type">
      <li class="yuimenuitem"><a class="yuimenuitemlabel"
          href="aboutme.html">About Me</a></li>
      <li class="yuimenuitem"><a class="yuimenuitemlabel"
          href="images.html">Images</a>
        <div id="images" class="yuimenu">
          <div class="bd">
            <ul>
              <li class="yuimenuitem"><a class="yuimenuitemlabel"
                  href="photography.html">Photography</a></li>
              <li class="yuimenuitem"><a class="yuimenuitemlabel"
                  href="fantasy.html">Fantasy Art</a></li>
              <li class="yuimenuitem"><a class="yuimenuitemlabel"
                  href="Corporate.html">Corporate Logos</a></li>
```

```
            </ul>
          </div>
        </div>
      </li>
      <li class="yuimenuitem"><a class="yuimenuitemlabel"
          href="blog.html">My Blog</a></li>
      <li class="yuimenuitem"><a class="yuimenuitemlabel"
          href="contact.html">Contact Me</a></li>
      <li class="yuimenuitem"><a class="yuimenuitemlabel"
          href="imagelinks.html">Image Resources</a>
        <div id="links" class="yuimenu">
          <div class="bd">
            <ul>
              <li class="yuimenuitem"><a class="yuimenuitemlabel"
                  href="http://www.flickr.com">Flickr</a></li>
              <li class="yuimenuitem"><a class="yuimenuitemlabel"
                  href="http://www.b3ta.com">B3ta</a></li>
              <li class="yuimenuitem"><a class="yuimenuitemlabel"
                  href="http://yotophoto.com">Yoto Photo</a></li>
            </ul>
          </div>
        </div>
      </li>
    </ul>
  </div>
</div>
```

The submenus take the same format as the top-level menu—an outer container `<div>` with a class of `yuimenu` forms the basis of the submenu, followed by an inner body `<div>`. Each submenu, like the overall Menu, is built from a standard unordered list (`<ul>`) element where each menu item is comprised of a single list item (`<li>`). The structure of the menu is very similar to that of the overall page because it has a distinct body section (`<div class="bd">`) and can also be given `hd` and `ft` sections if required.

Creating the Menu Object

Implementing a basic menu takes just a little bit of YUI-targeting JavaScript. You can add the following `<script>` block to the `<body>` of the page directly above the closing `</body>` tag:

```
<script type="text/javascript">
  //set up the namespace object for this example
  YAHOO.namespace("yuibook.menu");
```

```
    //define the initMenu function
    YAHOO.yuibook.menu.initMenu = function() {
      var menu = new YAHOO.widget.Menu("navmenu",
                                      { position:"static" });

      menu.render();
    }
    //call the initMenu function when the DOM is ready
    YAHOO.util.Event.onDOMReady(YAHOO.yuibook.menu.initMenu);
  </script>
```

The script consists of a very small function and the constructor. The `initMenu()` function first sets a variable which holds the Menu object created with the `YAHOO.widget.Menu` constructor. The constructor takes the `id` of the element that the menu should be constructed from, and a configuration object containing just one menu property—`position:"static"`.

There are many of these configuration properties that can be used to control the behavior of the Menu control, but the static positioning rule is the only one that is mandatory, and is required in order for the menu to function correctly.

The `.render()` method is then called on the object holding our menu instance, which is what actually draws the menu on the page. We call this function using the Event utility's `onContentReady` method so that the menu is created as soon as the `navmenu` element and its next sibling are detected in the DOM. Save this file as `menu.html` in your `yuisite` directory.

Styling the Page

Let's add some basic styling that will help to pick out and separate the different elements of our page and generally make it look a little better, it is supposed to be a portfolio site for a graphic designer after all!

We can still keep things relatively simple; a couple of background colors and some positional rules should be more than adequate. In a new file in your text editor, add the following selectors and rules:

```
#hd {
  height:80px;
  background:url(headbg.gif) repeat-x;
  border:2px solid #7fb0f1;
  margin-bottom:10px;
}
#hd h1 {
  margin:20px 10px;
  font-size:197%;
```

```
    font-weight:bold;
    color:#ffffff;
    text-align:right;
  }
  .content-head {
    font-size:153.9%;
  }
  #ft {
    height:40px;
    background:url(footbg.gif) repeat-x;
    border:2px solid #7fb0f1;
    margin-top:10px;
  }
  .ftext {
    margin:12px 10px;
    font-weight:bold;
    font-size:93%;
    color:#ffffff;
  }
```

Save this as `mymenu.css` in the `yuisite` directory. Don't forget to link to the CSS file using the following code in the `<head>` of the page:

```
<link rel="stylesheet" type="text/css" href="mymenu.css">
```

The new styles should format our page as shown below:

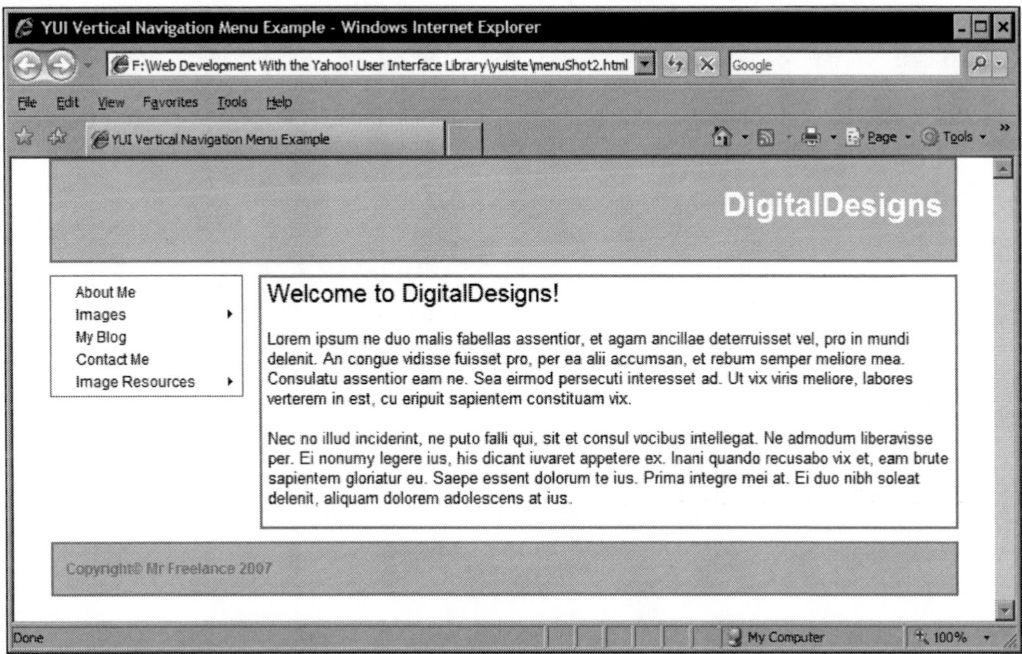

There is still more we can do however. You'll notice in the previous screenshot that our menu (and any subsequent submenus) is automatically given a black border. While this can look great in some situations, in our example it looks a little out of place. We need to override the default styling of the Menu object.

The default menu styles are controlled by the `sam` skin, which we are using in this implementation, so to change different aspects of the menu we just need to target the element accordingly:

```
.yui-skin-sam .yuimenu .bd {
  border:2px solid #579ffc;
}
```

Now the border for our menu matches that of the rest of the page, as you can see in the following screenshot:

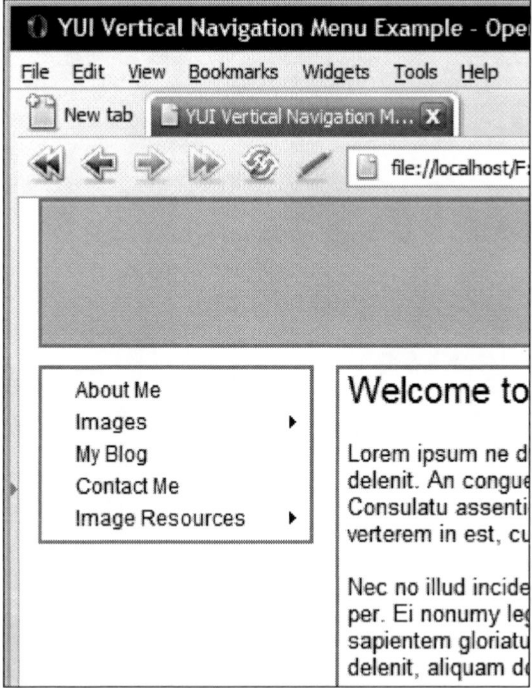

Using the ContextMenu

Let's move on to take a look at another menu type—the context, or right-click menu. The navigation menu on our portfolio site provides links to three different image pages. We can use one of these pages to showcase a series of thumbnail images and add right-click functionality to each thumbnail image.

The page that these thumbnail images will reside on can be structurally almost identical to the page that we've just created. Everything can be the same except for the content of the yui-main div.

Save another copy of menu.html, but this time rename it as fantasy.html. To display the images, the following code should be placed into the yui-b container, within the yui-main <div>, overwriting the existing *lorum-ipsom* design text:

```
<p class="content-head">Fantasy Art Images</p>
<div class="images">
  <img class="thumb" src="images/image1_thumb.jpg"
       title="Right-click for options
        (Opera users will need to use the Ctrl key + left-click)"
       alt="thumb1">
  <img class="thumb" src="images/image2_thumb.jpg"
       title="Right-click for options
        (Opera users will need to use the Ctrl key + left-click)"
       alt="thumb2">
</div>
```

We'll keep it simple and just use two images for this exercise. You'll need a couple of images of course in order to complete this part, which should be placed in your yuisite directory within a folder entitled images.

Some basic styling will also be required. Save a copy of mymenu.css, but rename it to fantasy.css. The following CSS can be added to the existing selectors and rules:

```
.images {
  margin:10px;
}
.thumb {
  margin-right:10px;
  border:1px solid #579ffc;
}
```

ContextMenu Scripting

Now for the JavaScript that will create our custom ContextMenu. This can be done entirely programmatically, without building on existing mark up (except for the images of course), making the contextmenu very easy and quick to implement.

The screenshot shows how the contextmenu should appear by the end of this example:

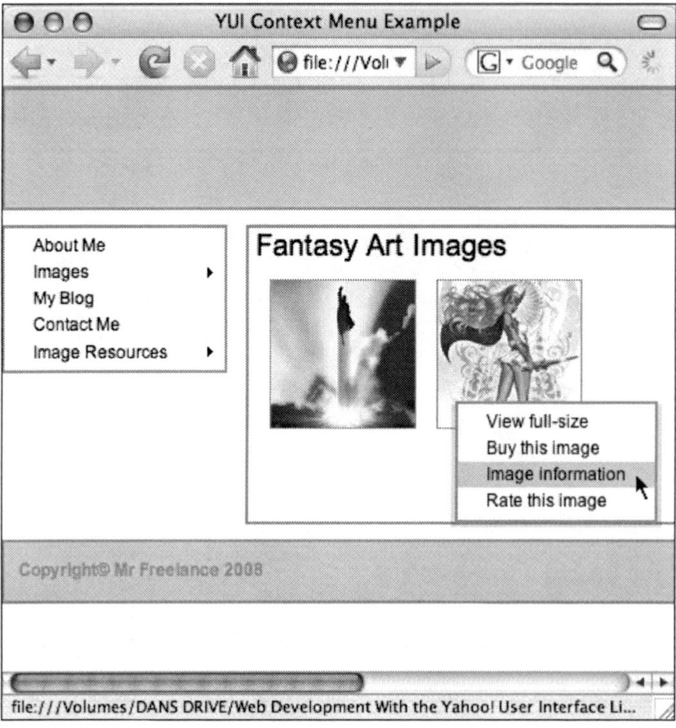

Add the following code to the existing `<script>` block near the bottom of the page. It will need to appear directly after the `.onDOMReady()` method:

```
//define the addContext function
YAHOO.yuibook.menu.addContext = function() {
  //obtain thumbnails from the page
  var images = YAHOO.util.Dom.getElementsByClassName("thumb");
  //use the context constructor to create a context menu
  var context = new YAHOO.widget.ContextMenu("imagecontext",
                                       { trigger: images });
  //define the context menuitems
  context.addItem("View full-size");
  context.addItem("Buy this image");
  context.addItem("Image information");
  context.addItem("Rate this image");
  //render the context menu (it will remain hidden until the
```

```
                                trigger is clicked)
    context.render(document.body);
    }

    //call the addContext function when the DOM is ready
    YAHOO.util.Event.onDOMReady(YAHOO.yuibook.menu.addContext);
```

We first obtain an array of all of the images on the page that have the class name `thumb` using the Dom utility's `.getElementsByClassName()` method. This array variable is then passed to the context menu constructor as the `ContextMenu` trigger.

The trigger is defined using a name:value pair that appears as a member of the literal configuration object and is the element (or in this case array of elements) upon which a right-click will trigger the display of our context menu.

The first argument of the constructor can be used to tell the script the `id` of the element holding the context menu items, but all of our items are added dynamically by script, so in this example the value of the first argument is given to the context menu as an `id` property.

The second argument of the constructor sets the trigger element. We've supplied the name of our image array, so each element in the array, and therefore each image on the page, has the trigger property attached to it and will display the context menu when it is right-clicked on

To add the menu items to our context menu, the `.addItem()` method is used. Once we have specified all of our items, the `.render()` method is used. This time however we need to tell the method where the context menu should be rendered to.

We've specified `document.body` in this example, so the context menu is appended to the body of the document. It is hidden by default and only displayed when it is triggered, and it is also repositioned so that it is displayed by the mouse pointer when it is shown on screen.

It's interesting to note that the default context menu supplied by the browser is completely replaced by our YUI context menu, which is a small step towards protecting the images from being downloaded if this is something that you wanted to do.

It's true that all one has to do to circumvent this is to switch off JavaScript in the browser, but another step that you could take would be to display the images using JavaScript as well, so if it is switched off the images themselves aren't even shown.

As you can see, the context menu has picked up the custom styling of our main navigation menu without any intervention from us. None of the menu items will actually do anything at this stage because we haven't wired in any additional functionality other than displaying the context menu itself.

Wiring Up the Backend

Adding functionality for the ContextMenu items is extremely easy. The first option in our contextmenu is to view a full size version of the thumbnail image. This could be easily accomplished using the Panel container (in fact, we can come back to this example when we look at the container family in more detail in the next chapter), but for the purpose of this example, we can just send out an alert.

Add the following function directly beneath the last function:

```
//define the viewFull function
YAHOO.yuibook.menu.viewFull = function() {
  alert("You chose the full view option!");
}
//execute viewFull when the first context menu item is clicked
YAHOO.util.Event.addListener("yui-gen11", "click",
                                        YAHOO.yuibook.menu.viewFull);
```

Now when the first ContextMenu item is selected, the alert will be produced. Other functions to cater from any other options that you wish to add can also be coded in this way to produce a fully working context menu.

Each of the menu items are automatically given an `id` attribute of `yui-gen` followed by a zero-based index number, just like a standard JavaScript array, so to refer to the second context menu item you would use `yui-gen12` and so on and so forth.

Note however, that this `id` may change depending on what other library components you have on your page. If this function doesn't work as expected, the best thing to do is use a DOM inspector to check the `id` that the context menu item has been assigned.

The Application-style MenuBar

The last member of the menu family is the menu bar, which creates a horizontal application style menu bar. Like both of the other menu types, the menu bar is exceptionally easy to create and work with.

For this example, we can create a basic user interface for a web-based text editor. Creating a fully working online application which can be used to create or open `.txt` files is beyond the scope of this chapter, but we can at least see how easy it would be to create the interface itself.

The page that we're going to finish up with should look like this:

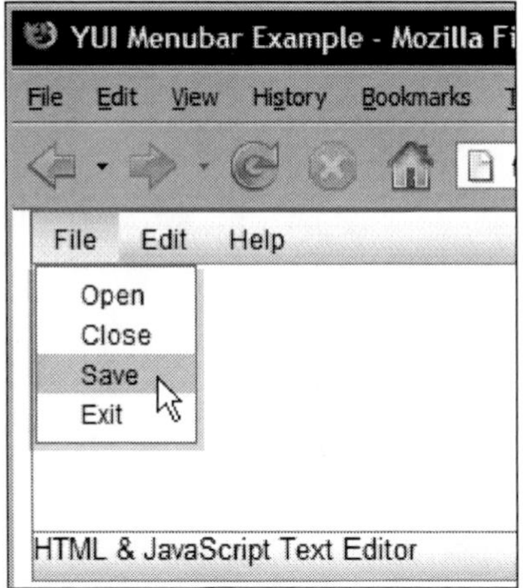

Start out with the following HTML in a blank page of your text editor:

```
<!DOCTYPE HTML PUBLIC "-//W3C//DTD HTML 4.01//EN"
                                "http://www.w3.org/TR/html4/strict.dtd">
<html lang="en">
  <head>
    <meta http-equiv="content-type" content="text/html;
                                                charset=utf-8">
    <title>YUI Menubar Example</title>
    <script type="text/javascript" src="yui/build/
                  yahoo-dom-event/yahoo-dom-event.js"></script>
    <script type="text/javascript"
            src="yui/build/container/container_core-min.js"></script>
    <script type="text/javascript"
            src="yui/build/menu/menu-min.js"></script>
    <link rel="stylesheet" type="text/css"
          href="yui/build/assets/skins/sam/menu.css">
    <link rel="stylesheet" type="text/css"
          href="yui/build/reset-fonts-grids/reset-fonts-grids.css">
  <body class="yui-skin-sam">
    <div id="doc">
      <div id="hd">
      </div>
      <div id="bd">
        <textarea class="ed"></textarea>
      </div>
      <div id="ft">
         HTML & JavaScript Text Editor v 1.0
    </div>
  </body>
</html>
```

The MenuBar can be created from underlying mark up. Add the mark up for it to the `hd` section of the page:

```
<div id="appmenu" class="yuimenubar">
          <div class="bd">
            <ul class="first-of-type">
              <li class="yuimenubaritem first-of-type">
                <a class="yuimenubaritemlabel" href="">File</a>
                <div id="file" class="yuimenu">
                  <div class="bd">
                    <ul>
                      <li class="yuimenuitem first-of-type">
                        <a class="yuimenuitemlabel"
                           href="">Open</a></li>
                      <li class="yuimenuitem">
                        <a class="yuimenuitemlabel"
                           href="">Close</a></li>
                      <li class="yuimenuitem">
                        <a class="yuimenuitemlabel"
                           href="">Save</a></li>
                      <li class="yuimenuitem">
                        <a class="yuimenuitemlabel"
                           href="">Exit</a></li>
                    </ul>
                  </div>
                </div>
              </li>
              <li class="yuimenubaritem">
                <a class="yuimenubaritemlabel" href="">Edit</a>
                <div id="edit" class="yuimenu">
                  <div class="bd">
                    <ul>
                      <li class="yuimenuitem">
                        <a class="yuimenuitemlabel"
                           href="">Cut</a></li>
                      <li class="yuimenuitem">
                        <a class="yuimenuitemlabel"
                           href="">Copy</a></li>
                      <li class="yuimenuitem">
                        <a class="yuimenuitemlabel"
                           href="">Paste</a></li>
                    </ul>
                  </div>
                </div>
              </li>
              <li class="yuimenubaritem">
```

```
                <a class="yuimenubaritemlabel"
                   href="test.html">Help</a>
                <div id="help" class="yuimenu">
                  <div class="bd">
                    <ul>
                      <li class="yuimenuitem">
                        <a class="yuimenuitemlabel"
                           href="about.html">About</a></li>
                      <li class="yuimenuitem">
                        <a class="yuimenuitemlabel"
                           href="help.html">Help</a></li>
                    </ul>
                  </div>
                </div>
              </li>
            </ul>
          </div>
        </div>
```

Structurally, it's exactly the same as the standard vertical navigation menu. All that's changed are the class names for the top-level menu items where `yuimenubar`, `yuimenubaritem`, and `yuimenubaritemlabel` are used instead of `yuimenu`, `yuimenuitem`, and `yuimenuitemlabel`.

Now let's add the JavaScript that will transform our mark up into an application style menu bar. We need to define a callback function that will generate the menu, as well as a handler to call this function.

Add the following `<script>` block to the `<body>` of the document directly after the underlying mark up for the MenuBar:

```
<script type="text/javascript">
  //set up the namespace object for this example
  YAHOO.namespace("yuibook.menu");
  //define the initmenu function
  YAHOO.yuibook.menu.initMenu = function() {
  //create the MenuBar object
  var menu = new YAHOO.widget.MenuBar("appmenu",
                                   { autosubmenudisplay: true });
  //draw the menu on screen
  menu.render();
  }
  //create the menubar object when the DOM is ready
  YAHOO.util.Event.onDOMReady(YAHOO.yuibook.menu.initMenu);
</script>
```

We specified another literal configuration object in the constructor for our MenuBar, this time making use of the `autosubmenudisplay` property. This means that the submenus on our MenuBar will automatically display when the mouse pointer hovers over them. Other configuration properties can be set in the same way.

Save the file in your `yuisite` folder as `textEditor.html` or similar and view it in a browser. At this point it should appear like this:

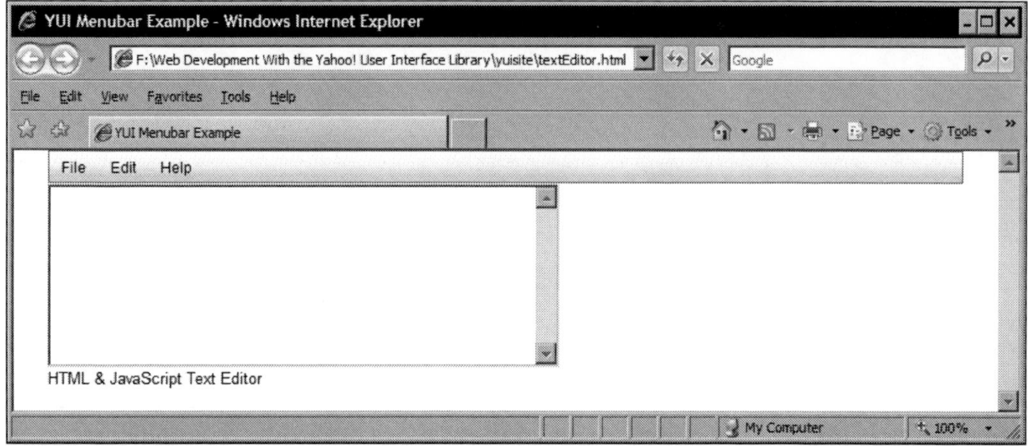

We need to tidy the page up a little, which we can do with the following CSS, which should be added to a blank page in your text editor:

```
.yui-skin-sam .ed {
  margin-top:-2px;
  width:748px;
  *width:749px;
  border:1px solid #7f9db9;
  height:200px;
  overflow:auto;
}
.yui-skin-sam #ft {
  margin-top:-2px;
  width:748px;
  *width:749px;
  border:1px solid #7f9db9;
  height:22px;
  background:url(yui/build/assets/skins/sam/sprite.png) repeat-x;
}
```

Save this new file as `texteditor.css` in your `yuisite` folder. These two selectors will style the page so that the `<textarea>` is a more reasonable size and so that the MenuBar and the footer sections all line up with the main body of the text editor. Again, don't forget to link to the CSS file in the usual way:

```
<link rel="stylesheet" type="text/css" href="texteditor.css">
```

The only striking rule in the above CSS is that we're making use of the `sam` skin's default background image for the MenuBar to style our footer section of the page. This is an efficient way to make the page design appear consistent. The screenshot shows how the page should look with the addition of the custom styling:

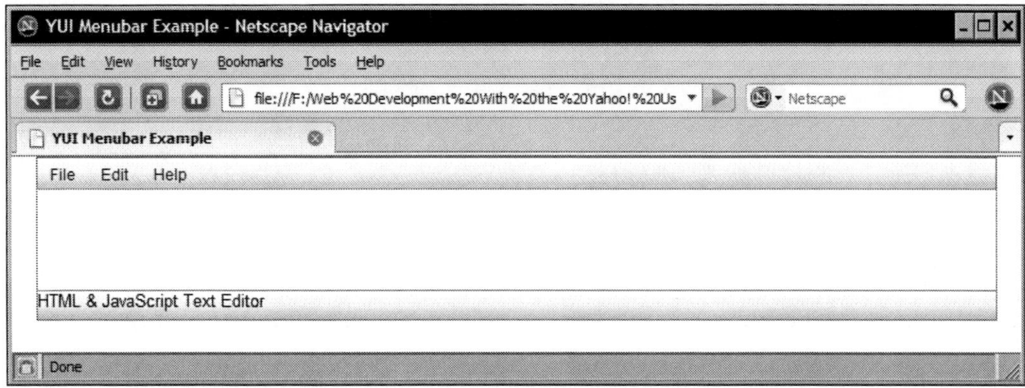

Look Ahead with the AutoComplete Control

The AutoComplete control allows you to add a useful typing suggestion facility that presents a drop-down list which holds suggested words when a visitor types into a text field. It's just the front-end, so you'll need to consume third party web services or construct your own back-end data source which the suggestion engine receives data from.

The screenshot shows an example of an AutoComplete control that has been interacted with in this way:

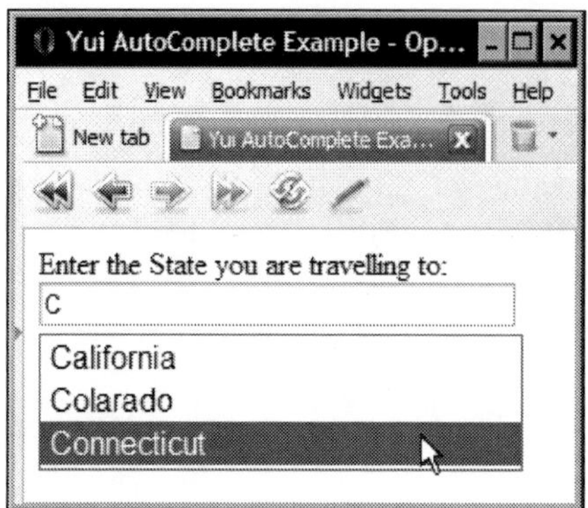

AutoComplete Components

There are several different components that go together to make up an AutoComplete instance. The control is built from underlying HTML based on a standard text `<input>` element. An empty container element is also required by the control, which will be used to display the suggestions returned by the control.

A DataSource object is also required, which is where the suggestions for the AutoComplete are returned from. There are currently four different types of DataSource that may be used with the AutoComplete control (although this list may grow in time):

- DS_JSArray—Live data returned as strings from an array
- DS_JSFunction—Live data returned as strings from a function
- DS_ScriptNode—Live data returned as JSON via the Get utility
- DS_XHR—Live data returned via the Connection Manager utility

Each data source has their pros and cons and your specific requirements will dictate which DataSource is best suited to the task at hand. Overall, JavaScript arrays or functions are useful for working with smaller datasets and tend to show the suggestions returned from the data source quicker, while XHR is better able to manage larger datasets returned from a database on the server.

Each type of DataSource, as well as the AutoComplete object itself are generated using their respective constructors. Let's have a quick look at each constructor in a little more detail.

The Constructors

Each of the classes of the AutoComplete control has their own constructors which are used to instantiate each of the different components needed to build a working AutoComplete object.

The `YAHOO.widget.AutoComplete` constructor takes up to four arguments: the first is the HTML input element that the AutoComplete control is associated with and can be either an `id` string or DOM reference, the second is the container element to be used to house the suggestions and again can be either an `id` string or DOM reference, the third argument is a reference to a DataSource instance and the fourth, optional argument is an object literal containing configuration parameters.

While the `YAHOO.widget.DataSource` class does have a constructor defined, it does not need to be instantiated manually by you in your scripts. One of its three subclasses is instantiated instead, depending on the requirements of your application.

Each of the request-type subclasses has their own constructor as well, with varying arguments depending on the request. `YAHOO.widget.DS_JSArray` and `YAHOO.widget.DS_JSFunction` have almost identical constructors; they both take either name of the array or the name of the function that holds the data as their first argument, and an optional configuration object as the second.

The `YAHOO.widget.DS_XHR` and `YAHOO.widget.DS_ScriptNode` are also very similar to each other. These constructors differ from the first two in that they take a different set of arguments: the first argument is the name of the script that returns the data, the second argument is the data schema definition of the set of results, and the third argument is again an optional configuration object.

Custom Styling and Visual Impact

It is very easy to change the style of your AutoComplete suggestion `<div>` as well, so you can specify a different highlight color for when results are navigated by the visitor and whether or not the first result is automatically highlighted. You can also easily add a tasty looking drop-shadow to the `<div>` when it is open or even set different highlight colors depending on whether the mouse or keyboard is used to navigate through the results.

To add flair to your AutoComplete, you can choose to animate the opening transition of the suggestion `<div>` populated by the AutoComplete and create a roll-down vertical effect, or a fly-out horizontal effect. You'll need to include a reference to the Animation utility to achieve these effects.

A Rich Event Portfolio

The AutoComplete control provides two distinct packages of events. The first set, defined as members of the `YAHOO.widget.AutoComplete` class provide custom events that handle the following interactions:

- itemArrowFromEvent
- itemArrowToEvent
- itemMouseOutEvent
- itemMouseOverEvent
- itemSelectEvent
- textBoxBlurEvent
- textBoxFocusEvent
- textBoxKeyEvent

All of these fire when the user does something either in the text box that the control is associated with, or the results `<div>` containing the suggestions. Most of them should be completely clear, but for the record the arrow events correspond to the arrow keys on a keyboard being used to navigate the suggestions in the results `<div>` instead of the mouse.

Along with these interaction events, there are also several execution events, including events that mark when the suggestions `<div>` collapses or expands, when query results are not received due to an error, when data is requested and when it is received, or when the input field is pre-filled as a result of the `typeAhead` feature.

The second package of events consists of members of the `YAHOO.widget.DataSource` class and like most of the properties and methods defined by the DataSource classes, they are inherited by the three DataSource subclasses.

The events defined by this class are:

- cacheFlushEvent
- cacheQueryEvent
- dataErrorEvent
- getCachedResultsEvent
- getResultsEvent
- queryEvent

Implementing AutoComplete

Let's jump straight into the coding with no further ado. Our page layout for this example can be very simple, we don't even need to make use of one of the `grids.css` layout templates, although we will be making use of the `sam` skin once again to add the basic styling of the results `<div>`.

First of all, let's focus on a basic implementation—a store search box which AutoComplete's the names of the companies whose products the store sells. Begin with the following HTML in a new file in your trusty text editor:

```
<!DOCTYPE HTML PUBLIC "-//W3C//DTD HTML 4.01//EN"
                          "http://www.w3.org/TR/html4/strict.dtd">
<html lang="en">
  <head>
    <meta http-equiv="content-type" content="text/html;
                                     charset=utf-8">
    <title>Yui AutoComplete Example</title>
    <script type="text/javascript"
            src="yui/build/yahoo-dom-event/yahoo-dom-event.js">
    </script>
    <script type="text/javascript"
            src="yui/build/autocomplete/autocomplete-min.js">
    </script>
    <link type="text/css" rel="stylesheet"
          href="yui/build/assets/skins/sam/autocomplete.css">
  </head>
  <body class="yui-skin-sam">
    <div id="companySearch">
      <input id="searchBox" type="text">
      <div id="suggestionContainer"></div>
    </div>
  </body>
</html>
```

As you can see from the above code, only a minimal amount of mark up is required for the basic AutoComplete. We have just an outer container `<div>` within which resides a standard `<input>` element and a second, empty `<div>` element.

The standard `<input>` control will be transformed by the YUI into a fully functional AutoComplete control, which is why we have given it an `id`. The second `<div>` element will hold the suggestion entries returned by the AutoComplete object.

Now we just need a few lines of code and we're away. There are at least two objects that need to be created for any AutoComplete implementation, one is the AutoComplete control itself and the other is the DataSource.

Our live data source will be relatively small in this example and so can be stored as a JavaScript array and pulled in to the AutoComplete object at runtime. Please remember that the following code would normally be placed into a JavaScript file of its own rather than being placed directly in the page, that way it could be shared between AutoComplete controls on separate pages and would reduce the overall size of this page.

Add the following JavaScript code directly above the closing `</body>` tag of the document:

```
<script type="text/javascript">
  //set up the namespace for this example
  YAHOO.namespace("yuibook.autoComp");
  //define our live data
  var companyData = [
    "amd", "asus", "belkin", "benq", "coolermaster", "corsair",
    "d-link", "dfi", "elpida", "enermax", "foxconn", "fujitsu",
    "gainward", "gigabyte", "hitachi", "hp", "intel", "infineon",
    "jbl", "keyscan", "kingston", "labtec", "logitech", "leadtek",
    "microsoft", "msi", "nec", "nvidia", "origen", "ocz", "patriot",
    "pny", "qimonda", "qtec", "razer", "realtec", "s3", "sony",
    "thermaltake", "trust", "umax", "us robotics", "via", "viewsonic",
    "western digital", "winfast", "xfx", "xg", "yamaha", "yukon",
    "zalman", "zoom"
  ];
  //define the initAutoComp function
  YAHOO.yuibook.autoComp.initAutoComp = function() {
    //define the datasource object
    var dataSource = new YAHOO.widget.DS_JSArray(companyData);
    //define the AutoComplete object
    var autoComp = new YAHOO.widget.AutoComplete("searchBox",
                              "suggestionContainer", dataSource);
  }
    //execute the initAutoComp function when the DOM is ready
    YAHOO.util.Event.onDOMReady(YAHOO.yuibook.autoComp.initAutoComp);
</script>
```

Once we've setup the namespace object for this example, the first thing we do is define our dataset, which in this example is a simple array.

The code that generates the AutoComplete instance is wrapped in the `initAutoComp()` function so that we can easily create the required objects using the `.onDOMReady()` method.

As our data is held in an array, we create a new `DS_JSArray` object, passing in the name of the array as an argument. We then create a new AutoComplete object specifying following arguments:

- The `id` of the element to turn into the AutoComplete control
- The `id` of the empty `<div>` used to display the results
- The name of the DataSource object

Save the page as `autocomplete.html` in your `yuisite` folder. If you run the page in your browser and type the letter **a** you should have something identical to the screenshot below:

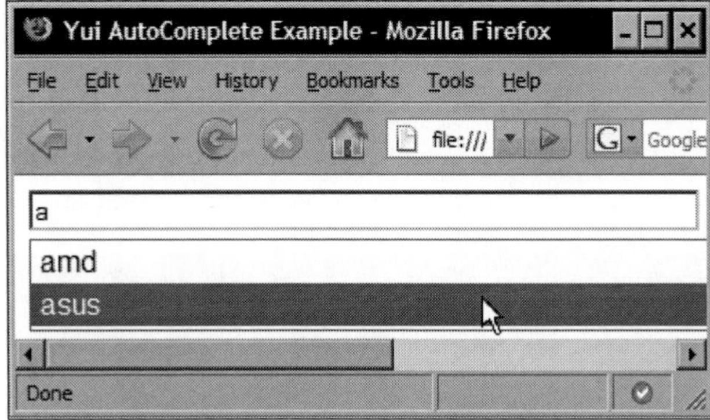

Adding Bling to Your AutoComplete

You have a range of options to consider when adding effects to your AutoComplete implementation including animations provided by the Animation utility, as well as some general settings of the AutoComplete control itself that can be adjusted.

Using the Animation utility is as simple as including a reference to it in the `<head>` of your page directly above the `<script>` tag linking to the `autocomplete-min.js` file:

```
<script type="text/javascript"
        src="yui/build/animation/animation-min.js"></script>
```

If the animation utility is linked to in this manner, the AutoComplete control will automatically animate the results `<div>` vertically with no additional configuration.

To animate the results horizontally, the following line of code should be added to the `initAutoComp()` function directly below the `autoComp` object definition:

```
//enable animation
autoComp.animhoriz = true;
```

Another nice effect that you can make use of is the drop-shadow and again, all it takes is the switch of a single object property to invoke. Set the following property directly after the animation property we just set:

```
//enable drop-shadow
autoComp.useShadow = true;
```

That's all you need to do (the documentation recommends that you define a CSS class called `.yui-ac-shadow` in order to enable the shadow, but if you look in the `autocomplete.css` skin file, you'll see that this class already exists). The screenshot below shows the results of these two properties:

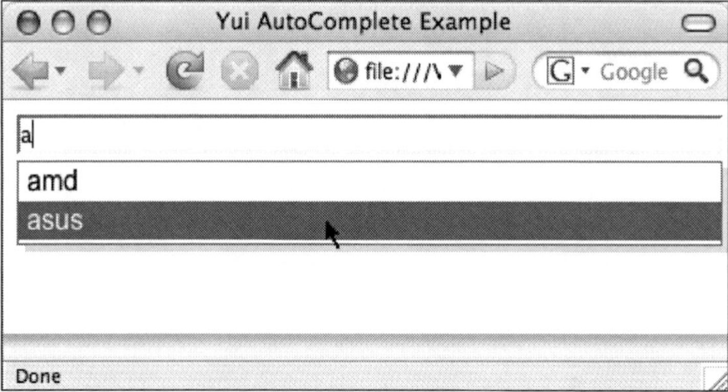

In addition to the properties we have looked at, there are others which let you control things. For example, you can control whether the first suggestion is highlighted in the results `<div>`, the minimum number of letters that should be typed before the suggestions `<div>` is displayed, and the delay between the visitor typing into the `<input>` and the suggestions being displayed among other things.

Working With Other DataSources

We saw how easy it was to work with an in-line JavaScript array as the DataSource connected to the AutoComplete control. While this method is fine for smaller data sets, the bigger the data set gets, the less efficient this method becomes.

There were 52 items in our example array earlier in the chapter, not a great deal in the grand scheme of things, but I think that any more than this would be pushing it a bit in terms of processing requirements (remember, we'll be running this example on a local test server and don't need to worry about other factors that may affect performance on the Internet). So what happens when you want to work with larger data sets?

For this next part of the tutorial, we'll use data stored in a mySQL database which we'll interact with using PHP over an `XMLHttpRequest` via the Connection Manager utility. Let's say that an `<input>` field is asking a visitor to select their country of origin and the suggestion `<div>` will receive the list of suggested countries as flat text data returned by a PHP file.

This book isn't an introduction to the language of PHP or mySQL and relational databases, so I'm going to assume that you know how to install a web server such as Apache (or Microsoft's IIS), and then install PHP and mySQL, as well as configure them all, and create and populate a mySQL database.

Installing the required components is very easy, and I will show you the basic PHP code used to query the database and produce and return the response data though so that you can better understand the mechanics of the whole process.

Bring on the Data

We'll create a new web page for this example. Begin with the following HTML in a new page in your text editor:

```
<!DOCTYPE HTML PUBLIC "-//W3C//DTD HTML 4.01//EN"
                              "http://www.w3.org/TR/html4/strict.dtd">
<html lang="en">
  <head>
    <meta http-equiv="content-type" content="text/html;
                                     charset=utf-8">
    <title>Yui AutoComplete Example 2</title>
    <script type="text/javascript"
            src="yui/build/yahoo-dom-event/yahoo-dom-event.js">
    </script>
    <script type="text/javascript"
            src="yui/build/connection/connection-min.js">
    </script>
    <script type="text/javascript"
            src="yui/build/autocomplete/autocomplete-min.js">
    </script>
    <link type="text/css" rel="stylesheet"
          href="yui/build/assets/skins/sam/autocomplete.css">
  </head>
  <body class="yui-skin-sam">
```

```
    <div id="countrySearch">
      Enter your country of origin: <input id="countryBox"
                                            type="text">
      <div id="suggestionContainer"></div>
    </div>
  </body>
</html>
```

Everything is pretty much the same so far as it was in the previous example. The files linked to are exactly the same except this time we link to the `connection-min.js` file as well. Structurally, the page is also practically identical.

Next add the following `<script>` block to the `<body>` of the page, directly below the final closing `</div>` tag:

```
<script type="text/javascript">
  //setup the namespace object for this example
  YAHOO.namespace("yuibook.autoComp");
  //define the initXHRAutoComp function
  YAHOO.yuibook.autoComp.initXHRAutoComp = function() {
  //define our external datasource
  var dataSource = new YAHOO.widget.DS_XHR("getCountries_flat.php",
                                          ["\n"]);
  //define the responseType property
  dataSource.responseType = YAHOO.widget.DS_XHR.TYPE_FLAT;
  //define the AutoComplete object
  var autoComp = new YAHOO.widget.AutoComplete("countryBox",
                                "suggestionContainer", dataSource);
      }
  //execute the initXHRAutoComp function when the DOM is ready
  YAHOO.util.Event.onDOMReady(YAHOO.yuibook.autoComp.initXHRAutoComp);
</script>
```

We use the `YAHOO.widget.DS_XHR` constructor to create the DataSource object this time, specifying the remote application that will pass back our data, and a schema used to map the data returned into array items that our AutoComplete instance can use.

The PHP file (which we'll create next) uses the newline character `\n` to separate the plain text entries of the suggestions, so this is the character we specify in our schema. The `responseType` property tells the control which type of data will be returned, since it is plain text we use the `YAHOO.widget.DS_XHR.TYPE_FLAT` data type.

Save this page as `autoComplete_flat.html`. This file will need to go into a content-serving directory that your web server has access to (don't forget to place a copy of the library in the same folder too).

Now for Some PHP

The PHP file consists of the following server-side scripting code (please note that this is the minimum amount of required code, there is probably much more that could be done including security and error checking):

```
<?php
  /* connection information */
  $host = "localhost";
  $user = "root";
  $password = "yourpasswordhere";
  $database = "mydata";
  /* make connection */
  $server = mysql_connect($host, $user, $password);
  $connection = mysql_select_db($database, $server);
  /* get querystring parameter */
  $param = $_GET['query'];
  /*protect from sql injections */
  mysql_real_escape_string($param, $server);
  /* query the database */
  $query = mysql_query("SELECT * FROM countries WHERE country LIKE
                      '$param%'");
  /* loop through and return matching entries */
  for ($x = 0; $x < mysql_num_rows($query); $x++) {
    $row = mysql_fetch_assoc($query);
    $output = $row['country']."\n";
    echo $output;
  }
  mysql_close($server);
?>
```

We first create a series of variables that represent the information we need to connect to the mySQL server, and then we make the connection to the server. Next we pull the data out of the database table and write each record back, followed by the newline character referred to by the schema in our HTML file.

The `DS_XHR` object sends a parameter to the server program using the query string. We can obtain this using the `$_GET` superglobal variable (because it's a `GET` request as opposed to a `POST` request).

We then use this to obtain matching items from the mySQL database. So if a 'z' is typed into the AutoComplete control, only items beginning with 'z' will be extracted from the database.

If you've got your web server setup, place all of the required files (the PHP file, the HTML page, and all of the necessary YUI files) into the directory it serves content from and give the page a try. You should see something like that shown in the screenshot when the **u** character is typed into the AutoComplete control.

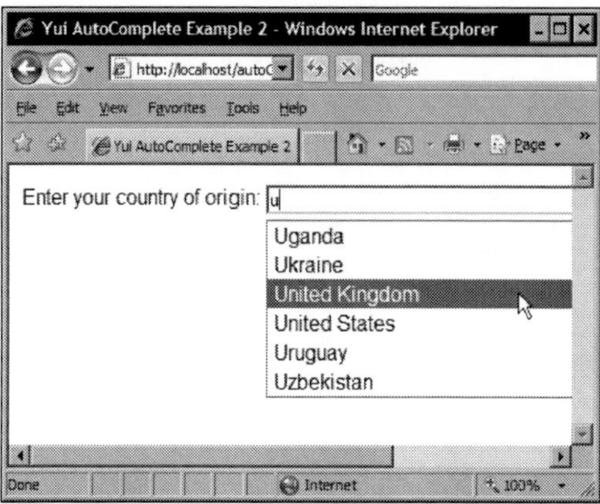

Using XHR in conjunction with some kind of database allows you to work with much larger data sets and there are a range of different configurations involving the cache and the number of results returned which allow you to fine tune your specific setup for maximum performance.

This example depends heavily on having the correct web server setup. You'll also need to request the page correctly in the first place. If you try to open the file by simply double-clicking it, you'll get a JavaScript error stating that **The required resource could not be contacted**. Instead, you need to request the page from the server by typing its full address in the address bar of your browser, which will be something like **http://localhost/autoComplete_flat.html**.

Summary

The menu control is a versatile and easy to use control which you'll probably want to implement in many of your web creations. As we've seen, there are three distinct menu types: the standard vertical or horizontal navigation menu, the right-click context menu, and the application style menu bar. Customizing these different types of menu is as easy as overriding the default styling if you don't want to stick with the standard skin.

The AutoComplete control has a better defined niche to cater for, but it's just as easy to add to any web forms or text inputs featured on your site or application. The functionality provided by this control is fantastic, and with a range of data types to play with, it should stand up to almost anything you throw at it.

8
Content Containers and Tabs

Content can live in all kinds of containers, usually `<div>`'s, `<p>`'s, and the like. When using the YUI you have a whole range of new containers in which to keep your content, each of which is designed to meet the needs of a specific implementation. In this chapter we'll be looking at all of them in detail.

A tabbed interface allows you to fit more content together on the same page without cluttering it up, distributing related items across different tabs. Doing this manually can lead to design nightmares, so the TabView control from the YUI library can really help you to cut corners code-wise without sacrificing presentational style or functionality.

While the Container and TabView controls are completely separate, tabs can still be looked upon as content containers, which is why these two controls have been included together in this chapter.

Skills that you will take away from this chapter include:

- The primary purpose of each of the different types of container
- How to implement each container
- Skinning the different containers
- Adding transition animations to applicable containers
- The different methods of adding tabbed content
- Adding content to tabs dynamically

Meet the YUI Container Family

The Container control is not in itself a control, but rather a family of container-like controls that can add visual appeal and enhancements to any web page or application. The Container family has been created in order to allow you to easily create different types of content containers which each serve a specific purpose.

The Container family is split up into six different individual containers; two of these form the core containers and can be used with the smaller `container_core-min.js` library file. The remaining four containers are built upon these and add additional properties, methods, and events specific to the functionality they provide. These require the full `container-min.js` file in order to function.

The different types of container available are:

- Module
- Overlay
- Panel
- Dialog
- SimpleDialog
- Tooltip

The following figure shows a visual representation of the structure of the Container family, the arrows indicate the direction of inheritance:

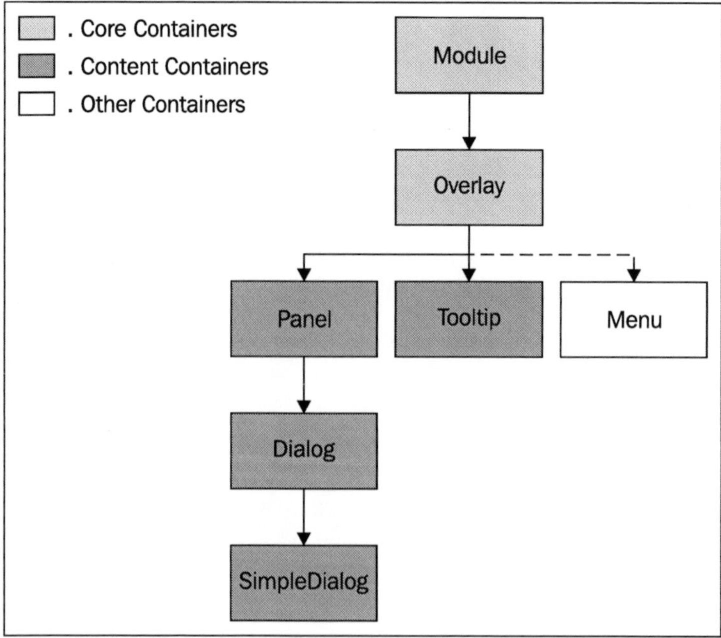

Let's now look at each member of the Container family in greater detail.

Module

Module is the fundamental unit and base class of all the Container classes, and is the foundation from which all of the other containers are derived from. Modules can be defined either in your HTML mark up or exclusively through JavaScript. They enable you to create a JavaScript object representation of any HTML container defined using Standard Module Format (SMF).

SMF, a Yahoo! standard for defining blocks of content, consists of a container `<div>` element and three child `<div>` elements which correspond to the header, body, and footer of the module. Many components of the library use SMF (think of the Menu objects from the last chapter and even the overall page structure advocated by Yahoo!, which we examined in detail when looking at the CSS tools).

The `YAHOO.widget.Module()` constructor, used to create the most basic type of containers, is very simple and takes just two arguments: a string representing the `id` of the module or an element reference pointing to the module, and an optional configuration object used to set different properties of the module. The configuration object can take the following properties:

- `visible`—a boolean indicating whether the Module's display property is set to 'block' or 'none'
- `monitorresize`—another boolean which indicates whether to create a hidden element that monitors for text size changes made by the visitor
- `effect`—an object or array of objects used to specify either fade or slide effects during animation

The module class also defines a rich set of properties, method, and events, most of which are also passed on to the subclasses. Some of the properties include references to the different sections making up a module, which allow you to get the content of each section programmatically:

- `header`
- `body`
- `footer`

Other properties deal with the browsing environment:

- `browser`
- `platform`
- `id`
- `isSecure`

Most of the properties defined in the `YAHOO.widget.Module` class are inherited by each of the subclasses.

A wide range of methods are also defined in the Module base class, including:

- `.appendToHeader()`
- `.appendToBody()`
- `.appendToFooter()`
- `.setHeader()`
- `.setBody()`
- `.setFooter()`

Other methods deal with the visibility of Containers, such as:

- `.destroy()`
- `.hide()`
- `.show()`
- `.render()`

The `.render()` method is especially important, as this is the method that you will call in your code in order to generate the container.

If your module is defined in your HTML mark up, the method is called without the need for any arguments. If creating the module via script, the argument you must supply refers to the node in the DOM to which the module will be appended to, and can be either a string or an element reference.

Overlay

An Overlay is very similar to a Module except that it is absolutely positioned above the flow of the page. It extends the Module class, and while it inherits most of Module's properties, it also defines a few of its own, most of which are used to align the Overlay such as:

- `YAHOO.widget.Overlay.TOP_LEFT`
- `YAHOO.widget.Overlay.TOP_RIGHT`
- `YAHOO.widget.Overlay.BOTTOM_LEFT`
- `YAHOO.widget.Overlay.BOTTOM_RIGHT`

A wide range of methods are defined as members of the Overlay class, most of which are event handlers that fire when different things take place, such as when different positional properties are changed, when the window is resized or when the window is scrolled.

The most interesting aspects of the Overlay class are the additional configuration attributes that it defines, giving you much more control over this type of Container. Properties that you are able to use in conjunction with a literal configuration object when using the `YAHOO.widget.Overlay()` constructor include:

- `constrainviewport` — a boolean that controls whether the overlay should be prevented from being positioned outside of the viewport. The default is false
- `context` — an array of arguments used to anchor a specific corner of an overlay to a specific corner of the anchor element
- `fixedcenter` — a boolean that anchors the overlay to the center of the viewport
- `height` and `width` — the dimensions of the overlay
- `x` and `y` — the absolute coordinates of the overlay
- `xy` — an array of the absolute X and Y positions of the overlay
- `iframe` — a boolean indicating whether the overlay should have a protective shim to cushion it from select elements in IE6 and below. This attribute is true if the browser is IE6 or below and false if not
- `zindex` — the CSS z-index of the overlay

Overlay also inherits the three configuration attributes defined by the Module class.

Panel

The `YAHOO.widget.Panel` class extends the Overlay class, and allows you to create a floating container which acts very much like an operating system window, allowing your visitors to drag it around or close it at will. It also adds support for modality to the Overlay.

Unlike the previous two containers that we have looked at so far, the Panel comes with pre-defined styling which is controlled by the `sam` skin and creates a default appearance for Panel elements.

The Panel Container inherits far more properties than are defined in its own class; just four of them are native and two of those are private and are used internally by the control. The two properties that are not private are constants and you probably won't need to use them in most implementations.

Most of the methods available to the Panel are also inherited and those that aren't are mostly event handlers that deal with events specific to the Panel. The two methods that you'll probably use most often are:

- `.destroy()` — this removes the Panel from the DOM and sets all of its child nodes to null
- `.render()` — this initially creates the Panel, using either underlying mark up from the page, or content defined by script

An excellent feature of the Panel is its modal capabilities. When the modal attribute is set, the Panel causes a semi-transparent mask to obscure the body of the document until the Panel has been closed.

Like the other Container elements, the Panel defines its own set of configuration attributes including:

- `close` — a boolean indicating whether a close button should be displayed on the Panel
- `draggable` — another boolean, indicating whether the Panel should be draggable. If the Drag-and-Drop utility is included, this defaults to true, otherwise it defaults to false
- `keylisteners` — this attribute makes use of the `YAHOO.util.KeyListener` class to specify a keypress (or array of keypresses) which the Panel should listen for. The keylistener(s) is enabled when the Panel is opened and disabled when it closes
- `modal` — this boolean dictates whether the Panel should be modal or not. Modality behavior requires a user response such as **ok** or **cancel** before the Panel can be closed
- `underlay` — a string which sets the type of underlay to use for the panel. Your options are `shadow`, `matte` or `none`, with `shadow` being the default

Tooltip

The Tooltip Container is a highly specialized control that generates a Tooltip object that is displayed when the visitor mouses-over a specified element on the page, just like a standard browser tooltip. Like the Panel, the Tooltip class extends the Overlay class, inheriting many of its members, while also adding a few more of its own.

This container is designed to be very easy to implement and configure and therefore requires a minimal amount of code. The `YAHOO.widget.Tooltip()` constructor is required of course, but like the other Container elements, it's very simple to use and takes just two arguments. These are the `id` of the element or an element reference to make the Tooltip from, and an optional configuration object.

There are few default properties and a large range of methods defined by the Tooltip class, but because the Tooltip is so specialized, you'll rarely need anything other than the methods that are inherited all the way from the basic Module class, such as `.setBody()`.

One striking difference between the Tooltip control and the other Containers is that you don't need to call the render method to generate the Tooltip(s) you use on your page. The Tooltip is automatically rendered in an invisible state when the page loads and is then ready to appear as soon as the visitor hovers over the Tooltip's context element (the element the Tooltip is attached to) with the pointer.

As with the preceding Containers, the section of the class that you'll be exposed to most often when working with Tooltip controls is the configuration attributes specific to this Container. The Tooltip class defines the following configuration attributes:

- `text` — a string representing the text displayed in the Tooltip
- `context` — a string or element reference specifying the element or elements that the Tooltip should be anchored to
- `container` — a string element reference specifying the container element that the Tooltip should be rendered into
- `preventoverlap` — a boolean which specifies whether the Tooltip should be prevented from overlapping its context element. The default is true
- `showdelay` — a number specifying the number of milliseconds the Tooltip should wait before appearing on a mouse-over of the context element. The default is 200
- `hidedelay` — a number specifying the number of milliseconds to wait before hiding a Tooltip after its context element has been moused-over. The default is 250
- `autodismissdelay` — the number of milliseconds the Tooltip should wait before dismissing the Tooltip after the mouse has been resting on the context element. The default is 5000

Like the Panel, the Tooltip has a default CSS skin file, controlled by the `sam` skin, to give it its attractive appearance.

Dialog

The Dialog Control extends the Panel, and the primary difference between the two is that the Dialog must be used to submit data, much like an operating system prompt. To facilitate this you can either include a form in your mark up, or the control will generate one automatically for you.

You can create the Dialog using SMF in your HTML mark up, or create and configure it via script. The `YAHOO.widget.Dialog` class provides a range of properties, methods, and configuration attributes that make it easy to create an array of button objects which the visitor can use to cancel or submit the dialog.

Dialog also allows you to submit the data that it has collected from the visitor using one of three methods: the standard form submission method which relies on the `action` attribute of your HTML form, via XHR using the Connection Manager utility (which also uses the `action` attribute), or by using no submission method, whereby additional code in your script detects and responds to the submitted data.

You have many methods available to make use of when programming the Dialog. It inherits a large number of them from the superclass chain, but it also defines quite a number of them natively. Some of the methods that you may find yourself using most include:

- `.cancel()` — cancels the dialog without submitting data
- `.doSubmit()` — submits the data captured in the form
- `.focusDefaultButton()` — sets the focus to the button designated as the default button. A button object is defined as the default button with the `isDefault` attribute
- `.focusFirstButton()` — sets the focus to the first button object
- `.focusLast()` — sets the focus to the last button object
- `.getData()` — returns the data captured by the form in a JSON compatible data structure
- `.submit()` — submits the form data using the specified submission method and hides the dialog
- `.validate()` — allows you to perform validation, if required, on the data submitted by the visitor

Inheritance is also the method by which this control obtains most of its custom events, but it still defines a few of its own including:

- `asyncSubmitEvent` — this is fired prior to the data being submitted using XHR
- `formSubmitEvent` — this occurs with form-based submission
- `manualSubmitEvent` — this notifies you of a manual submission

You can also pinpoint the moments before and after a submission, or detect the dialog being cancelled with:

- `beforeSubmitEvent`
- `submitEvent`
- `cancelEvent`

Dialog also defines the `buttons` configuration attribute which refers to the button objects used on your Dialog. This is an object literal with three members:

- `text`—provides the label for the button.
- `handler`—specifies the handler which will react to the button being clicked.
- `isDefault`—controls whether the button is focused by default.

SimpleDialog

The `YAHOO.widget.SimpleDialog` class extends the Dialog class and forms the last link in the subclass chain. It is designed to be used in circumstances where input is required from the visitor, but only in the form of a single answer, such as a simple **yes** or **no**.

You don't need to define it using HTML mark up, and it doesn't need a full HTML form in order to function (although one can be defined using the `.registerForm()` method if this is required).

Like the Tooltip, this control is highly specialized and very easy to create and use. As it appears at the end of the subclass chain (that is, it has no known subclasses, but several superclasses), a large number of its class members are inherited, giving you access to many of the features and configuration properties of the other Containers. As with the other types of Container, the SimpleDialog class also defines some of its own native members.

The main highlights of the class definition are once again the configuration attributes specific to this control. In addition to those inherited, it also defines:

- `icon`—a string which defines the icon to be used in the SimpleDialog, which can be one of six constant properties; `ICON_ALARM`, `ICON_BLOCK`, `ICON_HELP`, `ICON_INFO`, `ICON_TIP`, or `ICON_WARN`
- `text`—the text displayed in the SimpleDialog

As with the standard Dialog control, SimpleDialog allows you to create a button object whose members represent the buttons you would like to be displayed on the SimpleDialog.

The SimpleDialog is the last member of the Container family that represents a control visible to your visitors, but there are a couple of other relevant classes used by the Container family, which we will take a brief look at now.

Container Effects

I mentioned before that by including the Animation utility with implementations of some of the different containers, transition effects can be defined for when the container is displayed to the visitor or when it is hidden from view.

The `YAHOO.widget.ContainerEffect` class manages these transition effects for you and interacts with the Animation utility in order to generate them. Using this class, you can easily specify that containers fade in-and-out or slide in-and-out.

These transitions are specified as configuration attributes in each of the Container control's configuration objects. The `FADE` and `SLIDE` methods are very easy to use and each takes just two parameters: the container to apply the animation to and a number representing the duration of the animation. If the first parameter is not specified it will default to the current container in use.

OverlayManager

The `YAHOO.widget.OverlayManager` class is used to manage the focus states of multiple Overlay instances. An Overlay (or array of Overlays) is registered with the OverlayManager using the `.register()` method. The method returns **true** if the register operation was successful.

Once registered, the Overlay receives `focus` and `blur` methods and events which allow you to easily change the currently focused Overlay or determine programmatically the currently focused Overlay, as well as detect when the focus changes.

Other methods which you may find beneficial when using the OverlayManager class include:

- `.blurAll()` – removes the focus from all registered Overlays
- `.find()` – looks for and returns the specified Overlay if it exists
- `.getActive()` – returns the currently focused Overlay
- `.hideAll()` – hides all registered Overlays
- `.remove()` – removes the specified Overlay
- `.showAll()` – shows all registered Overlays
- `.toString()` – returns a string representing the OverlayManager

Two configuration attributes are available for use with the OverlayManager: the `focusevent` attribute which specifies the DOM event used to focus an Overlay, and `overlays` which is the collection of Overlays in use.

Creating a Panel

We'll work through examples of each of the out-of-the-box YUI containers that we have just looked at, so you can see exactly how easy they are to implement and work with. Creating custom containers is also possible, but won't be discussed in this book.

To showcase the ease in which Panel objects can be created, we can return to one of the examples from the last chapter. In the ContextMenu example, we added a custom right-click menu with a few dummy options on it. One of the options was to display a full size version of the thumbnail image that had been clicked on.

For this example we'll add some more code to this file which will result in a full size image being displayed in a Panel that floats above the rest of the document and can be dragged around at will.

Once we have finished, our Panel will appear like this:

Preparation

Make a new copy of the following files in the **yuisite** folder:

- `fantasy.html`
- `fantasy.css`

Rename them to:

- `panels.html`
- `panels.css`

Make sure you also have the following images in your **images** folder:

- `image1_thumb.jpg`
- `image1_full.jpg`
- `image2_thumb.jpg`
- `image2_full.jpg`

The New Code

The CSS file will only require one new rule, which should be added to the end of the file:

```
.panel {
  display:none;
}
```

The reason for this rule is to counteract the content-flicker that can occur if the page loads a little slowly. The flicker occurs because the panels are initially part of the page before they are hidden by each Panel's initialization function. Setting their `display` property to `none` makes sure they are always hidden.

We'll need to make some substantial changes to `panels.html` before it will function correctly, and will require additions to both the HTML and the JavaScript in order to function correctly.

We'll look at the additional HTML first. Change the underlying mark up of the page so that it appears the same as below, the new code has been highlighted:

```
<!DOCTYPE HTML PUBLIC "-//W3C//DTD HTML 4.01//EN"
                              "http://www.w3.org/TR/html4/strict.dtd">
<html lang="en">
  <head>
    <meta http-equiv="content-type" content="text/html;
                                     charset=utf-8">
```

```
    <title>YUI Context Panel Example</title>
    <script type="text/javascript"
            src="yui/build/yahoo-dom-event/yahoo-dom-event.js">
    </script>
    <script type="text/javascript"
            src="yui/build/dragdrop/dragdrop-min.js">
    </script>
    <script type="text/javascript"
            src="yui/build/container/container-min.js"></script>
    <script type="text/javascript"
            src="yui/build/menu/menu-min.js"></script>
    <link rel="stylesheet" type="text/css"
          href="yui/build/reset-fonts-grids/reset-fonts-grids.css">
    <link rel="stylesheet" type="text/css"
          href="yui/build/assets/skins/sam/menu.css">
    <link rel="stylesheet" type="text/css"
          href="yui/build/assets/skins/sam/container.css">
    <link rel="stylesheet" type="text/css" href="panels.css">
  </head>
```

The changes made to the `<head>` of the new page reflect the additional library files and the new CSS files (the Container skin file and our own custom CSS file) that are needed to use the Panel Container in this example.

The `<body>` of the page will need to have the underlying mark up from which the Panels will be created added to it. This has been highlighted so that you can easily see where the new code should be placed:

```
<body class="yui-skin-sam">
  <div id="doc" class="yui-t1">
    <div id="hd">
      <h1>DigitalDesigns</h1>
    </div>
    <div id="bd">
      <div class="yui-b">
        <div id="navmenu" class="yuimenu">
          <div class="bd">
            <ul class="first-of-type">
              <li class="yuimenuitem first-of-type">
                <a class="yuimenuitemlabel"
                   href="aboutme.html">About Me</a></li>
              <li class="yuimenuitem">
                <a class="yuimenuitemlabel"
                   href="images.html">Images</a>
                <div id="images" class="yuimenu">
                  <div class="bd">
                    <ul>
```

```
                    <li class="yuimenuitem">
                      <a class="yuimenuitemlabel"
                         href="photography.html">Photography</a>
                    </li>
                    <li class="yuimenuitem">
                      <a class="yuimenuitemlabel"
                         href="fantasy.html">Fantasy Art</a></li>
                    <li class="yuimenuitem">
                      <a class="yuimenuitemlabel"
                         href="Corporate.html">Corporate
                                                Logos</a></li>
                  </ul>
                </div>
              </div>
            </li>
            <li class="yuimenuitem">
              <a class="yuimenuitemlabel"
                 href="blog.html">My Blog</a></li>
            <li class="yuimenuitem">
              <a class="yuimenuitemlabel"
                 href="contact.html">Contact Me</a></li>
            <li class="yuimenuitem">
              <a class="yuimenuitemlabel"
                 href="imagelinks.html">Image Resources</a>
              <div id="links" class="yuimenu">
                <div class="bd">
                  <ul>
                    <li class="yuimenuitem">
                      <a class="yuimenuitemlabel"
                         href="http://www.flickr.com">Flickr</a>
                    </li>
                    <li class="yuimenuitem">
                      <a class="yuimenuitemlabel"
                         href="http://www.b3ta.com">B3ta</a></li>
                    <li class="yuimenuitem">
                      <a class="yuimenuitemlabel"
                         href="http://yotophoto.com">Yoto
                                                Photo</a></li>
                  </ul>
                </div>
              </div>
            </li>
          </ul>
        </div>
      </div>
```

```
      </div>
        <div id="yui-main">
          <div class="yui-b">
          <p class="content-head">Fantasy Art Images</p>
          <div class="images">
            <img id="img1" class="thumb"
                 src="images/image1_thumb.jpg" title="Right-click
                 for options (Opera users will need to use the Ctrl
                                   key + left-click)" alt="thumb1">
            <img id="img2" class="thumb"
                 src="images/image2_thumb.jpg"
                 title="Right-click for options
                   (Opera users will need to use the Ctrl key +
                                         left-click)" alt="thumb2">
          </div>
          <div id="panel1" class="panel">
            <div class="hd">Image 1</div>
            <div class="bd"><img src="images/image1_full.jpg"
                                 alt="fullsize1"></div>
            <div class="ft">Copyright &copy; The Extremist
                                                       2008</div>
          </div>
          <div id="panel2" class="panel">
            <div class="hd">Image 2</div>
            <div class="bd"><img src="images/image2_full.jpg"
                                 alt="fullsize2"></div>
            <div class="ft">Copyright &copy; The Extremist
                                                       2008</div>
          </div>
        </div>
       </div>
     </div>
     <div id="ft">
       <p class="ftext">Copyright&copy; Mr Freelance 2008</p>
     </div>
   </div>
   <script type="text/javascript">
     //javascript to go here
   </script>
  </body>
</html>
```

Each Panel is built using Yahoo's SMF mark up style, and has individual `hd`, `bd`, and `ft` sections. Each of these sections has a small amount of content relevant to this example within it. Now, let's look at the additional JavaScript required to create and use our new Panel instances:

```
//set up the namespace object for this example
YAHOO.namespace("yuibook.menu");
//define the initPage function
YAHOO.yuibook.menu.initPage = function() {
  var target;
  //define the initMenu function
  YAHOO.yuibook.menu.initMenu = function() {
    var menu = new YAHOO.widget.Menu("navmenu", { position:"static" });
    menu.render();
  }
  //call the initMenu function when the DOM is ready
  YAHOO.util.Event.onDOMReady( YAHOO.yuibook.menu.initMenu);
  //define the addContext function
  YAHOO.yuibook.menu.addContext = function() {
    //obtain thumbnails from the page
    var images = YAHOO.util.Dom.getElementsByClassName("thumb");
    //use the context constructor to create a context menu
    var context = new YAHOO.widget.ContextMenu("imagecontext",
                                              { trigger:images });

    //define the context menuitems
    context.addItem("View full-size");
    context.addItem("Buy this image");
    context.addItem("Image information");
    context.addItem("Rate this image");
    //render the context menu (it will remain hidden until the
    //trigger is clicked)
    context.render(document.body);
    //obtain id of element context event was a target of
    YAHOO.yuibook.menu.getTarget = function() {
      target = this.contextEventTarget.id;
    }
    //execute getTarget when the context menu is shown
    context.showEvent.subscribe(YAHOO.yuibook.menu.getTarget);
  }
  //call the addContext function when the DOM is ready
  YAHOO.util.Event.onDOMReady(YAHOO.yuibook.menu.addContext);
```

```
//define the initPanel function
YAHOO.yuibook.menu.initPanel = function() {
  //define the panels
  var panel1 = new YAHOO.widget.Panel("panel1", {
    close:true,
    visible:false,
    modal:true,
    width:"457px",
    fixedcenter:true
  });
  var panel2 = new YAHOO.widget.Panel("panel2", {
    close:true,
    visible:false,
    modal:true,
    width:"457px",
    fixedcenter:true
  });
  //render the panels
  panel1.render();
  panel2.render();
  //define viewfull function
  YAHOO.yuibook.menu.viewFull = function() {
    if (target == "img1"){
      YAHOO.util.Dom.setStyle("panel1", "display", "block");
      panel1.show();
    } else {
      YAHOO.util.Dom.setStyle("panel2", "display", "block");
      panel2.show();
    }
  }
  //attach a listener for a click on the show full context menuitem
  YAHOO.util.Event.addListener("yui-gen11", "click",
                                    YAHOO.yuibook.menu.viewFull);
}
//render the panels when the DOM is structurally complete
YAHOO.util.Event.onDOMReady(YAHOO.yuibook.menu.initPanel);
}
//execute the initPage function when the DOM is ready to be
 //manipulated
YAHOO.util.Event.onDOMReady(YAHOO.yuibook.menu.initPage);
```

The first change is the addition of an outer function, called `initPage()`, within which all of the other functions (both existing and those added for this example) reside. This is so that the `target` variable, which needs to be available to several different functions, does not become a global variable of the `window` object. It's not strictly necessary, we could just make the variable global after all, but this would negate the reason for namespacing our code with the `YAHOO.namespace()` method.

Next is the addition of the `getTarget()` function, which we've inserted into the `initContext()` function. This sets the value of our `target` variable to the `id` of the element that the Context menu was opened against. It obtains this value using the `id` property of the `contextEventTarget` object. The `this` keyword ensures that we get the `id` of the element that was right-clicked. The `getTarget()` function is executed when the custom `showEvent` of the Context, which we subscribe to, is detected.

A major addition to the code is the new `initPanel()` function. This function creates two new Panel objects. In each Panel constructor, we specify the `id` of the HTML element on the page from which the Panel is to be constructed, and a literal object of configuration properties.

We can use this configuration object to specify a close button for the Panel, its width, modality, and that it should be shown in the middle of the viewport. Because we don't want the panel to be displayed until the relevant Context MenuItem is selected, we set the `visible` property to `false`. Within the `initPanel()` function we also call each Panel's `.render()` method, which creates the Panel, but does not show it on screen.

In `fantasy.html` we had a `viewFull()` function which alerted a simple message to the visitor. In `panels.html`, we can take away the alert and use this function to show the Panel instead. Each Panel, as well as not being visible until the `.show()` method is called, is also currently set to `display:none` by `panels.css`. We can use the Dom utility's `.setStyle()` convenience method to set the `display` property to `block`, so that when we call the `.show()` method, the Panel is visible.

Note that the `viewFull()` function, as well the code used to execute it when the `click` event is detected on the relevant Context MenuItem, is also placed within the `initPanel()` function. We again make use of the `.onDOMReady()` method to execute the function.

Finally, we close off the outer function `initPage()` and once again make use of the `.onDOMReady` method to execute the outer function. When the DOM becomes available, the master function is executed, which in turn initializes each of the individual components. Running this page in a browser now and then selecting a view full option from the right-click context menu will give you a page like the screenshot shown at the beginning of this section.

To extend this page even further we can also make use of the `Dialog` and `SimpleDialog` Container controls to wire up some of the other items on the context menu as well.

Working with Dialogs

In this section we'll add an AJAX enabled Dialog box that will let visitors rate either of the images. Using Dialog is very similar in many ways to using the Panel. The underlying mark up for Dialog follows the same SMF, and the constructors are also very similar.

One of the benefits of Dialog over Panel is that you can send and receive data asynchronously between the Dialog and an application running on the server. This makes use of all of the AJAX facilities provided by the YUI with very little intervention from us.

We'll also write the PHP code that will carry out the rating request. Like the last time we looked at an AJAX application with the YUI, we need a full web server environment for this example to work correctly.

By the end of this section, we'll have something that looks like this:

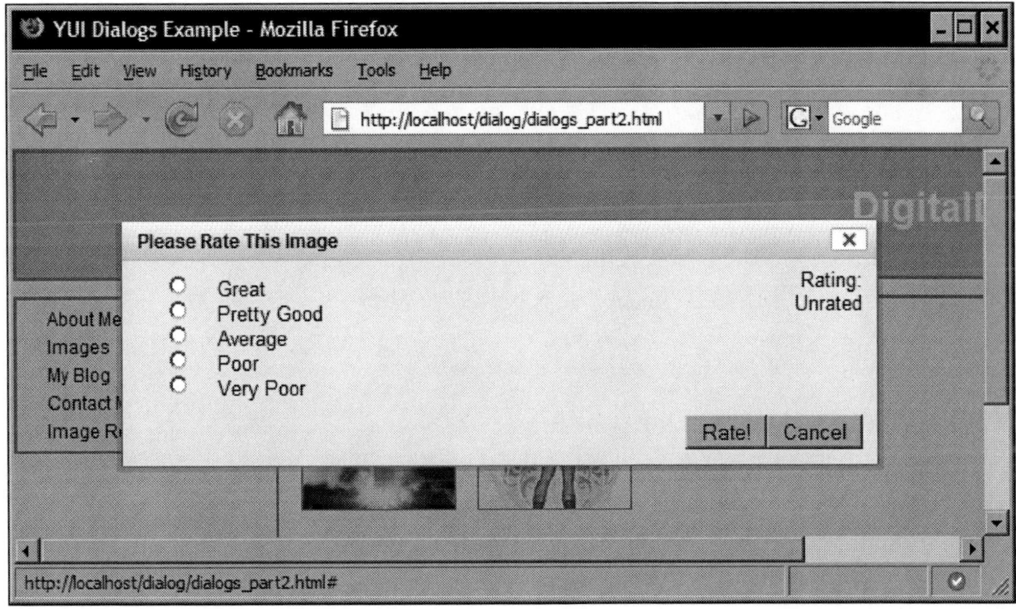

Preparation

Once again, it's probably best to make copies of the existing file to preserve the changes made between the implementation of each type of Container. Copy the following files:

- `panels.html`
- `panels.css`

Then rename them respectively to:

- `dialogs.html`
- `dialogs.css`

You'll also need to create two new text files, one called `img1Rating.txt` and the second called `img2Rating.txt`, and place these in the **yuisite** folder. Each file should contain just the simple string `unrated`. Ensure that PHP has permission to write to them both.

Additional Library files

The Dialog used on our page will make use of the `ContainerEffect` class to add fade-in and fade-out effects. To use these effects, we'll need the Animation utility. We'll also be making use of the Connection Manager utility, so will need to add references to both of these library files in the `<head>` of `dialogs.html`:

```
<!DOCTYPE HTML PUBLIC "-//W3C//DTD HTML 4.01//EN"
                                "http://www.w3.org/TR/html4/strict.dtd">
<html lang="en">
  <head>
    <meta http-equiv="content-type" content="text/html;
                                          charset=utf-8">
    <title>YUI Dialogs Example</title>
    <script type="text/javascript"
            src="yui/build/yahoo-dom-event/yahoo-dom-event.js">
    </script>
    <script type="text/javascript"
            src="yui/build/animation/animation-min.js"></script>
    <script type="text/javascript"
            src="yui/build/dragdrop/dragdrop-min.js"></script>
    <script type="text/javascript"
            src="yui/build/connection/connection-min.js"></script>
    <script type="text/javascript"
            src="yui/build/container/container-min.js"></script>
    <script type="text/javascript"
            src="yui/build/menu/menu-min.js"></script>
```

```
  <link rel="stylesheet" type="text/css"
        href="yui/build/reset-fonts-grids/reset-fonts-grids.css">
  <link rel="stylesheet" type="text/css"
        href="yui/build/assets/skins/sam/menu.css">
  <link rel="stylesheet" type="text/css"
        href="yui/build/assets/skins/sam/container.css">
  <link rel="stylesheet" type="text/css"
        href="dialogs.css">
</head>
```

Changes to the HTML

Now we can add the additional HTML that will form the foundation of our Dialog control. Like the Panel, the Dialog is built from underlying HTML in Yahoo's SMF coding style. The new code should be added directly after the mark up for the Panel. Here's the complete `dialogs.html` file, again the new code has been highlighted for easy readability:

```
<body class="yui-skin-sam">
  <div id="doc" class="yui-t1">
    <div id="hd">
      <h1>DigitalDesigns</h1>
    </div>
    <div id="bd">
      <div class="yui-b">
        <div id="navmenu" class="yuimenu">
          <div class="bd">
            <ul class="first-of-type">
              <li class="yuimenuitem first-of-type">
                <a class="yuimenuitemlabel"
                   href="aboutme.html">About Me</a></li>
              <li class="yuimenuitem">
                <a class="yuimenuitemlabel"
                   href="images.html">Images</a>
                <div id="images" class="yuimenu">
                  <div class="bd">
                    <ul>
                      <li class="yuimenuitem">
                        <a class="yuimenuitemlabel"
                           href="photography.html">Photography</a>
                      </li>
                      <li class="yuimenuitem">
                        <a class="yuimenuitemlabel"
                           href="fantasy.html">Fantasy Art</a></li>
                      <li class="yuimenuitem">
                        <a class="yuimenuitemlabel"
```

```
                    href="Corporate.html">Corporate
                                                Logos</a></li>
                </ul>
              </div>
            </div>
          </li>
          <li class="yuimenuitem">
            <a class="yuimenuitemlabel"
               href="blog.html">My Blog</a></li>
          <li class="yuimenuitem">
            <a class="yuimenuitemlabel"
               href="contact.html">Contact Me</a></li>
          <li class="yuimenuitem">
            <a class="yuimenuitemlabel"
               href="imagelinks.html">Image Resources</a>
            <div id="links" class="yuimenu">
              <div class="bd">
                <ul>
                  <li class="yuimenuitem">
                    <a class="yuimenuitemlabel"
                       href="http://www.flickr.com">Flickr</a>
                  </li>
                  <li class="yuimenuitem">
                    <a class="yuimenuitemlabel"
                       href="http://www.b3ta.com">B3ta</a></li>
                  <li class="yuimenuitem">
                    <a class="yuimenuitemlabel"
                       href="http://yotophoto.com">Yoto
                                                Photo</a></li>
                </ul>
              </div>
            </div>
          </li>
        </ul>
      </div>
    </div>
  </div>
   <div id="yui-main">
     <div class="yui-b">
      <p class="content-head">Fantasy Art Images</p>
      <div class="images">
        <img id="img1" class="thumb"
             src="images/image1_thumb.jpg"
             title="Right-click for options
               (Opera users will need to use the Ctrl key +
                                    left-click)" alt="thumb1">
```

```
  <img id="img2" class="thumb"
       src="images/image2_thumb.jpg"
       title="Right-click for options
         (Opera users will need to use the Ctrl key +
                               left-click)" alt="thumb2">
</div>
<div id="panel1" class="panel">
  <div class="hd">Image 1</div>
  <div class="bd"><img src="images/image1_full.jpg"
                       alt="fullsize1"></div>
  <div class="ft">Copyright &copy; The Extremist
                                                2008</div>
</div>
<div id="panel2" class="panel">
  <div class="hd">Image 2</div>
  <div class="bd"><img src="images/image2_full.jpg"
                       alt="fullsize2"></div>
  <div class="ft">Copyright &copy; The Extremist
                                                2008</div>
</div>
<div id="dialog">
  <div class="hd">Please Rate This Image</div>
  <div class="bd">
    <form method="POST" action="ratings.php">
      <div><input type="hidden" name="image"></div>
      <div class="radioContainer">
        <input type="radio" name="rating" value="Great">
          <span class="opt">Great</span></div>
      <div class="radioContainer">
        <input type="radio" name="rating"
               value="Pretty Good">
          <span class="opt">Pretty Good</span></div>
      <div class="radioContainer">
        <input type="radio" name="rating"
               value="Average">
          <span class="opt">Average</span></div>
      <div class="radioContainer">
        <input type="radio" name="rating"
               value="Poor">
          <span class="opt">Poor</span></div>
      <div class="radioContainer">
        <input type="radio" name="rating"
               value="Very Poor">
          <span class="opt">Very Poor</span></div>
      <p><span class="rating">Rating:</span></p>
    </form>
```

```
                </div>
                <div class="ft"></div>
              </div>
            </div>
          </div>
      </div>
      <div id="ft">
        <p class="ftext">Copyright&copy; Mr Freelance 2008</p>
      </div>
    </div>
    <script type="text/javascript">
      //javascript to go here…
    </script>
  </body>
</html>
```

We'll create a very basic Dialog for this example, consisting of just some simple text for the Dialog heading and a series of radio buttons. The text used in the hd section will form the title bar text of the Dialog control. The Dialog's buttons are automatically placed in the ft section of the control.

Our Dialog also contains a hidden <input> element called image, this is used to tell the PHP file which image the rating we are submitting is for. The value of this field is set by JavaScript later on using the target property that was so useful to us in the Panel example earlier in the chapter.

Some Additional CSS

We created a new CSS file, dialogs.css, at the start of this section. The new CSS file will need to have the following selectors and rules added to the bottom of it in order to style our Dialog:

```
#dialog {
  display:none;
}
input {
  margin-right:15px;
  margin-left:20px;
}
.opt {
  margin-right:5px;
  margin-left:5px;
}
.rating {
```

```
  position:absolute;
  top:30px;
  *top:5px;
  right:10px;
}
.result {
  position:absolute;
  top:45px;
  *top:20px;
  right:10px;
}
```

Firefox and IE calculate the `top` of the `rating` and `result` paragraphs differently. IE calculates it from the bottom of the `hd` (the titlebar) section of the dialog, whereas Firefox calculates it from the top of the `hd` section. In order to present the correct values to each browser we need to use the `*` hack, which FireFox will ignore, but IE will use.

Dialog's Required JavaScript

Let's review how the `<script>` tag within `dialogs.html` should look for this example, new code added for this example is again shown in bold:

```
//set up the namespace object for this example
YAHOO.namespace("yuibook.menu");
//define the initPage function
YAHOO.yuibook.menu.initPage = function() {
  var target;
  //define the initMenu function
  YAHOO.yuibook.menu.initMenu = function() {
    var menu = new YAHOO.widget.Menu("navmenu",
                                     { position:"static" });
    menu.render();
  }
  //call the initMenu function when the DOM is ready
  YAHOO.util.Event.onDOMReady(YAHOO.yuibook.menu.initMenu);
  //define the addContext function
  YAHOO.yuibook.menu.addContext = function() {
    //obtain thumbnails from the page
    var images = YAHOO.util.Dom.getElementsByClassName("thumb");
    //use the context constructor to create a context menu
    var context = new YAHOO.widget.ContextMenu("imagecontext",
                                       { trigger:images });
```

```
    //define the context menuitems
    context.addItem("View full-size");
    context.addItem("Buy this image");
    context.addItem("Image information");
    context.addItem("Rate this image");
    //render the context menu (it will remain hidden until the
    //trigger is clicked)
    context.render(document.body);
    //obtain id of element context event was a target of
    YAHOO.yuibook.menu.getTarget = function() {
      target = this.contextEventTarget.id;
    }
    //execute the getTarget function when the context menu is shown
    context.showEvent.subscribe( YAHOO.yuibook.menu.getTarget);
  }
  //call the addContext function when the DOM is ready
  YAHOO.util.Event.onDOMReady(YAHOO.yuibook.menu.addContext);
  //define the initPanels function
  YAHOO.yuibook.menu.initPanel = function() {
    //define the panels
    var panel1 = new YAHOO.widget.Panel("panel1", {
      close:true,
      visible:false,
      modal:true,
      width:"457px",
      fixedcenter:true
    });
    var panel2 = new YAHOO.widget.Panel("panel2", {
      close:true,
      visible:false,
      modal:true,
      width:"457px",
      fixedcenter:true
    });
    //render the panels but don't show them yet
    panel1.render();
    panel2.render();
    //define viewfull function
    YAHOO.yuibook.menu.viewFull = function() {
      if (target == "img1"){
        YAHOO.util.Dom.setStyle("panel1", "display", "block");
        panel1.show();
```

```
      } else {
        YAHOO.util.Dom.setStyle("panel2", "display", "block");
        panel2.show();
      }
    }
    //attach listener for a click on the show full context menuitem
    YAHOO.util.Event.addListener("yui-gen11", "click",
                                  YAHOO.yuibook.menu.viewFull);
  }
  //render the panels when the DOM is complete
  YAHOO.util.Event.onDOMReady(YAHOO.yuibook.menu.initPanel);
  //define the initDialog function
  YAHOO.yuibook.menu.initDialog = function() {
    //define the dialog button handlers
    var handleRate = function() {
      dialog.submit();
    }
    var handleCancel = function() {
      dialog.cancel();
    }
    //define the dialog control
    var dialog = new YAHOO.widget.Dialog("dialog", {
      width:"500px",
      fixedcenter:true,
      visible:false,
      modal:true,
      constraintoviewport:true,
      postmethod:"async",
      buttons: [
        {text:"Rate!", handler:handleRate},
        {text:"Cancel", handler:handleCancel}
      ],
      effect: {effect: YAHOO.widget.ContainerEffect.FADE,
                                              duration: 0.5}
    });
    //render the dialog but don't show it
    dialog.render();
    //define the success and failure response handlers
    var onSuccess = function(o) {
      alert(o.responseText);
```

```
      }
      var onFailure = function(o) {
        alert("Failure! " + o.status);
      }

      //execute whichever handler is appropriate
      dialog.callback.success = onSuccess;
      dialog.callback.failure = onFailure;
      //define the showDialog function
      var showDialog = function() {
        //show the dialog
        YAHOO.util.Dom.setStyle("dialog", "display", "block");
        dialog.show();
      }
  //execute showDialog when the appropriate context menuitem is clicked
      YAHOO.util.Event.addListener("yui-gen14", "click", showDialog);
    }
    //execute the initDialog function when the DOM is ready
    YAHOO.util.Event.onDOMReady(YAHOO.yuibook.menu.initDialog);
  }
  //execute the initPage function when the DOM is ready
  YAHOO.util.Event.onDOMReady(YAHOO.yuibook.menu.initPage);
```

Let's walk through the new code and see what we're using to achieve the end result. The `initDialog()` function wraps up all of the Dialog code and is executed when the DOM is ready, exactly the same as with the rest of the other library components already on the page.

We first define the callback functions `handleRate()` and `handleCancel()`. These callbacks will be associated with the buttons on the Dialog (which we'll look at the code for next).

When the **Rate!** button is clicked, the Dialog's form is automatically submitted using the `.submit()` method, according to the `method` and `action` defined in the form element. If the Cancel button is clicked instead, the `.cancel()` method closes the Dialog and discards any selection made by the visitor.

Next, the Dialog's constructor takes the `id` of the HTML element that contains the dialog mark up, and we again make use of an object literal containing the configuration attributes that we want. Some of these we used in Panel, but others, like the `postmethod` and `buttons` attributes, are specific to the Dialog (and SimpleDialog) control.

The buttons are defined as literal objects within the `buttons` configuration attribute. We can add as many button objects to the Dialog as we want to with this. All we need to specify is the text on the face of each button and the callback function to be associated with it.

Because we've specified `async` as the `postmethod`, the Dialog will automatically use the Connection utility to submit the data from our form to the server-side script specified in the form's `action` attribute.

We don't need to use the `.asyncRequest()` method of the Connection Manager utility, or interact with it directly in any way. The library handles all communication between the two Controls, sending and receiving all of the information that flows between them autonomously.

The final configuration attribute used in this example is the effect attribute, which allows us to add an effect powered by the Animation utility. The effect is created using another object literal, this time the object's members are `key:value` pairs.

The members we've specified are `effect`, whose value we've set to the `YAHOO.widget.ContainerEffect.FADE` constant from the `ContainerEffects` class. The next member, `duration`, allows us to specify the duration of the effect, which we have set to `0.5` seconds for this example.

After the Dialog object definition, we use the `.render()` method to render the Dialog to the page, but remember, this doesn't show it on the screen. To actually reveal the Dialog we need another function, `showDialog()`, which we'll look at in just a moment..

Once the Dialog exists, we can define the success and failure handlers. Both the `onSuccess()` and `onFailure()` functions are callbacks that are executed by the `dialog.callback.success` and `dialog.callback.failure` handlers respectively. We haven't coded the PHP file yet, so if we were to run this page in a browser now, open the dialog, and try to submit a rating, we'd trigger the `onFailure()` callback and get an alert stating **Error: 404**.

The `showDialog()` function simply uses the DOM utility's `.setStyle()` method to set the Dialog's style property to block, then uses the Dialog's `.show()` method to show the Dialog on the screen.

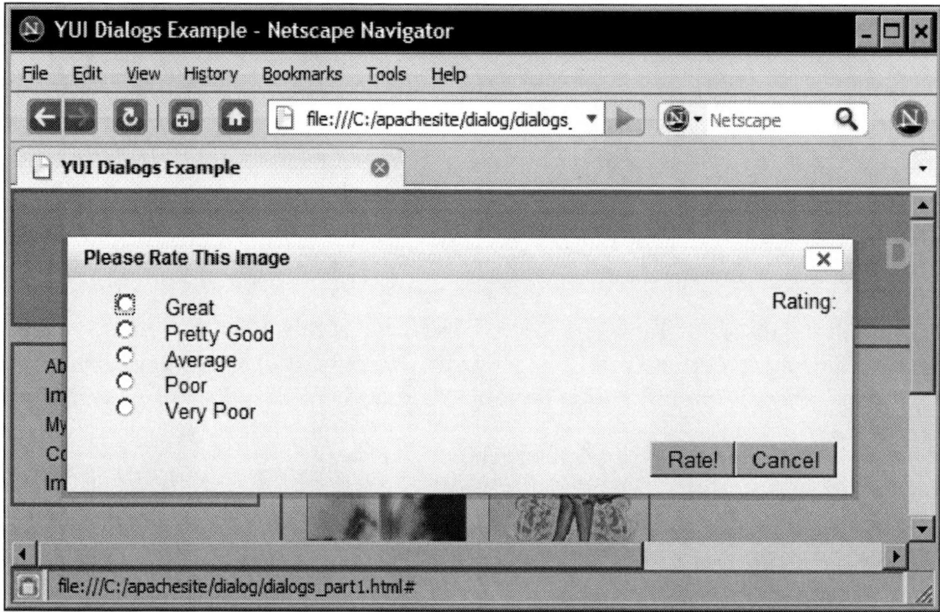

Extending the Dialog

We'll focus on achieving two things in this part of the example: first of all, when our Dialog opens initially, we'll need to get the current rating for the image by reading the appropriate `Rating.txt` file and then display it in the Dialog. Once the visitor selects a rating and submits the Dialog, we'll then update the stored rating and confirm success or failure.

We'll need to use the Connection Manager utility manually this time, so you'll get to see all of the code that you didn't need to write when the Dialog was automatically communicating with the Connection Manager for us! We'll add the additional JavaScript to `dialogs.html` first (see `dialogs_part2.html`). We can make use of the existing `showDialog()` function for our new code:

```
//define the showDialog function
var showDialog = function() {
  //define the transaction success and failure handlers
  var responseSuccess = function(o) {
    //remove existing rating
```

```
      var mydialog = YAHOO.util.Dom.get("dialog");
      var fchild = YAHOO.util.Dom.getFirstChild(mydialog);
      var nsib = YAHOO.util.Dom.getNextSibling(fchild);
      var lsib = YAHOO.util.Dom.getLastChild(nsib);
      if (lsib.className != "") {
        lsib.parentNode.removeChild(lsib);
      }
      //create the new rating
      var p = document.createElement("p");
      YAHOO.util.Dom.addClass(p, "result");
      var rating = document.createTextNode(o.responseText);
      p.appendChild(rating);
      dialog.appendToBody(p);
    }
    Var responseFailure = function(o) {
      alert(o.status);
    }
    //define the transaction callback object
    var callback = {
      success:responseSuccess,
      failure:responseFailure
    }
    //initiate the transaction
    var trans = YAHOO.util.Connect.asyncRequest("POST",
                   "getratings.php", callback, "image=" + target);
    dialog.form.image.value = target;
    YAHOO.util.Dom.setStyle("dialog", "display", "block");
    dialog.show();
  }
```

This addition to the `showDialog()` function first removes any existing rating (for example if both images are rated during the same page visit) and then creates and adds the current rating from the appropriate text file when the Dialog is opened.

We first define our success callback function `responseSuccess()`. In this function we create a new paragraph element which will hold the rating retrieved from the text file. This will be passed back to Dialog by the PHP file and will be available under the `o.responseText` property. The `responseFailure()` function simply alerts the failure message in a similar fashion to our `onFailure()` function earlier in the script.

As we're working with the Connection Manager manually, we use a literal object to specify each handler (whereas before we were able to use Dialog's built in `callback.success` and `callback.failure` handlers). We use `key:value` pairs as the members of our callback object in order to specify the handlers to execute on success or failure.

Once this has been done we can initiate the transaction using the `YAHOO.util.Connect.asyncRequest()` constructor, specifying the HTTP method, the remote file, our callback object, and some post data as arguments. The post data in this case will inform the PHP file of which image we want to get the rating for and again makes use of our `target` variable, which is set to whichever image the ContextMenu was attached to. We can also set a hidden `<input>` value using `target`.

A normal ratings system would probably store its data in a database and would use a complicated algorithm for determining the new rating after adding the visitors rating to the existing rating.

We're not going to do either of these however, we will store our data in simple text files instead of a database, and will simply overwrite the old rating with the new rating.

We'll need two PHP files to complete this example. The first one will need to retrieve the current rating for display in the Dialog, and the second will need to take the new rating from the Dialog and update the appropriate text file. Let's create the two PHP files now.

The PHP Needed by Dialog

The two new PHP files will deal with initially getting the current rating out of the text file, and updating the stored rating when an image is rated. On a new page in your text editor, add the following code:

```
<?php
  $imageFile = $_POST['image'];
  $path = $imageFile."Rating.text";
  $fHandler = fopen($path, 'r') or die("Could not open file");
  $curRating = fread($fHandler, 11);
  fclose(fHandler);
  echo $curRating;
?>
```

Save this as `getratings.php` in your **yuisite** folder. For the second PHP file, use the following code:

```
<?php
  $imageFile = $_POST['image'];
  $newRating = $_POST['rating'];
  $path = $imageFile."Rating.txt";
  $fHandle = fopen($path, 'w') or die("Cannot open file");
  fwrite($fHandle, $newRating);
  fclose($fHandle);
  echo("Thanks! the new rating is: ".$newRating);
?>
```

Save the second file as `ratings.php`, also in the **yuisite** folder.

If you save the `dialogs.html` file now and run it in your browser, the first time you see the Dialog you should see the **Unrated** message under rating. This has been retrieved from the text file using the `getRatings.php` file:

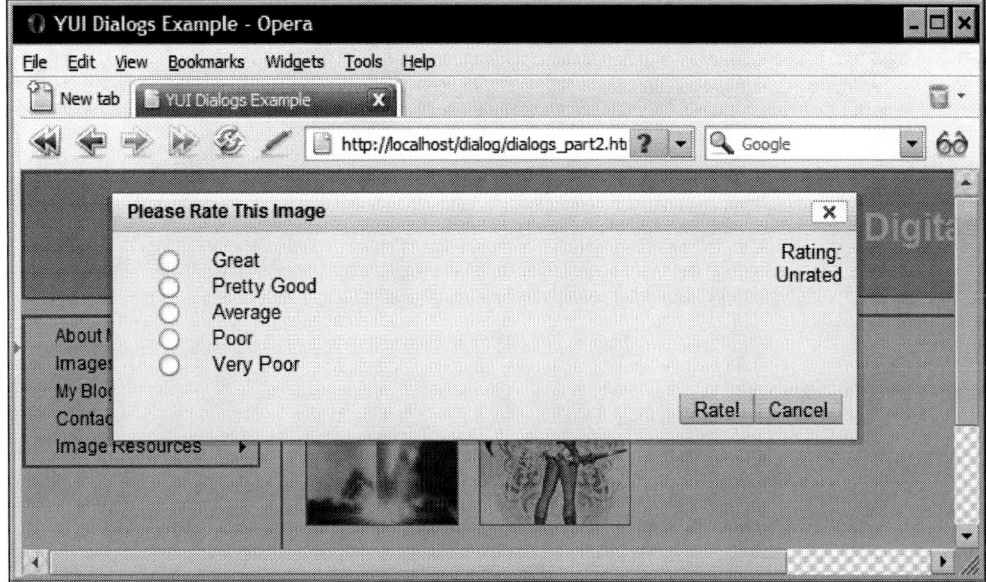

Now choose a rating for the image using the radio buttons, then refresh the page and open the Dialog again, this time the rating that you just chose should be displayed when the Dialog first opens:

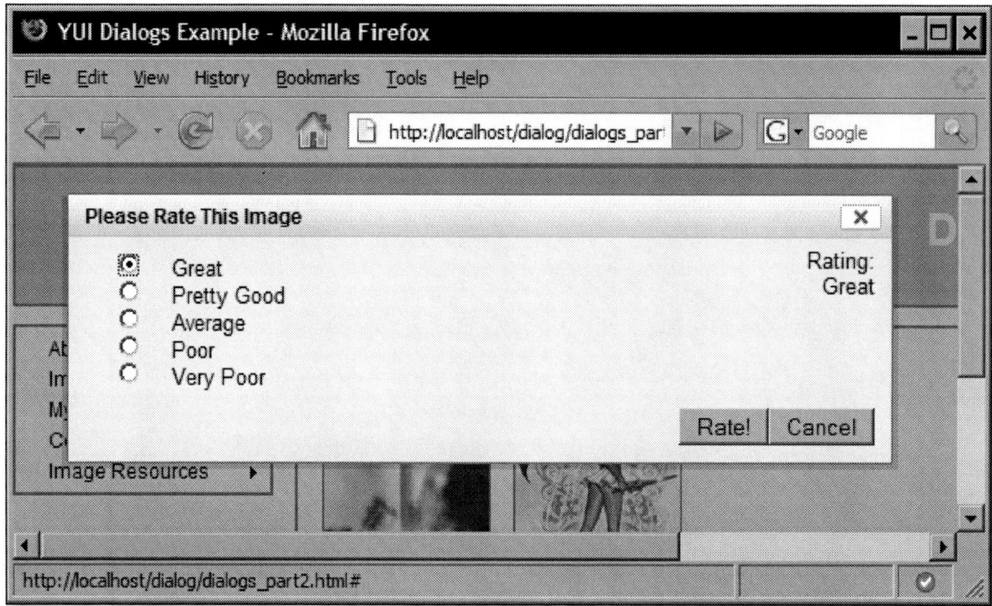

If you open up the text file for the image you just rated, you should also see the new rating in there. Depending on your web server environment, you may only be allowed to make one rating per page visit. If you try to rate an image twice, the Dialog may display the **Cannot open File** message generated by the PHP file. If this is the case, a page refresh between ratings will fix the issue.

A Quick SimpleDialog

The SimpleDialog extends the Dialog. It's used to get the result of a single question, much like a standard JavaScript confirm box, but with a lot more power. It can also be styled, by using the default `sam` skin, or by overriding this to add custom styling.

The example for this section will make use of the SimpleDialog to display an information box that displays some details about each of the example pictures. Like Dialog, this element also has full AJAX capabilities.

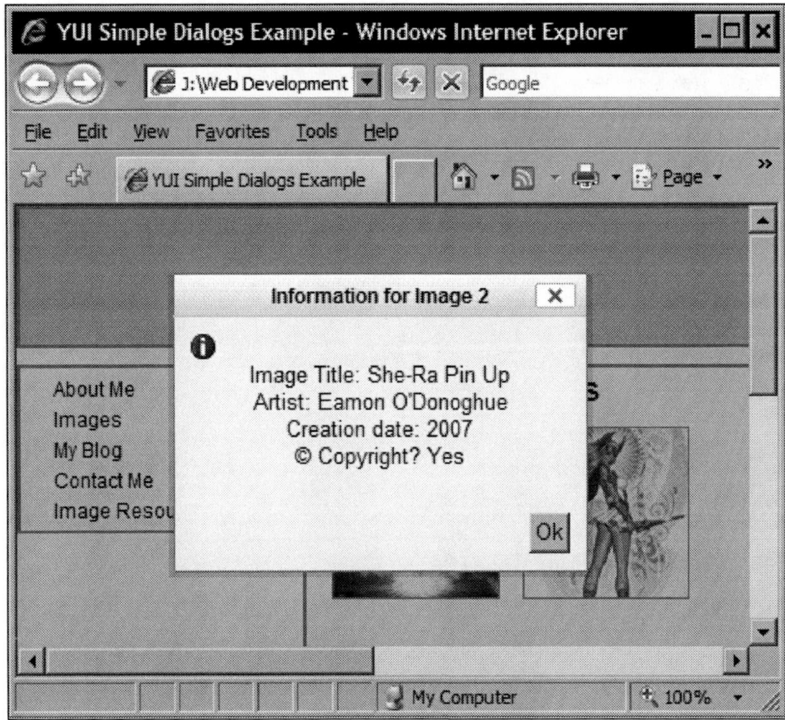

To get started, you'll need to copy the following file:

- `dialogs_part2.html`

Then rename it to:

- `simpleDialogs.html`

Unlike previous examples, the SimpleDialog requires no additional CSS so we can use the `dialogs.css` file from the last example.

Additonal JavaScript for SimpleDialog

Unlike the previous Container examples, we don't need to add any new underlying HTML for the SimpleDialog, everything is done from script. Let's see the new JavaScript we need to add to implement our SimpleDialog control. Here's how the complete `<script>` tag will need to look:

```
<script type="text/javascript">
  //set up the namespace object for this example
  YAHOO.namespace("yuibook.menu");
  //define the initPage function
```

```
YAHOO.yuibook.menu.initPage = function() {
var target;
//define the initMenu function
YAHOO.yuibook.menu.initMenu = function() {
  var menu = new YAHOO.widget.Menu("navmenu",
                                        { position:"static" });
  menu.render();
}
//call the initMenu function when the DOM is ready
YAHOO.util.Event.onDOMReady(YAHOO.yuibook.menu.initMenu);
//define the addContext function
YAHOO.yuibook.menu.addContext = function() {
  //obtain thumbnails from the page
  var images = YAHOO.util.Dom.getElementsByClassName("thumb");
  //use the context constructor to create a context menu
  var context = new YAHOO.widget.ContextMenu("imagecontext",
                                        { trigger:images });
  //define the context menuitems
  context.addItem("View full-size");
  context.addItem("Buy this image");
  context.addItem("Image information");
  context.addItem("Rate this image");
  //render the context menu (it will remain hidden until the
  //trigger is clicked)
  context.render(document.body);
  //obtain id of element context event was a target of
  YAHOO.yuibook.menu.getTarget = function() {
    target = this.contextEventTarget.id;
  }
  //execute the getTarget function when the context menu is shown
  context.showEvent.subscribe( YAHOO.yuibook.menu.getTarget);
}
//call the addContext function when the DOM is ready
YAHOO.util.Event.onDOMReady( YAHOO.yuibook.menu.addContext);
//define the initPanels function
YAHOO.yuibook.menu.initPanel = function() {
  //define the panels
  var panel1 = new YAHOO.widget.Panel("panel1", {
    close:true,
    visible:false,
    modal:true,
    width:"457px",
    fixedcenter:true
  });
  var panel2 = new YAHOO.widget.Panel("panel2", {
```

```
      close:true,
      visible:false,
      modal:true,
      width:"457px",
      fixedcenter:true
    });
    //render the panels but don't show them yet
    panel1.render();
    panel2.render();
    //define viewfull function
    YAHOO.yuibook.menu.viewFull = function() {
      if (target == "img1"){
        YAHOO.util.Dom.setStyle("panel1", "display", "block");
        panel1.show();
      } else {
        YAHOO.util.Dom.setStyle("panel2", "display", "block");
        panel2.show();
      }
    }
    //attach listener for a click on the show full context menuitem
    YAHOO.util.Event.addListener("yui-gen11", "click",
                                        YAHOO.yuibook.menu.viewFull);
  }
  //render the panels when the DOM is complete
  YAHOO.util.Event.onDOMReady(YAHOO.yuibook.menu.initPanel);
  //define the initDialog function
  YAHOO.yuibook.menu.initDialog = function() {
    //define the dialog button handlers
    var handleRate = function() {
      dialog.submit();
    }
    var handleCancel = function() {
      dialog.cancel();
    }
    //define the dialog control
    var dialog = new YAHOO.widget.Dialog("dialog", {
      width:"500px",
      fixedcenter:true,
      visible:false,
      modal:true,
      constraintoviewport:true,
      postmethod:"async",
      buttons: [
        {text:"Rate!", handler:handleRate},
        {text:"Cancel", handler:handleCancel}
      ],
```

```
    effect: {effect: YAHOO.widget.ContainerEffect.FADE, duration:
                                                            0.5}
  });
  //render the dialog but don't show it
  dialog.render();
  //define the success and failure response handlers
  var onSuccess = function(o) {
    alert(o.responseText);
  }
  var onFailure = function(o) {
    alert("Failure! " + o.status);
  }
  //execute whichever handler is appropriate
  dialog.callback.success = onSuccess;
  dialog.callback.failure = onFailure;
  //define the showDialog function
  var showDialog = function() {
    //define the transaction success and failure handlers
    var responseSuccess = function(o) {
      //remove existing rating
      var mydialog = YAHOO.util.Dom.get("dialog");
      var fchild = YAHOO.util.Dom.getFirstChild(mydialog);
      var nsib = YAHOO.util.Dom.getNextSibling(fchild);
      var lsib = YAHOO.util.Dom.getLastChild(nsib);
      if (lsib.className != "") {
        lsib.parentNode.removeChild(lsib);
      }
      //create the new rating
      var p = document.createElement("p");
      YAHOO.util.Dom.addClass(p, "result");
      var rating = document.createTextNode(o.responseText);
      p.appendChild(rating);
      dialog.appendToBody(p);
    }
    var responseFailure = function(o) {
      alert(o.status);
    }
    //define the transaction callback object
    var callback = {
      success:responseSuccess,
      failure:responseFailure
    }
    //initiate the transaction
    var trans = YAHOO.util.Connect.asyncRequest("POST",
                "getratings.php", callback, "image=" + target);
```

```
    dialog.form.image.value = target;
    //show the dialog
    YAHOO.util.Dom.setStyle("dialog", "display", "block");
      dialog.show();
    }
    //execute showDialog when the appropriate context menuitem is
     clicked
    YAHOO.util.Event.addListener("yui-gen14", "click", showDialog);
  }
  //execute the initDialog function when the DOM is ready
  YAHOO.util.Event.onDOMReady( YAHOO.yuibook.menu.initDialog);
  //define the initSimpleDialog function
  YAHOO.yuibook.menu.initSimpleDialog = function() {
    //handle the ok button click
    var handleOk = function() {
      if (target == "img1"){
        imageInfo1.hide();
      } else {
        imageInfo2.hide();
      }
    }
    //define the SimpleDialog objects
    var imageInfo1 = new YAHOO.widget.SimpleDialog("sdialog1", {
      width:"250px",
      fixedcenter:true,
      modal:true,
      visible:false,
      icon: YAHOO.widget.SimpleDialog.ICON_INFO,
      buttons:[{text:"Ok", handler:handleOk}]
    });
    var imageInfo2 = new YAHOO.widget.SimpleDialog("sdialog2", {
      width:"250px",
      fixedcenter:true,
      modal:true,
      visible:false,
      icon: YAHOO.widget.SimpleDialog.ICON_INFO,
      buttons:[{text:"Ok", handler:handleOk}]
    });
    //set the content of the SimpleDialogs
    imageInfo1.setHeader("Information for Image 1");
    imageInfo1.setBody("<br>Image Title: Superman<br>Artist:
                 The Extremist<br>Creation date: 2006<br>&copy;
                 Copyright? Yes");
    imageInfo2.setHeader("Information for Image 2");
    imageInfo2.setBody("<br>Image Title: She-Ra Pin Up<br>Artist:
                The Extremist<br>Creation date: 2007<br>&copy;
```

```
                                      Copyright? Yes");
        //render the SimpleDialogs
        imageInfo1.render(document.body);
        imageInfo2.render(document.body);
        //show the SimpleDialog
        var showSimpleDialog = function() {
          if (target == "img1"){
            imageInfo1.show();
          } else {
            imageInfo2.show();
          }
        }
        //call showSDialog when the appropriate context menuitem is
         selected
        YAHOO.util.Event.addListener("yui-gen13", "click",
                                                  showSimpleDialog);
      }

      //execute initSimpleDialog when DOMis ready
      YAHOO.util.Event.onDOMReady(YAHOO.yuibook.menu.initSimpleDialog);
    }
    //execute the initPage function when the DOM is ready
    YAHOO.util.Event.onDOMReady( YAHOO.yuibook.menu.initPage);
  </script>
```

We start off again with an initialization function wrapper for our new SimpleDialog code. Our first task is to add the `callback` function that handles the `ok` button on the SimpleDialog object being clicked.

We're not worried about passing information to the server or receiving the answer to a question from the visitor, so in this example we can simply close the SimpleDialog control when the `ok` button is clicked.

Next we define our SimpleDialog objects. The format of the constructor should be pretty familiar by now as it's almost identical to the constructors used in the previous examples. Again, most of the code goes into the configuration object which allows us to configure various properties of the SimpleDialog object.

With SimpleDialog we can make use of additional configuration properties such as the `icon` property, which allows us to define an icon that is placed within the SimpleDialog. Here we've used the `INFO` icon.

As there isn't any HTML on which to base the control, we have to set the content of each SimpleDialog with script instead, which is where the `.setHeader()` and `.setBody()` methods come into play. We also have to specify where in the DOM the control should be rendered. For the purpose of this example `document.body` is fine to use.

Each SimpleDialog is rendered, but remember this doesn't actually show the SimpleDialog on the screen, it just creates it ready for display at a later point. To show the SimpleDialog Controls, we use the `showSimpleDialogs()` function. This uses the `target` variable to determine which SimpleDialog to show, then calls the `.show()` method to display it on screen.

Easy Tooltips

The Tooltip control is one of the easiest components of the library to use; with just a couple of lines of code, you can have a custom Tooltip just like the one shown in the screenshot below:

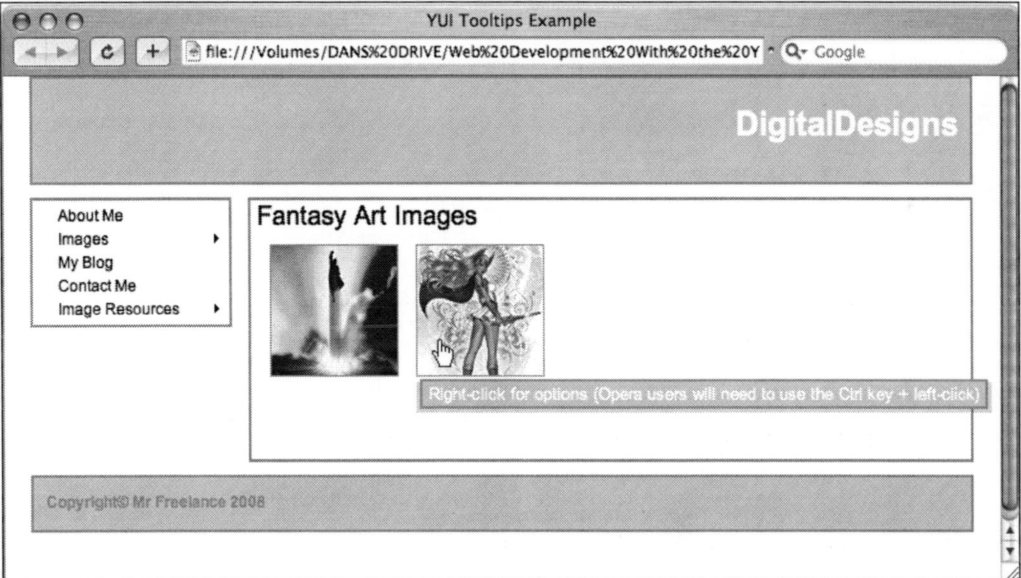

Preparation

Copy the following files:

- simpleDialogs.html
- dialogs.css

Rename them to:

- tooltips.html
- tooltips.css

Like the SimpleDialog, the Tooltip Control should be created dynamically with script rather than building from any underlying HTML. The underlying mark up of the page will stay the same for this example, but the `<script>` block will need to be changed so that it appears like follows:

```
<script type="text/javascript">
  //set up the namespace object for this example
  YAHOO.namespace("yuibook.menu");
  //define the initPage function
    YAHOO.yuibook.menu.initPage = function() {
    var target;
    var images;
    //define the initMenu function
    YAHOO.yuibook.menu.initMenu = function() {
      var menu = new YAHOO.widget.Menu("navmenu",
                                       { position:"static" });
      menu.render();
    }
    //call the initMenu function when the DOM is ready
    YAHOO.util.Event.onDOMReady(YAHOO.yuibook.menu.initMenu);
    //define the addContext function
    YAHOO.yuibook.menu.addContext = function() {
      //obtain thumbnails from the page
      images = YAHOO.util.Dom.getElementsByClassName("thumb");
      //use the context constructor to create a context menu
      var context = new YAHOO.widget.ContextMenu("imagecontext",
                                       { trigger:images });
      //define the context menuitems
      context.addItem("View full-size");
      context.addItem("Buy this image");
      context.addItem("Image information");
      context.addItem("Rate this image");
```

```
    //render the context menu (it will remain hidden until the
    //trigger is clicked)
    context.render(document.body);
    //obtain id of element context event was a target of
    YAHOO.yuibook.menu.getTarget = function() {
      target = this.contextEventTarget.id;
    }
    //execute the getTarget function when the context menu is shown
  context.showEvent.subscribe( YAHOO.yuibook.menu.getTarget);
}
//call the addContext function when the DOM is ready
YAHOO.util.Event.onDOMReady( YAHOO.yuibook.menu.addContext);
//define the initPanels function
YAHOO.yuibook.menu.initPanel = function() {
//define the panels
var panel1 = new YAHOO.widget.Panel("panel1", {
  close:true,
  visible:false,
  modal:true,
  width:"457px",
  fixedcenter:true
});
var panel2 = new YAHOO.widget.Panel("panel2", {
  close:true,
  visible:false,
  modal:true,
  width:"457px",
  fixedcenter:true
});
//render the panels but don't show them yet
panel1.render();
panel2.render();
 //define viewfull function
 YAHOO.yuibook.menu.viewFull = function() {
   if (target == "img1"){
     YAHOO.util.Dom.setStyle("panel1", "display", "block");
     panel1.show();
   } else {
     YAHOO.util.Dom.setStyle("panel2", "display", "block");
     panel2.show();
   }
 }
```

```
    //attach listener for a click on the show full context menuitem
    YAHOO.util.Event.addListener("yui-gen11", "click",
                                    YAHOO.yuibook.menu.viewFull);
  }
  //render the panels when the DOM is complete
  YAHOO.util.Event.onDOMReady(YAHOO.yuibook.menu.initPanel);
  //define the initDialog function
  YAHOO.yuibook.menu.initDialog = function() {
    //define the dialog button handlers
    var handleRate = function() {
      dialog.submit();
    }
    var handleCancel = function() {
      dialog.cancel();
    }
    //define the dialog control
    var dialog = new YAHOO.widget.Dialog("dialog", {
      width:"500px",
      fixedcenter:true,
      visible:false,
      modal:true,
      constraintoviewport:true,
      postmethod:"async",
      buttons: [
        {text:"Rate!", handler:handleRate},
        {text:"Cancel", handler:handleCancel}
      ],
      effect: {effect: YAHOO.widget.ContainerEffect.FADE, duration:
                                                                0.5}
      });
      //render the dialog but don't show it
      dialog.render();
      //define the success and failure response handlers
      var onSuccess = function(o) {
        alert(o.responseText);
      }
      var onFailure = function(o) {
        alert("Failure! " + o.status);
      }
      //execute whichever handler is appropriate
      dialog.callback.success = onSuccess;
      dialog.callback.failure = onFailure;
```

```
  //define the showDialog function
  var showDialog = function() {
    //define the transaction success and failure handlers
    var responseSuccess = function(o) {
      //remove existing rating
      var mydialog = YAHOO.util.Dom.get("dialog");
      var fchild = YAHOO.util.Dom.getFirstChild(mydialog);
      var nsib = YAHOO.util.Dom.getNextSibling(fchild);
      var lsib = YAHOO.util.Dom.getLastChild(nsib);
      if (lsib.className != "") {
        lsib.parentNode.removeChild(lsib);
      }
      //create the new rating
      var p = document.createElement("p");
      YAHOO.util.Dom.addClass(p, "result");
      var rating = document.createTextNode(o.responseText);
      p.appendChild(rating);
      dialog.appendToBody(p);
    }
    var responseFailure = function(o) {
      alert(o.status);
    }
    //define the transaction callback object
    var callback = {
      success:responseSuccess,
      failure:responseFailure
    }
    //initiate the transaction
    var trans = YAHOO.util.Connect.asyncRequest("POST",
              "getratings.php", callback, "image=" + target);
      dialog.form.image.value = target;
    //show the dialog
    YAHOO.util.Dom.setStyle("dialog", "display", "block");
    dialog.show();
  }
  //execute showDialog when the appropriate context menuitem is
  //clicked
  YAHOO.util.Event.addListener("yui-gen14", "click", showDialog);
}
//execute the initDialog function when the DOM is ready
YAHOO.util.Event.onDOMReady( YAHOO.yuibook.menu.initDialog);
//define the initSimpleDialog function
```

```
YAHOO.yuibook.menu.initSimpleDialog = function() {
  //handle the ok button click
  var handleOk = function() {
    if (target == "img1"){
      imageInfo1.hide();
    } else {
      imageInfo2.hide();
    }
  }
  //define the SimpleDialog objects
  var imageInfo1 = new YAHOO.widget.SimpleDialog("sdialog1", {
    width:"250px",
    fixedcenter:true,
    modal:true,
    visible:false,
    icon: YAHOO.widget.SimpleDialog.ICON_INFO,
    buttons:[{text:"Ok", handler:handleOk}]
  });
  var imageInfo2 = new YAHOO.widget.SimpleDialog("sdialog2", {
    width:"250px",
    fixedcenter:true,
    modal:true,
    visible:false,
    icon: YAHOO.widget.SimpleDialog.ICON_INFO,
    buttons:[{text:"Ok", handler:handleOk}]
  });
  //set the content of the SimpleDialogs
  imageInfo1.setHeader("Information for Image 1");
  imageInfo1.setBody("<br>Image Title: Superman<br>Artist:
              The Extremist<br>Creation date: 2006<br>&copy;
              Copyright? Yes");
  imageInfo2.setHeader("Information for Image 2");
  imageInfo2.setBody("<br>Image Title: She-Ra Pin Up<br>Artist:
             The Extremist<br>Creation date: 2007<br>&copy;
             Copyright? Yes");
  //render the SimpleDialogs
  imageInfo1.render(document.body);
  imageInfo2.render(document.body);
  //show the SimpleDialog
  var showSimpleDialog = function() {
    if (target == "img1"){
      imageInfo1.show();
    } else {
```

```
            imageInfo2.show();
          }
        }
        //call showSDialog when the appropriate context menuitem is
          selected
        YAHOO.util.Event.addListener("yui-gen13", "click",
                                                    showSimpleDialog);
      }
      //execute initSimpleDialog when DOMis ready
      YAHOO.util.Event.onDOMReady(YAHOO.yuibook.menu.initSimpleDialog);
      //define the initTooltip function
      YAHOO.yuibook.menu.initTooltip = function() {
        //define the Tooltip object
        var toolt = new YAHOO.widget.Tooltip("imgTip", {
          context:images,
          text:"Right-click for options (Opera users will need to use
                                         the Ctrl key + left-click)"
        });
      }
      //execute initTooltip when the DOMis ready
      YAHOO.util.Event.onDOMReady(YAHOO.yuibook.menu.initTooltip);

    }
    //execute the initPage function when the DOM is ready
    YAHOO.util.Event.onDOMReady( YAHOO.yuibook.menu.initPage);
  </script>
```

One of the requirements of the Tooltip is that although it isn't built from existing HTML, the context element that it is attached to must exist in the DOM before the Tooltip is initialized. The `.onDOMReady()` method ensures that this happens. As we need to reference the `images` variable used by the ContextMenu, we have had to move it so that it is created with the `target` variable.

The Tooltip control itself is created with the Tooltip constructor, specifying the `id` to be given to the Tooltip object, and a configuration object which makes use of the `context` and `text` configuration properties.

The `context` property allows us to supply a reference to the HTML element the Tooltip is to be attached to, while the `text` property lets us define the text that will appear within the Tooltip.

Run the page in a browser now and you should see the Tooltip control when you hover over one of the images on the page:

The Tooltip is styled automatically by the `sam` skin just like the rest of the Container types. It's also given an attractive drop shadow and will automatically close after a set amount of time (5 seconds). This can be adjusted using the `hideDelay` configuration property if required.

Another configuration attribute, `effect`, can let us easily specify animations to occur when the Tooltip control is shown and hidden. Change the `initTooltip()` function so that it appears as follows:

```
//define the initTooltip function
YAHOO.yuibook.menu.initTooltip = function() {
  //define the Tooltip object
  var toolt = new YAHOO.widget.Tooltip("imgTip", {
    context:images,
    text:"Right-click for options (Opera users will need to use the
                                        Ctrl key + left-click)",
    hideDelay:"300",
    effect: {effect: YAHOO.widget.ContainerEffect.SLIDE, duration:
                                                              0.5}
  });
}
//execute initTooltip when the DOMis ready
YAHOO.util.Event.onDOMReady( YAHOO.yuibook.menu.initTooltip);
```

This time, we've used the `YAHOO.widget.ContainerEffect.SLIDE` constant to set a neat slide-in and slide-out effect on the Tooltip.

The Tooltip control will automatically replace the tooltips that are generated by the browser when elements have a `title` attribute. You could remove the title attributes from the `<img>` elements in our underlying mark up for the page, however the `alt` text, as well as our Tooltip object, will both be displayed when the pointer hovers over an image. Therefore you should still use the `title` attribute in your HTML.

Overriding Sam

If you don't like the default styling or if it just doesn't fit in with your existing site scheme, overriding the default appearance is very simple. In the `tooltips.css` file that we created, add the following selector and rule set to the bottom of the page:

```
.yui-skin-sam .yui-tt .bd {
  background-color:#B3D4FF;
  color:#ffffff;
  border:2px solid #085394;
}
```

Now the Tooltips will match the rest of the page. As you can see in the screenshot at the start of this section, the Tooltip component is as easy to style personally as it is to implement on your page.

The YUI TabView Control

A visit to almost any area of the expansive Yahoo! web portal is practically guaranteed to result in your exposure to a TabView control in action. It's easy to see why; tabbed content is both attractive and functional, and helps to maximize the content on any one page without overcrowding it.

Unlike manually creating your own tabbed interface, which takes a lot of time, skill and of course, debugging, using the TabView control is both quick and easy. Just like the Menu control, it is constructed using a logical unordered list, and like many of the library components, it can be built from underlying mark up or entirely from simple JavaScript.

Whether your TabView control is built from HTML or script, its API provides a rich and varied set of properties, methods and events which allow you to programmatically switch between tabs, create, or destroy them, and manipulate the content contained in them with ease.

To make more of a visual impact with your tabbed content containers, you can include the Animation utility and define transition effects that occur when the active tab changes. Using the Connection Manager utility, you can even pull in the data for your tabs asynchronously.

TabView Classes

The TabView control consists of two classes: `YAHOO.widget.Tab` and `YAHOO.widget.TabView`. Both are subclasses of `YAHOO.util.Element` and inherit a few properties, methods, and events from it. The TabView class is the class from which the complete TabView control is derived, whereas the Tab class represents one tab and its content. Both have their uses so let's look at them quickly now, starting with their constructors.

The `YAHOO.widget.TabView()` constructor that is used to create a TabView control on the page takes two arguments. The first is optional and can be one of the following:

- a string
- an attributes object
- an HTML element

If neither a string nor an HTML element is supplied as the first argument, an attributes object specifying which element to use to create the TabView control should be provided instead. If a string or HTML element is provided as the first argument, an attributes object can, optionally, be provided as the second argument.

The constructor for `YAHOO.widget.Tab` also has an optional first argument: a string or HTML element. You don't need to specify each `<li>` element that should represent a tab because the control will create these elements itself. The second argument, the object containing the configuration properties is required however, and is used to specify among other things: the label text, the content associated with the tab, and whether it is active by default.

So the TabView constructor creates the overall tabbed control and the Tab constructor is used to create individual tabs and their content. One point that is not instantly obvious is that even when generating a tabbed control entirely from script using the two constructors, your HTML mark up still needs to have an empty container `<div>` with `id` and `class` attributes explicitly defined for the control to be rendered into.

Properties, Methods, and Events

The properties that are defined natively to both classes revolve mostly around CSS class names given to different parts of the TabView element such as the following found in the `YAHOO.widget.TabView` class:

- `CLASSNAME` — the name of the class for the containing element when building a TabView control from scratch. The default is **yui-navset**
- `CONTENT_PARENT_CLASSNAME` — the name of the class for the element containing the content. The default is **yui-content**
- `TAB_PARENT_CLASSNAME` — the name of the element containing the tab elements. The default is **yui-nav**

As well as the following properties in the `YAHOO.widget.Tab` class:

- `ACTIVE_CLASSNAME` — the name of the class applied to active tabs. The default is **on**
- `DISABLED_CLASSNAME` — the name of the class applied to disabled tabs. Defaults to **disabled**
- `LOADING_CLASSNAME` — the name of the class applied to tabs that obtain their content dynamically while the content is being loaded. Again, defaults to **disabled**

There are a few others, and both classes also inherit a small number of them.

As for the methods, the Tab class defines only two of its own methods: `initAttributes`, which is used automatically by the control to initialize the attributes within the configuration object, and the `toString` method which returns the name of the tab.

The `YAHOO.widget.TabView` class defines a much larger number of native methods, including the following:

- `.addTab()` — used to add a new tab to the control. The tab instance to add to the control should appear as the first argument and the second, optional argument is the index position to add it at
- `.getTab()` — used to obtain the tab at the index specified by its only argument
- `.getTabIndex()` — used to obtain the index of a tab specified in its single argument
- `.removeTab()` — removes the specified tab instance

Both classes define a series of custom events so that you can capture the most interesting moments during interactions with the TabView control. The most useful events deal with before and after active tab changes.

Adding Tabs

In this example, let's suppose that we're making a website for a computer hardware retailer; on pages that display items for sale we'll use a tabbed interface to provide extended product information displayed on a series of tabs.

We'll just create one page of this imaginary site, and as the data for the products would probably come out of a database, we'll also look at adding content to tabs dynamically using the Connection Manager. The finished page should end up looking something like this:

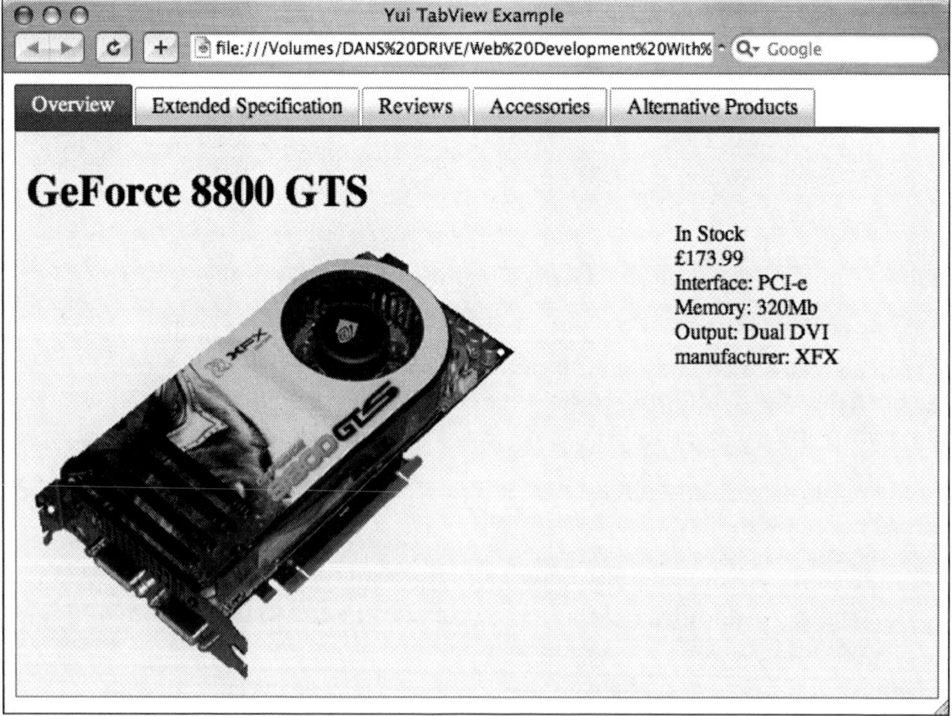

The Underlying Mark Up

Begin in a blank page in your text editor with the following HTML:

```
<!DOCTYPE HTML PUBLIC "-//W3C//DTD HTML 4.01//EN"
                                  "http://www.w3.org/TR/html4/strict.dtd">
<html lang="en">
  <head>
    <meta http-equiv="content-type" content="text/html;
                                    charset=utf-8">
    <title>Yui TabView Example</title>
    <script type="text/javascript"
            src="yui/build/yahoo-dom-event/yahoo-dom-event.js">
    </script>
    <script type="text/javascript"
            src="yui/build/element/element-beta-min.js"></script>
    <script type="text/javascript"
            src="yui/build/connection/connection-min.js"></script>
    <script type="text/javascript"
            src="yui/build/tabview/tabview-min.js"></script>
    <link rel="stylesheet" type="text/css"
          href="yui/build/assets/skins/sam/tabview.css">
    <link rel="stylesheet" type="text/css"
          href="yui/build/tabview/assets/border_tabs.css">
    <link rel="stylesheet" type="text/css" href="tabview.css">
  </head>
```

As always, the order in which the library files are linked to is important so make sure you follow the above format. Next we can add the underlying HTML for the page. This will form the foundation of the TabView control:

```
  <body class="yui-skin-sam">
    <div id="productTabs" class="yui-navset">
      <ul class="yui-nav">
        <li class="selected">
          <a href="#tab1"><em>Overview</em></a></li>
        <li><a href="#tab2"><em>Extended Specification</em></a></li>
        <li><a href="#tab3"><em>Reviews</em></a></li>
      </ul>
      <div class="yui-content">
        <div>
          <h1>GeForce 8800 GTS</h1>
          <img src="images/gcard.gif" alt="GeForce 8800 GTS">
          <div class="descText">
            In Stock<br>
            &pound;173.99<br>
            Interface: PCI-e<br>
            Memory: 320Mb<br>
```

```
          Output: Dual DVI<br>
          manufacturer: XFX<br>
        </div>
      </div>
      <div>
        <h1>Full Spec</h1>
        Memory Interface: 320bit<br>
        Memory Type: DDR3<br>
        RAMDACs: Dual 400 MHz<br>
        Memory Bandwidth: 64GB/sec<br>
        Fill Rate: 24 billion/sec<br>
        Graphics Core: 500 MHz<br>
        Clock Rate: 580 MHz<br>
        Chip Set: GeForce &trade; 8800 GTS<br>
        Interface: PCI-e
      </div>
      <div><h1>Consumer Reviews</h1>
        <p>The 8800 GTS is the best thing ever, woot. Lorem ipsum
                                                              etc…</p>
        <p>In et lorem, etc…</p>
        <p>Phasellus non erat etc…</p>
      </div>
    </div>
  </div>
 </body>
</html>
```

The outer container for the TabView control is a simple `<div>` element. We can give it an `id` attribute which will be fed to the constructor and a `class` so that it can be targeted by the `sam` skin for styling.

The Tab headings are created from a simple `<ul>` that has been given the class name `yui-nav`. The content areas of the tabs are created from `<div>` elements that appear as child nodes of the `<div class="yui-content">` element. You need to ensure that there are the same number of `<li>` elements in the tab headings list as there are `<div>` elements in the tab content container.

The JavaScript Needed by TabView

We'll only need a tiny bit of JavaScript to initially build our basic TabView control. Directly before the closing `</body>` tag, add the following `<script>` block:

```
<script type="text/javascript">
  //create the namespace object for this example
  YAHOO.namespace("yuibook.tabs");
  //define the initTabs function
  YAHOO.yuibook.tabs.initTabs = function() {
    //define the TabView object
    var tabs = new YAHOO.widget.TabView("productTabs");
  }
  //execute initTabs when the DOM is ready
  YAHOO.util.Event.onDOMReady(YAHOO.yuibook.tabs.initTabs);
</script>
```

The `YAHOO.widget.TabView()` constructor takes just the `id` of the container element and this one line of code creates the whole TabView control! If you save this file and run it your browser now, you'll see the `sam`—styled and fully functional control.

A Little CSS

Normally, you'd be using the TabView control with other elements on the page, probably inside one of the `grid.css` page layouts, but as the tabbed container is the only element on the page, it stretches the entire width of the page. We can easily fix this by overriding the `sam` skin with some CSS of our own. Any aspect of the skin can be changed using this same method.

In a new page in your text editor, add the following code:

```
.yui-sam-skin .yui-navset {
  width:700px;
}
.desctText {
  position:absolute;
  top:100px;
  left:500px;
}
```

View the page in your browser again, it should now look like this:

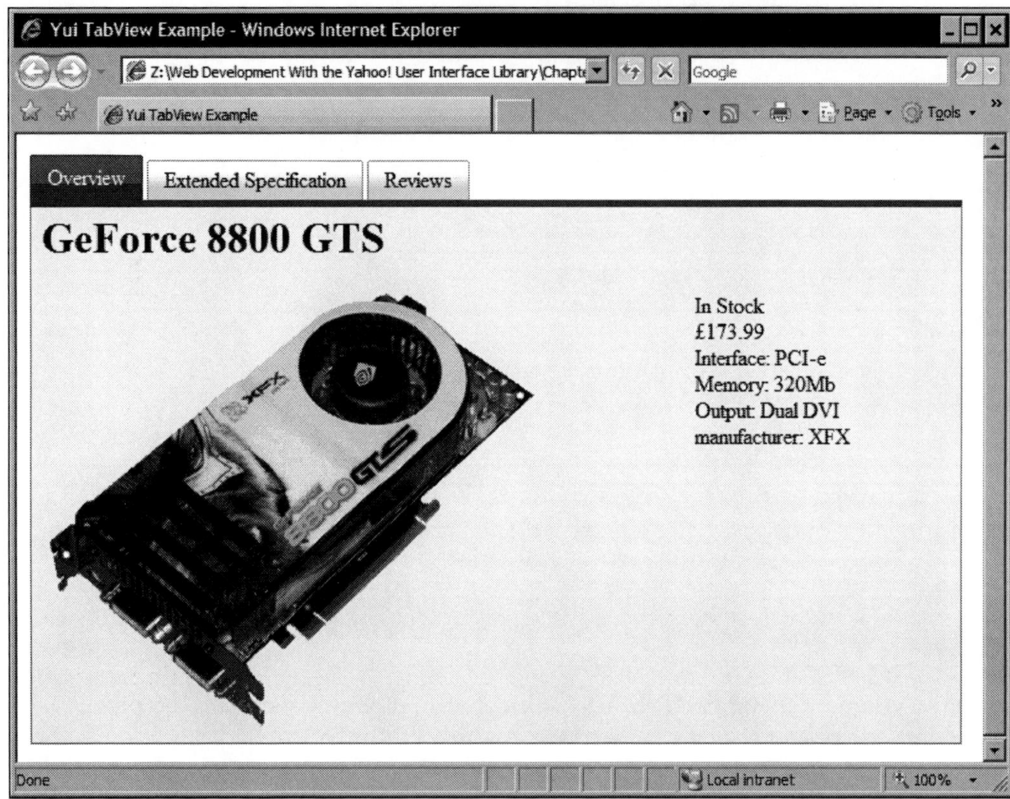

We talked about adding tabs via script and adding content dynamically earlier on so let's extend this example a little to look at both of these in more detail. First we'll generate a whole new tab and its content via script. Add the following code to the existing `<script>` block. It will need to appear directly after the TabView constructor:

```
//add a new tab programmatically
tabs.addTab(new YAHOO.widget.Tab({
  label:"Accessories",
  content:"SLI bridge<br>4 pin molex to 6 pin PCI-e adapter<br>
                                              DVI to DSUB converter"
}));
```

That's all you need. The `.addTab()` method uses the `YAHOO.widget.Tab` constructor to create a new `Tab` element. We don't specify the `id` of any underlying elements, instead we use an object literal to create the tab label and the tab content.

Now when you run the page, you should get the new tab:

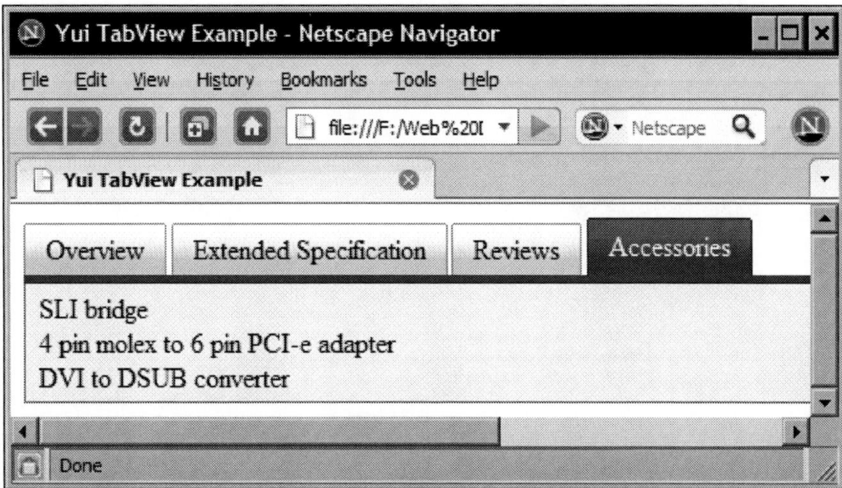

Let's move on to adding content to a Tab dynamically using the Connection utility. For this example, we'll use PHP to read and return data from an XML file. The Connection utility will query the PHP file and receive the response from it, which will then be displayed as content in another dynamically generated tab.

Begin by adding the following additional JavaScript directly below the new tab we just defined:

```
//add another new tab
tabs.addTab(new YAHOO.widget.Tab({
  dataSrc:"altprods.php",
  label:"Alternative Products"
}));
```

The `dataSrc` configuration attribute allows us to specify the location of an external application and tells the TabView control to communicate with the Connection Manger to retrieve the content of the tab. This is why we don't need to define the content using the `content` key, we only need to specify the `label`. All we have to worry about now are the XML and PHP files that are also required for this example to work.

Again you'll need to place the relevant files into a content-serving directory of your web server, and PHP (ideally the latest version) must be installed and configured. We'll create the XML file first so that we know how it is structured in order to write the correct PHP code.

In a blank page in your text editor, add the following code:

```
<?xml version="1.0"?>
<altprods>
  <prod>
    <thumb>img1.jpg</thumb>
    <name>GeForceFX 5500</name>
    <stock>Out of stock</stock>
    <price>£49.99</price>
  </prod>
  <prod>
    <thumb>img2.jpg</thumb>
    <name>S3 Chrome</name>
    <stock>In Stock</stock>
    <price>£29.99</price>
  </prod>
  <prod>
    <thumb>img3.jpg</thumb>
    <name>Matrox Millenium</name>
    <stock>In Stock</stock>
    <price>£79.99</price>
  </prod>
</altprods>
```

We have three product elements, each containing child nodes which hold information about the alternative products. Save this file as `altprods.xml`.

Now we're ready to create the PHP file. All the script will need to do is open the XML file, cycle through the nodes in the XML file and echo back the results. In another blank page of your text editor, add the following PHP code:

```
<?php
  if (!$altprods = simplexml_load_file("altprods.xml")) {
    echo "Error reading file";
  }
  foreach($altprods as $prod) {
    echo "<p><div><img src='images/".$prod->thumb."'></div>
             <div class='altText'>".$prod->name."<br>"
               .$prod->stock."<br>".$prod->price."</div></p>";
  }
?>
```

Luckily PHP 5 has many built-in methods for parsing XML, so the amount of PHP coding we need to do is minimal, just like the JavaScript that's required of us. Save this as `altprods.php`. Finally add the following CSS to the bottom of `tabview.css`:

```
.altText {
  position:absolute;
  left:120px;
  margin-top:-70px;
}
```

When you run the `tabview.html` file in your browser now and select the **Alternative Products** tab, you should see something like this:

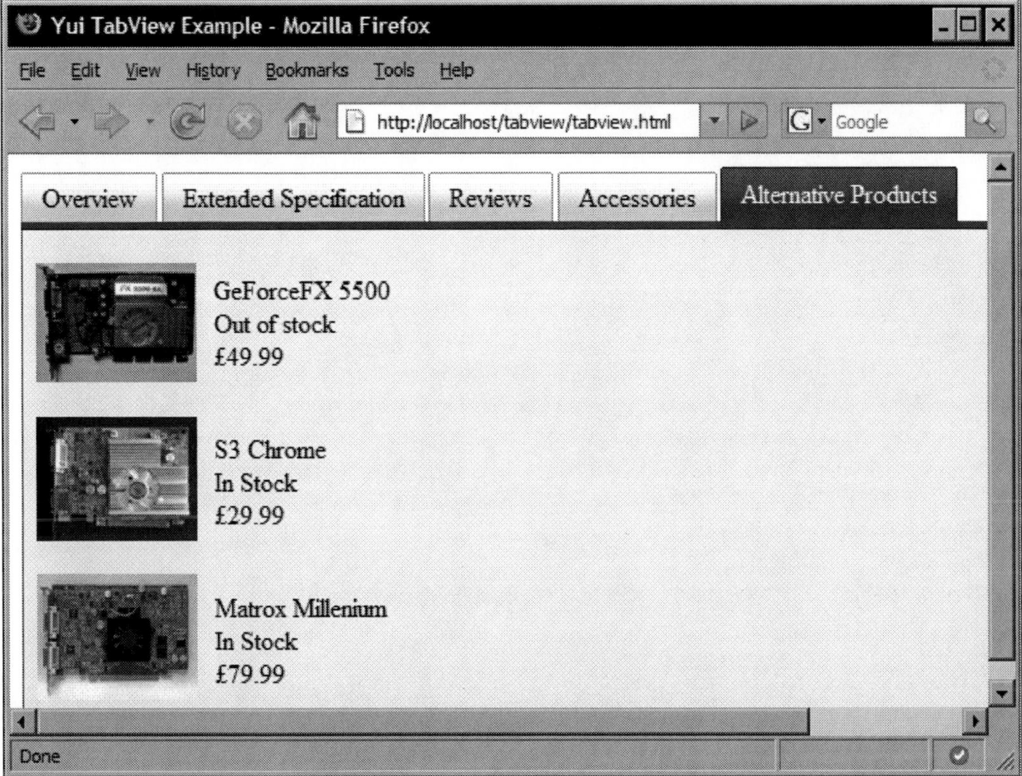

Summary

The Container family of controls found in the YUI provides an important series of components that allow you to add elements to your web applications which make them look and feel more like desktop applications.

All of the different containers are highly configurable and come pre-styled for your convenience. Using them takes surprisingly little code, so you can focus more on your content instead of worrying about how to present it.

TabView offers a flexible approach to grouping related chunks of content in an attractive tabbed interface, and gives you full control over the tab headings and tab content, allowing you to add new tabs and new data on the fly from a variety of sources.

9

Drag-and-Drop with the YUI

I remember the excitement I felt after drag-and-drop operations on web pages first became possible with the advent of DHTML and the release of capable browsers. The feeling soon wore off, it was messy, it took an awful lot of code, and browser support was haphazard at best.

Now thanks to the YUI, that same giddy feeling of joy has returned, and this time I can't see the bubble bursting so quickly. Drag-and-drop with Yahoo's library is extremely easy to implement, completely clean, and cross-compatible with the entire spectrum of A-grade browsers.

We've already had a little exposure to the usefulness of drag-and-drop in the previous chapter, as this is the mechanism which allows Panels and Dialogs to be dragged around the viewport (provided this attribute is enabled). In this chapter we're going to examine this utility in more detail.

Dynamic Drag-and-Drop without the Hassle

When we configured our Panel and Dialog boxes to be draggable in the last chapter, that's all we had to do—no additional configuration was required and the library handled everything for us.

Like most of the other library components, when creating your own drag-and-drop elements, there are a range of different options available to you that allow you to tailor those objects to your requirements. These properties, like those of most other library components, can be set using an object literal supplied with the constructor, but in most cases even this is not required.

The most challenging aspects of any drag-and-drop scenario in your web applications are going to center around the design of your specific implementation rather than in getting drag-and-drop to work in the first place. This utility is yet another example of the huge benefits the YUI can provide in reducing the amount of coding and troubleshooting that you need to concern yourself with.

The Different Components of Drag-and-Drop

In addition to the configurable properties used in your object literal, you also have several constructors that can be used to enable drag-and-drop. The first constructor `YAHOO.util.DD` allows for drag-and-drop at its most basic level. The supplied element will be transformed into an object that can be dragged around the page.

The mechanics of drag-and-drop result in a burden of fairly high processing. The library has to keep track of the mouse pointer whilst it is moving, the draggable object needs to be repositioned, and different events are almost continually firing while the drag is taking place.

In order to minimize the amount of information that needs to be processed, especially when the draggable object is fairly large, you can make use of a proxy element that will track across the page with the mouse pointer. When the proxy element reaches its final destination, it disappears and is replaced by the actual element.

If a proxy element is required, we can use the `YAHOO.util.DDProxy` constructor instead of the basic constructor. As the proxy element is just an empty `<div>`, it's much easier to track and can even be shared between different drag objects on the page, reducing the overall processing that's required.

Personally I think the default appearance of the proxy element is perfectly adequate, however you can also create your own custom elements to use as a proxy. The figure below shows the default proxy-element appearance:

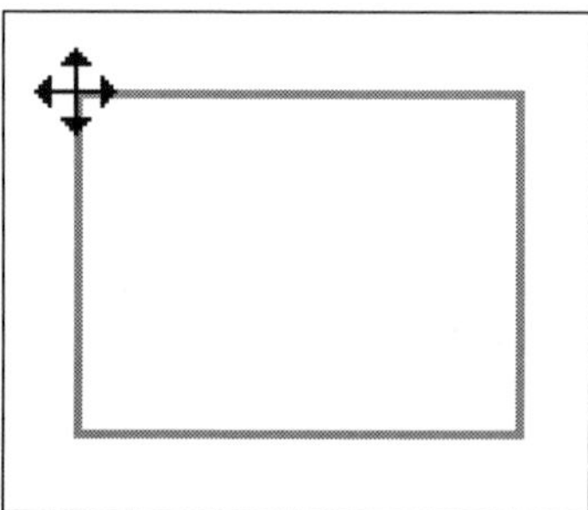

Design Considerations

When working with DragDrop implementations, it is useful to consider the following aspects of the design:

- Can any part of the drag object be clicked on to initiate the drag, or should a drag handle be defined?
- Can the object be dropped on to any part of the page or should a specific drop target be defined?
- Should anything occur whilst the object is being dragged?
- Should anything occur when the item is dropped on a non-valid target?
- Should anything occur when the object is dropped on to a valid target?

Events

Events are an integral aspect of many DragDrop situations. Sometimes, however, like in the Panel examples from the last chapter, being able to move something around the screen is the only behavior that's required, but generally you'll want something to happen either while the object is being dragged, or when it is dropped.

The `YAHOO.util.DragDrop` utility provides a series of custom events which allow you to hook into and respond to events such as `startDrag`, `endDrag`, `onDrag`, `onDragDrop`, and `onInvalidDrop`. Valid targets also expose events of their own including `onDragEnter`, `onDragOut`, and `onDragOver`. We will be looking at a number of these events during the example that follows.

Allowing Your Visitors to Drag-and-Drop

The Drag-and-Drop utility uses tried and tested DHTML techniques, as well as some innovative new features, to allow you to easily create objects that can be dragged and then dropped. All that you need to do to make an element on your page dragable is to create a new instance of the `YAHOO.util.DD` class and feed in the `id` or element reference of the element that drag is to be enabled for.

DragDrop Classes

The base class of the Drag-and-Drop utility is `YAHOO.util.DragDrop`, but you'll use one of its extending subclasses, like `YAHOO.util.DD`, most of the time. This subclass inherits all of the properties and methods of the base class and even adds a few of its own, so it's more than capable of handling most of your drag-and-drop requirements.

The `YAHOO.util.DD` class also has its own subclasses to deal with additional drag-and-drop requirements for different situations. The subclasses are `YAHOO.util.DDProxy` and `YAHOO.widget.SliderThumb`. As you can see, the Drag-and-Drop utility provides some of the basic functionality of another of the controls found in the YUI, the Slider Control (which we will look at in more detail towards the end of this chapter). Let's examine the `DDProxy` class, as that is relevant specifically to the Drag-and-Drop utility.

Creating a proxy object that tracks with the cursor when a drag object is being dragged instead of allowing the actual drag object to track can prevent problems that arise with large drag objects not tracking properly or obscuring other content on the page. The proxy object is a small, empty object that represents the drag object and shows only its borders.

The proxy object is created on the `mouseDown` event of the drag object and the actual drag object does not move to its new position until the `mouseUp` event is fired. Using a proxy object is both visually appealing and better overall for all but the simplest of implementations performance wise.

The Constructor

The constructor for an instance of the DragDrop object can also take a second or third argument when you are instantiating objects for dragging. The second argument, which is optional, specifies the group to which the element being dragged belongs.

This refers to interaction groups—the object being dragged can only interact with and fire events with other elements in its interaction group. The third argument, which is also optional, can be used to supply a configuration object, the members of which hold additional optional configuration properties that can easily be accessed and set.

Every object instantiated with the drag-and-drop constructor is a member of one or more interaction group(s), even if the second argument is not passed. When the argument is not supplied, the object will simply belong to the 'default' group instead. There is no limit as to how many groups an object can belong to.

The API provides just two methods that relate to group access. `.addToGroup()` is used to add the object to more than one group, so the first group membership is defined with the constructor and subsequent groups with the `.addToGroup()` method. To remove an object from a group, just call the `.removeFromGroup()` method.

Target Practice

There is no doubt that drag-and-drop adds a hands-on, fun element to surfing the net that is way more engaging than simple point-and-click scenarios, and there are many serious applications of this behavior too.

But dragging is only half of the action; without assigned drop targets, the usefulness of being able to drag elements on the page around at leisure is almost wasted.

Drop targets have a class of their own in the Drag-and-Drop utility. Which extends the `YAHOO.util.DragDrop` base class to cater for the creation of drag elements that aren't actually dragable and this is the defining attribute of a drop target.

The constructor is exactly the same as for the DD and Proxy classes with regard to the arguments passed, but `YAHOO.util.DDTarget` is used instead. The Target class has no methods or properties of its own, but it inherits all of the same methods and properties as the other two classes, including all of the events.

Get a Handle on Things

By default, holding down the mouse button whilst hovering over a drag object results in the mouse pointer 'picking up' the drag object. The pointer can be over any part of the drag object and the drag action will still be initiated.

Handles change this default behavior and become the only part of the drag object that responds to the `mouseDown` event. You can define multiple handles on a single drag object and the handle can even be completely external to the drag object.

To use a handle (or handles) for dragging, the draggable element itself is defined in the same way, but a child element is specified in the underlying HTML as the handle. It is then created by the library by calling the `.setHandleElId()`, or the `.setOuterHandleElId()` methods.

Both of these methods take just one parameter—the `id` of the element to use as the handle. The first method is used for handles that appear within the boundaries of the drag object, the second method is used when the handle appears outside the drag object.

There are several other useful methods that revolve mostly around allowing you to specify child elements of drag handles that should not initiate a drag interaction, or for indicating a CSS class or HTML element type that should not act as a drag handle or react to `mouseDown` events. This is useful for creating elements within the drag-and-drop element that react to clicks in a different way.

The Drag-and-Drop Manager

The page-wide manager of all drag-and-drop interactions is `YAHOO.util.DragDropMgr`. It features a huge API stuffed to the brim with properties and methods (although a number of the methods are marked as deprecated).

There's a lot in this class but fortunately, you don't need to take much notice of it as it works in the background during drag interactions to make sure everything proceeds as it should. There are a few helper methods that can be hugely useful however, so it is worth taking at least a quick look at the source file to see what they are.

The `getBestMatch()` function is useful for when a drag object overlaps several drop targets and helps you decide which target the element should actually be dropped on. This method is only used in intersect mode (see the next section) and takes an array of the targets as its argument. It returns the best match based on either the target that the cursor is over or the element with the greatest amount of overlap.

There are also a couple of properties that are used to initiate the dragging of an object. The first property is the pixel threshold (`clickPixelThresh`) which tells the script how many pixels the cursor should move while the mouse button is held down before a drag begins, the default is three pixels.

The second property is the time threshold (`clickTimeThresh`) which defines how long the button needs to be held down whilst the pointer is stationary before it is recognized as a drag. The default for this one is 1000 milliseconds.

Interaction Modes

The utility supports two types of interaction: point mode and intersect mode (although there are actually two types of intersect). Point mode means that as soon as any point of the mouse cursor touches any point of the drop target, the `dragOver` event fires. Alternatively, in intersect mode, as soon as the drop target is touched at any point with the drag object (even by just 1 pixel), the `dragOver` event fires.

To switch between the two modes programmatically, the DragDropManager has a property called `mode` (`YAHOO.util.DDM.mode`), which can be set to one of three values: `YAHOO.util.DDM.POINT`, `YAHOO.util.DDM.INTERSECT` or `YAHOO.util.DDM.STRICT_INTERSECT`.

With intersect mode, the interaction is defined by either the cursor or the amount of overlap, but with strict intersect the interaction is defined just by the amount of overlap. POINT mode is the default value.

Implementing Drag-and-Drop

To highlight some of the basic features and considerations of drag-and-drop we'll create a shopping basket application, which can be used by visitors to drag products they want to buy into the basket.

The page that we'll end up with by the end of this example will look like this:

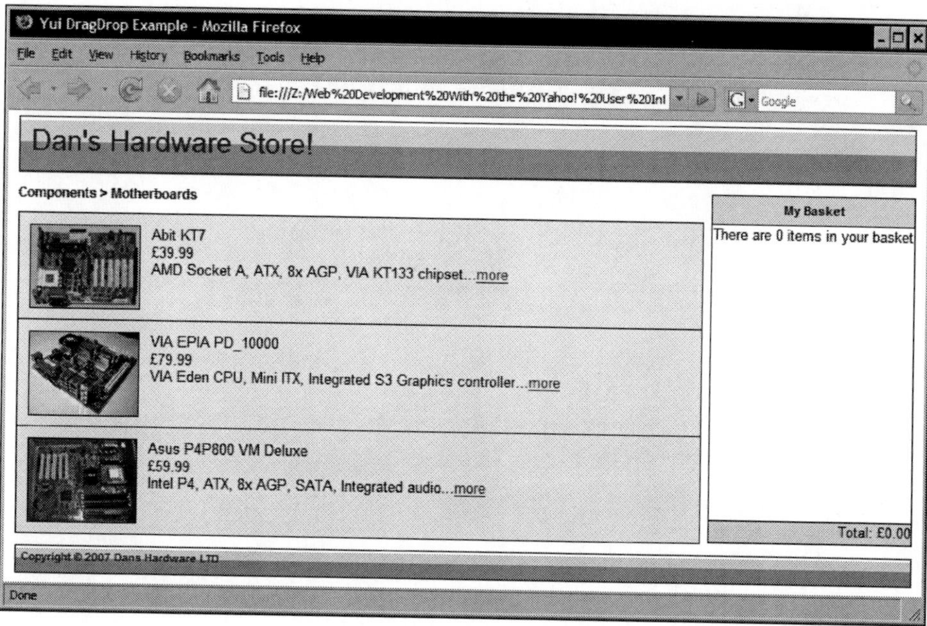

In a blank page in your text editor, begin with the following basic HTML page:

```
<!DOCTYPE HTML PUBLIC "-//W3C//DTD HTML 4.01//EN"
                               "http://www.w3.org/TR/html4/strict.dtd">
<html lang="en">
  <head>
    <meta http-equiv="content-type" content="text/html;
                                     charset=utf-8">
    <title>Yui DragDrop Example</title>
    <script type="text/javascript"
            src="yui/build/yahoo-dom-event/yahoo-dom-event.js">
    </script>
    <script type="text/javascript"
            src="yui/build/dragdrop/dragdrop-min.js"></script>
    <link rel="stylesheet" type="text/css"
          href="yui/build/reset-fonts-grids/reset-fonts-grids.css">
    <link rel="stylesheet" type="text/css"
          href="basket.css">
  </head>
```

```
  <body>
    <div id="doc3" class="yui-t6">
      <div id="hd"><h1>Dan's Hardware Store!</h1></div>
      <div id="bd">
        <div id="yui-main">
          <div class="yui-b">
            <div class="yui-g"></div>
          </div>
        </div>
        <div class="yui-b"></div>
      </div>
      <div id="ft">Copyright © 2007 Dans Hardware LTD</div>
    </div>
  </body>
</html>
```

We'll use the `doc3` 100% fluid page layout and the `t6` template to give us a convenient right-hand side bar into which we can place our shopping basket. We can also add the link for the external stylesheet that we'll create shortly.

Let's add the code for the products listing first. Normally, this kind of data would come out of a database dynamically when the page was loaded, but in this example, the data will be will be hard-coded into the page. We are inputting the data this way so that we can focus purely on the drag-and-drop aspect.

To keep things simple, we'll just show a couple of products; insert the following code into the `yui-g` div:

```
<div class="crumbTrail">Components > Motherboards</div>
<div class="listing_green"><img id="prod1"
                          src="images/prod1.jpg" alt="image1">
                          <div id="prod1info" class="info">
                          Abit KT7<br>£39.99<br>AMD Socket A, ATX,
                          8x AGP, VIA KT133 chipset...
                          <a href="">more</a></div></div>
<div class="listing_grey"><img id="prod2"
                         src="images/prod2.jpg" alt="image2">
                         <div id="prod2info" class="info">
                         VIA EPIA PD_10000<br>£79.99<br>VIA Eden
                         CPU, Mini ITX, Integrated S3 Graphics
                         controller...
                         <a href="">more</a></div></div>
<div class="listing_green"><img id="prod3"
                          src="images/prod3.jpg" alt="image3">
                          <div id="prod3info" class="info">
                          Asus P4P800 VM Deluxe<br>£59.99<br>Intel
                          P4, ATX, 8x AGP, SATA, Integrated
                          audio...<a href="">more</a></div></div>
```

We can add a few of the things that you'd expect to find on a page such as this, like the breadcrumb trail links and `more` links. Clicking on these obviously won't do anything in our example, but it helps set the overall effect of the page.

Now let's add the mark up for the shopping basket itself. Add the below code to the `yui-b` container `<div>`:

```
<div id="basket">
  <div id="title">My Basket</div>
  <div id="basketBody">There are <span id="basketTotal">0</span> items
in your basket</div>
  <div id="total">Total: &pound;
    <span id="basketCost">0.00</span></div>
</div>
```

Save what we've added so far as `dragdropbasket.html` in your `yuisite` folder.

The Required CSS

As drag-and-drop itself is behavior-based rather than a UI control, we don't need to worry about using `sam` skin files. However, in order to set the page up correctly, we will be making use of the grids CSS tool, as well as our own custom stylesheet.

At this stage, there's nothing particularly spectacular about the collection of elements that make up the basket. In order for both aspects of the page to look right, we also need to add some basic CSS. In a new file in your text editor, add the following CSS code:

```
#hd {
  font-size:197%;
  height:44px;
  background: url(images/headbg.gif) repeat-x;
  color:#000099;
  padding-top:5px;
  border:1px solid #000099;
  margin:5px 0px 10px 0px;
  padding-left:10px;
}
.crumbTrail {
  font:bold 93% arial, sans-serif;
  margin-bottom:10px;
}
.listing_green {
  width:99%;
  height:75px;
```

```
    background-color:#d8f2e0;
    padding:10px;
    border:1px solid #000000;
  }
  .listing_grey {
    width:99%;
    height:75px;
    background-color:#e9eae9;
    padding:10px;
    border:1px solid #000000;
    border-bottom:0px;
    border-top:0px;
  }
  img {
    border:1px solid #000000;
    float:left;
    margin-right:10px;
  }
  #prod1, #prod2, #prod3 {
    cursor:move;
  }
  .info {
    width:80%;
    float:left;
  }
  #basket {
    width:95%;
    height:311px;
    float:right;
    border:1px solid #000000;
  }
  #title {
    height:20px;
    font:bold 85% arial, sans-serif;
    text-align:center;
    border-bottom:1px solid #000000;
    padding-top:5px;
    background-color:#dbdbff;
  }
  #basketBody {
    text-align:center;
    height:265px;
    border-bottom:1px solid #000000;
  }
```

```
#total {
  width:100%;
  text-align:right;
  background-color:#dbdbff;
  height:19px;
}
#ft {
  font:bold 77% arial, sans-serif;
  margin-top:10px;
  background: url(images/footbg.gif) repeat-x;
  height:21px;
  border:1px solid #000099;
  color:#000099;
  padding:3px 0px 0px 5px;
}
```

This is it for now as far as the CSS goes. We'll need some more in a little while, but for now save this file as `basket.css` in the same directory as the HTML page.

If you re-open the `dragdropbasket.html` file in your text editor again, we can begin adding the JavaScript that will bring this page to life. At this point, your page should now resemble the screenshot at the start of this section.

Scripting DragDrop

There are two ways that we could go about achieving our objective. We could take the easy way and treat each draggable object as an independent module, with its own independent properties and event handlers. This would make the code simpler, but would mean that we would require a good deal more of it.

If there are just one or two objects on your page which can be dragged and dropped then this way is fine. However, when you begin to have more than just a couple of objects that can be moved, the amount of code required to handle these objects efficiently increases dramatically.

The second way may be a little more complex and therefore will require a greater degree of understanding. However, this way allows for sharing properties and event handlers across similar drag-and-drop objects. This reduces the overall footprint of your application and saves us an incredible amount of typing.

Creating Individual Drag Objects

We can look at both methods, so you can see just how much work the second way saves us. We'll start with the easy method. Add the following `<script>` tag directly before the closing `</body>` tag:

```
<script type="text/javascript">
  //create the namespace object for this example
  YAHOO.namespace("yuibook.dd");
  //define the setDDs function
  YAHOO.yuibook.dd.setDDs = function() {
    //detect the useragent
    var ua = YAHOO.env.ua;
    if (ua.ie != 0) {
      ua.data = "ie";
    }
    //define variables
    var basketTotal = 0;
    var basketTot = 0;
    var Dom = YAHOO.util.Dom;
    //create the 3 DragDropProxy objects
    var dd1 = new YAHOO.util.DDProxy("prod1");
    dd1.isTarget = false;
    dd1.scroll = false;
    var dd2 = new YAHOO.util.DDProxy("prod2");
    dd2.isTarget = false;
    dd2.scroll = false;
    var dd3 = new YAHOO.util.DDProxy("prod3");
    dd3.isTarget = false;
    dd3.scroll = false;
    var basket = new YAHOO.util.DDTarget("basket");

    //define function to call when dd1 starts being dragged
    dd1.startDrag = function() {
      //set cursor position to top-left of proxy
      dd1.setDelta(0,0);
    }
    //define function to call when dd1 stops being dragded
    dd1.endDrag = function() {
    }
    //define function to call when dd1 enters basket
    dd1.onDragEnter = function(e, id) {
      //has dd1 been dragged into basket?
```

```
if (id == "basket") {
  //add 1 to the total number of items
  basketTotal += 1;
  var tot = YAHOO.util.Dom.get("basketTotal")
  tot.innerHTML = basketTotal;
  //create new p element to hold product summary
  var p = document.createElement("p");
  Dom.addClass(p, "prod");
  p.id = "prod" + basketTotal;
  //add icon for product 1 to basket
  var ico = document.createElement("img");
  ico.setAttribute("src", "images/prod1_ico.jpg");
  ico.id = "imageico" + basketTotal;
  Dom.addClass(ico, "icon");
  //add product 1 summary to basket
  p.appendChild(ico);
  Dom.get("basketBody").appendChild(p);
  //create new p element for product 1 title
  var p2 = document.createElement("p");
  var info = Dom.get("prod1info");
  //is the browser IE?
  if (ua.data == "ie") {
    var infos = info.innerHTML.split("<BR>");
  } else {
    var infos = info.innerHTML.split("<br>");
  }
  //set product 1 title
  var title = document.createTextNode(infos[0]);
  Dom.addClass(p2, "prodTitle");
  p2.id = "prodTitle" + basketTotal;
  //add title to basket
  p2.appendChild(title);
  Dom.insertAfter(p2, Dom.get(ico));

  //create p element for product 1 price
  var p3 = document.createElement("p");
  var price = document.createTextNode(infos[1]);
  Dom.addClass(p3, "prodPrice");
  p3.id = "prodPrice" + basketTotal;
  //add product 1 price to basket
  p3.appendChild(price);
  Dom.insertAfter(p3, Dom.get(p2));
```

```
      //update total basket price
      price = Dom.get(p3).innerHTML;
      var rawPrice = price.slice(1,6);
      var cost = parseFloat(rawPrice);
      basketTot += cost;
      var newBasketTot = Dom.get("basketCost");
      newBasketTot.innerHTML = basketTot;
    }
  }
  //define function to call when dd2 starts being dragged
  dd2.startDrag = function() {
    dd2.setDelta(0,0);
  }
  //define function to call when dd2 stops being dragged
  dd2.endDrag = function() {
  }
  //define function to call when dd2 enters basket
  dd2.onDragEnter = function(e, id) {
    if (id == "basket") {
      //add 1 to the total number of items
      basketTotal += 1;
      var tot = YAHOO.util.Dom.get("basketTotal")
      tot.innerHTML = basketTotal;

      //create new p element to hold product summary
      var p = document.createElement("p");
      Dom.addClass(p, "prod");
      p.id = "prod" + basketTotal;
      //add icon for product 2 to basket
      var ico = document.createElement("img");
      ico.setAttribute("src", "images/prod2_ico.jpg");
      ico.id = "imageico" + basketTotal;
      Dom.addClass(ico, "icon");
      //add product 2 summary to basket
      p.appendChild(ico);
      Dom.get("basketBody").appendChild(p);
      //create new p element for product 2 title
      var p2 = document.createElement("p");
      var info = Dom.get("prod2info");
      //is the browser IE?
      if (ua.data == "ie") {
        var infos = info.innerHTML.split("<BR>");
      } else {
```

```
            var infos = info.innerHTML.split("<br>");
          }
          //set product 2 title
          var title = document.createTextNode(infos[0]);
          Dom.addClass(p2, "prodTitle");
          p2.id = "prodTitle" + basketTotal;
          //add title to basket
          p2.appendChild(title);
          Dom.insertAfter(p2, Dom.get(ico));
          //create p element for product 2 price
          var p3 = document.createElement("p");
          var price = document.createTextNode(infos[1]);
          Dom.addClass(p3, "prodPrice");
          p3.id = "prodPrice" + basketTotal;
          //add product 2 price to basket
          p3.appendChild(price);
          Dom.insertAfter(p3, Dom.get(p2));
          //update total basket price
          price = Dom.get(p3).innerHTML;
          var rawPrice = price.slice(1,6);
          var cost = parseFloat(rawPrice);
          basketTot += cost;
          var newBasketTot = Dom.get("basketCost");
          newBasketTot.innerHTML = basketTot;
        }
      }

      //define function to call when dd3 starts being dragged
      dd3.startDrag = function() {
        dd3.setDelta(0,0);
      }
      //define function to call when dd3 stops being dragged
      dd3.endDrag = function() {
      }
      //define function for when dd3 enters basket
      dd3.onDragEnter = function(e, id) {
        if (id == "basket") {
          //add 1 to the total number of items
          basketTotal += 1;
          var tot = YAHOO.util.Dom.get("basketTotal")
          tot.innerHTML = basketTotal;
          //create new p element to hold product summary
```

```
var p = document.createElement("p");
Dom.addClass(p, "prod");
p.id = "prod" + basketTotal;
//add icon for product 3 to basket
var ico = document.createElement("img");
ico.setAttribute("src", "images/prod3_ico.jpg");
ico.id = "imageico" + basketTotal;
Dom.addClass(ico, "icon");
//add product 3 summary to basket
p.appendChild(ico);
Dom.get("basketBody").appendChild(p);
//create new p element for product 3 title
var p2 = document.createElement("p");
var info = Dom.get("prod3info");
//is the browser IE?
if (ua.data == "ie") {
  var infos = info.innerHTML.split("<BR>");
} else {
  var infos = info.innerHTML.split("<br>");
}

//set product 3 title
var title = document.createTextNode(infos[0]);
Dom.addClass(p2, "prodTitle");
p2.id = "prodTitle" + basketTotal;
//add title to basket
p2.appendChild(title);
Dom.insertAfter(p2, Dom.get(ico));
//create p element for product 3 price
var p3 = document.createElement("p");
var price = document.createTextNode(infos[1]);
Dom.addClass(p3, "prodPrice");
p3.id = "prodPrice" + basketTotal;
//add product 3 price to basket
p3.appendChild(price);
Dom.insertAfter(p3, Dom.get(p2));
//update total basket price
price = Dom.get(p3).innerHTML;
var rawPrice = price.slice(1,6);
var cost = parseFloat(rawPrice);
basketTot += cost;
var newBasketTot = Dom.get("basketCost");
```

```
            newBasketTot.innerHTML = basketTot;
          }
        }
      }
      //execute setDDs when DOM is ready
      YAHOO.util.Event.onDOMReady(YAHOO.yuibook.dd.setDDs);
    </script>
```

All of the code here sits within the `setDDs()` function, which is called using the Event utility's `onDOMReady()` method.

The first section of code within the `setDDs()` function uses the `.env.ua()` method of the YAHOO global object to determine the user-agent string of the browsing environment. We can use this as a quick and easy way of detecting the browser being used to view the page.

The `ie` property exists within the `ua` object even if IE is not in use, but if it isn't in use, the property is set to 0. Therefore, if the `ie` property does not equal to 0 it means that IE is the browser currently being used. In this case, the ie property will hold an integer representing the version of IE in use. When IE is being used, we set the data property of our `ua` variable to the string `ie`.

We then create a series of variables for use in the script. The last variable is created purely for convenience. We'll be making heavy use of the DOM utility during this example, so defining that first part of the DOM call as a short variable helps make things easier on us.

Next we create all three of the individual `DDProxy` objects. Remember, in this implementation, each object has to have its own properties and event handlers defined for it. We also define the basket as a `DDTarget` so that we can make use of the `.onDragEnter()` method.

Because we want each product to interact only with our shopping basket and not the other products on the page, we have to set the `.isTarget` property to false. As well as being able to specifically create drop targets using the `YAHOO.util.DDTarget` class, any drag object is by default also a drop target. Additionally, we can switch off the `.scroll` property, which causes the viewport to scroll indefinitely when the dragged object exceeds the window boundary.

Using DragDrop Events

Three event handlers are required for this example: `startDrag`, `endDrag`, and `onDragEnter`. The `startDrag` event fires as soon as the left mouse button has been held down for the required length of time on a drag object, or the pointer moves the specified number of pixels.

The `.setDelta()` method used in the `startDrag` event handler allows us to control where the pointer is relative to the drag object, or in this case, the proxy element. By specifying `0,0` as arguments for this method, we are instructing the pointer to appear at the top-left corner of the proxy element. This is needed so that the element is placed back where it began instead of where the pointer was relative to the drag object when the drag began.

The `endDrag` event fires when a `mouseup` event is detected on the object being dragged. The anonymous function here has a very special purpose, even though it is just an empty function. What it does is ensure that the item being dragged is returned to its original position once it has been dropped instead of remaining where it was dropped. This is important because if we didn't keep the listing pictures in their proper locations, the page would soon be littered with abandoned drag objects.

The `onDragEnter` event fires when the moving object is dragged over a legal target. Since the shopping basket is the only valid target on the page, this will fire whenever a `product` object is dragged over the basket. This function is where the bulk of our code lies.

Two arguments are specified for this function. The first is the event object, which is automatically passed to our handler. The second argument is the `id` of the element that triggered the event, which in this example will be the basket.

We first use our `YAHOO.util.Dom` shortcut to get the `<span>` element displaying the number of items in the basket, then use the `innerHTML` property to alter this value in accordance with the `basketTotal` variable.

We create a new paragraph element and give it a class of `prod`. This new element will act as a container for a short summary of the item placed in the basket. We can go ahead and create the different items that will make up this short description of the product that has been purchased.

A new `<img>` element is created and stored in the `ico` variable. Its `src` attribute is set to the icon representing the product. We then give it a `class` name so that we can style it and an `id` attribute so that we can identify it. Once created and configured, we can append the `<img>` to the new `<p>` element, and then append the `<p>` element to the body of the basket. Now let's work on extracting some of the listing description to display in the basket.

We create another new `<p>` element and give it a class of `prodTitle`. We then need to do more detection to determine which product was dropped, getting the full listing text of the product in the `title` variable once we have.

Each part of the listing text is separated by a `<br>` element, so we can create an array of each different bit of information contained in the listing text using the `.split()` method. This is the part of the script where we use the information gathered from the `ua` property earlier on.

IE for some reason capitalizes all HTML elements in the DOM. This means that IE sees `<BR>` tags, while other browsers see `<br>`, and is the reason we need the if statement to determine the browser in use.

The first item in the `infos` array is the name of the product, so we can use this as the title for the product summary and create a new `textNode` based on it. This title element is then inserted into the DOM directly after the icon element using the DOM utility's `.insertAfter()` method, which takes the element to insert and the element it should be inserted after as arguments.

For good measure, let's add the price of the product to the product summary. A final `<p>` element is created to hold a new textNode comprised of the second item in the infos array, which happens to be the price of the product. The class for the new `<p>` element is set and it is then inserted as a sibling of the previous element that was created.

At the bottom of our basket is a price indicator showing the total cost of all items in the basket; we can easily update this using the same method as we updated the basket contents total earlier on. We recycle the price variable, updating it with the HTML element from the basket.

As the price is currently a text string rather than a number, we have to convert it. Before we can do this however, we need to remove the currency symbol from the front of it, which we can do with the `.slice()` method.

Then we can use the standard JavaScript parseFloat math function to convert the remaining string into a true floating-point number. We can then update the current cost by adding the cost of the dropped product to it. Finally, we set the `innerHTML` property of the `basketCost` span element to the new total.

As each drag object is completely independent, the rest of our script is made up of identical event handlers tied to the other drag objects (products 2 and 3). This is what bloats our code to three times the size it actually needs to be, and imagine how much typing would need to be done if there were 30 products on the page!

Additional CSS

As our basket creates a series of new elements when products are dragged into it, we can add some additional CSS to target and style these new elements. In `basket.css`, add the following new selectors and rules:

```
.prod {
  position:relative;
  height:40px;
  width:250px;
  padding:5px;
}
.prodTitle {
  margin:11px auto auto 5px;
  text-align:left;
  float:left;
  width:100px;
}
.prodPrice {
  margin-top:15px;
  width:50px;
  float:left;
}
```

The basket should now function as we want it to within the confines of this example. If you run the page and then drag a product into the basket, the basket should be updated accordingly, as in in the screenshot below:

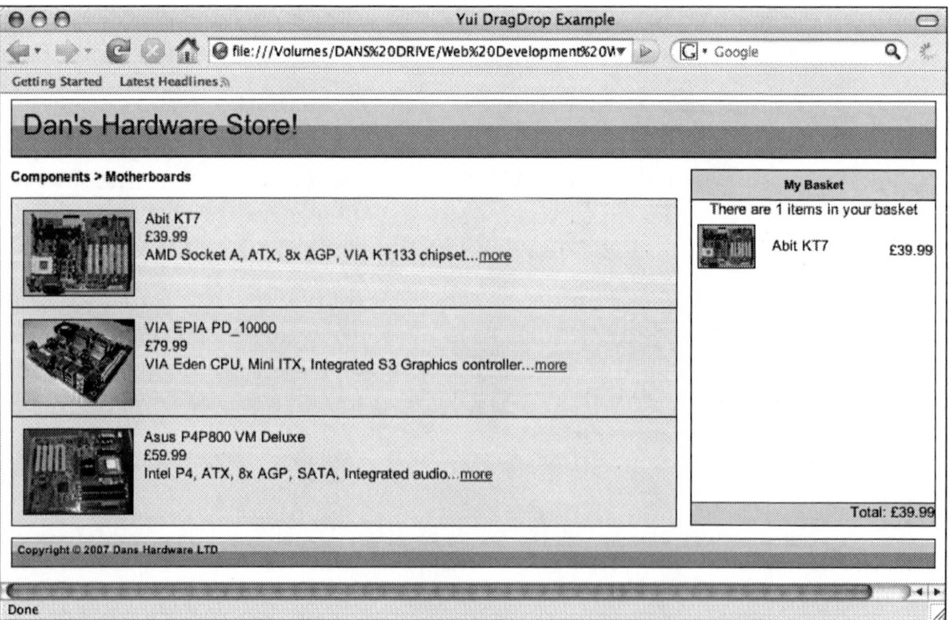

Extending the DDProxy Object

Now we'll look at using the YAHOO global object's `.extend()` method to streamline our code and cut down on unnecessary duplication. Instead of having to define properties and event handlers for each DDProxy object individually, we can customize the DDProxy object itself so that every instance of the object has them already built in.

Here is the complete script:

```
<script type="text/javascript">
  //setup the namespace object for this example
  YAHOO.namespace("yuibook.dd");
  //define the setDDs function
  YAHOO.yuibook.dd.setDDs = function() {
    //detect the useragent
    var ua = YAHOO.env.ua;
    if (ua.ie != 0) {
      ua.data = "ie";
    }
    //define variables
    var basketTotal = 0;
    var basketTot = 0;
    var Dom = YAHOO.util.Dom;
    //apply the initProd function to all product objects
      product = function() {
      product.superclass.constructor.apply(this, arguments);
      this.initProd();
    }
    //extend the DDProxy class
    YAHOO.lang.extend(product, YAHOO.util.DDProxy, {
      //define the initProd function
      initProd: function() {
        this.isTarget = false;
        this.scroll = false;
      },
      //define the startDrag function
      startDrag: function() {
        this.setDelta(0,0);
      },
      //define the endDrag function
      endDrag: function() {
      },
```

```
        //define the onDragEnter function
        onDragEnter: function() {
          //add 1 to the total number of items
          basketTotal += 1;
          var tot = Dom.get("basketTotal");
          tot.innerHTML = basketTotal;
          //create a new p element to hold product info
          var p = document.createElement("p");
          Dom.addClass(p, "prod");
          var ico = document.createElement("img");
          //create a new img element and get matching icon
          var ico = document.createElement("img");
          ico.setAttribute("src", "images/" + this.id + "_ico.jpg");
          Dom.addClass(ico, "icon");
          //add product to the basket
          p.appendChild(ico);
          Dom.get("basketBody").appendChild(p);
          //create p element for product title
          var p2 = document.createElement("p");
          Dom.addClass(p2, "prodTitle");
          //get product info
          var info = Dom.get(this.id + "info");
          //is the browser IE?
          if (ua.data == "ie") {
            var infos = info.innerHTML.split("<BR>");
          } else {
            var infos = info.innerHTML.split("<br>");
          }
          //add product title to basket
          var title = document.createTextNode(infos[0]);
          p2.appendChild(title);
          Dom.insertAfter(p2, Dom.get(ico));

          //create p to hold product price
          var p3 = document.createElement("p");
          var price = document.createTextNode(infos[1]);
          Dom.addClass(p3, "prodPrice");
          p3.appendChild(price);
          //add price to basket
          Dom.insertAfter(p3, Dom.get(p2));
          price = Dom.get(p3).innerHTML;
          //update total basket price
```

```
            var rawPrice = price.slice(1,6);
            var cost = parseFloat(rawPrice);
            basketTot += cost;
            var newBasketTot = Dom.get("basketCost");
            newBasketTot.innerHTML = basketTot;
          }
        });
        //define the products array
        var prods = [
          new product("prod1"),
          new product("prod2"),
          new product("prod3"),
        ];
        var basket = new YAHOO.util.DDTarget("basket");
      }
      //execute setDDs function when the DOM is ready
      YAHOO.util.Event.onDOMReady(YAHOO.yuibook.dd.setDDs);
    </script>
```

The first part of the script is the same, we still enclose our code in the `setDDs()` function and execute it as soon as the DOM is in a usable state. We still need to detect the user-agent in the same way, and we'll still need to use the same set of variables.

The first new addition defines a `product` function, which will act as the constructor used to create new product objects. These objects are our customized version of the DDProxy object, so we'll use this function, instead of the `YAHOO.util.DDProxy()` constructor to produce our drag objects. All this function does is apply the `.initProd()` method to the existing methods found in the `YAHOO.util.DDProxy` class. Every time a new product object is created, the `.initProd()` method will be called.

`Next we need to use the .extend() method of the YAHOO global object.` `The .extend()` method takes three arguments: the first is the object being used to do the extending and the second is the class which we want to extend. The third argument is an object literal that consists of a series of 'name:value' pairs which we can use to define the functions, properties, and event handlers specific to our implementation.

The first pair in our literal object is the `.initProd()` method which we use to set the `isTarget` and `scroll` properties. Although we've only configured the `.isTarget` and `.scroll` properties once, any newly created `product` object will inherit them automatically. This is the power of the `superclass`.

As you can see, we use our custom constructor to create each new drag object. All we need to pass in is the `id` of the corresponding element on the page which is to be made draggable, exactly as if we were using the `YAHOO.util.DDProxy` constructor directly.

We still need to define the shopping basket as a legal target. As we aren't using our custom constructor but the `YAHOO.util.DDTarget` constructor instead, none of our custom properties we be applied to it and the basket will be a standard drop target for our drag objects.

The event handlers used in this example are the same as before—we still only require `startDrag`, `endDrag`, and `onDragEnter`. This time they are added to our `.extend()` method so that they are applied to all new drag objects which negates us having to code them for each object individually. This saves us a huge amount of code.

Our main event, `onDragEnter`, is very similar as before but there are some subtle differences. The part of the script that gets the correct icon image to display in the basket for example, makes use of the `this` keyword to address the object. This keeps us from having to work with specific file names. When we come to extract the product info for whichever product has been dragged into the basket, we can again use the `this.id` property to easily obtain the product title and price.

The final difference is the way the drag objects are created. This time we use a neat and efficient array, each item of which creates a new product object using our new `product` constructor.

The code used in this second method is much, much more efficient. We only have three products on the page, yet the total amount of JavaScript code required to make the first example work was an excessive 252 lines!

In the second example we have just 107 lines of code, and not only do we create all three existing drag objects from the first example, but we can have an unlimited number of additional drag objects. All we need to do for each one is add a new call to the product constructor in our product array. The screenshot below shows the second example in use:

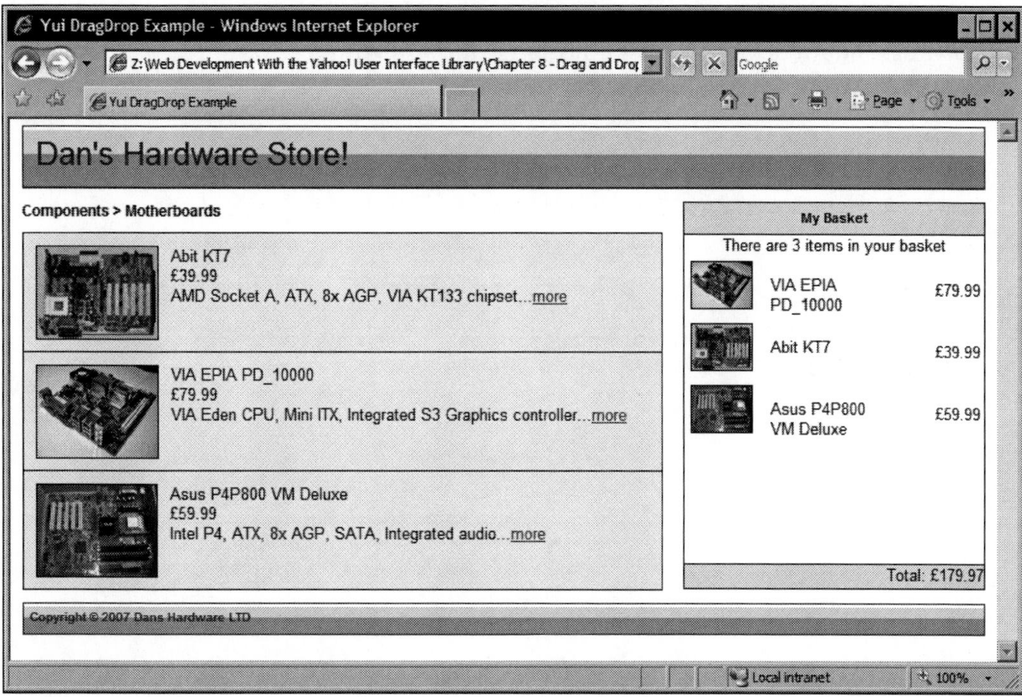

Although our demonstration pages work as intended and look passable, extensive testing reveals that they are little more than a practical demonstration of the capabilities and considerations of the Drag-and-Drop utility rather than a full solution to an online store.

To turn this into a fully working application that you could use on a live site, far more work would need to be done. For example, there is no notion of state within our test application and essential basket features such as removing items from the basket, or proceeding to some kind of checkout area simply aren't there.

Visual Selection with the Slider Control

So far in this chapter we've focused on the functionality provided by the Drag-and-Drop utility. Let's shift our focus back to the interface controls section of the library and look at one of the components which is related very closely to drag-and-drop—the Slider control.

A slider can be defined using a very minimal set of HTML. All you need are two elements: the slider background and the slider thumb, with the thumb appearing as a child of the background element:

```
<div id="slider_bg" title="the slider background">
  <div id="slider_thumb" title="the slider thumb">
    <img src="images/slider_thumb.gif"></div>
</div>
```

These elements go together to form the basic Slider control, as shown in below:

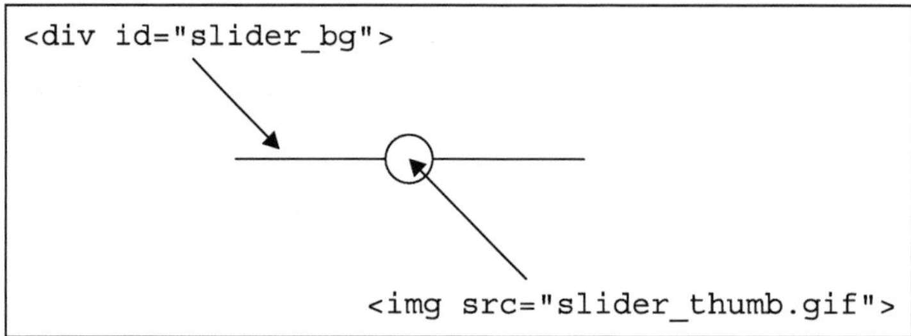

The Slider control works as a specific implementation of DragDrop in that the slider thumb can be dragged along the slider background either vertically or horizontally. The DragDrop classes are extended to provide additional properties, methods, and events specific to Slider.

One of the main concepts differentiating Slider from DragDrop is that with a basic slider, the slider thumb is constrained to just one axis of motion, either X or Y depending on whether the Slider is horizontal or vertical respectively.

The Slider is another control that can be animated by including a reference to the Animation control in the head of the page. Including this means that when any part of the slider background is clicked on, the slider thumb will gracefully slide to that point of the background rather than just moving there instantly.

The Constructor and Factory Methods

The constructor for the slider control is always called in conjunction with one of the three factory methods, depending on which type of slider you want to display. To generate a horizontal slider the `YAHOO.widget.Slider.getHorizSlider` is called, with the appropriate arguments.

To generate a vertical slider, on the other hand, the `YAHOO.widget.Slider.getVertSlider` would instead be used. There is also another type of slider that can be created—the `YAHOO.widget.Slider.getSliderRegion` constructor and factory method combination creates a two-dimensional slider, the thumb of which can be moved both vertically and horizontally.

There are a range of arguments used with the different types of slider constructor. The first two arguments are the same for all of them, with the first argument corresponding to the `id` of the background HTML element and the second corresponding to the `id` of the thumb element.

The type of slider you are creating denotes what the next two (or four when using the SliderRegion) arguments relate to. With the horizontal slider or region slider the third argument is the number of pixels that the thumb element can move left, but with the horizontal slider it is the number of pixels it can move up. The fourth argument is either the number of pixels which the thumb can move right, or the number of pixels it can move down.

When using the region slider, the fifth and sixth arguments are the number of pixels the thumb element can move up and down, so with this type of slider all four directions must be specified. Alternatively, with either the horizontal or vertical sliders, only two directions need to be accounted for.

The final argument (either argument number five for the horizontal or vertical sliders, or argument number seven for the region slider) is optional and refers to the number of pixels between each tick, also known as the tick size. This is optional because you may not use ticks in your slider, therefore making the Slider control analogue rather than digital.

Class of Two

There are just two classes that make up the Slider control—the `YAHOO.widget.Slider` class is a subclass of the `YAHOO.util.DragDrop` class and inherits a whole bunch of its most powerful properties and methods, as well as defining a load more of its own natively.

The `YAHOO.widget.SliderThumb` class is a subclass of the `YAHOO.util.DD` class and inherits properties and methods from this class (as well as defining a few of its own natively).

Some of the native properties defined by the Slider class and available for you to use include:

- animate—a boolean indicating whether the slider thumb should animate. Defaults to true if the Animation utility is included, false if not

- animationDuration—an integer specifying the duration of the animation in seconds. The default is 0.2
- backgroundEnabled—a boolean indicating whether the slider thumb should automatically move to the part of the background that is selected when clicked. Defaults to true
- enableKeys—another boolean which enables the home, end and arrow keys on the visitors keyboard to control the slider. Defaults to true, although the slider control must be clicked once with the mouse before this will work
- keyIncrement—an integer specifying the number of pixels the slider thumb will move when an arrow key is pressed. Defaults to 25 pixels

A large number of native methods are also defined in the class, but a good deal of them are used internally by the slider control and will therefore never need to be called directly by you in your own code. There are a few of them that you may need at some point however, including:

- .getThumb()—returns a reference to the slider thumb
- .getValue()—returns an integer determining the number of pixels the slider thumb has moved from the start position
- .getXValue()—an integer representing the number of pixels the slider has moved along the X axis from the start position
- .getYValue()—an integer representing the number of pixels the slider has moved along the Y axis from the start position
- .onAvailable()—executed when the slider becomes available in the DOM
- `.setRegionValue()` and `.setValue()`—allow you to programmatically set the value of the region slider's thumb

More often than not, you'll find the custom events defined by the Slider control to be most beneficial to you in your implementations. You can capture the slider thumb being moved using the `change` event, or detect the beginning or end of a slider interaction by subscribing to `slideStart` or `slideEnd` respectively.

The `YAHOO.widget.SliderThumb` class is a subclass of the DD class; this is a much smaller class than the one that we have just looked at and all of the properties are private, meaning that you need not take much notice of them. The available methods are similar to those defined by the Slider class, and once again, these are not something that you need to concern yourself with in most basic implementations of the control.

A Very Simple Slider

What we're aiming to achieve over the course of this example is to produce a small widget that visitors to your site could use to dynamically change the font size of text on the page in a visually appealing manner.

I know that the font-size of any given page can easily be adjusted by your visitors using the native method of their browser's UI, but it's a nice effect to have directly on your own pages, it promotes usability, and would sit nicely in a 'user control panel' area of your site/page.

The screenshot below demonstrates how our slider will appear by the end of this example:

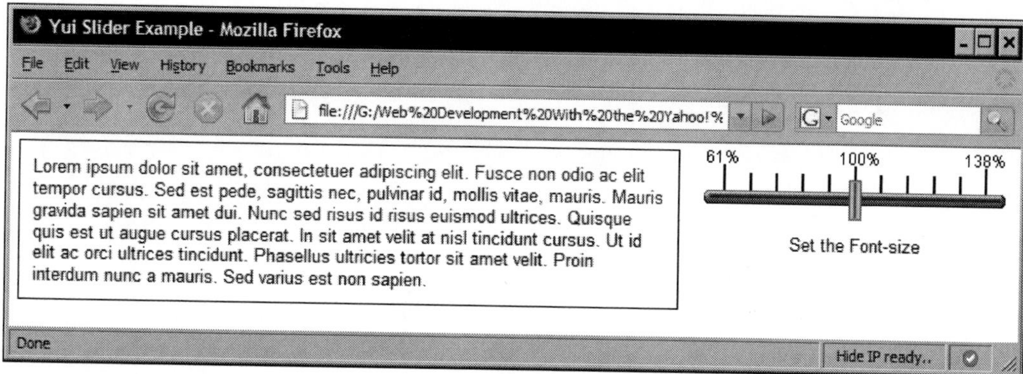

Getting Started

All instances of the Slider control must be built not only from underlying HTML and JavaScript, but also CSS. Certain aspects of the control can only be set using a stylesheet. When using this control styling is just as important as the other two aspects, but we'll come to that in just a moment.

We'll also be making use of the `reset-fonts-grids.css` tool for this example as well. Yahoo! recommends the use of this file in all library implementations so that you get a consistent look across browsers.

In a blank page in your text editor, begin with the following basic page:

```
<!DOCTYPE HTML PUBLIC "-//W3C//DTD HTML 4.01//EN"
                                "http://www.w3.org/TR/html4/strict.dtd">
<html lang="en">
  <head>
    <meta http-equiv="content-type" content="text/html;
                                    charset=utf-8">
```

```
        <title>Yui Slider Example</title>
        <script type="text/javascript"
                src="yui/build/yahoo-dom-event/yahoo-dom-event.js">
        </script>
        <script type="text/javascript"
                src="yui/build/dragdrop/dragdrop-min.js"></script>
        <script type="text/javascript"
                src="yui/build/slider/slider-min.js"></script>
        <link rel="stylesheet" type="text/css"
              href="yui/build/reset-fonts-grids/reset-fonts-grids.css">
        <link rel="stylesheet" type="text/css" href="slider.css">
      </head>
      <body>
        <div id="doc" class="yui-t5">
          <div id="bd">
            <div id="yui-main">
              <div class="yui-b">
                <div class="content" id="content">
                  <div>Lorem ipsum etc…</div>
                </div>
              </div>
            </div>
            <div class="yui-b">
              <div id="sli_bg" title="font size slider">
                <div id="sli_thumb"><img src="images/sli_thumb.gif"
                     alt="slider_thumb"></div>
              </div>
              <p class="sli_legend">Set the Font-size</p>
            </div>
          </div>
        </div>
      </body>
    </html>
```

A lot of the nested `<div>` elements are required for the `doc3` and `yui-t5` CSS template used to layout our example page. Don't worry too much about those (just make sure they're all there), the key part of the code is the mark up defining the underlying slider.

The slider thumb, `sli_thumb`, has the image making up the slider thumb hard-coded directly into it as opposed to being set with CSS, as the slider background is, and is defined as a child of the slider background element `sli_bg`. Save what we have so far as `slider.html` in the `yuisite` folder.

Adding the CSS

As I mentioned before, CSS is essential to the correct layout and functioning of the slider object and is used to set the background image of the outer slider `<div>` element among other things. In a new page in your text editor, add the following CSS:

```
#sli_bg {
  position:relative;
  width:240px;
  height:50px;
  background:url(images/sli_bg.gif) no-repeat;
  margin:5px auto auto 5px;
}
#sli_thumb {
  position:absolute;
  top:20px;
  left:110px;
}
```

These two selectors target the slider background and thumb components respectively; both elements of the slider must have a specified `position` for the control to work. The main rule for the slider background is the `background` property which is used to display the slider background image. Save this file as `slider.css`.

In our example, the middle of the slider is the default position so when the page loads, it is important for the slider thumb to be centered over the background image. This is done by positioning the image with CSS, instead of using a property of the slider object as you may do with other controls.

We'll also need just a couple of other selectors specific to this demonstration page:

```
  .content {
    font-size:100%;
    margin-top:5px;
    padding:10px;
    border:1px solid black;
  }
  .sli_legend {
    font-size:100%;
    margin-top:10px;
    text-align:center;
  }
</style>
```

Adding the JavaScript

Now we're ready to move on to the final part of this example—the JavaScript that will turn a couple of images into a fully working Slider element. Make sure `slider.html` is open in your text editor. Just before the closing `</body>` tag, add the following code:

```
<script type="text/javascript">
  //setup the namespace object for this example
  YAHOO.namespace("yuibook.slider");
  //define the initSlider function
  YAHOO.yuibook.slider.initSlider = function() {
    //define the slider object
    var fontslider = YAHOO.widget.Slider.getHorizSlider
                         ("sli_bg", "sli_thumb", 110, 110, 20);
    //subscribe to the change event
    fontslider.subscribe("change", setFontSize);
    //define the sizes object
    var sizes = {
      "-100":61,
      "-80":69,
      "-60":77,
      "-40":85,
      "-20":93,
      "0":100,
      "20":108,
      "40":116,
      "60":123,
      "80":131,
      "100":138
    };
    //define the setFontSize function
    function setFontSize() {
      //get the position of the slider thumb
      var val = fontslider.getXValue();
      //set the new font-size according to the slider position
      var newSize = sizes[val] + "%";
      YAHOO.util.Dom.setStyle("content", "font-size", newSize);
    }
  }
  //execute initSlider when DOM is ready
  YAHOO.util.Event.onDOMReady( YAHOO.yuibook.slider.initSlider);
</script>
```

The `.onDOMReady()` method kicks everything off as soon as the DOM is in a complete state which will ensure that our slider is available as soon as the page has loaded. The rest of the code then goes within the curly brackets of the `setSlider()` function.

The `Slider.getHorizSlider` constructor has five arguments. The first is the element with an `id` attribute of `sli-bg`, the second is the element with an id of `sli_thumb`. The next two arguments indicate how far the slider thumb can travel in left and right directions, it is important that the distance does not exceed the boundary of the slider background or the thumb will be able to leave the slider background.

The final parameter sets up the tick marks for the slider, making it digital instead of analogue. The visible lines that mark each tick are part of the picture itself and are not created automatically by the control.

We want the text size to increase or decrease depending on the position of the thumb. To achieve this we'll need to find out how far the slider has moved in either direction and then translate this into the corresponding font-size. We also need to tell the script 'when' the font-size should be changed.

We start off by addressing that last point first, which is going to be very easy to do using one of the custom events built into the Slider control.

The change event fires every time the position of the slider thumb changes. We can easily subscribe a callback function to the event which we can use to execute the code which changes the size of the text. We use a literal object to map the slider positions to `font-size` values, we can then refer to items in the object using a simple string.

The `.getXValue()` method provided by the `YAHOO.widget.Slider` class allows us to retrieve the number of pixels the thumb has moved from the start position. Each time the thumb is moved, we can use this to determine its new position and store it in the `val` variable.

As we've defined tick marks of 20 pixels, the `val` variable will only be holding a value which matches one of the strings used in the associative array. So the `newSize` variable will hold one of the values from the array, which correspond (mostly) to a small range of the font sizes used in `fonts.css`.

We also need to concatenate a percentage symbol onto the end of the value returned from the object. This is in order to avoid the value being treated as the default of points, as this would make the text ridiculously large.

Finally, we make use of the `.setStyle()` DOM method to physically change the size of the text contained in the content element. The format of the arguments supplied to the method is: the element reference to target, the style property you wish to change, and the value by which to change it.

It's as easy as that, no further coding is needed for the slider to work as intended. Save the page and view it in your browser of choice, it should appear as shown here:

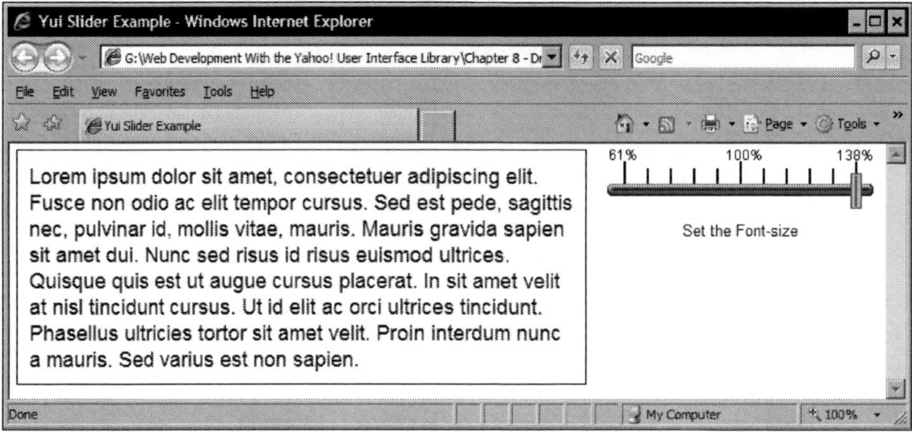

When designing a slider implementation, it is important to take into account the sizes of the slider background and thumb images when configuring properties such as the pixel distance the thumb can travel and the distance between ticks, to make sure everything looks as it should.

Summary

The code required to make the images on our product listing page draggable could best be described as minimal. It's also very easy code to get to grips with. As the example highlighted, it's the mechanics of what you want to achieve with the Drag-and-Drop utility's functionality that takes far more consideration.

A close descendant of Drag-and-Drop, the Slider, is even easier to implement and can be a very effective and visually appealing addition to your pages. Although this control is relatively basic and compact, it still provides a series of custom events to hook into and a range of configurable properties.

10
Advanced Debugging with Logger

Unlike the rest of the library, the Logger is not an Interface control that is designed to be used in production applications. The Logger control is just for you, the developer, to assist you primarily in the design phase of your site or application, but also in maintenance or upgrade phases as and when required.

Like any of the controls provided by the library, Logger is both easy to implement and easy to use. It provides a mechanism for both the writing and reading of log messages generated by your application at key moments during its use.

JavaScript provides no console support natively. It is usually left to the browser or interpreting environment to manage and report runtime errors, and as I'm sure you're aware, browsers don't always provide as robust or intelligible results that we as developers would like!

The Purpose of Logger

The Logger has been built to be used directly in connection with the `-debug.js` versions of each individual library component. The Logger is primarily used to display the different messages that are produced by each of the different library components at different points during their execution, allowing you to see exactly what is going on throughout the progress of your script.

As well as providing error messages to assist you with debugging and troubleshooting, each library component is configured to log informational messages when different custom events fire. This allows you to keep track of the different things that happen during the course of a particular interaction. When first beginning to use the library, this feature of Logger can provide valuable insights into the inner workings of each component.

You needn't rely solely on the different messages hard-coded into each library component either. It is very simple to log your own custom messages to the Logger control at any point during your script so the Logger control can help you regardless of whether you are using any of the other library components or not.

The Logger control is different from the other controls in the respect that it is something that the visitors to your site will rarely, if ever, see. You can add it to a public page of course; there is certainly nothing to stop you. The Yahoo! development team are quick to point out that it could be extended for other uses by more adventurous developers.

The main reason why you wouldn't have an instance of the Logger sitting happily on your application's landing page are based on the performance hit your application is likely to take when managing the interactions your visitor is making, while at the same time processing and displaying log messages. Some of the examples on the YUI documentation site are testament to this!

Additionally, the Logger is designed to work with the `-debug` versions of the library files, rather than the `-min` versions, the latter of which you should be using in a production application. The `-min` versions are the ones served by Yahoo! and have been optimised for quick downloading and therefore have no Logger targeting code routines in them.

Using the Logger control when designing your pages or applications gives you an insight into what is going on in the library files you are using at different points during their execution. If you look through one of the `-debug` versions of any of the library files, you'll see various statements that log messages to the Logger which can help you to understand why something isn't working the way it should if.

You can also log your own custom messages when building an application to help with troubleshooting and debugging your own code. I've always used the standard JavaScript `alert` to test what information is being passed around in a function and to provide guidance when things haven't been going right. But with the Logger, you have far greater control over the format of the messages that you can output, and the interface used to view them is a lot more pleasant than an intrusive and ugly alert.

The Logger provides advanced functionality including built-in methods for easily showing and hiding, pausing and resuming, or collapsing and expanding the Logger control. It also maintains an internal message stack into which logged messages are saved for reference, and even a buffer which can store log messages while the Logger is paused.

The Purpose of the –debug Library Files

As well as having all of the comments, plenty of white space, and more sensible variable names, the `-debug.js` versions of each of the different library components also have plenty of additional code that outputs messages for the Logger component to display. At their most fundamental level the `-debug.js` and standard files are just much more human-readable and much easier to make sense of than the `-min.js` versions.

If you open up one of the `-debug.js` versions of one of the library components in your text editor, you'll be able to see all of this extra code for yourself first-hand instead of just taking my word for it. Let's look at both the standard non-suffixed and `-debug.js` versions of the Animation utility:

```
YAHOO.util.Anim = function(el, attributes, duration, method) {
    if (!el) {
    }
    this.init(el, attributes, duration, method);
};
```

This is the very first function found in the `animation.js` file, note the empty `if` statement which checks that the `el` object exists. Now let's take a look at exactly the same function, but this time from the `animation-debug.js` file instead of the standard version:

```
YAHOO.util.Anim = function(el, attributes, duration, method) {
    if (!el) {
        YAHOO.log('element required to create Anim instance',
                 'error', 'Anim');
    }
    this.init(el, attributes, duration, method);
};
```

In this version of the file, the `if` statement contains a message to log to the Logger console. In this case the message alerts you (not the visitor) that you need to supply an element in order to create an animation. Each debug file is filled with additional code like this to alert you to potential problems with your code. Just for the sake of interest, let's view the `-min.js` version of the same function:

```
YAHOO.util.Anim=function(B,A,C,D){if(!B){}this.init(B,A,C,D);
};
```

Nice! Highly efficient for a browser to download and use, but not very helpful to the likes of you and me, and as you can clearly see, no log messages are generated.

Each component has varying amounts of Logger specific code in its `-debug` file depending on each utility or control's capacity for error. The above code snippets from the Animation utility are one of just a couple of lines of code related to the Logger. This is because it's a simple utility where little can go wrong.

The Connection Manager utility on the other hand, is filled with Logger targeting code due to its complexity, and the fact that there is a lot more that can go wrong when working with remote applications. The Logger can be extremely helpful debugging and troubleshooting Connection problems.

How the Logger Can Help You

The Logger can be a valuable asset when initially coding your application or site. If something isn't working as you'd expect, you can instantiate Logger and then replace the `-min.js` file for the `-debug.js` version and see exactly where your code is falling down. As I mentioned before, it can also be extremely helpful when upgrading an application to run on a newer version of the library.

When creating a new implementation, debugging usually consists of adding alerts to your code to check that variable values are being passed from function to function correctly and as pointers to how far a script progresses before it halts. This is true whether involving components from the YUI or just coding a standard, non-library assisted JavaScript application.

So if you've added five alerts to different parts of your script and only see four of them during execution, you can pin-point (with varying degrees of success) exactly where the problem lies. Sometimes however, depending on what your script does, the mere presence of an alert can throw a spanner in the works.

Debugging the Old Way

Let's look at a simple web page, which uses a basic script that obtains an element from the DOM and then passes it to several functions, alerting different properties of the element along the way:

In your text editor, add the following page:

```
<!DOCTYPE HTML PUBLIC "-//W3C//DTD HTML 4.01//EN"
                              "http://www.w3.org/TR/html4/strict.dtd">
<html lang="en">
  <head>
    <meta http-equiv="content-type" content="text/html;
                                     charset=utf-8">
    <title>Old Style Debugging Example</title>
  </head>
```

```
  <body>
    <div id="div1" class="divClass"></div>
    <script type="text/javascript">
      var initPage = function() {
        var el = document.getElementById("div1");
        getTheClass(el);
      }
      var getTheClass = function(el) {
         alert("The div's class is " + el.className);
         getTheId(el);
      }
      var getTheId = function(el) {
        alert("The div's id is " + el.id);
        getTheType(el);
      }
      var getTheType = function(el) {
        alert("The el variable is of type " + typeof(el));
      }
      window.onload = initPage;
    </script>
  </body>
</html>
```

If you run the page in your browser, you should see each of the alerts and therefore know that the script has progressed as planned. The existence of the alerts however disturbs the natural flow of the script and is a less than satisfactory way of checking variables and properties.

Debugging the YUI Way

We can use the Logger to check the same objects and properties in a much friendlier way:

```
<!DOCTYPE HTML PUBLIC "-//W3C//DTD HTML 4.01//EN"
                              "http://www.w3.org/TR/html4/strict.dtd">
<html lang="en">
  <head>
    <meta http-equiv="content-type" content="text/html;
                                     charset=utf-8">
    <title>YUI Style Debugging Example</title>
    <script type="text/javascript"
            src="yui/build/yahoo-dom-event/yahoo-dom-event.js">
    </script>
    <script type="text/javascript" src="yui/build/logger/
                                        logger-min.js"></script>
    <link type="text/css" rel="stylesheet"
          href="yui/build/logger/assets/skins/sam/logger.css">
  </head>
  <body class="yui-skin-sam">
```

```
      <div id="div1" class="divClass"></div>
      <script type="text/javascript">
        YAHOO.namespace("yuibook.logger");
        YAHOO.yuibook.logger.initPage = function() {
          var myLogger = new YAHOO.widget.LogReader();
          var el = YAHOO.util.Dom.get("div1");
          getTheClass(el)
        }
        var getTheClass = function(el) {
          YAHOO.log("The div's class is " + el.className, "info");
          getTheId(el);
        }
        var getTheId = function(el) {
          YAHOO.log("The div's id is " + el.id, "info");
          getTheType(el);
        }
        var getTheType = function(el) {
          YAHOO.log("The el variable is of type " + typeof(el), "info");
        }
        YAHOO.util.Event.onDOMReady(YAHOO.yuibook.logger.initPage);
      </script>
    </body>
  </html>
```

This time the page loads and all of the functions execute, without waiting for you to click each alert. All of the information we wanted to find out is displayed in the Logger as shown here:

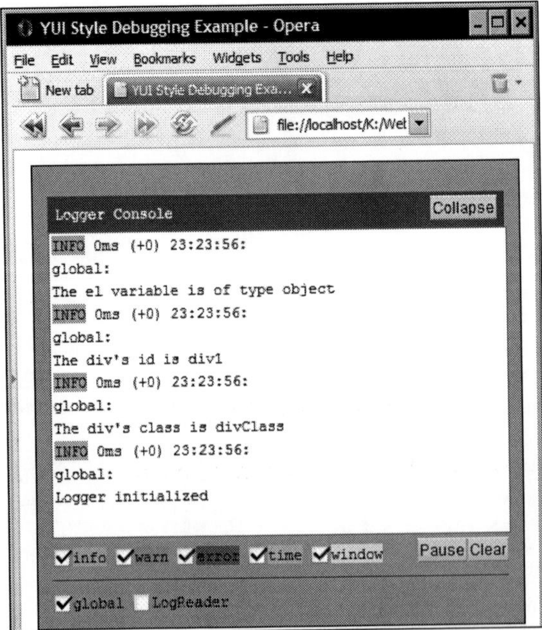

Logger negates the need for littering your code with numerous alerts in the first place. This also has the added benefit of meaning that you don't need to go back through your code once the problem has been eradicated to remove all of the alerts.

Instead of using alerts to test the values of a variable or to mark different events, you can make a simple call to the `YAHOO.log` method, specifying the text that forms the main message and the category of message. For example, in order to check that something is loading, you could include:

```
YAHOO.log("Component X has loaded!", "info");
```

Or for clarification of the value of a particular variable, something like the following should suffice:

```
YAHOO.log ("The current value of myspecialvariable is: " +
           myspecialvariable, "info");
```

This is just as easy as using alerts but much more elegant and won't interfere with your application the way alerts sometimes can (and you won't have to put up with the irritating beep either).

Some components, especially those designated as beta or subject to change in new revisions, can even alert you to the fact that a method or property that you are using has been deprecated, This makes Logger the ideal companion when migrating to newer versions of the library.

Log Message Types

Logger provides access up to five different types of default message. Each message can be specified as one of the following categories:

- TIME
- ERROR
- WARNING
- INFO
- WINDOW

Each category of message is color coded within the Logger interface so it's easy to see at a glance exactly which category of message has been logged. The **TIME** category can be used to profile the speed at which particular features of your implementation execute.

Category **ERROR** messages clearly indicate that something isn't working or something that is required is not present, and **WARNING** messages indicate potential non-fatal errors in your code. **INFO** messages are logged when components are initialized and at the beginning and end of key interactions.

The extremely rare **WINDOW** category is only used by the Logger control itself, and is generated when the Logger causes a window error by being out of the scope of an event handler.

In addition to the Logger interface provided by the YUI for the display of log messages, the Logger control also allows you to log messages directly to some browser consoles, such as Firebug in Firefox.

Logger Layout

Like many of the different components available under the YUI, the Logger control is comprised of three sections of underlying mark up, adhering to the SMF: the header (`yui-log-hd`), the main body (`yui-log-bd`), and a footer section (`yui-log-ft`). These three components are created automatically by the control when a new Logger instance is generated, you don't need to add them to your page.

The header section contains a UI button that allows for the expansion and collapse of the control and a brief explanatory title. The header also serves as the drag handle by which the control can be dragged, if this feature is enabled. If the Drag-and-Drop utility is referenced in the head of the page, the Logger will be dragable automatically without further intervention.

The body of the logger is where all messages sent to the Logger are displayed. By default, new messages appear at the top of this viewing pane, although this can be configured so that new messages are added to the bottom of the pane. It is also very easy to configure the logger to be collapsed by default so that only the header section is initially visible.

The Logger footer contains most of the UI for customizing the type and source of displayed log messages and allows you to filter out the category messages that you aren't interested in, or their source, and also contains buttons for you to pause and resume log reading. If necessary, the footer section can be disabled so that it is not displayed at all. When this option is configured, the filtering options are still available programmatically.

The UI control itself is also simple and easy to use and provides buttons for collapsing or expanding the control, pausing or resuming it or clearing the message window. It also allows you to filter the log messages based on the category or whether the log message came from the global `.log()` method, or the `LogReader` class. You can even alter the styles of the different categories of log message and the title used in the head of the Logger.

The screenshot below shows the default Logger interface (highlighted by one of the Logger examples from the YUI documentation example space):

In this example just one message has been logged. Let's break down the message and take a look what each part of it refers to or represents.

The highlighted prefix shows the category of the message; in this case it is a simple INFO message. Next is the ongoing count, which is a continuous timer that begins when the Logger is initialized. The number following in brackets is a count since the previous log message and the final snippet of information on the first line is a full timestamp of when the message occurred.

The second line features the source of the message. As you can see in the footer section, global messages are enabled. If you uncheck the **global** box, the above message will disappear from view (although it will still be available to the control).

Finally, on the third line, the actual log message is displayed. This is the standard format of log messages by default, although the property `verboseOutput` can be set to **false** so that all messages are compacted to one-line entries.

Logger Styling

The first screenshot also shows us how the Logger appears by default. Like most of the other controls, its default appearance is controlled by the `sam` skin, so a reference to this must be included in the head of any page on which the Logger is to appear.

Like the other components styled by `sam`, it's very easy to configure the Logger to suit your own implementations. Although unless you were providing an extended version of Logger for your users to interact with, there isn't really much point in worrying about styling. The default appearance is functional and easy to make sense of, so overriding style rules simply adds to your workload.

Logger is not Omnipotent or Infallible!

The logger is an excellent addition to the library and can help you understand any process within any component in greater detail. I should point out however that the component cannot detect every problem with your code, and some fatal errors result in the Logger not even being displayed on the page, so it can't be relied upon to troubleshoot any and all errors. If you look at the source of the Debug utilities, you'll see that **INFO** category messages are by far the most common.

An example of where the Logger can fall down when troubleshooting is when the required utilities are not present. The Drag-and-Drop utility can present a category **ERROR** message when the Event utility is not present, but on a page without the Event utility, Logger won't even render. This means you won't see the message advising that `event.js` is not present.

The Logger Classes

Four classes provide the functionality of the Logger control: the `YAHOO.widget.Logger` singleton class, the tiny `YAHOO.widget.LogMsg` class, and the input and output classes `YAHOO.widget.LogReader` and `YAHOO.widget.LogWriter`. Let's take a look at each of them in turn.

The static `YAHOO.widget.Logger` class manages the core functionality of processing and displaying log messages. It's a static class because it contains no constructor and therefore the properties and methods defined by the class can be used without an instance of the Logger. It receives log messages generated by the global `.log` function or by LogWriter instances. It can also use the native console of the browser to log messages to, when supported by the browser and enabled.

This class acts as part of the logic behind the Logger control so you won't have to interact with it directly very often, but a property that you will probably want to manipulate from time to time is `maxStackEntries`, which allows you to limit the number of messages in the internal stack. The default number is 2500 which can be lowered to claim back some of that performance cost if required.

There are also a few useful methods, including:

- `disableBrowserConsole`—prevents messages being logged to the browsers native console
- `enableBrowserConsole`—logs messages to the browsers native console using the `console.log` function. The `browserConsole` is disabled by default
- `log`—saves a log message to the internal stack and browser console if enabled
- `reset`—clears the internal stack and resets the `_startTime` property. The Logger remains enabled

A series of events are also defined by this class to mark different points in the operation of the Logger. These events are:

- `categoryCreateEvent`—this is fired when a new category has been created, which occurs when a log message is assigned to an unknown or custom category
- `logResetEvent`—fired when the reset method has been called
- `newLogEvent`—fires when a new log message is created
- `sourceCreateEvent`—this is fired when a new source has been created, which occurs when a log message is from an unknown source

None of the other classes define any events for the Logger control, so short of creating your own, this is all you have to work with in a basic implementation.

LogMsg Structure

The `YAHOO.widget.LogMsg` class is tiny. It consists of just a constructor and five properties. It defines a single log message and while you probably won't need to call it yourself (it is used by the Logger class that we have just discussed), it is useful to see the structure of an individual message.

The constructor takes just one argument and that is the literal object containing the five message properties. These properties are:

- `category`—the category of the log can be either **info, warn, error, time, window** or a new category of your choice. Each category is styled and any custom categories you add can also easily be styled using the `.yui-log` class. `Info` is the default class, used when a category is not specified
- `msg`—holds the textual message of the log, it should be a simple string, expressing the message displayed in the Logger
- `source` and `sourceDetail`—relate to the source of the log. The source can consist of one or more words, where the first word appears as `source` and any subsequent words (after the first blank space delimiter) are stored as `sourceDetail`. Messages without a specified `source` are assigned as `global`
- `time`—the property which refers to when the log occurred

Generate the UI Interface with LogReader

The `YAHOO.widget.LogReader` class is what is used to render the log message viewer on the page, and is where the Logger class passes messages to be displayed. This is the biggest class in the control by far, defining a wide range of both private and public properties and methods, many of which you can put to good use in your own implementations. Properties you may find useful include:

- `draggable`—specifies whether the Logger control can be dragged and dropped. Defaults to true, if the Drag-and-Drop utility is present on the page
- `footerEnabled`—a boolean specifying whether the footer is enabled
- `newestOnTop`—If true (the default) this adds new log messages to the top of the Loggers display panel
- `thresholdMax`—the maximum number of messages to display on the display panel. Defaults to 500
- `thresholdMin`—the minimum number of messages. Used when a Logger control reaches `thresholdMax`, resetting the display to the number specified
- `verboseOutput`—when false, text wrapping, and whitespace are used to make the log messages more readable. Default is true

A large amount of methods are also defined by LogReader—of these, a large number are private and used internally by the class, but some that you will definitely want to use are:

- `clearConsole`—this method clears all messages from the Logger window but doesn't actually delete them from the stack

- `collapse`—collapses the Logger
- `expand`—expands the Logger
- `hide`—hides the Logger
- `hideCategory` and `hideSource`—hides individual log messages based on the category or source
- `pause`—pauses the Logger
- `resume`—resumes the Logger
- `show`—shows the Logger
- `showCategory` and `showSource`—shows individual messages based on the category or source

The LogWriter Class

`YAHOO.widget.LogWriter` allows you to write log messages from a particular source, which can be useful when debugging a class, which may generate many log messages. This is another specialized and compact class containing just the constructor, one private property and four methods.

The simple constructor takes just one argument which should be a string specifying the source of the LogWriter instance. This then appears as the `_source` property. The methods defined consist of:

- `getSource`—a public accessor method which returns a string referring to the source of the LogWriter
- `log`—as before, the simple log method logs a message to the stack, although this time it is attached to the LogWriter source. Arguments passed with this method are a string specifying the log message and a string specifying the category name
- `setSource`—allows you to programmatically set the LogWriter source
- `toString`—returns the unique name of the LogWriter instance as a string

All of the members of each class can be used to build a rich and easily implemented infrastructure for receiving and displaying log messages, or generating custom messages, in a friendly and unobtrusive interface.

How to Use Logger

The Logger control has few dependencies and can be instantiated with just one line of code. For the most part, using the logger is passive. You just invoke it and sit back while it receives and displays the messages fired by different parts of each component. Let's look at this aspect of its use first.

Make sure the `logger-min.js` file is placed in your `yui` folder and begin with the following basic HTML page:

```
<!DOCTYPE HTML PUBLIC "-//W3C//DTD HTML 4.01//EN"
                            "http://www.w3.org/TR/html4/strict.dtd">
<html lang="en">
  <head>
    <meta http-equiv="content-type" content="text/html;
                                       charset=utf-8">
    <title>Yui Logger Example</title>
    <script type="text/javascript"
            src="yui/build/yahoo-dom-event/yahoo-dom-event.js">
    </script>
    <script type="text/javascript"
            src="yui/build/dragdrop/dragdrop-debug.js"></script>
    <script type="text/javascript"
            src="yui/build/logger/logger-min.js"></script>
    <link type="text/css" rel="stylesheet"
          href="yui/build/logger/assets/skins/sam/logger.css">
  </head>
  <body class="yui-skin-sam">
  </body>
</html>
```

The `<head>` of the page contains the references to the required dependencies of the Logger, as well as the Logger source file itself, and the `sam` skin file that controls its appearance. Now let's display the logger on the page. Within the `<body>` of the document, add the following code:

```
<script type="text/javascript">
  //create the namespace object
  YAHOO.namespace("yuibook.logger");
  //initialise logger
  YAHOO.yuibook.logger.initLogger = function () {
    //define logger instance
    var myLogger = new YAHOO.widget.LogReader();
  }
  //execute initLogger when DOM is ready
  YAHOO.util.Event.onDOMReady( YAHOO.yuibook.logger.initLogger);
</script>
```

Ok! So I said it could be instantiated with one line of code, yet including the above function and event handler, that's four lines. Well, usually Logger would be placed on the page with other components that would need to be initialized in the normal way anyway, so really it's just the LogReader object constructor in the above code which is unique to this example.

If you save what you have so far, as `logger.html` or similar, and view it in a browser, you'll see the logger control on the page, but as there's nothing else for it to interact with, it will only display two messages, the Logger initialization message and the LogReader initialization message.

Because we haven't specified an underlying container for the Logger, a new container is generated for it automatically by the control and is inserted into the DOM. The default positioning of the control pushes it to the right-hand edge of the page.

Let's liven things up a little and build on this simple example. The Logger will automatically become a drag object if the Drag-and-Drop utility is included in the head of the page. Go ahead and add a reference to the `dragdrop-min.js` file with the other dependencies (it should appear in between the `yahoo-dom-event.js` and the `logger-min.js` references):

```
<script type="text/javascript" src="yui/dragdrop-min.js"></script>
```

Save the file again and view it in your browser once more. Nothing has changed, except that the Logger control should now be drag-able. If you now substitute the minified `dragdrop-min.js` file for `dragdrop-debug.js` and view the page a third time, suddenly there're a whole lot more messages.

These messages reveal exactly what happens when the page loads and the order in which things occur. Every time you interact with the Logger, by say dragging it, more messages are logged, informing you that the mouseDown event was detected and the startDrag event was detected, and so on.

Next, we can take this opportunity to look at logging our very own custom messages to the Logger. We don't need to rely on the `-debug.js` versions of each file to add our own custom messages either; for additional clarity you should switch back to the `-min.js` version of DragDrop so that our message isn't lost amongst those generated by this control. Add the following code to the existing `onDOMReady()` function just below the LogReader object initialization:

```
<script type="text/javascript">
  //create the namespace object
  YAHOO.namespace("yuibook.logger");
  //initialize logger
```

```
    YAHOO.yuibook.logger.initLogger = function () {
      //define logger instance
      var myLogger = new YAHOO.widget.LogReader();
      //define a callback for the click event
      function clickCallback() {
        //log a message
        YAHOO.log("Don't click there!", "warn");
      }
      //add listener for the click event
      YAHOO.util.Event.addListener("yui-gen0", "click", clickCallback);
    }
    //execute initLogger when DOM is ready
    YAHOO.util.Event.onDOMReady( YAHOO.yuibook.logger.initLogger);
  </script>
```

The container for the Logger is automatically given an `id` attribute of `yui-gen0` so we can use this to attach an event handler that listens for the click event on the Logger control.

When this is detected, the YAHOO global method `.log()` allows us to add our custom message. Clicking anywhere on the logger will result in the message as shown below:

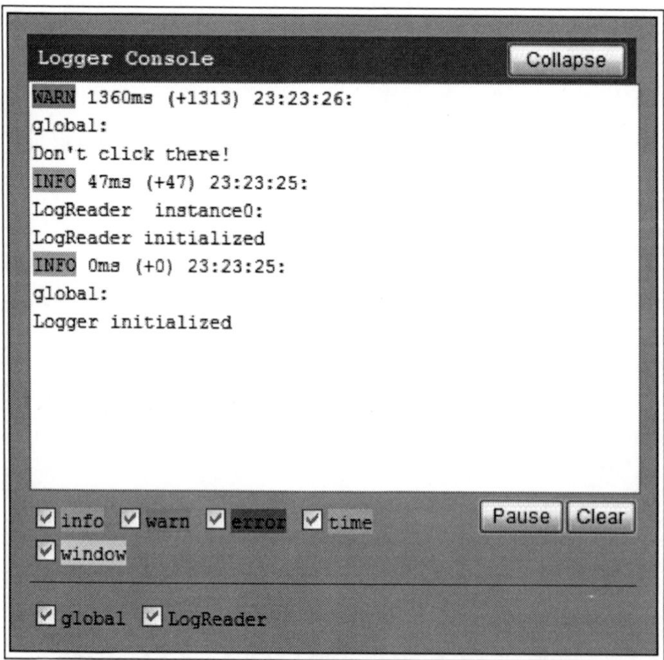

For reference, the default category of message is **INFO**. In our custom message example above, if we don't specify that our message is of category **WARN** in the `.log()` constructor, it will automatically be categorized as **INFO**.

For the final part of this simple use exercise, we can look at using a custom configuration object to alter some of the default properties of our instance of the Logger control. Add the following object literal declaration to the very first part of the `initLogger()` function:

```
<script type="text/javascript">
  //create the namespace object
  YAHOO.namespace("yuibook.logger");
  //initialise logger
  YAHOO.yuibook.logger.initLogger = function () {
    //define configuration object
    var myConfObj = {
      width:"250px",
      height:"250px",
      footerEnabled:false,
      thresholdMax:5,
      thresholdMin:5
    }

    //define logger instance
    var myLogger = new YAHOO.widget.LogReader(null, myConfObj);
    //define a callback for the click event
    function clickCallback() {
      //log a message
      YAHOO.log("Don't click there!", "warn");
    }
    //add listener for the click event
    YAHOO.util.Event.addListener("yui-gen0", "click", clickCallback);
  }
  //execute initLogger when DOM is ready
  YAHOO.util.Event.onDOMReady( YAHOO.yuibook.logger.initLogger);
</script>
```

We adjust the size of the Logger using the `width` and `height` properties, and can also easily disable the footer (we want to see any category of message from any source anyway, and could always change the filter via code later if we wanted).

The `thresholdMax` and `thresholdMin` properties should be used in conjunction with each other. If we set a `thresholdMax` but not a `thresholdMin` value, the Logger messages will simply be cleared when the threshold is reached. This way, we ensure that the five most recent messages are always on display.

Now we just need to add a reference to our configuration object to the existing LogReader constructor. Alter the constructor so that it appears as follows:

```
var mylogger = new YAHOO.widget.LogReader(null, myConfObj);
```

The optional object literal should be added as the second argument in the constructor. The first argument accepts a reference to the `HTMLElement` being used to contain the logger, but as we aren't using this particular feature, we need to pass in a `null` value. View the page again, and you should see something resembling like this:

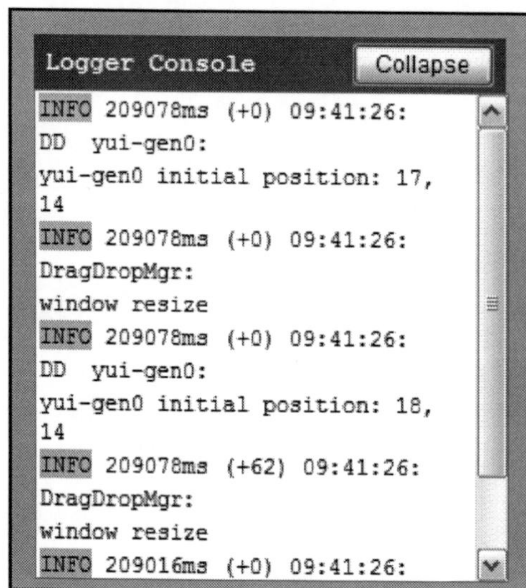

Component Debugging with Logger

Let's look at a basic example of how errors in your code can be easily exposed and corrected with the assistance of the Logger control. We'll use the Animation utility for this example, and will make a new file, so in a blank page in your text editor begin with the code shown below:

```
<!DOCTYPE HTML PUBLIC "-//W3C//DTD HTML 4.01//EN"
                              "http://www.w3.org/TR/html4/strict.dtd">
<html lang="en">
  <head>
    <meta http-equiv="content-type" content="text/html;
                                     charset=utf-8">
```

```
    <title>Yui Logger Example 2</title>
    <script type="text/javascript"
            src="yui/build/yahoo-dom-event/yahoo-dom-event.js">
    </script>
    <script type="text/javascript"
            src="yui/build/animation/animation-debug.js"></script>
    <script type="text/javascript"
            src="yui/build/logger/logger-min.js"></script>
    <link type="text/css" rel="stylesheet"
          href="yui/build/logger/assets/skins/sam/logger.css">
    <link type="text/css" rel="stylesheet" href="animError.css">
  </head>
  <body class="yui-skin-sam">
    <div id="animDiv"></div>
    <div>
      <button id="makeAnim">Animate!</button>
    </div>
  </body>
</html>
```

Then, directly preceding the `</body>` tag, add the following Logger initialization function:

```
<script type="text/javascript">
  //define namespace object
  YAHOO.namespace("yuibook.logger");
  //define the initLogger function
  YAHOO.yuibook.logger.initLogger = function() {
    //define a logger instance
    var myLogger = new YAHOO.widget.LogReader();
  }
  //execute initLogger when DOM is ready
  YAHOO.util.Event.onDOMReady( YAHOO.yuibook.logger.initLogger);
</script>
```

Our initial page is pretty much identical to what we started with in the previous example. Next we can begin to add the Animation specific code. We'll just make use of a simple animation for this example to highlight its error handling capabilities:

```
<script type="text/javascript">
  //define namespace object
  YAHOO.namespace("yuibook.logger");
  //define the initLogger function
  YAHOO.yuibook.logger.initLogger = function() {
    //define a logger instance
```

```
      var myLogger = new YAHOO.widget.LogReader();
      //define animation attributes
      var atts = {
        width: { to: 200}
      };
      //define callback function for click event
      YAHOO.util.Event.on("makeAnim", "click", function() {
        //define the animation instance
        var myAnim = new YAHOO.util.Anim(null, atts);
        //animate!
        myAnim.animate();
      });
    }
    //execute initLogger when DOM is ready
    YAHOO.util.Event.onDOMReady( YAHOO.yuibook.logger.initLogger);
  </script>
```

The `atts` variable contains an object literal holding the animation attributes; in this case it specifies that the width of the target element will grow to 200 pixels wide.

Next is the animation object's constructor followed by an event handler to detect when the `makeAnim` button is clicked, which will in turn cause the animation to occur. Save the page so far as `animError.html` in your `yuisite` folder.

We will also need to add some page-specific styling to our `<div>` element. In a new file in your text editor, add the following CSS:

```
#animDiv {
  height:100px;
  width:100px;
  background-color:red;
  margin-bottom:10px;
}
```

This is all that's required for our basic example. Save it as `animError.css`, also in the `yuisite` folder. At this stage, running the page and clicking the button should give you something similar to the screenshot below:

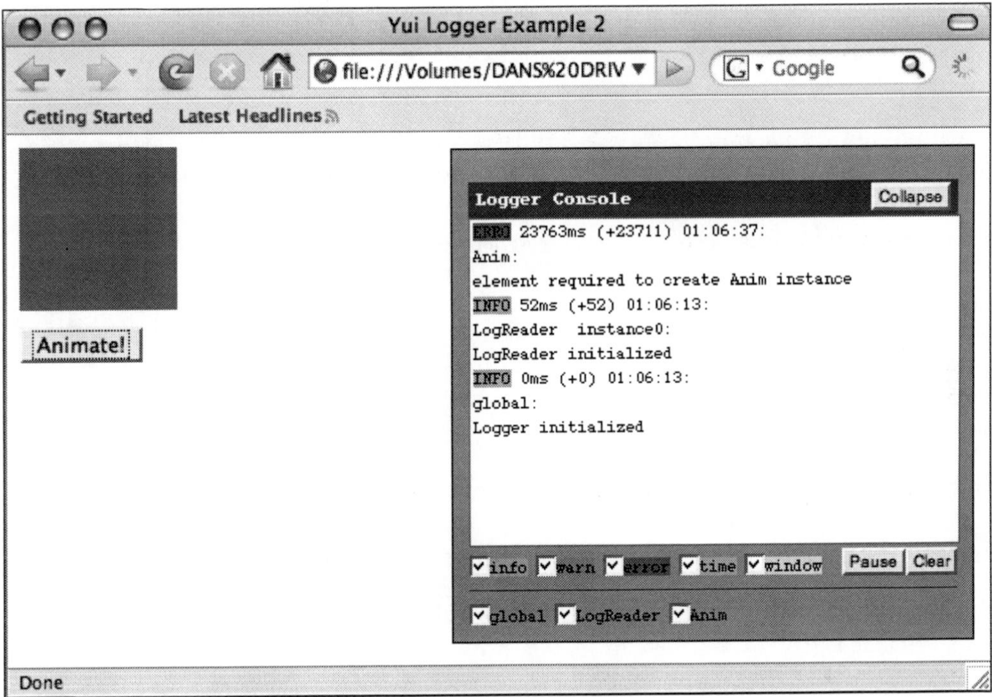

As you probably noticed, we passed in a `null` reference as the first argument in the animation constructor. This is not allowed. In order to animate an element, the constructor needs to know what that element is, and when it receives a null value it logs an appropriate ERROR category message from the source: `Anim`.

I'm sure you'll agree that the example is tenuous at best. We have to supply a null value in the constructor in order to receive the category ERROR message in Logger. If we simply passed in an element reference for an element that didn't exist, the error would not be generated because the utility would just assume that the element referenced would eventually exist. So it's pretty unlikely that as a developer you'd generate this message in a proper debugging scenario.

Nevertheless, it does highlight the functionality provided by some of the debugging versions of the YUI components. For fun, you might want to go back and correct the constructor, passing in the correct element reference as the fist argument. Now when the page loads, the error message is not generated and a click of the button will animate our red `<div>`.

Logging with a Custom Class

We've already looked at writing our own simple log messages using the global `YAHOO.log()` method from within YUI-specific code. Now let's look at using the Logger control with a custom class or source. We'll need to define our very own class for this example but don't worry, for the sake of simplicity we'll be keeping the class relatively small.

The Yahoo! library itself is class-based, with each utility and control constructed from a range of interlinked classes which give the components their functionality and behavior. This next example should not only improve your understanding of the Logger control but also of the workings of the overall library, and even of JavaScript itself.

Let's assume that we're working on the user interface for a web-based music application; it could be a store that sells records and allows visitors to preview records they intend to purchase. Part of this interface will feature a turntable object which visitors can interact with in different ways.

To facilitate this, we'll need to add several properties and methods to the object. We can also add some code that specifically targets the Logger control, allowing us to quickly and easily log messages from within our custom object.

If this were a real implementation, the page would no doubt be full of interesting things. As this is just a demonstration, we won't clutter things up with unnecessary content. Begin with the following basic page:

```
<!DOCTYPE HTML PUBLIC "-//W3C//DTD HTML 4.01//EN"
                          "http://www.w3.org/TR/html4/strict.dtd">
<html lang="en">
  <head>
    <meta http-equiv="content-type" content="text/html;
                                     charset=utf-8">
    <title>Yui Logger Example Three</title>
    <script type="text/javascript"
            src="yui/build/yahoo-dom-event/yahoo-dom-event.js">
    </script>
    <script type="text/javascript"
            src="yui/build/logger/logger-min.js"></script>
    <link type="text/css" rel="stylesheet"
          href="yui/build/logger/assets/skins/sam/logger.css">
  </head>
  <body class="yui-skin-sam">
  </body>
</html>
```

Here's the first part of the script, add it within the `<body>` tag:

```
<script type="text/javascript">
  //create the namespace object
  YAHOO.namespace("yuibook.logger");
  //define the initLogger function
  YAHOO.yuibook.logger.initLogger = function() {
    //create a new logger instance
    var myLogger = new YAHOO.widget.LogReader();
    myLogger.hideSource("global");
    myLogger.hideSource("LogReader");
    myLogger.hideCategory("time");
    myLogger.hideCategory("window");
  }
    //execute initLogger when DOM is ready
    YAHOO.util.Event.onDOMReady( YAHOO.yuibook.logger.initLogger);
</script>
```

We instantiate a Logger control in the usual way, and as we're only interested in messages from our turntable source we can hide the other sources displayed by default. We won't be using any category TIME or WINDOW messages either, so we can hide these as well. We can now move on to defining our own custom class. Add the following code directly after the initial `YAHOO.namespace()` method at the start of the script (new code highlighted):

```
<script type="text/javascript">
  //create the namespace object
  YAHOO.namespace("yuibook.logger");
  //define the turntable object constructor
  YAHOO.yuibook.logger.turntable = function(brand) {
    //set object properties
    this.brand = brand;
    this.playing = "false";
    this.startStop = YAHOO.yuibook.logger.startOrStop;
  }
  //define the initLogger function
  YAHOO.yuibook.logger.initLogger = function() {
    //create a new logger instance
    var myLogger = new YAHOO.widget.LogReader();
    myLogger.hideSource("global");
    myLogger.hideSource("LogReader");
    myLogger.hideCategory("time");
    myLogger.hideCategory("window");
```

```
    }
    //execute initLogger when DOM is ready
    YAHOO.util.Event.onDOMReady( YAHOO.yuibook.logger.initLogger);
  </script>
```

This function defines our `turntable` class and acts as a constructor for the turntable object. We give it two properties and a method (except that the method, `.startstop`, won't actually be a method until we add a function for it in a minute). Each property and method is added using the `this` keyword which is how objects refer to themselves.

Real turntables have a button that either starts or stops the record platter spinning. Our turntable object can also have a mechanism by which it is started or stopped. Add the following function to the page (new code highlighted):

```
  <script type="text/javascript">
    //create the namespace object
    YAHOO.namespace("yuibook.logger");
    //define the turntable object constructor
    YAHOO.yuibook.logger.turntable = function(brand) {
      //set object properties
      this.brand = brand;
      this.playing = "false";
      this.startStop = YAHOO.yuibook.logger.startOrStop;
    }
    //define startOrStop function
    YAHOO.yuibook.logger.startOrStop = function() {
      //is the property already false?
      if (this.playing == "false") {
        //set playing property
        this.playing = "true";
        //write a custom message to Logger
        YAHOO.log("The " + this.brand + " is playing!", "info",
                  "turntable");
      } else {
        //set playing property
        this.playing = "false";
        //write a custom message to Logger
        YAHOO.log("The " + this.brand + " has stopped!", "info",
                   "turntable");
      }
    }
```

```
    //define the initLogger function
    YAHOO.yuibook.logger.initLogger = function() {
      //create a new logger instance
      var myLogger = new YAHOO.widget.LogReader();
      myLogger.hideSource("global");
      myLogger.hideSource("LogReader");
      myLogger.hideCategory("time");
      myLogger.hideCategory("window");
    }
    //execute initLogger when DOM is ready
    YAHOO.util.Event.onDOMReady( YAHOO.yuibook.logger.initLogger);
  </script>
```

The function (which is actually a method of our custom class) first examines the `playing` property to see whether or not the turntable is playing. If not, we set the property to `true` and output an appropriate message to the console.

We can also include the brand property of the object within the log message. If the playing property is already true we do the opposite and stop the turntable, outputting a similar message.

Next we can create an instance of our turntable object, specifying the brand name as an argument, and then calling the `.startStop()` method on it (this code should be added to the `initLogger` function, see `turntableLogger.html` for clarification):

```
<script type="text/javascript">
  //create the namespace object
  YAHOO.namespace("yuibook.logger");
  //define the turntable object constructor
  YAHOO.yuibook.logger.turntable = function(brand) {
    //set object properties
    this.brand = brand;
    this.playing = "false";
    this.startStop = YAHOO.yuibook.logger.startOrStop;
  }
  //define startOrStop function
  YAHOO.yuibook.logger.startOrStop = function() {
    //is the property already false?
    if (this.playing == "false") {
      //set playing property
      this.playing = "true";
      //write a custom message to Logger
      YAHOO.log("The " + this.brand + " is playing!", "info",
                "turntable");
    } else {
      //set playing property
      this.playing = "false";
      //write a custom message to Logger
```

```
        YAHOO.log("The " + this.brand + " has stopped!", "info",
                "turntable");
      }
    }
    //define the initLogger function
    YAHOO.yuibook.logger.initLogger = function() {
      //create a new logger instance
      var myLogger = new YAHOO.widget.LogReader();
      myLogger.hideSource("global");
      myLogger.hideSource("LogReader");
      myLogger.hideCategory("time");
      myLogger.hideCategory("window");
    }
    //create a new turntable object
    var tt = new YAHOO.yuibook.logger.turntable("technics");
    tt.startStop();
    //execute initLogger when DOM is ready
    YAHOO.util.Event.onDOMReady( YAHOO.yuibook.logger.initLogger);
  </script>
```

Save the page so far as `turntableLogger.html` and view it in your browser, you should see something similar to the following screenshot (I've un-ticked the `window` and `time` categories so that our custom log message is shown alone in the Logger):

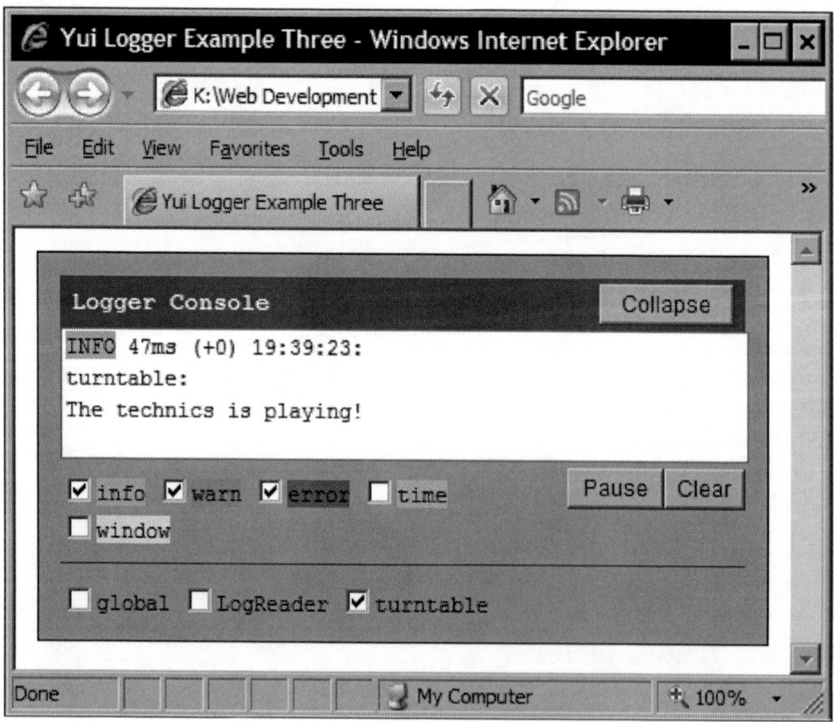

If you add another call to the `.startStop()` method directly below the first, the logger will display both the above message as well as a message advising that **The technics has stopped**.

We can also add our own debugging messages as well; we've specified that a `brand` argument should be supplied to our constructor. We can easily output an error message if this argument isn't provided. Change the `turntable` class function so that it appears as follows:

```
//define the turntable object constructor
YAHOO.yuibook.logger.turntable = function(brand) {
  //log message if brand not specified
  if (brand == undefined) {
    YAHOO.log("Please specify a brand of turntable", "error",
              "turntable");
  } else {
    this.brand = brand;
    this.playing = "false";
    this.startStop = startOrStop;
  }
}
```

If you now remove the brand from the following statement:

```
var tt = new turntable();
```

And view the page again, you should see this:

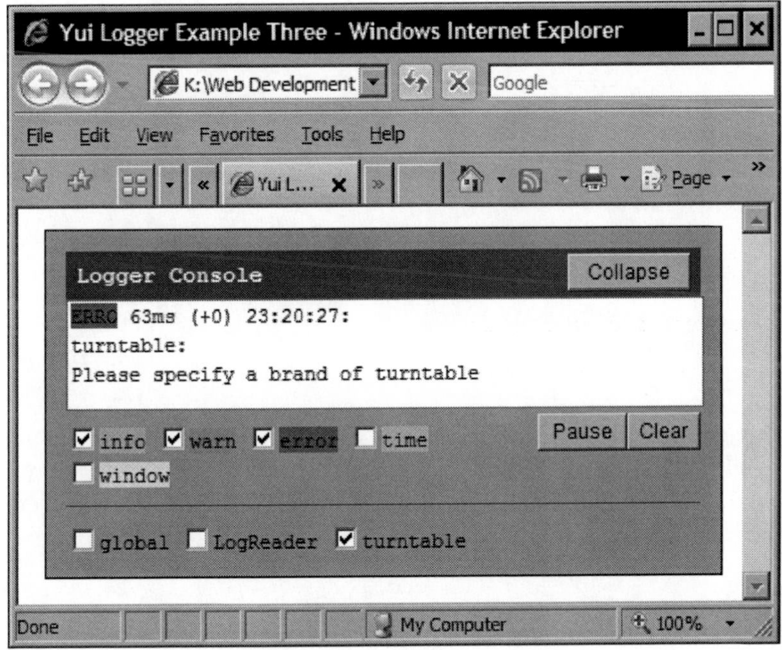

The class we've defined in this example is extremely simple and only outputs three lines of Logger code. If our class was part of a fully functional web application, there would no doubt be many more lines of Logger targeting message code. In this scenario, we would probably want to define our own named source using the LogWriter class provided by the Logger control.

We can add a few more log messages for good measure and can generate the new messages using a new property and a new method. Change the turntable class function so that it is as shown below:

```
//define the turntable object constructor
YAHOO.yuibook.logger.turntable = function(brand, speed) {
  //log message if brand not specified
  if (brand == undefined) {
    YAHOO.log("Please specify a brand of turntable", "error",
              "turntable");
  } else {
    //set object properties
    this.brand = brand;
    this.playing = "false";
    this.startStop = startOrStop;
    this.speed = speed;
    this.setSpeed = setRPMSpeed;
    this.myLogWriter = new YAHOO.widget.LogWriter("turntable");
  }
}
```

First we add a new argument to the object constructor, which is then set to a new property of the object, and a new method is also added. Next we define our custom LogWriter which will be used to add our messages. Now let's add the `.setRPMSpeed()` method:

```
function setRPMSpeed(rpm) {
  this.speed = rpm;
  this.myLogWriter.log("You've changed the speed to " + rpm + "
                                                    RPM", "info");
}
```

Notice how we call the `.log()` method of our own custom LogWriter instance instead of the global `YAHOO.log` method. We can also omit the third argument of the `.log()` method, which can help shrink our code by a few bytes (don't forget that this is a cumulative saving—the more message logging statements you have in your code, the more you will save).

Alter the remaining message logging statements so that they make use of the custom LogWriter:

```
//define startOrStop function
YAHOO.yuibook.logger.startOrStop = function() {
  if (this.playing == "false") {
    //set playing property
    this.playing = "true";
    //write a custom message from our custom class
    this.myLogWriter.log("The " + this.brand + " is playing at " +
                                        this.speed + " RPM", "info");
  } else {
    //set playing property
    this.playing = "false";
    //write a custom message from our custom class
    this.myLogWriter.log("The " + this.brand + " has stopped!",
                                                          "info");
  }
}
```

Now that our constructor requires an additional argument and we have a new method to play with, the code that creates a new turntable object and works with its methods will also need to be changed:

```
var tt = new turntable("technics", "33");
tt.startStop();
tt.setSpeed("45");
```

Save the changes to the file and view it one more time in your browser. Logger should now resemble that shown in the screenshot below:

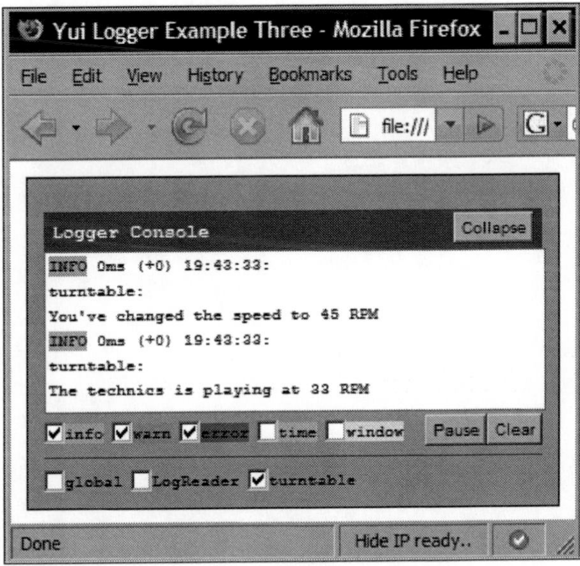

Summary

The focus of this chapter has been solely on the Logger control. This control can significantly reduce your learning curve when working with the `-debug.js` versions of the different library components and provides a window through which the inner workings of each component can be examined in detail.

Like the CSS tools provided by the YUI, Logger is a component that you can use even when not implementing any of the other library components directly. Logger can easily be included within an application that you are creating yourself so that you can log messages from different parts of your code to check that everything is functioning correctly.

Index

Symbols

A

B

C

D

E

F

G

R

S

T

U

X

Y

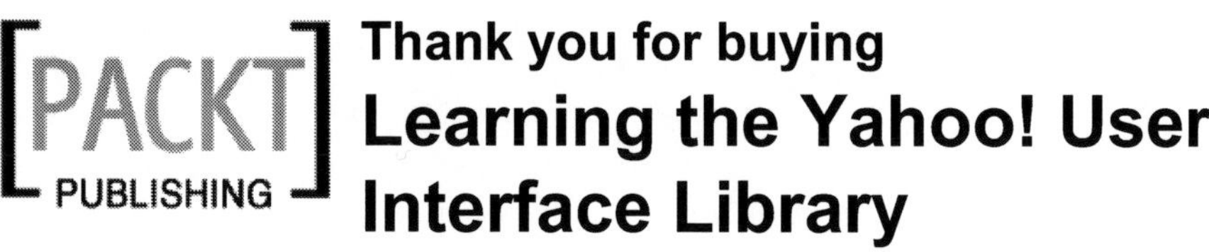

Packt Open Source Project Royalties

When we sell a book written on an Open Source project, we pay a royalty directly to that project. Therefore by purchasing Learning the Yahoo! User Interface Library, Packt will have given some of the money received to the Yahoo! User Interface Library project.

In the long term, we see ourselves and you—customers and readers of our books—as part of the Open Source ecosystem, providing sustainable revenue for the projects we publish on. Our aim at Packt is to establish publishing royalties as an essential part of the service and support a business model that sustains Open Source.

If you're working with an Open Source project that you would like us to publish on, and subsequently pay royalties to, please get in touch with us.

Writing for Packt

We welcome all inquiries from people who are interested in authoring. Book proposals should be sent to `authors@packtpub.com`. If your book idea is still at an early stage and you would like to discuss it first before writing a formal book proposal, contact us; one of our commissioning editors will get in touch with you.

We're not just looking for published authors; if you have strong technical skills but no writing experience, our experienced editors can help you develop a writing career, or simply get some additional reward for your expertise.

About Packt Publishing

Packt, pronounced 'packed', published its first book "Mastering phpMyAdmin for Effective MySQL Management" in April 2004 and subsequently continued to specialize in publishing highly focused books on specific technologies and solutions.

Our books and publications share the experiences of your fellow IT professionals in adapting and customizing today's systems, applications, and frameworks. Our solution-based books give you the knowledge and power to customize the software and technologies you're using to get the job done. Packt books are more specific and less general than the IT books you have seen in the past. Our unique business model allows us to bring you more focused information, giving you more of what you need to know, and less of what you don't.

Packt is a modern, yet unique publishing company, which focuses on producing quality, cutting-edge books for communities of developers, administrators, and newbies alike. For more information, please visit our website: `www.PacktPub.com`.

Learning jQuery

ISBN: 978-1-847192-50-9 Paperback: 380 pages

jQuery: Better Interaction Design and Web Development with Simple JavaScript Techniques

1. Create better, cross-platform JavaScript code
2. Detailed solutions to specific client-side problems

PHP Web 2.0 Mashup Projects

ISBN: 978-1-847190-88-8 Paperback: 280 pages

Create practical mashups in PHP grabbing and mixing data from Google Maps, Flickr, Amazon, YouTube, MSN Search, Yahoo!, Last.fm, and 411Sync.com

1. Expand your website and applications using mashups
2. Gain a thorough understanding of mashup fundamentals
3. Clear, detailed walk-through of the key PHP mashup building technologies
4. Five fully implemented example mashups with full code

Please check **www.PacktPub.com** for information on our titles

jQuery Reference Guide

ISBN: 978-1-847193-81-0 Paperback: 225 pages

A Comprehensive Exploration of the Popular JavaScript Library

1. Organized menu to every method, function, and selector in the jQuery library
2. Quickly look up features of the jQuery library
3. Understand the anatomy of a jQuery script
4. Extend jQuery's built-in capabilities with plug-ins, and even write your own

---

AJAX and PHP

ISBN: 1-904811-82-5 Paperback: 275 pages

Enhance the user experience of your PHP website using AJAX with this practical tutorial featuring detailed case studies

1. Build a solid foundation for your next generation of web applications
2. Use better JavaScript code to enable powerful web features
3. Leverage the power of PHP and MySQL to create powerful back-end functionality and make it work in harmony with the smart AJAX client

Please check **www.PacktPub.com** for information on our titles

Made in the USA